# ENOUGH FOR ALL FOREVER

## A HANDBOOK FOR LEARNING ABOUT SUSTAINABILITY

---

*EDITED BY:*
*JOY MURRAY, GLENN CAWTHORNE,*
*CHRISTOPHER DEY & CHRIS ANDREW*

# ENOUGH FOR ALL FOREVER

## A HANDBOOK FOR LEARNING ABOUT SUSTAINABILITY

*EDITED BY:*
*JOY MURRAY, GLENN CAWTHORNE,*
*CHRISTOPHER DEY & CHRIS ANDREW*

Common Ground

First published in Champaign, Illinois in 2012
by Common Ground Publishing LLC
as part of the On Sustainability series

Library of Congress Cataloging-in-Publication Data

Enough for all forever : a handbook for learning about sustainability / Joy Murray,
editor...[et.al.].

    p. cm. -- (On sustainability)

Includes bibliographical references.
ISBN 978-1-61229-014-0 (pbk : alk. paper) -- ISBN 978-1-61229-015-7 (pdf)
1. Sustainability. 2. Sustainable living. 3. Environmentalism. I. Murray, Joy.

GE195.E555 2012
338.9'27--dc23

2011048648

Cover Image: John Murray, 2011

# Table of Contents

## Foreword

*Enough for All Forever* is an important book, and deserves to be read and taught widely. It deals with one of the most pressing issues of our time, namely how to live on our precious earth in a sustainable way—in a way that doesn't jeopardise the future.

There is a wide and diverse range of expert thinking in its many chapters. With its consistent focus on personal reflection, discussion points and personal action choices, this book is an especially useful resource for all of us, but will be particularly helpful to educators in many settings. The innovative approaches available to engage students, provide real life learning and link the curriculum with meaningful opportunities for personal action. For anyone keen to better understand the environment, the pressures it faces and the opportunities we have to act to preserve the gifts a healthy planet provides, it is a timely collection of scholarship, well suited to our times.

I commend *Enough for All Forever* to all who care about our world.

The Hon. Peter Garrett AM MP
Minister for School Education, Early Childhood and Youth
Parliament House
Canberra ACT 2600
Australia

# Preface

This book is for teachers who want to understand more about sustainability. In its chapters voices from around the world present some of the dilemmas associated with how to live sustainably and equitably within the limits of the earth's capacity to provide for healthy and fulfilling lives.

The book's purpose is to provide information about, and views on sustainability that will provoke thoughtful discussion and action. To this end it covers a wide range of perspectives from different people living and working in many different contexts – academics and practitioners from a whole range of backgrounds and areas of expertise.

All without exception realise that this sustainability predicament in which we find ourselves cannot be addressed from within any one area of knowledge. It will take an integration of knowledge; an understanding of how the different systems that govern our lives on earth fit together to sustain all living things.

Some of the chapters in this book also address those vexed questions around rights and wrongs and who's to blame: How did we get into this predicament? How can we get out and who should do the heavy lifting to get us out?

There's an old joke that goes something like this: Two intrepid adventurers, Bootsie and Sox, are tramping through the long grass when they come across a sleeping lion. Bootsie grabs a rock and throws it at the lion. The lion wakes up and Bootsie yells, run Sox run! Sox looks coolly at Bootsie and says, why should I run, you threw the rock!

Well it looks as though those of us in the developed world belong to the rock throwers. However unfair it is to the rest of the world who would like to have had the opportunity to do some throwing of their own, we are now all in this together; now we all have to run. But how fast we each must run and where to for safety are urgent questions; questions that are inevitably being answered from an array of different and often conflicting perspectives on the world and our place in it.

And that's where we hope this book might help out as a guide.

While the introduction provides a couple of maps of what ground we need to cover, sections one to six provide a look at some of the topography. However although we might be providing a map and some features to look out for, the map is certainly not the journey. The journey is an individual thing – lived by all of us and by our students from one minute to the next.

Towards the end of his famous motorcycle journey, in *Zen and the Art of Motorcycle Maintenance*, Robert Pirsig's protagonist says:

> *"My personal feeling is that this is how any further improvement of the world will be done: by individuals making Quality decisions and that's all." (Robert M. Persig (1974). Zen and the Art of Motorcycle Maintenance. Vintage, London. p. 362)*

We are all individuals with the ability to make quality decisions to improve the world. We make decisions large and small every minute of our day. We each have the wealth of our lineage, heritage and personal history out of which to make them. We also interpret the world out of this same lineage, heritage and history. Therefore every individual reader of this book will read through different eyes, interpret and make decisions about what is written here through different understandings of the world and how it works. In turn each of us will pass different messages on to our students depending on which chapters catch our eye, which messages fit into our belief system and connect with our[1] own experience of life.

For this reason we are presenting a range of views in a range of styles. All shed light on the same daunting challenge but they arise out of different life experiences and different spheres of influence: social, cultural, political, academic and business. Some chapters, for example, discuss the sustainability challenges to business and industry and how they must accept a fair share of responsibility for the social, economic and environmental effects of what they do. Other chapters suggest that such debates may be missing the point. In the face of our dire impact on the earth and all that lives on it there'll be no business if we can't get the environment right.

We have deliberately sought out experts committed to doing something about *sustainability* from wherever they stand; but where they stand – their areas of expertise or perspectives on life and sustainability – differs widely. In this way we hope to present at least some chapters that will immediately resonate with your own situation and interest and be useful in your professional or personal life. From there we hope that each chapter will lead you on to another.

Ultimately we want to say that everything is connected to everything else and our starting point for action can only ever be ourselves, the world we have now and all that is in it. There is no point in saying if I were travelling to a sustainable future I wouldn't start from here and I wouldn't start from now. We have no choice. We must start from *here*, which encompasses who and where we are as well as the social, cultural, political and economic edifices and infrastructure of our time; and we have to start from *now*, which is the early part of the 21st century with all of our accumulated history. How we interpret the fundamental message of this book will be through our own personal, idiosyncratic web of connections and from wherever we stand in time and place.

---

1. We say 'our' because we are all in this together. We (the editors) having read all the chapters of this book have gone through the process of adopting some ideas, arguing about others and making changes to our lives based on others according to our knowledge, beliefs, values and opportunities. We are all teachers so we'll use these materials in our teaching one way or another. The contributors too are teachers in their various spheres of influence and probably in due course will read each other's chapters and respond according to who and where they are and the opportunities that present themselves. So, when we say 'us' and 'our' we're counting all of us.

The book is organised around four broad principles of sustainability which provide the focus for sections two to five of the book:

1.  Sustainability is everyone's business
2.  We must share equitably the cost and the benefits of living sustainably with nature
3.  People need to be able to live healthy, fulfilling and sustainable lives
4.  Long-term solutions require a whole-system view; they are complex and multi-faceted.

Each principle implies certain questions (i.e. if this is what we believe about sustainability then the following questions need to be addressed). Chapters within each section address some of the many questions that arise.

Sections two to five are followed by case studies that showcase the work of dedicated and passionate individuals and organisations from around the world. The book ends with a section intended to bring the above threads together. It moves from a discussion of formal education into communities and students taking their learning into the world. The Epilogue provides a resource that may be useful to teachers who are working through the book with students, in which case you may want to read it before you begin. It suggests frameworks that may be useful for organising information and strategies for taking action.

Section one provides the introduction to the book. It consists of two invitations. The first is to 'sit together, share some food and talk about sustainability'. The invitation comes from Laklak Burarrwanga, Merrki Ganambarr and Banbapuy Ganambarr members of the oldest surviving culture on earth – the Indigenous culture of North East Arnhem Land in Australia's Northern Territory. Along with Sandie Suchet-Pearson and Kate Lloyd from Macquarie University and Sarah Wright from the University of Newcastle they discuss their conception of a connected world. This is followed by David Suzuki's 2010 speech to the Green Party of Aotearoa New Zealand, which invites us to appreciate the vast and magnificent interconnectedness of the world's systems. He shows us these systems through the eyes of "a scientist, a biologist and an elder". In doing so David Suzuki makes an impassioned plea to the world to hurry up and take action.

The remainder of the book is in support of that plea to 'take action'.

Sections two to five deal with each of the principles outlined above. The chapters within each section address some of the questions that need to be grappled with if we are to adopt the principle as something by which to live.

*Section two: Sustainability is everyone's business*

This section begins with our responsibility as citizens. It asks the questions: *How sustainable is my life style and how can I make it more sustainable.* Dan Moran of the University of Sydney and Mathis Wackernagel, President of the Global Footprint Network and co-creator of the Ecological Footprint, discuss how we can measure the footprints of populations around the world and ways in which we can reduce them through individual action. Iain Black, University of Edinburgh, examines the role of socio-cultural influences and pressures that defy many of our attempts at more sustainable lifestyles. He shows how our seemingly insatiable appetite for the acquisition of *stuff* drives greenhouse gas (GHG) emissions and ultimately climate disruption. In doing so he provides a toolkit for addressing overconsumption.

Having examined our role as individuals in sustainability the next chapter looks at sharing responsibility fairly among households. In this case Annemarie Kerkhof, a life-cycle analysis expert working with The Netherland's company Pré Consultants, deals with one particular aspect of responsibility. She examines the cost of mitigating greenhouse gas emissions across Europe. In doing so she considers the variation in household GHG emissions in various European countries and discusses the equity of burden sharing. She leaves us with the question of what is a fair share of responsibility.

We now move on to the role of business in sustainability. This chapter is written by Michiyo Morisawa from the Carbon Disclosure Project, Japan and Darian McBain Director of Blue Sky Green, Australia. It takes up the role of business and industry and discusses what is being done to help them address their responsibility towards creating a more sustainable world. Morisawa and McBain's chapter is followed by a chapter on how business and industry can share along their supply chains the responsibility for emissions, water use, land disturbance etc. Thomas Wiedmann, Senior Research Scientist at CSIRO Ecosystem Sciences, Australia and Chris Dey and Manfred Lenzen from the University of Sydney's Integrated Sustainability Analysis group discuss their technique for accounting for the social, environmental and economic effects of doing business. They show how responsibility for the good and the bad effects can be shared equitably along the supply chain.

The section concludes with an examination of the role of government in sustainability. Frank Stilwell, Professor of Political Economy at the University of Sydney discusses the central role of governments in securing a more sustainable society as they grapple with competing ideologies and the shift in mindset that is needed. However, he points out, this does not let us as individuals 'off the hook'; an educated citizenry has a collective responsibility to create the political climate necessary for change.

*Section three: Sharing in a sustainable future*

Section three begins with a short chapter form Harriet Nalukenge, Senior State Attorney from the Ministry of Justice and Constitutional Affairs in Uganda. In it she presents a summary of the ethics of sustainability, particularly in the context of developing nations and the challenge of poverty. She argues that in order to bring about a fundamental change we need new ways of understanding ourselves and our relationship with nature. She draws on her experiences in Uganda to illustrate what a new, fairer model of sustainability might look like. In doing so she provides us with guidance on how to work out what is fair and equitable. The next chapter is written by Gretchen

Daily, Heather Tallis and Anne Guerry from Stanford University. They explain what constitutes natural capital and discuss how the world's ecosystems can be seen as natural capital assets which, properly managed can yield a stream of vital 'ecosystem services'. They demonstrate how the value of natural capital is being mainstreamed into decisions. Ida Kubiszewsi and Robert Costanza from the Institute for Sustainable Solutions at Portland State University are concerned about how we can create systems in which sustainable and fair decisions can be made. They discuss a new way of sharing what they call the 'information commons' so that ecosystem services can be harnessed for public good. Following this discussion of the value of natural capital and ways in which it can be shared equitably, Sharon Beder, Visiting Professorial Fellow at the School of Social Sciences, Media and Communication at the University of Wollongong tackles the big questions about passing on this natural capital in as good a condition as we found it. She leaves us with some difficult questions about our responsibility towards people who have not yet been born.

Having discussed how we need to value and share natural capital the next section examines what needs to happen in order for all of us to be able to live well and at the same time live within our natural means.

*Section four: Living healthy, fulfilling, sustainable lives*

This section begins with the importance of considering the relationship between lifestyle and the environment. Shigemi Kagawa and Yuke Oshita from Kyushu University, Keisuke Nansai from Japan's National Institute for Environmental Studies and Sangwon Suh from the Bren School of Environmental Science and Management at the University of California, show how consumption affects our carbon footprint using food as an example. Garry Egger, Professor of Health and Human Sciences from Southern Cross University also discusses food. In his chapter on health he focuses on the modern obesity epidemic and our obsession with economic growth with its consequences for our health and that of the planet. Our next chapter is by Richard Stirzaker, Principal Research Scientist at CSIRO Land and Water. He writes about hunger caused by poverty and hunger caused by scarcity and asks the question 'Can we feed the world a nutritious diet at a price they can afford both now and into the foreseeable future?' Closely allied to sustainable agriculture is access to water. Sergey Volotovsky from the Water Corporation of Western Australia writes about water security. He takes us through the various issues that threaten the supply of fresh water around the world and what we can do to conserve it.

Tied up with our ability to provide food and water as well as health services are our access to transport and our need for dwellings, infrastructure and art. The following three chapters take up these themes. Peter Newman from Curtin University discusses sustainable transport. He ask the fundamental question of how our cities need to change so that sustainable transport becomes viable and effective. Phil McManus from the University of Sydney takes us through the issues surrounding sustainability and the built environment. He reminds us that the quest for sustainable cities is part of a long tradition of improvement to make cities more liveable. Maja Fowkes and Reuben Fowkes discuss art and sustainability. They present the work of artists who directly address socio-cultural and environmental sustainability. Examples range from the effects of an oil pipeline on peoples' lives to the protection of indigenous products and customs. The authors also examine the ecological footprint of art itself, especially in relation to exhibitions and biennale. This section of the book ends with a chapter on happiness. Catherine O'Brien from the Department of Education, Cape Breton University, Nova Scotia, introduces the concept of sustainable happiness, which, she says, is about everyone thriving but not at the expense of other people, other species or the natural environment.

In keeping with our first principle – that sustainability is everyone's business – most of the above chapters end with two actions for the reader. The first asks you to think through what you have read and decide where you stand on the debate. The second asks you to take action. That action could be as simple as a personal choice to do something differently in your life or it could be a project that you develop with a class or group, a community or at an even broader level. Whatever you decide to do will have consequences. So the final question is what are those consequences and what other aspects of sustainability do they affect: what broader human and ecological systems are linked to your action. The Epilogue at the end of the book provides some pointers for how you might address these questions and suggests a mind map or some other device for keeping track of your learning.

*Section five: Sustainability – a whole-system view*

This section focuses on a systems view of the universe. The following three chapters take a different look at the connectedness that we began with as we sat down by the water with Laklak Burarrwanga, Merrki Ganambarr and Banbapuy Ganambarr. David Salt from the Australian National University explains the concept of *resilience* as it applies to ecosystems. He discusses the complexity and self-organising capabilities of natural and social systems. Michael Ben-Eli, founder of The Sustainability Laboratory, based in New York, provides a new framework which includes five core sustainability principles. These principles, derived from a holistic- systems view, are used as the conceptual foundation for the work of the Lab. The principles have been used widely and are being applied in his ground breaking project with a Bedouin community in the Negev desert of Israel, developing a model for a sustainable agriculture in arid environments.

Ray Ison, Professor of Systems at the Open University, UK and of Systems for Sustainability at the Monash Sustainability Institute, Australia, provides a cybersystemic framework for taking practical action. He introduces us to cybersystemic thinking to help us break out of the traps associated with our current ways of thinking and acting.

*Section six: Demonstrating sustainability – case studies*

This section presents five case studies, two are from education systems, one is from a school and two are from individuals who offer insights into how we might live in a simpler way. These chapters are offered as examples of what we know is being done by committed people everywhere. You may already be engaged in something similar yourself or you may know people who are.

Krista McKinzey from Climate Change Schools in the UK describes an initiative that has provided support for a large number of schools to become showcases for climate change teaching, learning and positive action in their communities. Catherine Nielsen from the New South Wales Department of Education and Training tells about an environmental education program – *Murder under the Microscope* – that has engaged around 100,000 students from around Australia and elsewhere over the past four years. In the program students compete online, working in teams to solve an 'environmental crime'. The next chapter describes the work of Annukka Alppi at the Mahnala Environmental School in Hameenkyro Municipality in Finland. It is co-written by Mauri Åhlberg from the University of Helsinki and tells of their collaboration in the development of this international sustainability award winning school. The case study that advocates a simpler way of life is a tour of Pigface Point, the home of Ted Trainer who has been a sustainability icon and inspiration to generations of student at the University of New South Wales in Australia. The final chapter in this section written by cartoon artist, Joe Francis, provides us with one example of the role of the Arts in achieving a sustainable future. Through the eyes of *Tomorrow, Man* whose crusade is to get the world to slow down, we see a reflection of Western society and a way to counter its self-destruction.

*Section seven: Out of the classroom and into a sustainable world*

This section consists of four chapters. Their role is to focus on what needs to change within the education sector and how student and community learning about sustainability can be taken out beyond the school gate to the village and to the world. The first chapter, written by Paul Ehrlich and Anne Ehrlich from the Center for Conservation Biology at Stanford University, lays out what everyone should know about our environmental predicament and what should be included in a foundational and comprehensive sustainability curriculum. The second chapter is written by Syd Smith, who pioneered environmental education in Australia, and is now a senior advisor to the Environment and Schools Initiative (ENSI) group, based in Switzerland. He addresses the challenges for educators in implementing sustainability programs when most education systems still operate on an industrial age model of inputs, processes and products.

The third chapter is by Manfred Max-Neef from the Economics Institute, Universidad Austral de Chile. His chapter – *Implementation: From the Village to a Global Order*[2] – looks at what we can do with our learning. He takes a bottom-up grassroots point of view and shows us the numerous projects that are quietly building an alternative paradigm of development that goes upwards, from the village to a global order. The final word goes to Fabian

---

2.First published in Smith, P. B. & Max-Neef, M. (2011) *Economics Unmasked*, Green Books, UK. The chapter is copyright Philip B. Smith and Manfred Max-Neef.

Sack who is a consultant at the Dusseldorp Skills Forum and an Honorary Associate at the University of Sydney. He examines how students, having learned much about sustainability can move out into the world and make a difference through their work.

*Section eight: Epilogue*

The epilogue suggests ways of organizing and using the information contained in these chapters. It is provided as a resource that may be helpful in sorting through the complexity and deciding where and how to begin. You may want to skim this section first before you read the book.

The paintings that introduce each section of the book are by Australian artist John Murray. They are from two series of paintings: *Landscapes* (2008-11) and *Mindscapes* (2010-11). Murray lives and works on the Australian coast in a self-built house constructed mostly from local and recycled materials. Solar panels provide his energy needs and rainwater is collected for washing and cooking. Much of his food is grown locally. The native forest surrounding his house and the local coastline and ocean provide the inspiration for much of his work.

## *Sustainability*

Finally a word about the meaning of *sustainability*. We have purposely not provided a definition, neither did we offer a definition to the book's contributors as a guide for their writing. Different meanings arise out of different world-views. If we had imposed one meaning we would have constricted the debate and undermined our purpose. Besides, we live in an inseparable web of relationships. The word *sustainability* may initially suggest the *environment* but environmental systems are not independent of social systems with all that they entail. This makes for messy definitions that provoke a myriad questions: What are we actually trying to sustain? How long do systems need to continue into the future to be called *sustained?* Don't all systems – social and ecological – rise and fall naturally? Can they be called *sustainable?*

Resilient environmental systems can absorb shocks and re-organise without losing their identity. Likewise resilient social systems can sustain themselves over generations of changing membership retaining their identity through the continuation of rituals, arts and stories. Like my old broom that's had four new handles and six new heads, the system goes on. Is this what we mean by a *sustainable system?* Is *sustainability* always a work in progress? Is *sustainability* more to do with mediating equitable social/environmental interrelationships and interdependencies over time – local or global communities in constant struggle towards living together without exploitation in an ever-changing world?

This sounds like sustainability-as-process, learning to manage in a shifting world as we living systems, in communication with ourselves in reflection and others in discussion, find novel ways to deal with the tensions created by ethical dilemmas and competing demands. Perhaps it is sufficient to *strive towards* sustainability, in which case we may need a framework to guide our actions.

We hope that this book will help you to build up such a framework as you work your way through it, discussing the ideas presented here, trying things out and documenting your learning. We hope that out of this process will emerge your own definition of *sustainability* and your own sustainable process of learning and living.

Joy Murray
Glenn Cawthorne
Christopher Dey
Chris Andrew

Sydney
October, 2011

## Acknowledgements

The editors would like to thank Nik Dawson for transcribing David Suzuki's speech to the Green Party of Aotearoa New Zealand; and Sebastian Brunsdon, Alice Ossowski, Klaus Ossowski, Fabian Sack and Stuart Smith for their valuable feedback on various chapters.

# List of Contributors

**Mauri Åhlberg,** Professor of Biology and Sustainability Education, University of Helsinki, Finland

**Annukka Alppi,** MSc (Education), The ENSI Program, Finland, annukka.alppi@hameenkyro.fi

**Chris Andrew,** Greening Australia

**Sharon Beder,** Visiting Professorial Fellow, School of Social Sciences, Media and Communication, University of Wollongong, Australia

**Michael Ben-Eli,** The Sustainability Laboratory, New York

**Dr Iain Black,** University of Edinburgh Business School, University of Edinburgh Iain.Black@ed.ac.uk

**Laklak Burarrwanga,** Bawaka Cultural Experiences

**Glenn Cawthorne,** New South Wales Department of Education and Training

**Robert Costanza,** Institute for Sustainable Solutions, Portland State University

**Gretchen Daily,** Professor, Department of Biological Sciences, Director, Centre for Conservation Biology, Stanford University, USA

**Christopher Dey,** Senior Research Fellow, Integrated Sustainability Analysis (ISA) School of Physics, University of Sydney, Sydney, Australia

**Garry Egger,** Professor, Health and Human Sciences, Southern Cross University, Lismore, NSW

**Anne H. Ehrlich,** Senior Research Scientist, Policy Coordinator, Center for Conservation Biology, Stanford University, Stanford, CA 94305 aehrlich@stanford.edu

**Paul R. Ehrlich,** Bing Professor of Population Studies, Professor of Biology, President, Center for Conservation Biology, Stanford University, Stanford, CA 94305 pre@stanford.edu

**Maja Fowkes,** Art historian and curator, translocal.org

**Reuben Fowkes,** Art historian and curator, translocal.org

**Joe Francis,** Cartoon artist, Sydney http://www.tomorrowmancomics.com/

**Banbapuy Ganambarr,** Bawaka Cultural Experiences

**Merrki Ganambarr,** Bawaka Cultural Experiences

**Anne Guerry,** The Natural Capital Project, Stanford University

**Ray Ison,** Professor of Systems, Communication & Systems Department, The Open University, UK; Professor, Systems for Sustainability, Monash Sustainability Institute, Clayton, Australia

**Shigemi Kagawa**, Associate Professor of Economic Statistics, Faculty of Economics, Kyushu University, Japan

**Annemarie Kerkhof**, PRé Consultants b.v., The Netherlands

**Ida Kubiszewski**, Institute for Sustainable Solutions, Portland State University

**Manfred Lenzen,** Professor of Sustainability Research, Integrated Sustainability Analysis (ISA) School of Physics, University of Sydney, Sydney, Australia

**Kate Lloyd,** Department of Environment and Geography, Macquarie University

**Darian McBain,** Director, Blue Sky Green; Integrated Sustainability Analysis (ISA) School of Physics, University of Sydney

**Dr Krista McKinzey,** Climate Change Schools Project Manager, Science Learning Centre North East, Durham University, United Kingdom www.climatechangeschools.org.uk

**Phil McManus**, School of Geosciences, University of Sydney

**Tomorrow, Man,** Superhero, The Future

**Manfred Max-Neef,** Director, Economics Institute, Universidad Austral de Chile

**Dan Moran**, Integrated Sustainability Analysis, University of Sydney

**Michiyo Morisawa,** Carbon Disclosure Project, Japan & UN Principles for Responsible Investment (PRI)

**John Murray,** Freelance artist, Crescent Head, NSW, Australia johnfrancismurray@hotmail.com and www.sowsearsilk.com.au

**Joy Murray,** Senior Research Fellow, Integrated Sustainability Analysis (ISA) School of Physics, University of Sydney, Sydney, Australia

**Harriet Nalukenge**, Senior State Attorney, Ministry of Justice and Constitutional Affairs, Uganda

**Keisuke Nansai,** Senior Researcher, Research Center for Material Cycles and Waste Management, National Institute for Environmental Studies, Japan and Visiting Professor of Sustainability Research, Integrated Sustainability Analysis (ISA), School of Physics, University of Sydney

**Peter Newman,** Curtin University Sustainability Policy (CUSP) Institute, Curtin University, Australia

**Catherine Nielsen**, New South Wales Department of Education and Training

**Catherine O'Brien**, Dept of Education, Cape Breton University, Nova Scotia, Canada

**Yuko Oshita**, Ph.D. candidate, Faculty of Economics, Kyushu University, Japan

**Fabian Sack,** Consultant, Dusseldorp Skills Forum & Honorary Associate, University of Sydney

**David Salt**, ARC Centre of Excellence for Environmental Decisions (CEED), The Fenner School of Environment and Society, College of Medicine, Biology & Environment, Australian National University

**Syd Smith**, Senior adviser to the Environment and Schools Initiative (ENSI) group, Switzerland; former manager Environmental Education Unit, NSW Dept of Education and Training

**Frank Stilwell**, Professor of Political Economy, University of Sydney

**Richard Stirzaker**, CSIRO, Land and Water

**Sandie Suchet-Pearson**, Department of Environment and Geography, Macquarie University

**Sangwon Suh**, Assistant Professor, Bren School of Environmental Science and Management, University of California, Santa Barbara

**David Suzuki**, Professor Emeritus, University of British Columbia; Co-Founder of the David Suzuki Foundation http://www.davidsuzuki.org/

**Heather Tallis**, The Natural Capital Project, Stanford University

**Ted Trainer**, School of Social Work, University of New South Wales

**Sergey Volotovsky**, Climate Resilience Strategy and Policy Advisor, Water Corporation of Western Australia, Perth, Australia

**Mathis Wackernagel**, President, Global Footprint Network

**Thomas Wiedmann**, Senior Research Scientist, CSIRO Ecosystem Sciences, Canberra, Australia; Integrated Sustainability Analysis, University of Sydney, Australia; Centre for Sustainability Accounting (CenSA), York Science Park, York, UK

**Sarah Wright**, Discipline of Geography and Environmental Studies, The University of Newcastle

## Editor bios

Joy Murray is a Senior Research Fellow with the Integrated Sustainability Analysis (ISA) group in the School of Physics at the University of Sydney. Before joining ISA Joy worked for over 25 years in education, teaching students from pre-school to post-graduate.

Glenn Cawthorne is an educator with a strong commitment to the environment and to sustainability. He has over 30 years' teaching experience with a focus on Early Childhood and English as a Second Language.

Christopher Dey is a Senior Research Fellow in the Integrated Sustainability Analysis (ISA) team in the School of Physics at the University of Sydney. His research interests are in energy technologies, greenhouse accounting and sustainability analysis.

Chris Andrew began his working life as an engineer. His journey over the past 25 years took him through roles in the oil, mining, finance, education and clean energy sectors before finally leading him to biodiversity conservation.

# Part I

## An Invitation:
## Two Songs for a Sustainable World

*looking south across the bay* (detail)
**watercolour**

# Chapter 1
## Learning from Indigenous Conceptions of a Connected World

*Laklak Burarrwanga*
*Merrki Ganambarr*
*Banbapuy Ganambarr*
*Bawaka Cultural Experiences*
**Sandie Suchet-Pearson**
**Kate Lloyd**
*Macquarie University*
**Sarah Wright**
*The University of Newcastle*

Come here everyone. We would like to invite you who are reading this book to come here with us now, come, sit on this beautiful mat under the djomula and look across the peaceful waters of Port Bradshaw. Djomula means casuarina trees in Yolŋu matha, our Yolŋu language here in Arnhem Land. Have some cool gapu, water, to drink. It's lovely to have all you teachers here at our homeland Bawaka. This land Bawaka is our life, and our purpose in life is to educate people about how we Yolŋu co-exist with nature in all of its beauty and richness.

So we will sit under these beautiful trees and listen to them whisper to us. We will sit together, share some food and talk about sustainability. We hope that by all talking together, you can learn something about the Yolŋu way of living. We've been here a long time, the longest time, longer than any other culture. Our culture is strong and we will teach you a little bit about it here. We'll share with you about how we relate to Country – to the land, the animals, the winds, the spirit beings, the water, the rocks and everything around us. And we'll talk with you about how we care for Country, how it is so important to us. We care for it, and it cares for us. Animals and plants, seasons and winds, water and ceremony, stars and shells, these are all sentient, they all have knowledge, they are all connected to us. We are not separate and we are not above them. We have a responsibility to each other. To care for one is to care for all. It's our culture and our Law.

Yolŋu people look at things in a connected way. The land and the nature are all kin. We don't separate the environment as something different from us. It's not a 'thing.' We understand that everything is our kin, everything is connected. We humans with our knowledge and our language and our song are no different from the animals, plants and everything around us, which have their own knowledges, their own languages and their own songs. Everything has a rightful place in the world. If you change your thinking this way, maybe you can begin to see the world a bit differently. Maybe you can begin to see something of the Yolŋu way.

My name is Laklak Burarrwanga and I'm a Datiwuy Elder, eldest sister and Caretaker for Gumatj. I'm a qualified teacher and taught many children through primary school here at Bawaka between 1982 and 1991. I've taught many, many others Yolŋu knowledge. The children come out from town to learn here on Country. Now I teach non-Indigenous people, tourists and visitors too. They come here to learn. And Merrki and Banbapuy here, my sisters, are also teachers. They teach our children at the Yirrkala School. Merrki has been a teacher since 1983 and Banbapuy started teaching four years later. You saw Yirrkala, the Aboriginal community, before the two-hour drive to Bawaka didn't you? (Figure 1). And before that had you flown into Nhulunbuy from your homes? Did you fly via Darwin or Cairns? Sandie, Kate and Sarah here, they've been adopted as our sister, daughter and granddaughter and they teach university students in Sydney and Newcastle so they know how long that journey can be. We've all worked together on different projects teaching non-Indigenous people about Yolŋu knowledge here at Bawaka.

Figure 1: Location of Bawaka homeland, North East Arnhem Land, Australia
(Source: Olivier Rey-Lescure)

Let's get you all a nice cuppa tea now and my son Djawa and daughter Djawundil will make sure the wakun, mullet, is cooking nicely. See it over there, sitting on the djilka leaves over the coals? Before we have something to eat let me tell you about Bawaka. This is important. Bawaka is our wäŋa, our place, our homeland, what we call in Aboriginal English *Country*. Aboriginal people all have particular relationships to certain areas of Country and these determine our obligations and responsibilities. Our knowledges and what we do in attending to Country, all relate to our particular areas of Country, our knowledge is localised and we would never, ever presume to speak for someone else's Country. This is different to the Western science taught in schools, isn't it? There, children are taught about knowledge that can be applied generally, in all situations. They tend to learn from the top down if you like, from the broad knowledge of how things 'work', down to the particular situations. We learn the other way round, we learn from feeling, doing and knowing the connections and relationships on the ground. So remember, everything we tell you today is from Bawaka and about Bawaka. But the lessons you learn about knowing the world have importance beyond Bawaka. Maybe these lessons will help you to think about your own ways of teaching, learning, thinking and doing. That is what we are hoping will happen after we talk together.

The first important lesson is that you mustn't think that culture is the same for Aboriginal people everywhere in Australia, or for Torres Strait Islanders or for other Indigenous people elsewhere in the world. People often think that all Aboriginal people or Indigenous people think the same or have the same way of understanding and relating to the world. But no, everyone is different and the ways people understand the world always depends on where they are and who they are and of course people are always using new things and seeing things differently. We didn't always drive to Bawaka in a troopie 4WD like you did today. That troop carrier is pretty new for us, I remember walking to Bawaka with my family when I was much younger. But it's a long way out to Bawaka and we certainly use our troopie now. And of course our solar panels and generator let us have power for our freezer and for lights and fans and a phone. And we can get our bush food much more easily now using guns and outboard motors for our boats.

So, many things change for us, but the underlying things stay the same. The Law, our Rom (what you may know as Dreaming), that stays the same. Our connections with each other and the land are always there, never changing. Our responsibilities - they are enduring. We care for the land, the sea, the water, we look after the trees. We use the land when people go out hunting. All that knowledge is in the land. That's why the old people paint. That art, that's the story about the land. It's like a book, a dictionary that tells about the land. In Canberra, all the politicians have to stand in one place. There the government can change their laws. But our law, our constitution, is on our land. It never changes, for generations and generations to use. I can't change it, it will be the same until the day I die and for all the generations. These things never change.

So you are at Bawaka and learning about Bawaka, walking on our raŋi, our beach. Can you feel the white sand oozing through your toes as you walk? Do you sense the peace, the healing and the learning that can take place here? Do you hear the sand speaking to you as your toes squeak through the fine grains? That is good because our Yolŋu way of learning is not through the pen and the book but by doing and feeling. We learn through the land and the landscape. We learn through experiencing rather than reading, questioning and answering. The land and everything in it are our teachers. So being here is good and it's the beginning of understanding a little bit of what it means to us to be Yolŋu and to live in the world. But remember, we don't have all that long to talk so you're just getting a tiny little glimpse into our knowledge.

Our connection to Country is everything. Country cares for us and we must respect it. What we must do first before anything else, is introduce you to Bawaka and to do this we need to have a smoking ceremony, a welcome to Country. Everyone who comes to Bawaka for the first time must have a smoking ceremony to cleanse them and their spirit, and to make sure that the Bawaka spirit will recognise and protect them. It is like an introduction making sure you belong here. Here, you see we have some smouldering leaves from the djilka tree and we'll brush them over all of you. Breathe deep now, close your eyes and smell that smoke. Now you are safe.

Bayini, who looks after Bawaka, will look after you too. Bayini is one of our ancestors. She still lives on here protecting us. Bayini is a beautiful young princess who came from Makassar in Indonesia a long, long time ago. Her spirit and eyes are still everywhere in Bawaka, looking after the land and the people. She is part of Country, part of what we talk about when we talk about our land. She's got knowledge too, of course.

So, you want to learn about sustainability to teach your students about sustainability. Tell me what do *you* mean by sustainability? We don't have a word for sustainability in Yolŋu matha. What we have is our Yolŋu Law where everything – people, animals, plants, sand dunes, clouds, rain, songs, rocks, sunsets, stars – is always connected, connected through the Rom. So I'm not going to tell you about Indigenous sustainability here because there is no such thing as one, general type of Indigenous sustainability. What I'm going to tell you about are our Bawaka Yolŋu connections. I'm going to introduce you to some of the relationships that weave everything together and mean we remain in balance. I'm going to tell you a little bit about the songs and stories and dances and actions that keep these relationships alive. And finally, I'll tell you a little bit about the obligations and responsibilities that come with these relationships and with starting to understand and know them. We will talk about some ways you might bring these ideas into your own lives and the lives of your students. As you hear our stories, hopefully you will also think about what they mean for you and how you can live in a connected way in your place.

So everyone, look. Can you see the tide slowly going down? Can you see those deep grey clouds in the sky? Can you see the oysters on the rocks at the ends of the raŋi? Hear that gukguk bird calling? There's Djawa turning that wakun on the fire. And the kids, see them running into the water, feeling with their toes and collecting pippies? All these things you can see, everything you can hear, taste, smell, feel, imagine, think about, experience, everything in our Yolŋu world is linked together in a great pattern, a great web of life.

Everything has a place in the web. I'm not just talking in a metaphorical way. We have many patterns, some complex, and some simple, that underpin our relationships, our connections, our responsibilities and our place in the world. The fundamental pattern, or structure, is that of Yirritja and Dhuwa. The anthropologists call Yirritja and Dhuwa moieties and they are the basis for our relationships and connections. All those things I just mentioned, the children, the fire, the fish, the clouds, the tide, the animals, the sand, they are all either Yirritja or Dhuwa. Like yin and yang, Yirritja and Dhuwa are complementary and together they make a whole. They ensure balance and determine responsibilities and obligations. Yirritja and Dhuwa are a cycle, a pattern that goes to infinity. You see my son Djawa there, he is Yirritja, that is because I, his mother, am Dhuwa. Djawa's wives must be Dhuwa just as my husband was Yirritja. You see everything must balance out, what you are determines how you connect and what relationships exist and must be nurtured. This wäŋa Bawaka is Yirritja and as my sisters and I are mothers of this land, we are Dhuwa. You see that rock there, in the

7

middle of the bay? That's the boundary between this Yirritja wäŋa and the next wäŋa, which is Dhuwa. You see, Dhuwa must have Yirritja and Yirritja must have Dhuwa, they can't exist without each other and it is only with each that they can be whole.

Not only must Dhuwa and Yirritja be in balance but they are intimately interconnected. Do you know the famous band from Yirrkala Yothu Yindi? You should play some of their music for your students. There's their song *Treaty* and we'll be talking more about *Djäpana*, sunset, at the end of this story. Go on, play Yothu Yindi's music for your students and you can tell them more about our Yolŋu interrelationships. That's because yothu means child and yindi means mother. This mother-child relationship is incredibly important for us. That's because it's not only about relationships between a mother and her children but about relationships between all people, and between people and everything else. Every person, every thing is a mother (they can be a man or a woman) and every person and thing is also a child. So yothu-yindi means that Dhuwa and Yirritja are always inter-related.

Yirritja and Dhuwa and yothu-yindi help show us where we belong. Are we a mother or a child in any particular relationship? Are we sisters and brothers or are we potentially husband and wife? And don't forget, it is not just people. You can be a sister to a whale or a mother to a particular rock too. There are so many patterns for us, so many ways of belonging. Belonging underpins everything and with it comes responsibility. Merrki plays a game with the children at school, which helps them see some of the layers of belonging. She puts on the music and when it stops she asks the kids to form a group based on their wäŋa, totem. All the kids that have the same totem e.g. python, shark, crocodile etc will gather in a group together. This shows the kids where they belong. Then she starts the music again and this time she tells them to get into groups based on their mälk, skin names. All the different skins come together. This time they see that they are in a different group but that there might be one or two other kids from their previous group in this group. They learn that there are different groups, but also that there are connections. We do this with a range of things, totem, skin names, bapurru, clan groups, e.g. Gumatj. Everyone fits in, in many different ways and these connections go beyond just people. No one and nothing is left out. Can you think of a game to play with your students like this one? I think it is harder for non-Indigenous people to think of ways to group each other so that everyone belongs in different ways. Perhaps there are examples that fit for your students and in your area. Perhaps the students could get into groups by hair colour, star sign, what sport they play, class name or whether they walked, rode, took the bus or drove to school.

Belonging is one of the ways we know our worlds. There are other ways we group things too. In our Yolŋu world we include things that you may not think of as animate, as relations, as family, as kin. That wakun on the fire, it is Dhuwa. Oysters, maypal, they are Yirritja. That gukguk bird, he is Dhuwa. Those rain clouds building up they are Dhuwa. Walu, the sun, is Dhuwa. So I, Laklak, am wakun, walu and gukguk's sister. Ŋalindi the moon is Yirritja so ŋalindi is my waku, my daughter. Baṉumbirr the morning star is family for Dhuwa people, Yirritja people are kin to Djurrpun the evening star. And of course we are inter-related because the yothu-yindi, the mother-child, relationship weaves all Dhuwa and Yirritja together.

Come now, why don't you teachers have a think about the ways you know your worlds. What are the categories and connections that you use to understand things? Think about your own schools, text books and lessons, think about your homes, your towns, farms, cities, families, pets, livestock, gardens, fields, suburbs, rivers, dams, streams. Why don't you ask your students to do this too – to start reflecting back on their own ways of thinking and knowing? You could challenge your students to think about some of the categories they use – for example how useful is it to use summer, winter, autumn, and spring as seasonal markers where they live? Do they see 'wild' fire as something that always needs to be put out? What about the plants and soils that need different types of fires to stay healthy? You could ask your students to break different things into groups based on some of the groups and patterns you use in your teaching? For example, what is nature and what is culture? How do humans fit into your picture? Are humans a part of nature or are they separate? If you had to count the animals in a certain area would you include humans in the count? What is economy and what is environment? Are these separate categories or are they in fact interdependent?

Are the groups you use to understand the world interconnected like the Yolŋu way or are things seen as separate? Do you think that maybe forgetting about or cutting some of those connections has caused so much damage and has meant we need to talk about sustainability today? You could spend time with your students considering some of the many connections that may have been forgotten or disrupted. I'm sure you do already. What about where food comes from and the many, different things that were part of your food's journey to your table? What about where your rubbish goes and the different webs of connection associated with your sewerage's journey – through pipes or perhaps into septic tanks or holes in the ground? Those mobile phones we all use so much, they're closely connected to mining and wars in Africa and what connections to Asia and beyond surround the palm oil used in your soap or shampoo? You could spend a long, long time tracing all the webs of life connected to turning on a light switch in the classroom, driving a car to school or producing a hand ball used at lunch time.

In our world, everything is not only connected but everything is alive. Things like animals, birds, and insects, the winds, the clouds, the rains and the flowers think and act and can communicate with us in different ways. They signal to us. Do you feel that wind now? It's a bit cool isn't it? That wind is telling us to hurry up and finish harvesting the yams, catching our fish and crabs, because the harvest time, the season of Midawarr, is drawing to a close. The world is always talking. The birds, butterflies and plants, they let us know what to do – but we need to pay attention to what they say.

When the dragonflies are out, it's the end of the wet season up here at Bawaka. Do you see dragonflies sometimes and not others? What do these dragonflies tell you? Why don't you and your students learn about the flowers, plants and animals in your area? You can go outside and try and find the connections yourselves. Listen to what the world is telling you. You can learn about native flowers and connect that flower to what is happening in your area. What is happening when a particular flower comes out at your school? You can explore and find out what the flowers, plants, winds or birds are telling you. People don't have the time to look around and pay attention nowadays. But here, we are always teaching our children to look around, to listen, to be aware, to notice when things happen. We know a certain flower will tell you that now is the time to catch a certain animal, to fish or to gather a certain fruit. See the connection? The pattern? You can go out and get fish anytime but you need to know the right time of year, the time when the fish are fat or else you'll be eating the fish at the wrong time and it won't be good for you. Or maybe you will be wasting your time because that fish might not be there at all. We take our kids out to learn how to read the signals, to look for food. You could take your students out too. And where ever you are there will be Indigenous people who can help you see and make the connections too. Why not make the effort to connect with them as well?

And these relationships do not exist in a vacuum. They need to be constantly nurtured and attended to. Our songs, dances and stories constantly make the relationships real and our interactions through hunting, eating, fishing, living on Country, burning Country are essential to keeping the webs of connection alive. Every Wednesday at school in Yirrkala, Merrki runs a Galtha workshop. Galtha refers to the way Yolŋu end a negotiation by piercing a spear into the ground. Galtha workshops are when we bring Yolŋu and Western knowledge together at our school; it is like a negotiation where all forms of knowledge are respected. This term, the students are learning about seasons, about what Midawarr, the harvest season is about. This is where we get different food. One group gets djitama, a very poisonous yam that needs to be properly prepared in fresh running water to be edible. The group goes out collecting yams, making sure there is plenty left over for more yams to grow up, and they learn how to prepare it for eating. Next term we will learn about a different season. Maybe you can do that with your students too, to see the connections and be part of making them at the same time. Sometimes in the classroom we also make a circle to represent the year. We cut out some animals and ask the students to place them on the circle for when they appear or when is the time to hunt or gather them. For us, that is bush foods but for your students, you could include some fish, wild animals and plants that they may eat or gather but what about encouraging them to connect with the rhythms of when certain fruits and vegetables grow, maybe in a vegetable garden at school, or at home or at the local markets, or when's the best time to eat certain animals and fish?

The land Bawaka is very important. It has lots of knowledge in it. Knowledge is in the sea and in the land. It is very important to Yolŋu people to look after and care for the land because it's our life. There will be no life if there is no land. Yolŋu people are lucky because we have our own land, our own promised land. Way back, ancestors made the land and they've got knowledge. They said, this land is for Gumatji, Galpu people, all the clans. We wouldn't be here without our ancestors. We wouldn't have language, culture, knowledge without our ancestors and without the land that they made and that made them. And so you can see what we do is so important as it cares for Country. But, don't forget Country cares for us too. And Country cares for itself.

Humans are not the centre of the Yolŋu world. Are they the centre of your worlds? Humans are not the only beings who can think, feel, understand, know. Everyone, every nature, every person living in Arnhem Land, they've got their own knowledge, even the trees, the water, the animals, the birds, they've got their own knowledge and language – same as people. We see the birds when they make a nest for their baby, they make a warm nest, where do they learn, where do they get their knowledge?

I understand that many scientists in Western thinking are also realizing that non-humans have intelligence and purpose, that they can live moral, emotional lives. Maybe you can spend some time thinking this through with your students so that humans are not always seen as superior and in control but rather a part of reciprocal, attentive and respectful relationships. Ask your students what they think sentience is – what thinking, living and the will to act – all involve. Does a plant dropping a fruit show a will to reproduce? What about the grass seed that gets stuck to your sock and makes you carry it to another place where it can grow? What happens if you all attend to your school grounds and take notice of the actions of the animals, insects, plants, rocks, grasses, stones, rain runoff, and soils? Where does that water want to go? What does that tree desire to live well?

Aah, look now at the sunset. The delicate crimson, orange and red colours all around you. The colours drift around the sun and into our hearts. All sunsets here on Yirritja Country are djäpana sunsets and all songs and stories from Bawaka, including this one, end with djäpana. We hope that you have enjoyed your time here and have experienced a little bit of Bawaka and learnt a bit too, a bit about our ways of knowing the world, but more importantly a bit about yourselves. We hope that you've learnt about our connections and relationships and about the ways we all work together to share and look after each other. We hope that learning a little about us, and our way of living, will help you reflect on what you know and what you teach your students. Stopping and reflecting on your own ways of understanding may help you to think about sustainability in a different way and may help you to make your own connections for a more balanced world wherever you may live.

Remember, balance is key to our world and part of keeping that balance is reciprocity. As we care for Country, Country cares for us. So we have obligations and responsibilities to know and nurture our relationships. Now that you've been welcomed to Bawaka and leant new things, you too have obligations and responsibilities. One of these is that you respect our know-ledge. We often hear stories of non-Indigenous people thinking Indigenous ways (medicines, techniques, songs, knowledges) are better and they steal them, exploit them and make money out of them and this is very wrong. But we are happy to share some of our knowledge with you and we now hope you will share it with others. That is part of your obligation. To share what you know respectfully. The reflections and thoughts you have, we hope they travel far and wide. We hope that we have inspired you to think carefully about what you know, do and teach, and that you use the learning with your students to not only think about how to live more respectfully in your own worlds, but to think about your obligations and responsibilities to attend to all things with care.

## *Further reading*

Bodkin, F. & Robertson, L. (2008). *D'harawal seasons and climatic cycles*. Sydney: Natural Heritage Trust.

Burarrwanga, L., Ganambarr, R., Ganambarr, M., Ganambarr, B., May-muru D., Suchet-Pearson, S., Wright, S., & Lloyd, K. (in draft). *Welcome to my country*.

Burarrwanga, L., Maymuru, D., Ganambarr, R., Ganambarr, B., Wright, S., Suchet-Pearson, S. & Lloyd, K. (2008). *Weaving lives together at Bawaka, North East Arnhem Land*. Newcastle, Callaghan: Centre for Urban and Regional Studies, University of Newcastle.

Christie, M. (1994). Grounded and ex centric knowledges: exploring Abori-ginal alternatives to Western thinking. In J. Edwards (Ed.), *Think-ing: International Interdisciplinary Perspectives (pp. 24-34)*. Victoria: Hawker Brownlow Education.

Rose, D.B. (1996). *Nourishing Terrains: Australian Aboriginal views of land-scape and wilderness*. Canberra: Australian Heritage Commission. http://www.environment.gov.au/heritage/ahc/publications/com-mission/books/pubs/nourishing-terrains.pdf

Sveiby, K. & Skuthorpe, T. (2006). *Treading lightly: The hidden wisdom of the world's oldest people*. Crows Nest: Allen & Unwin.

## *Resources*

Bawaka Cultural Experiences:
     http://www.bawaka.com.au/
Indigenous Concepts of Country and Sustainability:
     http://www.aries.mq.edu.au/projects/deewr_indigenous_con-cepts/index.php

Living knowledge: Indigenous knowledge in science education:
    http://livingknowledge.anu.edu.au/html/educators/index.htm
Yothu yindi:
    http://www.yothuyindi.com/


*Children's books*

Christophersen, J. & Christophersen, C. (2005). *My home in Kakadu*.
    Broome: Magabala Books.
Christophersen, J. (2007). *Kakadu Calling*. Broome: Magabala Books.

# Chapter 2
## From David Suzuki's Speech to the Green Party of Aotearoa New Zealand, November 12, 2010

*David Suzuki*
*University of British Columbia*

I hope you'll permit me to provide some context from the standpoint of my perspective as a scientist, a biologist and an elder.

*Part 1*

As a biologist I tend to look at human beings in terms of evolutionary time. Remember that life appeared on this planet perhaps 3.8 to 4 billion years ago, and of all the species that have existed, it's estimated that 99.9999% are extinct. Extinction is a natural process, necessary for life to evolve as conditions on the planet change over time. The average life span of a species is 1-2 million years. Modern human beings have been on earth for perhaps 150,000 years – we're an infant species; and yet, we're already creating conditions that make the possible extinction of humanity a very real one within the next few generations.

Africa was our birthplace, but we have now spread around the entire planet and one of the great keys to our success as a species has been our adaptability. We're not bound to a specific habitat or ecosystem by hereditary limits. We are so adaptable, we have learned to live very comfortably in environments as different as the Arctic tundra, steaming jungles and tropical rainforests, mountains, temperate rainforests, wetlands, prairies – we are a very adaptable species.

And now, we have entered a period of unprecedented rapid change and we've marginalised the very people who can provide some context and sense of the speed at which we're changing. That is, we've marginalised our elders. Our elders, who are a repository of memory, of culture, of experience, that provides us with a sense of assessing where we are today. There is a constant shifting of baselines, so we don't know where we've come from and therefore, where we're going.

A film shown on public broadcasting a few years ago called 'Empty Oceans, Empty Nets', had an interview with a very young skipper of a swordfish boat out of Boston. She said: "Oh yes, there are lots of swordfish in the ocean. We go up around Newfoundland and get our limit in a few weeks". She added, "A few weeks ago someone caught a 200 pound swordfish. There are big fish still left in the oceans." The film then cut to a man who must have been in his early 80s and had been a swordfisherman all his life. He told us he seldom had gone further than 4 or 5 miles out of Boston and had let anything under 200 pounds go. So the baseline has shifted to where a young swordfish skipper considered it normal to go all the way to Newfoundland to fish and a 200 pounder had become a big fish.

My wife and I have a cabin on an island in the Pacific and when we leave Vancouver and get on the last ferry to our island, we rejoice because we can see salmon, herring balls and eagles and we think "Oh it's so great to get back in nature". Then we talk to our neighbour who is in his 80s, and he remembers when you could hear the salmon miles away, they were so abundant that you could hear them splashing in the water. He remembers you could go out in a punt with a rake and rake herring off the kelp beds and fill a punt in 15 minutes. He describes an island that is unrecognisable today. But because we live in a fundamentally degraded environment of a city, to us, our cabin seems to be rich and we think "Oh this is what nature always was", because we don't have our elders to remind us of what once was.

I was born in Vancouver in 1936. My parents came through the Great Depression and they have taught us some of the lessons I have tried to instil in my own children. They taught us to live within our means. They taught us to save some for tomorrow. They taught us to help our neighbours because you never know when you might need their help. And they taught us to work hard to earn money because money is needed to buy the necessities in life. But you don't run after money as if having more money or stuff makes you a more important or better human being. We were taught to feel sorry for people who got caught up in running after money, more stuff and flashy clothes and cars.

Now we celebrate the super rich. There are magazines and programs about the wealthy and we look to them as role models, people we envy and aspire to become. Today we define ourselves not as parents, as churchgoers, as teachers, as plumbers, but as consumers. Our job in society today is to go out and buy stuff. It wasn't an accident or joke after 9/11, Mr Bush's first call to the American public was to go out and shop. That wasn't a joke. They had to go out and shop because 70% of the American economy is based on consumption. That consumption is not about providing our *needs*, or what my parents called the necessities of life, but the consumption based on our *wants* and there's no limit to what we want.

What is the issue today? Imagine a graph in which the X-axis is divided into 15 units, while each unit represents 10,000 years. Then on the Y-axis is population in billions. For 99% of 150,000 years, that time the curve is virtually flat on this graph. Ten thousand years ago, at the beginning of the agricultural revolution, there were about 10 million human beings on the entire planet. Agriculture heralded a huge shift in the way that we live, so that in only 8,000 years that number had increased by an order of magnitude. By the time Jesus Christ was thought to have been born, it's estimated that there were a hundred million people. On this graph, that's in the last pencil width of time. We reached the first billion people in the early 1800s and then in less than 200 years we reached 6.9 billion human-beings in 2010, and the curve is now going straight up off the page.

## Part 2

You can superimpose on that same 150,000-year chart, virtually everything from fishing catches to logging and the amount of carbon we produce and release into the atmosphere. And that's the challenge. This is all happening at once, but we have no baseline in our lives, we're really not aware of the incredible change in the human impact on the planet.

We are now the most numerous mammal on earth. There has never been as many of one species of mammal as there are of us today – 6.9 billion – and we are having a heavy impact on the planet. We have become so powerful with our numbers, technology, consumptive demand and the global economy that we're actually altering the physical, chemical and biological features of the planet on a geological scale. Geologists divide Earth's history based on major geological events into epochs like the Pleistocene, Eocene, Myocene and so on. Paul Crutzen, the Nobel prize winner, suggests that the present should be considered the Anthropocene epoch, the time when human beings have become so powerful that we are a geological force.

How did we get to this moment? We're not well endowed with size, speed, strength or sensory abilities. We're just a naked ape. But of course, we have one big advantage over the rest of creation, and that was the largest brain to brawn ratio ever achieved. The human brain more than compensated for our lack of physical and sensory ability. That brain endowed us with a massive memory, made us curious and impressively inventive. And those qualities more than compensated for our lack of other endowments.

We invented the concept of a future. The future doesn't exist; the only thing that exists is now and what we can remember of the past. But because the human brain invented the idea of a future we are the only creature that realised that we can affect the future by what we do today. With our accumulated knowledge, experience and observations, we can now look ahead and choose a path today to avoid dangers and exploit opportunities. I believe our great advantage over the rest of creation was *foresight* that enabled us to dream of a world to come, in which we could avoid dangers and exploit opportunities, and then work in the present toward achieving that. It brought us to our present dominance on the entire planet, and we have scientists and supercomputers that can act in the very best tradition of our species – pull together our accumulated knowledge then look ahead to see where it is leading us. And for 40 years, scientists have been warning us that we've been going down a very dangerous path. Scientists, acting in the best traditions of our species, have been looking ahead and seeing where the dangers and opportunities lie.

A remarkable document released in November of 1992 was called *World Scientists' Warning to Humanity*. When you look at the more than 1500 scientists who have signed this, these are not third or second-rate scientists these are the top scientists in the world. Over half of all scientists alive in 1992 signed this document. So, what were they warning us about?

> *"Human beings and the natural world are on a collision course. Human activities inflict harsh and often irreversible damage on the environment and on critical resources. If not checked, many of our current practices put at serious risk the future we wish for human society and may so alter the living world that it will be unable to sustain life in the manner that we know. Fundamental changes are urgent if we are to avoid the collision our present course will bring about."*

And then the document goes on to list the areas of collision: the atmosphere, water resources, oceans, soil, forests, living species and population. And then, the words grow even more bleak:

> *"No more than one or a few decades remain before the chance to avert the threats we now confront will be lost, and the prospects for humanity immeasurably diminished. We, the undersigned senior members of the world's scientific community hereby warn all humanity of what lies ahead. A great change in our stewardship of the earth and life on it is required if vast human misery is to be avoided, and our global home of this planet is not to be irretrievably mutilated."*

And then they list the five most urgent programs that must be started immediately.

This is a frightening document. Scientists of this stature don't often sign such strongly worded documents. But if this is a frightening warning, the response of the media around the world was terrifying. There was no response. I don't know about New Zealand, but in North America, none of the major television networks bothered to report it. In Canada, the CBC (our national broadcaster) didn't report it. Our only national newspaper at that time, the Globe and Mail, didn't bother to report it. So, you've got to wonder what we're being informed about when such a statement is basically ignored. I sat as a Board member of the Millennium Ecosystem Assessment, a UN Committee that was the largest study ever done on the state of ecosystems around the planet. Two years ago we completed the work, and it was a frightening document as you might expect and called for immediate action. The announcement of the final report was made in New York City.

Kofi Annan was still the UN Secretary General and attended the press conference to announce the results. In Canada, our national newspaper covered it. The very next day, the Pope got sick and went to hospital and his illness, death and succession pushed everything off the media agenda. So, what was the largest study ever carried out on the state of the globe's ecosystems was a one-day page 3 story in Canada. And then the media went on to other things.

I arrived in Australia, four weeks ago now, the day after it was announced that 20% of plant species on the planet are in danger of going extinct by the middle of the century, but when I landed, the banner headlines were "Australian dollar reaches parity with the American dollar"! Twenty per cent of plant species in danger of extinction, (last week, reports from Nagoya suggested that 20% of vertebrate species could be extinct by the middle of this century) yet media focus on fluctuations in the economy or the daily Dow Jones average. It shows you what our priorities are today.

## Part 3

The economy is the dominant issue that occupies our attention today. We talk today about the triple bottom line. Usually this is depicted by three circles of equal size that all intersect: society, the environment, the economy. This is the dumbest idea I have ever heard. There is one big circle and that is the biosphere, the zone of air water and land where all life exists. Carl Sagan, the late astronomer, told us if the earth were shrunk to the size of a basketball, the biosphere, where all 30 million species live, would be thinner than a layer of varnish painted onto that ball. That's it. It's fixed and can't grow and that's what allows life to exist. Within that biosphere you should have 30 million tiny circles representing all the other species that occupy the biosphere. But one of those circles now is about 40% of the area of the biosphere – that's us. We have now co-opted over 40% of the photosynthetic activity (what is called the net primary productivity) on this planet, and when we co-opt that activity we deny it to other species and therefore create an extinction crisis. We're on our way trying to co-opt 80% of the photosynthetic activity of the planet. This is absolutely suicidal for us. So within that sphere which represents our species, there should be an even smaller circle and that's the economy. And yet we've got this crazy idea that the economy can exist as the same size as the environment and society – this is just nuts.

The word economics is based on the same root Greek word as ecology. Oikos is the Greek words meaning household or domain. Ecology is the study of home. Economics is its management. Ecologists try to determine the conditions and principles that enable a species, any species, to survive and flourish. Not a bad bit of information. I would have thought that any group in society, any government, any corporation, before beginning any new program would say 'Oh wait a minute now. What were those ecologists telling us? What were those principles and conditions? Because whatever we do, we don't want to violate those principles or conditions.' But no, we don't do that we want to elevate the economy *above* ecology. Of the three amigos, George Bush, John Howard and Stephen Harper, only Harper remains but he continues their radical policy of climate change denial. And he maintains that doing anything to reduce greenhouse gas emissions will destroy the economy. So Canada's prime minister elevates the economy above the very atmosphere that keeps all life alive.

Our energy province in Canada is Alberta, comparable to the state of Texas. It's our petro state. And a past Alberta minister of the environment was quoted as saying 'Environmentalists should understand we can't afford to do what they're demanding if we don't have a strong growing economy.' So even the minister of the environment whose job is to protect the environment thinks the economy is our highest priority and as long as it's functioning well, then we can afford to do the things that keep us alive. This is absolutely crazy. I'm reminded of the most important children's tale that we teach our kids about the goose that laid the golden egg. And you know, as long as the goose was fat and healthy it laid a golden egg every day. But then, the owners of the goose got greedy. They wanted more at once, so they killed the goose to get more and discovered it was just a goose. The point is the goose is the biosphere. The goose is our forests, our soil, our oceans. And as long as we keep them as our highest priority, they are the source of economy, and provide our well-being and happiness. But we forget that.

We have forgotten that we live in a world that is shaped by realities, from principles that emerge from science. We know in the world of physics, the first and second laws of thermodynamics inform us that you cannot build a perpetual motion machine. The law of gravity says you can't have an anti-gravity machine here on earth. And certainly, the speed of light determines that we can't build a rocket that will travel faster than the speed of light. These are physical principles in the world that we live in and we live with them, we can't exceed them or change them – that's fact.

Chemistry dictates that there are principles, there are laws that regulate the kind of chemical reactions that we can have, the rate at which they can go on, the kind of molecules you can create by reacting various compounds and reagents. The rates of diffusion and reaction determine what we can do in the field of chemistry. And biology informs us that we are biological creatures – we're animals. And people don't like to be told that anymore. You can see our attitude if you call someone a chicken, a pig, a worm, a snake, a monkey – these are insults because we think somehow we are superior to these other creatures. A few years ago I went to a store in Calgary with a great big sign on the front door 'No animals allowed.' I told the owner if he enforced that sign he wouldn't have any customers. He didn't know what the hell I was talking about. That's the way we are.

We are animals, biology tells us, and we have an absolute requirement for clean air, clean water, clean soil, clean energy that comes from the sun and biodiversity. Without those things we sicken and die. Those, it seems to me, should be our highest priorities, because we're animals and we can't do anything about it. We need those things, just to stay healthy.

We live in a world that is shaped by principles and facts that emerge from the laws of physics, chemistry and biology. Other things like capitalism, free enterprise, corporations, the economy, currency and markets are not forces of nature, we invented them! We can't change the laws of nature; but we can sure as hell change these human creations. Indeed, we've got to change them, because they are totally out of sync, or out of balance, with the world that makes them possible. And we elevate them now as if they are forces of nature.

A few centuries ago people believed in dragons, demons and monsters. We really believed in them. If we thought they were mad at us we'd give them gold, jewels, sacrifice virgins – anything to get them off our back. Well nobody believes in dragons, demons and monsters today, we know they're figments of our imagination. But then what do we do? We replace them with another figment of our imagination: the economy. And by God, you read the headlines: 'The economy is not looking too healthy today'. Man do we get scared. I mean we give them gold, we give them jewels, we'll give them anything else. We just want them back up and running. What's going on? We can change the economy if it's not working.

## *Part 4*

In 2008, the global economic meltdown was an incredible opportunity to sit down and recognize something is wrong here. We can't go from dot-com boom to bust, housing boom to bust, this is crazy. Let's change the bloody system! But what did we do? The first thing Mr Bush did, and then Mr Obama after, was to pump hundreds of billions of dollars into the very banks that created the problem, into the auto-sector without any strings attached. All they asked was for them get back up and running and growing again.

Einstein said the definition of insanity is doing the same thing over and over and expecting a different result. And that's what we're doing. We can modify, we can change these human created things; we can't change the world of nature.

What kind of shift do we need? We need a shift from an anthropocentric point of view in which we think that we are so bloody important we can take over and manage the entire planet through the lenses of our self-importance. We think we're in control and it's ours to take charge. The reality is we need a biocentric point of view in which we see ourselves as one species among a community of other organisms that keep the planet habitable and healthy for animals like us. We are a part of and utterly dependent on that community. We are not the dominant animal in charge of the whole thing.

We have to stop trying to shoehorn nature into our economic, social and political priorities. We've got to live with nature as it is and try to do everything we can to ensure that nature, the goose, prospers and is fat and healthy. Then we will reap all the benefits that come from that.

But look at what's happened as a result of the way we try to do things. December 2009 in Copenhagen, 192 countries trying to negotiate the atmosphere as if it belonged to each of them. How can you look at what is a single system through 192 different national lenses? And each of the 192 countries has its own economic priorities and agendas. Then they all attempt to manage the atmosphere. It's madness! It can never work this way until we all agree the atmosphere is our highest priority, because that's what lets us live. And whatever we do, we've got to shoehorn our political agendas, our national agendas, our economic agendas into a way that will allow for the flourishing of the atmosphere.

Nagoya in 2010 we saw the same thing, a 192 countries came to Nagoya in Japan a couple of weeks ago, and tried to negotiate the future of biodiversity. Do you think other species care about economic or national borders? Of course not! And yet we're trying to determine the future of biodiversity on the planet through the same kind of international mechanisms. That won't work.

The planet has been fully occupied and fully developed by tens of million of species for millions of years. The Brundtland Commission Report, *Our Common Future*, was a groundbreaking report that coined the phrase *sustainable development* and advocated protecting 12% of our land base for the rest of nature. And that was shocking. We are one species out of 30 million, yet the report assumes it's our species' right to take over 88% of the planet's terrestrial surface as if it is not going to have enormous consequences. And now delegates at Nagoya raised the area to be protected to 17% as if taking over 83% of the land base and the vast bulk of the oceans will have little consequence for us.

Thank goodness there is a Green Party to constantly raise these issues and provide a desperately needed perspective. But so long as there's a Green Party, the environment is just another vested interest issue. We have to move to a society that understands to its core our utter dependence on the rest of creation for our health and well-being. Are there examples of success or role models to emulate? Everybody knows that Bhutan has a Gross Happiness Index instead of a Gross Domestic Product. The poor country of Bolivia has elected the first indigenous person as PM or president in any country in the world, and they've now enshrined Mother Nature in their constitution, so that forests, and fish, and birds have a constitutional right to exist and flourish. When people ask where to look to, I say Cuba is a model, where 80% of food consumed in their cities is grown right in the cities. Cuba is a poor country by our standards, yet ensures education to all right through university, medical care for all and one of the highest rates of literacy and birth survival. There are ways we can begin to shift from the current economic paradigm.

The problem with the economy right now is that it is so fundamentally flawed that however well meaning we are, if we don't toss this system up or radically modify it, we're still going to be led down a suicidal path. Leaders meeting at Bretton Woods in 1944, designed a post-war economy by creating the World Bank, the International Monetary Fund, tying world currency to the American greenback and so on. But they left out nature, which performs dozens of services that keep the planet healthy and habitable for us and make economies possible. To me, the most frightening report I've heard in years was when 70% of honeybees in North America suddenly vanished. That sent the biggest bolt of fear through me because if pollinators were to disappear, we would follow very quickly. It wouldn't be possible for humanity to exist without pollinators. And that's considered irrelevant by economists. It's an externality. Nature's performance is basically dismissed or overlooked by our conventional economic system. Now, I know there's a big push by ecological economists to internalise what we currently externalise, and that's an interesting exercise, but I happen to think that there are lots of things that are *sacred*. When you have something that is sacred, you cannot put a value on that because it's beyond economics. How do you incorporate the sacred? And I've learnt this through my indigenous brothers and sisters who have taught me in Canada, that the earth is literally our mother. How do you put an economic value on your mother? We are created out of the sacred elements: earth, air, fire and water. How do you put a value on things that are sacred?

And the other problem is that we've created an economic system in which growth has become the very definition of progress. Ask any politician, even a Green politician I bet, or a corporate executive: "How well did you do last year?" And the chances are, within a pico-second, they'll talk about growth in GDP, the economy, market share, jobs or profit. Growth is synonymous with progress. But what is growth? What does growth do for us? Growth is just a description of the state of a system. How can you make growth an end when it is just a means to something else? But when growth is progress, nobody wants to impede progress. So we never ask the important questions like what an economy is for? How much is enough? Are there no limits? Are we happier with all this stuff? We should be asking these questions, but even the discussion here was about fitting this economy and ensuring its health in growing. It can't grow, and you pointed out the example of lilies in the pond starting with one at time zero and doubling every minute until the pond is full at 30 minutes. Every scientist I have talked to agrees with me, we're past the 29th minute. And all this talk about grow, grow, grow, becomes suicidal. We've got to aim not just for a static economy, we've got to shrink our economy. We, 20% of the world in the rich countries are using over 80% of the planet's resources. And we love to say that the big problem is overpopulation, that it's those brown, black and yellow people, who are breeding like flies. But wait a minute, it's not just a function of numbers; it's how much you consume per person. We are consuming over 80% of the planet's resources and leaving a pittance for the developing world, and we act as if they're the problem. We're the major predator of Earth's finite resources and the only opportunity, if we're not going to go and slaughter people, is to cut back on our consumption and our economic growth.

So this is the challenge, the growth economy and what do we do about that. And what do we do about nature that doesn't even play a role in an economic system that is utterly dependent on it?

Thank you very much

# Part II

## Sustainability is Everyone's Business

*beranghi*
watercolour
12cm by 8cm

# Chapter 3
## Measuring Sustainability

*Dan Moran*
*Integrated Sustainability Analysis, University of Sydney*
*Mathis Wackernagel*
*Global Footprint Network*

Children today are growing up in a world in which the biosphere is stretched beyond the limits of its ability to provide for us. Our planet provides a critical supply of resources and services that we often take for granted. This is a new, and big, problem.

During most of human civilization humanity has been small compared to the planet. Homo sapiens was just one species in a biosphere with room for many. But today that is not the case. We dominate the planet. Humans, domesticated animals and our pets make up an estimated 95% of mammalian biomass[1]. We consume one quarter of the gross product of photosynthesis

---

1.Smil, V. (2003). *The Earth's Biosphere: Evolution, Dynamics, and Change*. Cambridge, MA: The MIT Press.

each year[2]. A recent scientific survey paper identified seven specific bio-sphere limits that are dangerous to cross (e.g. maximum alteration of biogeochemical cycles such as carbon and nitrogen, ozone layer thickness, annual biodiversity loss, acidification limits) and found that we have sur-passed three of them[3]. And our Ecological Footprint is so large it would re-quire 1.5 planets to renew all we use (or it takes one year and a half to renew what we use in one year)[4]. Some scientists propose that these changes are so significant that we are actually in a new geological era, the Anthropocene.

Today the biosphere is no longer an unlimited resource. We must learn to use it more carefully. We must learn to satisfy our needs and wants while putting less pressure on the planet. But how much less and how soon? This is what measuring sustainability is about. We need to know how much nature we have, and how much we need.

### *Ecological overshoot*

Ecological overshoot is the term for the situation we are currently in, whereby we are using natural resources more quickly than they are replen-ished.

The biosphere provides a huge flux of ecosystem services which form the foundation for all human life. The Millennium Ecosystem Assessment[5] (MEA) report by the UN is a comprehensive scientific survey of the health of all major ecosystem services. The MEA groups ecosystems into four cat-egories: *Provisioning services* such as fresh water, ocean fisheries, forests, rivers for hydropower, and much more. *Regulating services* include the nat-ural filtering of air and water, natural pollination, waste and sewage absorp-tion, climate regulation and $CO_2$ sequestration. *Supporting services* include nutrient cycling and seed dispersal. Finally, *cultural services* refer to the emo-tional and recreational benefits of enjoying nature, as well as the value of scientific discoveries based on natural phenomenon and materials. The au-

2. Haberl, H., Erb, K.H., Krausmann, F., Gaube, V., Bondeau, A., Plutzar, C., Gin-grich, S., Lucht, W. & Fischer-Kowalski, M. (2007). Quantifying and mapping the human appropriation of net primary production in earth's terrestrial ecosystems. *Proceedings of the National Academy of Sciences 104*(31), 12942-12947. Also see Vitousek, P.M., Mooney, H.A., Lubchenco, J. & Melillo, J.M. (1997). Human domination of Earth's ecosystems. *Science, 277*(5325), 494-499.

3. Rockström, J., W. Steffen, K. Noone, Å. Persson, F. S. Chapin, III, E. Lambin, T. M. Lenton, M. Scheffer, C. Folke, H. Schellnhuber, B. Nykvist, C. A. De Wit, T. Hughes, S. van der Leeuw, H. Rodhe, S. Sörlin, P. K. Snyder, R. Costanza, U. Sved-in, M. Falkenmark, L. Karlberg, R. W. Corell, V. J. Fabry, J. Hansen, B. Walker, D. Liverman, K. Richardson, P. Crutzen, & J. Foley. (2009). Planetary Boundaries: Ex-ploring the Safe Operating Space for Humanity. *Ecology and Society 14*(2), 32. Online at http://www.ecologyandsociety.org/vol14/iss2/art32/.

4. Global Footprint Network, (2010). Ecological Footprint Atlas 2010, www.footprintnetwork.org

5. http://maweb.org

thors say, "The bottom line of the MA findings is that human actions are depleting Earth's natural capital, putting such strain on the environment that the ability of the planet's ecosystems to sustain future generations can no longer be taken for granted."

Ecological overshoot occurs when we start drawing on these ecosystem services so heavily that the biosphere providing them gets damaged. One example is observed in some deep ocean fishing grounds. As populations of high value fish like tuna and salmon get fished out the fleets start harvesting smaller, lower trophic level fish. But these smaller fish are the main food for the larger fish and therefore the population of larger fish cannot recover. This is an example of a renewable resource (a fishery) being used so intensively that it becomes damaged and cannot provide as much as it could originally. Natural resources must be carefully managed to ensure they remain healthy for the next generation.

It is possible to exist in ecological overshoot for some time. The orange roughy is a good example. This deep-sea fish grows and reproduces very slowly. By some figures the average filet of orange roughy comes from a 50 year old fish. Not only do the fish grow slowly and mate rarely, the bottom-trawlers used to harvest the fish seriously damage its habitat. In Australia it took less than 20 years to fish out 90% of the orange roughy population and earn the fish a spot on the endangered species list. For those years the fishery was profitable, but in serious overshoot.

This same pattern appears all too often across different ecosystem services. Forests, in some areas, are harvested more quickly than they grow, groundwater and in some places even entire lakes have been drawn down more quickly than they refill, waste is emitted more quickly than it can be naturally absorbed – particularly greenhouse gases in the atmosphere; the list goes on. We can overexploit a resource for a while, but at some point it is damaged, the stock is used up, and eventually ecosystems collapse. And with it all who depend on those ecosystems.

Overshoot also contributes to resource conflicts and wars, mass migrations, famine, disease and other human tragedies – and tends to have a disproportionate impact on the poor, who cannot buy their way out of the problem by getting resources from somewhere else.

$CO_2$ accumulation is one of the most serious instances of global overshoot. For decades we have been emitting $CO_2$ more quickly than it can be sequestered by plants and trees. Essentially we are emitting $CO_2$ as waste more quickly than it can be absorbed. By August 21, 2010, humanity had used all the combined resource production and carbon sequestration capacity that the planet's ecosystems had available for that entire year. Since the mid-1970s, when global ecological overshoot first became a consistent reality, we have been drawing down the biosphere's principal rather than living off its annual interest. To support our consumption we have been liquidating resource stocks and allowing carbon dioxide to accumulate in the atmosphere.

## *Measuring our impact: the Ecological Footprint*

Humanity relies on the planet's ecological services to provide basic needs – food, clothing and shelter. But how much are we using, and how much do we have?

The Ecological Footprint is an accounting tool for answering these questions. The Footprint measures human demand on nature by tracking how much land and water area (i.e. forests, agricultural land, rivers, etc) a human population requires to produce the resources it uses and to absorb its wastes, using prevailing technology. Nature's ability to provide these services is called biocapacity. It is the source of clean water, grain for our bread, lumber for our houses, vegetable or animal fibres for making our clothes. Ultimately, the Footprint can assess the demand of any human activity by answering the question: How much nature does it take? Therefore this tool can be used for products, individuals, households, businesses, cities, countries and humanity as a whole.

Accounting for a country's consumption Footprint starts with tracking all goods and services produced in that country, then adding imports and subtracting exports.

Biocapacity is the area of productive land and water available to provide all ecological services, including production of biological resources and absorption of carbon dioxide waste, under current management practices. Both the Ecological Footprint and biocapacity are measured in standard units called global hectares (gha). One gha represents a biologically productive hectare such as a forest, cropland, grazing land or fishing grounds, with world average productivity.

It may not be wise for humanity to have an Ecological Footprint that occupies 100% of the Earth's biocapacity. After all, humanity is just one species and there may be at least 10 million other species with which we share this planet. How much do you suggest humanity leaves to other species? Ten percent of the Earth, or maybe twenty? The eminent Harvard professor of biology, E.O. Wilson, implores in his book *The Future of Life* to leave 50% of the planet's biocapacity untouched in order to guarantee a deep reserve of biodiversity. He considers biodiversity to be the main legacy we have. Many others agree with him, considering biodiversity to be crucial for the healthy operation of many ecosystem services.

While economies, populations and resource demands grow, the size of the planet remains the same. In 2007, humanity's Footprint exceeded global biocapacity by 50%. If even moderate United Nations' projections come true, the consequence would be growing human demand far beyond Earth's biocapacity. Following these 'moderate' trends would mean that by the late 2030s the capacity of two Earths would be needed to keep up with our consumption. But are such sustained levels of overshoot physically possible? Staying on this course of continuous overshoot would quickly diminish our room to manoeuvre and the wellbeing of many of the planet's residents would be increasingly at risk.

*Reducing your Ecological Footprint*

There are many ways to reduce your Ecological Footprint. Here are a few possibilities:

- Bike, bus or carpool to school. If you drive to school or if parents make a special trip to drive to school, that trip emits $CO_2$ and contributes to global warming. A bus emits much less $CO_2$ and a bike emits none!

- Eat less meat. Look up Peter Menzel's illuminating photo essay book *Hungry Planet* to see pictures of what different families around the world eat each week, and compare that to how much meat and energy-intensive processed foods your family usually eats. It takes a lot of feed, fuel and water to run a modern cattle ranch. In some places there's so much demand for meat that rainforest gets cut down illegally to make new ranches and soybean farms for cattle feed. Also, cattle emit methane from burps and flatulence – and methane is 26 times more potent per molecule than $CO_2$ as a greenhouse gas. Because of this, livestock produce a stunning 18% of all greenhouse gas emissions[6].

- Live locally. Eat locally grown food. It requires less $CO_2$ emissions to transport to your plate. Out of season fruits in particular may travel thousands of miles by truck or plane to get to the supermarket. Avoid air travel if possible. Plane travel is $CO_2$ intensive.

- Use efficient lighting. Compact florescent bulbs use much less electricity than old-fashioned incandescent bulbs. In fact, incandescent bulbs are so inefficient they are now banned in some countries.

- Reduce. Reuse. Recycle. Waste doesn't disappear once you put it into the trashcan. Trash fills up landfills and sometimes hazardous chemicals from waste leach into the water table. Reduce how much trash you generate by keeping things longer, choosing products with less packaging and not buying things you won't actually use. Reuse empty containers, shop at second-hand shops and think of creative ways to reuse old things. Recycle as much as you can.

- Many choices by adults of a household have large impacts on the family's Footprint. For instance, the house the family chooses to live in not only determines how much energy it takes to heat and cool it, but also how much transportation is required to get to all the places the family needs to get to, school, shops, work, sport, friends.

---

6. For a good summary of the environmental impacts of livestock, see the article from *The Independent* Cow 'emissions' more damaging to environment than $CO_2$ from cars' from 10 December 2006. http://www.independent.co.uk/environment/climate-change/cow-emissions-more-damaging-to-planet-than-cosub2sub-from-cars-427843.html

There are many resources online for tips on how to reduce your Footprint. Schoolchildren can have a big effect on their family's footprint because they can suggest new ideas to their parents about how to reduce their Ecological Footprint.

There are publications documenting how the Ecological Footprint is calculated and how it can be applied[7]

## *What drives our growing Footprint?*

Part of the increasing demand for resources is due to our growing population. United Nations' estimates assume that the worldwide population could grow to between nine and 10 billion by the middle of this century. Each individual wants a healthy, thriving, productive life. And even in the most efficient of all possible worlds this takes resources.

But population isn't the only reason for our growing Ecological Footprint. We're consuming more too. Many people around the world are consuming more and more. Many in China and Brazil are able to afford more comfortable lifestyles, but even in well-off US or Europe, consumer demands are still on the rise. Sadly there is a significant number of the world's population forced into living on smaller Footprints due to lack of resources. In order to sustainably support our larger human family we must learn to satisfy our needs and wants while putting less pressure on the biosphere.

Learning to be more eco-efficient is one key strategy – as long as we do not use more and more of the efficient products and services, losing thereby the efficiency gains.

The term $I=PAT$[8] is often used to summarize the sustainability challenge:

$$\text{Impact} = \text{Population} * \text{Affluence} * \text{Technology}$$

Affluence means how much we consume per person, and technology refers to how efficiently we create consumption goods from nature. To reduce our total impact on nature, we can reign in population growth, reduce consumption (for example by eating less meat) and become more eco-efficient.

## *Measuring sustainable development*

The verbal and general commitment to sustainable development as the common dream or necessary goal of humanity is ubiquitous in the global policy discourse. Yet hardly any institution systematically tracks its de-

---

7. www.footprintnetwork.org, Global Footprint Network – for example Atlas or Method paper, Wackernagel, M. & Rees, W. (1996). *Our Ecological Footprint: Reducing Human Impact on the Earth*. Gabriola Island, BC: New Society Press. Chambers, N., Simmons, C. and Wackernagel, M. 2000. *Sharing Nature's Interest: Ecological Footprints as an Indicator for Sustainability*, EarthScan, London.

8. Ehrlich, P.R. and Holdren, J. P. (1971). Impact of population growth. *Science 171*(3877), 1212-1217. The Wikipedia article on I=PAT provides a good summary.

cisions' impact on the sustainable development performance of its constituency. But a shortage of natural resources often frustrates development goals and sometimes even threatens recent development gains. Many global institutions such as the UN Environment Program and UN Development Programme are starting to recognize this connection. They now use the Human Development Index (HDI)-Footprint framework, a measurement approach to track human development gains in the context of resource constraints.

Can 'living well' be measured? The United Nations Human Development Programme developed an Index twenty years ago in an attempt to quantify human development. Their HDI tracks three key social outcomes that enable 'living well': life expectancy, basic education and literacy, and the ability to purchase needed goods and services. On a scale of 0 to 1 the UN defines in their latest version of the index, a score of 0.67 as the threshold that indicates a 'high' level of development.

But development can only be sustained if it is done within the Earth's ecological limits. This means that the average person's Ecological Footprint must not exceed the per capita biocapacity available on the planet – 1.8 global hectares, as of 2007 – or less if we want to leave some space for wild species.

This framework provides an empirically based, measurable map for core sustainable development characteristics. Figure 1 shows the position for about 150 countries across the world.

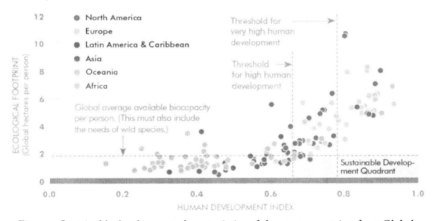

Figure 1: Sustainable development characteristics of about 150 countries; from Global Footprint Network with data from UNDP and National Footprint Accounts, 2010 edition

The quadrant formed by these two conditions represents where world average human development would need to be in order to live on a planet that provides thriving lives within the resource constraints of the planet. The countries below the biocapacity line have a Footprint that is globally replicable. But today, many of them still have a human development deficit. Many countries with high human development depend on very high Footprints too.

This framework gives a message of hope: countries can still make big gains in human development with a low Ecological Footprint cost. And countries with a high Footprint can reduce their Footprint without big sacrifices to their quality of life.

### *The Happy Planet Index*

The new economics foundation in the UK is proposing a similar approach, simplifying the challenge by marrying the two measures of ecological performance and human development. They start their inquiry from the human perspective, recognizing that many people feel that a society of runaway consumerism isn't just bad for the planet, it's pretty unpleasant too. So when we start to look beyond just how much stuff we consume (GDP) as a measure of how successful a country is, in addition to measures of resource demand we might also want to simply ask: how happy are people?

The Happy Planet Index (HPI) addresses this by claiming that we need to both live within resource constraints of the planet as well as enjoy long, happy lives. Therefore it advances this message with a simple efficiency measure: How many happy life-years can a country squeeze out of every global hectare of Footprint? We could call this *sustainability efficiency*.

Out of the three ingredients, *Footprints*, *life expectancy* and *happiness*, the first two we have already discussed. So how can we assess *happiness* in a country? The new economics foundation bases the happiness measure on results from surveys that ask people about factors such as wealth, free time, working conditions, and the quality of friends and community.

When you rank countries according to whom produces the most happy life-years per global hectare input you find industrialized nations such as Germany and Japan in the midfield, with the United States even lower on the list. Many Latin American and Asian countries lead the list including Costa Rica and Colombia, Vietnam and China[9].

What elements are keys to a happy life? What roles do friendship and education, faith or cultural roots play? What clothes, objects, and furniture in your room could you do without? And what is most valuable to you? Does a comparison with the possessions of others play a role?

### *Conclusion*

The Earth provides all that we need to live and thrive. So what will it take for humanity to live within the means of one planet? Individuals and institutions worldwide must begin to recognize ecological limits. We must begin to make ecological limits central to our decision-making and use human ingenuity to find new ways to live, within the Earth's bounds. This means

---

9. You can calculate your own Happiness Index at http://survey.happyplanetindex.org/

investing in technology and infrastructure that will allow us to operate in a resource-constrained world. It means taking individual action to choose a sustainable lifestyle.

# Chapter 4
## Consumers and Consumption

### What Influences us to Consume?

*Iain Black*
*University of Edinburgh, Scotland*

### *The issue*

This chapter explores the influences on consumers that have contributed to us leading materially unsustainable lives. It focuses on evolutionary psychology (our pre-programming) and culture (our programming) as the key influences on our consumption behaviour. It is these influences, plus governmental and technological factors that over the last 50 years have combined to throw out of balance our use of the Earth's resources and the Earth's ability to absorb pollution. This chapter puts consumer demand at the heart of the problem. This is good news as it allows us simultaneously to understand part of the solution.

### *How does consumer demand affect sustainability?*

Our choices of what to consume whether made as individuals, members of families or members of groups are the engine that drives all resource usage and pollution production. For example, we buy cars for personal use and pay taxes to the government. Governments then build the roads using mined and crushed rock and oil-based asphalt/bitumen. Large machines, petrol, oil, and servicing etc are required along with shovels, wheelbarrows, pouring cans and protective clothing for those doing the work. Each of these must be made, and in turn the machines that make these materials must be made and so on until the primary resources (iron, oil, chromium, etc) are extracted. This is just one example of how all other industrial demand is derived from consumer demand, in this case from our desire to travel by car. A key issue with this is that whereas we can easily imagine the resources used to make roads and cars, even small goods require enormous energy and material inflows to make them. Hence, even our small, individual purchase decisions have a considerable impact on the Earth.

### *Why do we consume?*

So what motivates us to purchase products and services? Beyond this, what has changed in the recent past (50 years) so that demand now significantly outstrips the Earth's ability to supply the resources and absorb the resultant pollution? What role have governments played in constructing the social and cultural environment for the development of a consumer led, materialist society?

We as a species must consume in order to maintain the basic metabolic processes of life. To consider how this affects our consumption, think about the proportion of a family budget (however a family is configured) that is spent on food, drink or shelter and their associated costs such electricity and gas for cooking, heating and cooling. For most this represents the majority.

Of course our needs go well beyond these basic requirements. Amongst the higher order motivations that lead to significant levels of consumption are:

- need to find and maintain partners
- need for status
- need to parent offspring
- need to form alliances.

This understanding is important as it is a core contention of this chapter that human consumption is driven by evolutionary processes.

### *What has changed?*

As evolution implies however, we have had these same motivations for thousands of years, so how come we find ourselves in the current environmental and social predicament? Much has been written on the economic causes that have, since the industrial revolution, seen a 10 fold increase in global per capita income. The rate of increase has, however, accelerated in the last 50 years as the economic policies of world governments have openly embraced globalisation.

These policies include:

- Reduction in trade barriers between countries so making foreign imports cheaper.
- Allowing and encouraging direct foreign investment in domestic companies.
- Relaxing media ownership laws allowing a relatively few multinational organizations to dominate.

These policies are coupled with important technological advances, including:

- Improvement in telecommunications and information technology that have vastly simplified communication and hence the control of diverse global locations.
- The simple 20 and 40 ft shipping container! This promotes the cost effective movement of components and finished goods across the globe.
- The growing harmonisation of cultures across the globe where western ideas and tastes for individuality and material wealth are exported and which in turn drive demand.

These changes mean that new sources of demand have been opened, production and distribution is more affordable and the capital required to fund this expansion is readily available. The outcome is that international trade in manufactured goods increased more than 100 times (from $95 billion to $12 trillion) between 1955 and 2010.

So in essence what has changed is that it is easier for companies to sell a vast array of inexpensive products to a growing world population that has the growing ability (via income and access to credit) and desire (innate and culturally motivated) to spend money on material possessions for the motivations described earlier. These companies also have the ability (through sophisticated marketing) to encourage and influence consumers' wants and desires to own these product.

To explore how the needs for products are formed and how desires for specific satisfiers are shaped (i.e. if we are hungry, why we might want a Big Mac) we turn to a key scientific debate that for many years has raged across the social sciences: What influences our behaviour? Is it our genes, our upbringing or both? We will examine these topics to answer two questions: Are we pre-programmed to consume or are we programmed to consume? The answer presented here is both.

### *Are we pre-programmed to consume?*

To explore the origins of our (over) consumption we first consider whether within our genetic make-up, there exist codes that actively encourage us to consume products and services. At a basic level, we must accept this assertion – we cannot survive without consuming food or water or without ensuring our core body temperature does not drop too low. However, our genes also influence more complex consumption desires and in this section Evolutionary Psychology (EP) is used to explore how our minds evolved and to explain our desires for many of the products we consume.

EP is the study of the how the human mind and its processes and capabilities have evolved. It is founded on the premise that just as our physical traits have evolved because of a superior fit to the environment, then so too has the human mind. Specifically, it purports that our minds and certain behaviours evolved to solve certain adaptive problems present during the Pleistocene period the "Era of Evolutionary Adaptedness" (EEA, 2 million – 10,000 years ago).

Table 1: Era of Evolutionary Adaptedness

| Characteristics of the EEA | Adaptive problems present during EEA |
|---|---|
| Low population density | Attracting and Choosing Mates |
| Simple technology | Caring for offspring and other relatives |
| Small kin-based groupings | Forming alliances |
| Hunter/gather subsistence existence | Eating the right food |
| Nomadic or semi-nomadic population | Avoiding predators |
| High infant mortality and low life expectancy | |
| Vulnerability (e.g. predators, disease) | |
| Few lifestyle options | |

Overcoming all of these problems was crucial for our ancestors so that they could pass on their genes. Hence our minds evolved to consist of specific modules that have proven beneficial in solving these concerns. Considering Table 1, with the exception of avoiding predators, these remain fundamental concerns humans and in particular teenagers, still face today. For example, teenagers are bombarded from an early age with messages regarding food and what is appropriate to eat, once they reach a certain age, they become preoccupied with finding a sexual partner and spend considerable time and energy ensuring they are liked and have friends. Indeed, it could be argued that for teenagers, much else in their lives is secondary to the concerns of partners and friends.

But what is the link between these adaptive problems, consumption and sustainability?

*Attracting and choosing mates*

According to EP, mate choice, mating strategies, traits desired in a prospective partner and those subsequently displayed to attract a mate, are fundamentally affected by differential parental investment. Differential parental investment explains how across the animal kingdom, differences typically exist between the genders regarding how much (and what) they invest in their offspring to increase the chances of its survival. Therefore, they look for their potential mate to provide what they cannot. For example, females most often invest more physical resources in child bearing and child rearing (gestation, feeding, protection) whereas males more often invest in supplying resources from the environment. Hence, following a resources matching process, the gender investing more physical resources tends to prefer partners who can provide the necessary environmental resources. In turn the gender providing the environmental resources looks for cues of fertility, ability to birth offspring and of faithfulness. It is very important to note that EP does not espouse biological determinism but instead is based on the interaction of biology and environment. The recent "Cougar" phenomenon highlights this. Here, older women with money and environmental resources of their own seek cues to reproductive fitness (i.e. younger physically attractive men). The key variable is not gender; it is seeking from a partner what they cannot provide for themselves.

So where does this leave human consumption and over-consumption? As partners are chosen based on their displays of desirable traits, competition between members of the same sex for access to higher quality partners (richer, more beautiful, more charming) means that the potential partner displaying the most/best of the desired trait often wins. So this in a nutshell is the problem: If men are chosen by women partly because of their wealth or ambition (as a cue to gaining wealth in the future) then men will compete with each other by displaying these traits. On the other hand, if women are chosen by men partly because of the way they look, women will compete amongst themselves in order to enhance these traits leading to consumption of clothes, jewellery, health and beauty products and certain foods.

*Parental care*

The most readily understandable behaviours that evolved in order for us to pass on our genes are to invest in our offspring and to care for them. There is a clear survival benefit for humans in caring for our babies and those parents that invest more are likely to see their offspring reach reproductive age. For modern humans with access to money and goods these inherited urges are played out by spending on a bewildering number of goods and services.

*Forming alliances, group formation and maintenance*

The Era of Evolutionary Adaptedness was a time where predation by animals, attack from other kin based groups and the hunting of large prey were common dangers. In these circumstances, having allies and friends was a distinct advantage as they could help you keep an eye on the environment, fight with you or work collaboratively on the hunt. Key traits in forming and maintaining alliances are *helping* and *reciprocity*, with reciprocity being more important when assisting those that are not closely related. In terms of consumption, gift giving is a key activity here as are social activities and the related travel, food, clothes, drink, etc.

*Food choice*

Without farming and keeping livestock, human's access to food was sporadic and during certain times of the year, scarce. It was beneficial under these conditions to evolve the desire and capacity to eat food with a high calorific content which helps one stay full and build up reserves. Foods with high levels of fat and protein fit this bill with protein having the added benefit of helping muscle and brain development. These preferences are still with us today but are now combined with the environmental circumstances where, in many countries, an overabundance of food of these types is available. These factors are therefore fuelling the rapid rise in obesity both in adults and children.

From an environmental perspective, this demand is partly satisfied with rearing of livestock for meat, which in turn relies on vast quantities of food and water. For example, the Simplot feedlot at Grand View Idaho (USA) annually fattens up to 150,000 cattle for beef. Each animal is fed approximately 12-14 kg of food and requires 30-40 litres of water per day. The amounts are so huge that a 100 carriage train is required to transport feed to the site. This grain in turn requires fertiliser and water to grow, with one tonne of grain requiring up to 1000 tonnes of water.

## Are we programmed to consume?

Whereas evolution can explain our desires to consume certain goods, it does not explain our choice of specific products nor the rapid recent growth in consumption levels. For answers to this we must turn to culture and marketing. These forces actively teach us to consume as well as how to behave, how to communicate, how to look and indeed how to live.

Culture is "a set of attitudes, values and beliefs shared by a group of individuals, which guide and influence behaviours and reactions to various stimuli" (Lambkin et al., 1998: 248). It is expressed via the use of symbols, language, food, clothes music, values, myths, norms and rituals. We learn culture via agents of socialisation such as family, friends, celebrities, role models, mass media, commercial organisations and governments.

*Values*

These are consensual views about what is appropriate and desirable. We typically learn these values in the stories we are told as children but latterly TV programmes have become more of a source of these ideas.

*Myths*

These are stories that express some key values of society. For example, in Australia and New Zealand the true stories of the Australian and New Zealand Army Corps (ANZAC) have undergone a mythical transition. Ideals such as mateship, success in the face of failure, punching above your weight, and larrikinism have been added to these heroic activities whilst non-conforming ideas are being lost.

*Norms*

These are the rules of behaviours used to organise our daily lives. For example, shaking someone's right hand or eating cereal for breakfast, not lunch.

*Rituals*

These are sets of symbolic behaviours that occur in a fixed sequence and tend to be repeated periodically. Rituals are often heavily intertwined with consumption of food, giving of gifts, wearing of certain clothes and have become heavily co-opted by a range of organisations. Companies now attempt to link the consumption of their products or services with rituals, for example, Lindt chocolate bunnies at Easter.

*Symbols*

Symbols are something that represents something else, though we have to learn the association. For example, golden arches do not in themselves contain any meaning that could be worked out, we learn over repeated exposure to associate this particular colour and shape with McDonald's restaurants. Advertising is full of symbolism, often to represent fear, danger or something unpleasant. Symbols may be visual or aural.

### *How do we learn culture?*

Culture is learnt through *enculturation* where agents of socialisation teach us what it means to be part of our culture and specific ways in which it is expressed. It is these agents that inform us, reward us and punish us directly or indirectly so we learn how and what to consume.

*Family*

Our direct family members are incredibly powerful influences over what and how we consume. From the specific breakfast cereals, toothpaste or brand of coffee we use, to cars and banks, our first experience of these products is likely to be from our family. It also teaches us our values.

*Friends and acquaintances*

To be liked or accepted often involves conforming to the norms of the group, for example, to dress like your friends, to listen to the same sort of music and use language in the same way.

*Celebrities/role models*

In recent years, celebrities and other role models such as sports stars have been recognised as a growing influence on culture. Their high status means they are mimicked and followed by others and as such what they wear, what they drive and what products they use, have become powerful influences on behaviour.

*Mass media*

It can be argued that the primary goal of commercial mass media is to deliver a receptive audience to its advertisers. It is very much in their interest to produce popular programmes that consumers with money to spend enjoy watching and that these consumers are primed to be receptive to the accompanying advertising messages. We can see this if we analyse mass media and the adverts they carry. They promote the importance of wealth, youth, power, competition and conformity and how possessions are required for living a fulfilling life. These values are promoted directly and indirectly to their audience. For example, TV channels and glossy magazines feature attractive, young models/actors (particularly for women) or older, less physically attractive but rich and powerful men and hold up such figures as role models. Family situations are featured frequently as are homes full of consumer goods and members engaging in consumption situations such as having dinner, going out or shopping. These characteristics reflect our culture and provide the lens by which we are told to view the world.

*Governments*

Governments of all levels have a profound impact on our culture. This is achieved through macro level interventions such as enacting laws or setting the economic framework and micro level interventions such as deciding what arts, sports, community groups and social marketing campaigns[1] should be funded and how they should be managed. In recent years governments have made economic growth their key target and with this have created the environment where we understand that our role in society is to shop and consume.

*Organisations such as commercial companies, charities and political parties*

These organisations reflect and inform culture through the use of marketing to promote their goods, services or ideas. Marketing, as many commentators have expressed, is a particularly powerful mechanism that contributes to our over-consumption.

It is the explicit intention of many organisations to persuade us to buy their goods and modern marketing is both sophisticated and successful in helping them achieve this. It is not this chapter's role to detail how marketing is practiced nor how it achieves this, instead to fully discuss the power of culture in shaping our consumption it is important to outline what marketing is, its main tools and highlight key mechanisms by which it influences us to consume.

---

1.Social marketing involves using marketing strategies and tactics to encourage or discourage certain individually or socially harmful behaviours such as smoking or taking illegal drugs.

*Marketing*

Marketing can simply be defined as a business process used to satisfy consumers' needs and wants whilst simultaneously satisfying the goals of the organisation. More recently this focus has been widened to include not only the interest of the company and consumers but also to include the interests of shareholder, consumer groups, charities and the environment. Hence marketing is now viewed as satisfying consumers' needs and wants without damaging the environment nor the culture or society of other groups. This wider focus is a form of more enlightened marketing and whilst long talked about in boardrooms across the world, the Earth is still awaiting wide scale adoption and adherence to these principles.

From this definition we understand that a company looking to successfully compete in the market place should focus on understanding the wants and needs of their existing (and potential) consumers. This understanding may include:

- What price are they willing to pay?
- How do they want to use the product?
- What should it look like and what should it do?
- What should the product say about the individual?
- How and where should it be available for purchase?

Having discovered these needs and wants, the firm then constructs a 'marketing mix' which involves making decisions on the following areas:

- Product – What is it made of, how does it function, what is its size, shape, packaging etc?
- Price – What price will it be sold at, what discounts are available, what promotion deals will be used?
- Promotion – How will it be advertised and communicated to the target audience e.g. internet or e-marketing, public relations, personal selling, sales promotions?
- Distribution – Where will it be sold e.g. in supermarkets and local shops or only available in exclusive, higher status outlets?

By relying on what people need and want, marketing is intrinsically linked to basic human consumption requirements described earlier. It is also adept at creating needs and wants, typically by framing the lack of a particular product as in some way damaging to a consumer's self-image.

Marketing professionals and academics have developed a very sophisticated understanding of how to influence people, what to say, when to say it and what offers increase likelihood of consumer action. One of the most powerful approaches is linking consumption to the consumer's self-concept. Such is the importance of this manipulation of self-concept that to complete our understanding of how culture programmes us to consume via marketing, we must explore this area in detail.

## Self-concept

Self-concept contains a personal self and a social (or collective) self. These represent ideas on who we perceive we are and how we are perceived by others such as our family and friends. Within our overall self-concept we have a number of identities and play a number of roles. These typically involve us behaving in a range of ways though relying on the same underlying values and beliefs. For example, we may be a son, brother, musician and a charity volunteer.

Inherent within this view of self, is that in some instances when acting out one particular role, we are confronted by a situation which requires us to act in a way which conflicts with another role. For example, mothers often find themselves in conflict between purchasing products their children want (and are expressions of love for them) but are made of non-recyclable plastic, are unlikely to last and are environmentally damaging. In this case, the mothering identity is in conflict with being an environmentally aware consumer. Which role takes precedence is down to an interplay of which identity and values are held more centrally to the person's overall self-image and the situational factors such as stress, convenience and the wider task being undertaken.

Families play a key role in children developing a basic sense of who they are. This occurs by experiencing the roles that are given to them by birth, observing how these should be carried out and subsequent reinforcement of 'right' and 'wrong' behaviour. Parental support and monitoring can create strong, positive self-image and esteem, however family and culture can also undermine a child's sense of who they are. This can lead to children defining themselves by what they own, not by the strength of their character or the contribution they make to society.

### Possessions and self-concept

Consumption is a meaningful activity indicating that the act of purchasing and the item purchased have meanings attached. This is true whether we are purchasing low-calorie corn flakes or a leather jacket or whether we are taking part in Oxfam's Big Fast or travelling to Thailand on holiday. Each of these consumption choices signals something about us to ourselves and other people. This has led us to the situation where what we own or (do not own) form a key part of our self-concept. This affects our relationship with consumption in the following ways:

To have is to be – Possessions and the extended self

> Possessions have become part of our extended self-concept though this occurs only if we feel that we created, controlled or have known them. Hence, shopping is not merely the acquisition of things, it can be used to buy an identity (or part of it).

Not to have is to be – Consumption resistance

> What we avoid and don't have is also significant for our sense of self, we may deliberately avoid Nike trainers because they represent conformity.

## To have is to belong – Consumption and social identification

Acquiring personal possessions expresses not only our individual sense of identity but also our sense of belonging to a group and group identity. By owning a Harley-Davidson motorcycle or an Apple computer we imagine a sense of belonging to a Harley-Davidson or an Apple tribe.

So how do marketers as socialisation agents use the notions of possessions and the self to influence consumption?

### Use of social comparison

This is a process by which consumers evaluate themselves by comparing themselves with others on attributes such physical attractiveness, social status, relationship status and job. This leads to judgements as to superiority or inferiority with this other person. Marketers use this process by highlighting how a particular good is integral to the success of the model used in the advertisements. Hence, if consumers compare themselves to the model and find that they fare badly, then purchasing the particular product becomes a way to reduce the perceived gap.

### Portraying real and ideal selves

A related tactic to social comparison is to use the notions of *ideal* and *real* selves and the gap that exists between them. The *ideal self* is a person's conceptualisation of who they would like to be and is partially molded by elements of a consumer's culture. A person's *real* self is their realistic appraisal of the qualities they do or do not possess.

Companies play on the gap between these images by using marketing to create a large discrepancy between these two ideas. They then highlight how ownership and use of a particular product can bridge this gap.

There are additional ways in which marketers use self-concept to persuade people to consume. These are typically linked to making the consumer feel that the product will help them be someone better, avoid harm or belong to a desirable group. For example:

- Linking products with membership of specific desirable groups and highlighting how a particular product is integral to a specific lifestyle, value or role.
- Positioning a product as a symbol of wealth and power.
- Positioning a product as creating envy in other people.
- Suggesting that you deserve a product or experience because of some beneficial trait (hard work, creativity or just being you).
- Suggesting that being without a certain product makes you a bad example of a particular identity or role.
- Suggesting that experience makes you a more interesting and enviable person.

### Criticisms of marketing

Marketing has been criticized (quite rightly) for this approach of connecting new, novel 'stuff' with self. This approach is implicated in:

- Environmental degradation
- Lower social cohesion
- Lower levels of happiness

It must be pointed out that marketing is an *amoral* business activity, i.e. it is itself neither good nor bad, right nor wrong. Its use has been quite rightly attacked for creating superficial desires, for encouraging unsustainable levels of consumption, making us purchase dangerous and indeed lethal products (smoking and alcoholic drinks), for undermining peoples self-esteem and influencing mental health issues. However, this is not the fault of marketing per se, it is the fault of those people (yes individuals within firms) who make decisions to use its tools for these purposes. It can and is also used by organisations for pro-social activities such as anti-smoking campaigns and by firms looking to sell sustainable products. Therefore, whereas marketing has undoubtedly contributed to unsustainable consumption it can also contribute to sustainable consumption.

## *Conclusion*

This chapter has sought to provide educators with an overview of the influences on our over-consumption. It has firmly placed individual and family decisions at the heart of this issue as they not only lead directly to resources being used but they also fuel all industrial and government production. Government action is no doubt essential to tackle the environmental issues described in this book. However, consumers should not be allowed to abdicate responsibility, as their actions not only have a direct influence on what is produced, used and wasted but they also signal to governments what issues are important to them. This 'consumption as voting' behaviour is a key tool in developing sustainability.

This chapter has sought to bring together both cultural and evolutionary explanations of behaviour into a model which helps us understand what influences us to consume at a product category level i.e. food, drink, clothes and shelter but also what influences us to purchase specific products and brands. Finally, by outlining these influences it also provides an overview on what tools we can use to balance consumers' desires within a level that the earth can sustainably satisfy.

*Thinking it through: where do I stand?*

This chapter takes a quite controversial position regarding the influences on our consumption behaviour. For many years the focus has been on the role of culture and how we have learnt to (over) consume. What do you and your class think? Are we programmed or preprogrammed to consume?

For each of these positions discuss the following:

What does this mean for sustainable development?
- Can we achieve it?
- How can we achieve?
- What are the major barriers to achieving it?

---

*Action: what can I do?*

Activity 1

Considering the adaptive problems discussed in this chapter and the consumption inheritance with which it has left us. Complete the table found in the *Resources* section below. Enter specific products or services your family has consumed that can be associated with each problem. Explain the connection between the product and the adaptive problem.

Activity 2

1) What possession of yours has particular meaning to you?

How did you acquire it?
How did marketing affect your desire for this product?
How does marketing maintain and develop your desire for this product?
What meaning does it have?
What does it say about you?

2) Discuss, in groups of 3-4, what you think your classmates' possessions say about them.

## *Further reading*

Jackson, T. (2009). *Prosperity without Growth? - The Transition to a Sustainable Economy*. London: Sustainable Development Commission.

Lambkin, M., Foxall, G., Heilbrunn, B. & van Raaij. F. (1998). *European Perspectives on Consumer Behaviour*. London: Prentice Hall.

Peattie, K., & Peattie, S. (2009). Social marketing: A pathway to consumption reduction?, *Journal of Business Research*, 62(2), 260-68.

Saad, G. (2007). *The Evolutionary Bases of Consumption*. Mahwah, NJ: Lawrence Erlbaum.

## *Resources*

Table for use in student activity 1

| Adaptive problems still relevant today | | | | |
|---|---|---|---|---|
| Mate choice | Mate assessment | Caring for offspring | Forming alliance | Food choice |
| Abercrombie & Finch T-Shirt | Revlon Super Lustrous Lipstick | Huggies Nappies | Cadburys Dairy Milk Chocolates | Big Mac Meal |
| | | | | |
| | | | | |
| | | | | |
| | | | | |
| | | | | |
| | | | | |

# Chapter 5
## Sharing the Costs of Climate Policies Among Households in Europe

*Annemarie Kerkhof*
PRé Consultants b.v.

### The issue

Households give rise to greenhouse gas (GHG) emissions by consuming goods and services. The amount of GHG emissions per household depends on several factors, including the consumption level and pattern. Variation in household GHG emissions may lead to unequal distributions of climate change mitigation costs across households. This chapter considers the variation in household GHG emissions in Europe and discusses the equity of burden sharing.

### Context

The invention of James Watt's steam engine in the late 18th century enabled an efficient energy conversion from fossil fuels to steam power. This invention increased production and consumption levels and was the main driving force behind the industrial revolution. At the same time the combustion of fossil fuels led to carbon dioxide ($CO_2$) emissions. As a result, global atmospheric concentrations of $CO_2$ have increased markedly since the industrial revolution, which may ultimately result in global warming and climate change.

In the last decades efforts have been made to reduce greenhouse gas (GHG) emissions, including $CO_2$, in order to mitigate climate change. An international agreement was achieved in Kyoto in 1997. The Parties involved in the Kyoto Protocol committed themselves to reducing their greenhouse gas emissions by an average of five percent below 1990 levels during the period 2008-2012. International negotiations are still taking place with the goal of reaching a post-2012 global agreement on climate change mitigation. At the regional and local level, measures and policies are already underway to further reduce GHG emissions. The European Union (EU), for example, has committed to reducing its GHG emissions by 20% below 1990 levels by 2020.

## Household CO2 emissions and cost distribution

Households purchase goods and services to support their lifestyles. By consuming goods and services, households give rise to greenhouse gas (GHG) emissions, both directly and indirectly. Heating a home or driving a car, for example, give rise to $CO_2$ emissions directly. Households also cause GHG emissions indirectly by purchasing goods and services in which GHG emissions from raw material acquisition, manufacturing and transport are embodied. Wearing clothes for example does not lead to GHG emissions directly, but manufacturing of clothes does. These direct and indirect GHG emissions related to products and services are often referred to as the carbon footprint of products.

The household $CO_2$ emissions may differ between countries as a result of different consumption levels and patterns. The consumption level and pattern of households may differ due to differences in household income, climate and geography. Households in a cold climate spend more money on heating a home than households in a warmer climate. The household $CO_2$ emissions may also differ as a result of national production technologies or the energy system. For instance, a high share of electricity is generated with natural gas and coal in the UK while a high share of electricity is generated with hydropower and nuclear power in Sweden. Burning natural gas and coal leads to higher $CO_2$ emissions than hydropower or nuclear power and as a result the electricity use in UK households leads to higher GHG emissions than the electricity use in Swedish households.

An international agreement, like the Kyoto Protocol, might not feature prominently in your daily consciousness but it can affect your household. In order to achieve emission reduction targets, producers need to purchase and implement emission reduction technologies or to purchase emission permits. The costs of these measures will be partly passed on through the product chain and will ultimately accumulate at the household level. Since household consumption and associated GHG emissions differ between countries, the costs of climate policies will probably not be equally distributed among households in Europe.

Are unequal costs for households also inequitable? The answer depends on your personal or society's notion of fairness. Fairness can be based on several principles. When fairness is based on the equality principle, which means that costs should be distributed equally, the unequal costs are indeed unfair. However, one could also argue that costs for climate policies should be distributed across households according to the households' contribution to climate change. This is known as the polluter pays principle. Another basis for cost distribution could be the principle of capacity, or the household's ability-to-pay. In other words, "the broadest shoulders should bear the greatest burden". If fact, there is no 'good' or 'bad' cost distribution, but all three options lead to different consequences for households.

The principles of fairness can form the basis of all kinds of cost sharing. They can be applied to share the costs of mitigating a wide range of environmental impacts, like particulate matter formation, toxicity and acidification. This chapter however focuses on climate change only.

### Case study: the Netherlands, UK, Sweden and Norway

The differences in household $CO_2$ emissions can be best illustrated with a case study. Figure 1 shows the total annual expenditures of an average household in the Netherlands, UK, Sweden and Norway around the year 2000. The figure shows the household expenditures on 12 main groups of products such as food, housing, transport and so on. The group *food* includes all expenditures on food including milk, meat, vegetables, bread, etc. The group *housing* includes rent, heating, electricity use, etc. In this way, figure 1 reflects the average shopping basket of households in the Netherlands, UK, Sweden and Norway.

Figure 1 shows some differences between shopping baskets in the four countries. First of all, the consumption level, or size of the shopping basket, differs among the countries. The Dutch household spent 23.8 k€/year, the UK household and Swedish household spent 26.9 k€/year, while the Norwegian household spent 31.7 k€/year. Moreover, the consumption patterns differ. This means that each shopping basket contains a different mix of products. The average Dutch household spent 12 percent of the total expenditure on transport, while the average Norwegian household spent 20 percent on transport. The share of expenditure on housing is relatively low in the UK (about 20 percent) as compared to the other countries (25-27 percent). The share of expenditures on restaurants and hotels ranges from 4 percent in Norway to 10 percent in the UK. The shares of expenditure on the remaining product groups are fairly similar for the four countries.

With information on the household expenditure and the $CO_2$ emissions from products and services, the $CO_2$ emissions of households can be calculated. Figure 2 shows these results for our case study. The household $CO_2$

emissions are the lowest in Sweden with 12.2 tons $CO_2$ per year, followed by the Norwegian households with 13.6 tons $CO_2$ per year. The household $CO_2$ emissions are the highest in the Netherlands and the UK with 19 and 20.2 tons $CO_2$ per year, respectively. These results do not reflect the average household expenditures in figure 1!

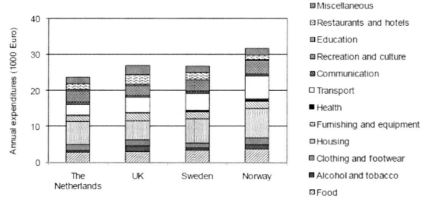

Figure 1: Total annual expenditures and expenditures per product group of the average households in the Netherlands, UK, Sweden and Norway *Source: Kerkhof et al. (2009)*

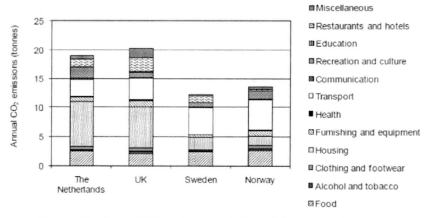

Figure 2: Total annual $CO_2$ emissions and $CO_2$ emissions per product group for the average household in the Netherlands, UK, Sweden and Norway
*Source: Kerkhof et al. (2009)*

Household $CO_2$ emissions are related to expenditures, but also to other factors like national energy supply, climate and geography. In our case study, the climate of the four countries differs only slightly. $CO_2$ emissions from housing are however higher in the Netherlands and the UK than in Sweden and Norway. This is a result of the way in which homes are heated in these countries. Each home is heated with a small natural gas burner in the Netherlands and UK, resulting in considerable amounts of $CO_2$ emissions. In contrast, homes are heated with district heating and electricity in

Sweden and with electricity in Norway. The electricity mixes in both countries have a low $CO_2$ emission intensity. The electricity in Sweden is generated with hydropower and nuclear power; the electricity in Norway is generated with hydropower. The difference in $CO_2$ emissions from housing can also be explained by the electricity mixes in the four countries. We already discussed that electricity generation in Sweden and Norway. In the Netherlands and the UK electricity is mainly generated with fossil fuels, like natural gas and coal, which results in higher $CO_2$ emissions.

In contrast, $CO_2$ emissions from transport are higher in Sweden and Norway in comparison to the Netherlands and the UK. In figure 1, we already saw that Swedish and Norwegian households spent more money on transport. This can be explained by the geography of those countries. The longer travel distances in Sweden and Norway lead to higher expenses on transport than in the Netherlands and the UK, resulting in higher $CO_2$ emissions.

From the results of the Netherlands, UK, Sweden and Norway, we can conclude that household $CO_2$ emissions depend on both average household expenditure and the direct and indirect $CO_2$ emissions associated with products and services. We also know that household expenditure and $CO_2$ emissions from products and services are country-dependent.

With this knowledge, we can go one step further. Assume that each household has to pay a tax for each kg of $CO_2$ emission it creates during consumption, either in a direct or indirect way. The EU or another governmental body may decide to impose such a tax in order to stimulate low carbon consumption[1]. A tax on $CO_2$ emissions will give an incentive to households to lower their $CO_2$ emissions. Household members could take the bicycle or train instead of the car. They could lower the heating of their home (or lower the air conditioning). The household could even purchase a solar cell for hot water if they have the money.

The tax on $CO_2$ emissions could be 20 € per ton $CO_2$. The total amount of money that a household needs to pay can then be calculated by multiplying the annual household $CO_2$ emissions with the tax of 20 €/ton $CO_2$. The average Dutch household in our case study emits 19 tons $CO_2$ per year. When we multiply this value with the tax of 20 €/ton $CO_2$, we get an amount of 380 €/year. This is the amount of money that the average Dutch household has to pay for emitting 19 tons $CO_2$ per year. The same calculations can be done for the average households in the UK, Sweden and Norway. The results are shown in Table 1.

---

1. A $CO_2$ Emission Trading Scheme (ETS) was launched in Europe in 2005. It is one of the measures for achieving the EU climate target in 2020. The example of the $CO_2$ tax in this chapter is simplified and theoretical and can therefore not be compared to EU ETS.

Table 1: Annual expenditures, $CO_2$ emissions, and tax payments per average household in the Netherlands, UK, Sweden and Norway in 2000

|  | Household expenditure (k€/year) | Household $CO_2$ emissions (ton $CO_2$/year) | $CO_2$ tax payments (€/year) | $CO_2$ tax payments (% of annual expenditures) |
|---|---|---|---|---|
| Netherlands | 23.8 | 19.0 | 380 | 1.60 |
| UK | 26.9 | 20.2 | 404 | 1.50 |
| Sweden | 26.9 | 12.2 | 244 | 0.91 |
| Norway | 31.7 | 13.6 | 272 | 0.86 |

What is your opinion? Are the $CO_2$ tax payments fairly distributed among the households in the four European countries?

At the beginning of this chapter, it was discussed that fairness can be based on several principles. When we take the polluter pays principle as a basis, the costs are fairly distributed across the households in the different countries. UK households have the highest $CO_2$ emissions and should therefore pay the highest costs. However, from the viewpoint of "the broadest shoulders should bear the greatest burden", we can conclude that the costs are not fairly distributed across households. The $CO_2$ tax comprises 1.50% of the total expenditure of UK households, while it only comprises 0.86% of the expenditure of Norwegian households. From the viewpoint of equality, the cost distribution is also not fair, because the households pay different taxes.

Table 2 gives an overview of the cost distribution according to the three principles of fairness: 1) Polluter pays principle, 2) Ability-to-pay, and 3) Equality. When the costs are distributed across households on the basis of ability-to-pay, the average households in the four European countries pay the same share of their expenditures on the $CO_2$ tax. In our case study, this implies that each household has to pay a tax of 1.19% of its annual expenditure. As a result, the average Dutch household would have to pay 283 €/year, which is a saving of €97 in comparison to the cost distribution according to the polluter pays principle. The UK household would have to pay 320 €/year, which is a saving of €84. However, the annual tax payments of Swedish and Norwegian households would go up €76 and €105, respectively. These are substantial differences. When the costs are distributed in accordance with the equality principle, each household has to pay the same amount of tax. In our case, each household has to pay 325 €/year.

Table 2: Annual tax payments per average household based on Polluter pays principle,
Ability-to-pay, and Equality

| | CO2 tax payments based on Polluter pays principle | | CO2 tax payments based on Ability-to-pay | | CO2 tax payments based on Equality | |
|---|---|---|---|---|---|---|
| | (€/ year) | (% of annual expenditure) | (€/ year) | (% of annual expenditure) | (€/ year) | (% of annual expenditure) |
| Netherlands | 380 | 1.60 | 283 | 1.19 | 325 | 1.37 |
| UK | 404 | 1.50 | 320 | 1.19 | 325 | 1.21 |
| Sweden | 244 | 0.91 | 320 | 1.19 | 325 | 1.21 |
| Norway | 272 | 0.86 | 377 | 1.19 | 325 | 1.03 |

The initial aim of introducing a CO2 tax was to stimulate households to reduce their CO2 emissions. The polluter pays principle provides a strong incentive for households to reduce their CO2 emissions. After all, a reduction in the household CO2 emissions lowers the costs of the tax, while an increase leads to higher costs. A direct relationship exists between the tax and the household CO2 emissions. The ability-to-pay and equality principle result in a more even cost distribution, but both cost distributions diminish the incentive for households to reduce their CO2 emissions. A combination of principles could lead to a CO2 tax that gives an incentive to households to reduce their CO2 emissions, but that also takes economic differences into account.

The Kyoto Protocol differentiates the GHG emission reduction targets (and associated costs) for different countries and regions in order to reflect their different economic, technological, and energy situations. However, no clear rule led to this differentiation. It was more the result of international politics.

*Thinking it through: where do I stand?*

1. How can the differences between figure 1 and figure 2 be explained?
2. Role play: In table 2, the costs of the CO2 tax are shared among households on the basis of three different principles: 1) Polluter Pays principle, 2) Ability-to-pay and 3) Equality.

   Split up into groups of four students. One student represents the Netherlands, one the UK, one Sweden and one Norway. Imagine that those four countries want to introduce a CO2 tax collectively in order to reduce their CO2 emissions. As in the case study, the tax rate is 20 €/ton CO2.

   Assignment: Represent a country and negotiate the lowest annual tax payments for the households in this country. For example, when you represent the UK, you should negotiate the lowest annual tax payments for the UK households.

   Note: the cost distribution should be based on one of the principles in table 2.

   What is the outcome of the negotiation? Which of the principles was selected as a basis for the cost distribution and why?

Which burden sharing is fair according to you? You can discuss your viewpoint with your group.

3. Household $CO_2$ emissions differ across European countries, due to differences in household income, consumption patterns, and national technologies and energy systems. At the global level, even larger differences exist. Can you name a few countries where you expect high household $CO_2$ emissions? Can you also name a few countries where you expect low household $CO_2$ emissions? Can you explain these differences? (See Table 3 in the Annex for some examples)

*Action: what can I do?*
- How could you reduce your personal or household $CO_2$ emissions?
- How could the school reduce its $CO_2$ emissions?
- What are the spin-off effects of your action? How will these impinge on other aspects of sustainability?

## *Further reading*

Blanchard, O., Criqui, P., Kitous, A. & Viguer, L. (2003). Combining Efficiency with Equity: A Pragmatic Approach. In I. Kaul, P. Conceição, K. Le Goulven, R. U. Mendoza (Eds.), *Providing Global Public Goods* (pp. 280-303). Oxford: Oxford University Press.

Hertwich, E.G. & Peters, G.P. (2009). Carbon Footprint of Nations: A Global, Trade-linked Analysis. *Environmental Science and Technology, 43*, 6414 – 6420. See also: http://www.carbonfootprintofnations.com/index.php

Kerkhof, A.C., Benders, R.M.J. & Moll, H.C. (2009). Determinants of variation in household $CO_2$ emissions between and within countries. *Energy Policy 37*, 1509 –1517.

## *Annex: Per capita GHG emissions worldwide*

Table 3 shows the per capita GHG emissions in different countries around the world[2]. The table shows that the per capita GHG emissions greatly differ among countries. These differences are mainly the result of the differences in per capita consumption expenditures. Not all differences can be explained by per capita expenditures though. For example the variation in GHG emissions for food consumption across countries is not so well explained by expenditure differences.

---

2. The values in table 3 are not comparable to the values in the case study used in this chapter, because table 3 represents the per capita emissions instead of household emissions. Moreover, the values in table 3 are obtained from another study.

Table 3: Per capita GHG emissions in different countries around the world in 2001

|  | Per capita GHG emissions (ton $CO_2$ equivalents/year) |
|---|---|
| Australia | 20.6 |
| Brazil | 4.1 |
| China | 3.1 |
| Germany | 15.1 |
| India | 1.8 |
| Russian Federation | 10.1 |
| US | 28.6 |
| Zimbabwe | 2.0 |

Source: Hertwich and Peters (2009)

# Chapter 6
## The Role of Business in a Sustainable Future

*Michiyo Morisawa*
*Carbon Disclosure Project, Japan & UN PRI*

*Darian McBain*
*Director, Blue Sky Green*
*Integrated Sustainability Analysis (ISA) School of Physics,*
*University of Sydney*

### The issue

Businesses provide us with what we eat, what we wear, the homes we live in, the services we utilise and tools for education. Along with the government and the community, business (both for profit and not for profit) and industry provide us with what we need to live and what we want to prosper. The American Economist Milton Freidman stated that "There is one and only one social responsibility of business – to use its resources and engage in activities designed to increase its profit so long as it stays with the rules of the game, which is to say, engages in open and free competition, without deception or fraud." However, increasingly the role of business and industry in helping to create a sustainable future is being emphasised. The Global Financial Crisis of 2008-09 showed us how interconnected we are, where financial crises travelled from continent to continent like shockwaves, as a result of business and government decisions. Similarly environmental and social crises are not contained to one city or even country but are closely tied to business decisions.

## *Context*

Businesses are increasingly recognising their role in sustainability. Many organisations' strategic planning now includes how they are contributing to the triple bottom line, whereby environmental performance and social progress are considered as well as the financial bottom line. It is common for companies to appoint a person or team of people dedicated to sustainability performance, link sustainability to position descriptions, have organisational sustainability key performance indicators and even give sustainability oversight to high-level decision makers such as Vice Presidents or Board members.

Whilst pollution of the air, water and soil first brought our attention to corporate impact on the environment drivers for change now include:

- efficiency and the rising cost of utilities such as energy, water and waste;
- environmental legislation and government incentive programs;
- employee and community expectations;
- supplier expectations;
- consumer sentiment; and
- socially responsible investment.

Even school children are having an impact on how businesses are run. Their familiarity with the concepts of sustainability and direct action through purchasing and recycling are having a knock on effect on their parents, who then take these ideas and principles to work. But how do we identify a sustainable business? Investors have for some time been applying evaluation models and methods in order to identify sustainable companies and global methodologies for accountability exist. However as yet there is not one fixed evaluation model and method.

The role of business in sustainability is further emphasised when considering their financial power. Individual businesses have a turnover greater than the Gross Domestic Product (GDP) of some countries. In many developed countries, the market capitalisation of listed companies is greater than their GDP. According to the World Bank, in 2010 this was true in at least 18 countries, including Australia, Canada, Chile, Malaysia, Singapore, South Africa, the UK and the USA. If this is the case, does business not have a greater responsibility to its stakeholders than returning a profit? Its stakeholders will include shareholders, employees, consumers, government and non-government organisations (NGOs) and the wider community. Stakeholders expect businesses to work towards sustainability because corporate activities have a powerful impact on our social, environmental and economic future. Companies provide goods and services that we want and need, but also have a role in creating a sustainable future.

*Historical*

Business responsibility beyond profits can be traced back over centuries. Socially Responsible Investment (SRI)[1] probably dates back to the Quakers and Christian groups in the eighteenth century. It was developed to address environmental and social issues resulting from business practices. Corporate Social Responsibility (CSR), the business equivalent of philanthropy, has also been around since commercial trade grew from individuals trading to organised 'businesses'. A good example of early CSR can be found by considering Cadbury, the well known chocolate and food producer.

*Case study: Early Corporate Social Responsibility*

"No man ought to be condemned to a place where a rose cannot grow." (George Cadbury).

John Cadbury[2] opened a grocer's shop in Birmingham, England is 1824. As well as groceries, he sold coffee, tea, cocoa and drinking chocolate, believing in providing hot drinks as an alternative to consuming alcohol. John Cadbury was a Quaker, and as such was committed to social justice and preventing human misery and deprivation. Other philanthropic activities he was involved in included leading the campaign to stop young boys being used to sweep chimneys and establishing an animal protection society (a forerunner to the RSPCA). In the 1840s a Royal Commission showed the poor quality of life for those living in the Birmingham slums, where most of his factory workers lived. In 1878 John's sons George and Richard moved the factory to Bournville, four miles from the centre of Birmingham. George believed that factory workers had the right to country air and activities, with clean water and away from the pollution of the cities.

The Cadburys built cottages for workers, and eventually schools, churches, recreation areas and created a thriving community. They created a charitable trust to preserve the community and green spaces that they created, welcoming others into the community and protecting it from overdevelopment. Their hard work paid off and in 1915 a study showed that the general death rate and infant mortality was lower in Bournville than in Birmingham. Cadbury continues with its CSR through the Cadbury Foundation, its environmental commitments and its sourcing policies.

*Political*

Governments have a role to play in encouraging businesses towards sustainability. Through policy, regulation, education, international agreements and

---

1.http://en.wikipedia.org/wiki/Socially_responsible_investing

2.Source: http://www.cadbury.co.uk/cadburyandchocolate/ourstory/Pages/ourstory-Flash.aspx

institutional frameworks governments enable businesses for the transition to a sustainable future. Some examples from governments around the world are outlined here.

The European Union Emissions Trading Scheme, EU ETS, is the largest multi-national emissions trading scheme in the world. It was launched in 2005 and is a major pillar of EU climate policy. Under the EU ETS, large emitters of carbon dioxide within the EU must monitor and annually report their $CO_2$ emissions. Based on their emissions allowance, they can either buy or sell their $CO_2$ emissions (emissions trading) depending on their actual annual carbon emissions for the year. The EU ETS engages companies to take energy efficiency measures to reduce their emissions through economic measures, forcing high emitters to pay for their emissions trading and those who have reduced their emissions to save.

Government policy can also influence businesses by encouraging sustainable consumption and production. The Japanese government set up The Top Runner Program in 1999 as a countermeasure to reduce energy consumption in the civil and transportation sectors. This program provides the standard of energy efficiency for products and is applied to 23 products of machinery, equipment and vehicles prescribed under the Energy Conservation Law. In 2002 the UK government published a 10 year Sustainable Production and Consumption Framework and in Germany in 2005 the Centre on Sustainable Production and Consumption was established.

Government policy has also influenced business sustainability through investment policy. The SRI Pensions Disclosure regulation in the UK came into force on 3 July 2000, which forced the investment market for pensions to become more transparent. According to the SRI Pensions Disclosure Regulation, schemes must disclose their SRI policy in their Statement of Investment Principles. Since 2000, there have been numerous developments and initiatives that have further fuelled the growth in the institutional SRI market. The concept of materiality in financial accounting standards and regulations has also had an impact on company investment transparency.

*Global*

There are many business associations and NGOs that promote and support the work of businesses towards sustainability. For example, the World Business Council for Sustainable Development (WBCSD) says that leading global companies of the future will be those that provide goods and services and reach new customers in ways that address the world's major challenges – including poverty, climate change, resource depletion, globalization and demographic shifts.

The UN Global Compact is a strategic policy initiative for businesses that are committed to aligning their operations and strategies within the areas of human rights, labour, environment and anti-corruption. It is a practical framework for the development, implementation, and disclosure of sustainability policies and practices, offering participants a wide spectrum of work streams, management tools and resources to help advance sustainable business models and markets.

OECD Guidelines on Multinational Enterprises is a recommendation for responsible business conduct covering social issues, environment and governance. For example on social issues the Guidelines promote respect for the internationally recognised human rights standards and the principles of the International Labour Organisation (ILO). They encourage local capacity building through close co-operation with the local community and encourage human capital formation, in particular by creating employment opportunities and facilitating training opportunities for employees. The Guidelines were updated in 2011 for the fourth time since they were first adopted in 1976.

The United Nations-backed Principles for Responsible Investment Initiative, PRI, was launched in 2006. It is a network of international investors working together to put its six Principles into practice. The Principles were devised by the investment community. They reflect the view that sustainability issues can affect the performance of investment portfolios and therefore must be given appropriate consideration by investors if they are to fulfil their fiduciary duty. The Principles provide a voluntary framework by which all investors can incorporate sustainability issues into their decision-making and ownership practices and so better align their objectives with those of society at large.

*Reporting and Disclosure*

Reporting of non-financial data is not mandatory in most countries, however many businesses are finding it an increasingly useful tool to communicate their vision and commitments to stakeholders. There are NGOs who assist companies to disclose and report their data voluntarily such as The Global Reporting Initiative (GRI) and Carbon Disclosure Project (CDP) and the International Organization for Standardization (ISO).

The GRI is a network-based organization based in the Netherlands. The GRI's main output is a reporting framework able to be applied to organisations worldwide regardless of size, industry or sector. The GRI has worked to develop industry sector appropriate supplements, and promote good reporting practice. The GRI's core goals include the mainstreaming of disclosure on environmental, social and governance performance. Sustainability reports based on the GRI Framework can be used to demonstrate organizational commitment to sustainable development, to compare organizational performance over time, to benchmark with other businesses and to measure organizational performance with respect to laws, norms, standards and voluntary initiatives.

The CDP seeks to accelerate solutions to climate change by putting relevant information at the centre of business and investment decisions. The process aims to increase transparency around climate-related investment risk and commercial opportunity in the global market place and drive investments towards a low carbon economy. Over 3,000 organizations in some 60 countries around the world now measure and disclose their greenhouse gas emissions, water management and climate change strategies through CDP, in order that they can set reduction targets and make performance improvements. These data are made available for use by a wide audience including: institutional investors, corporations, policymakers and their advisors, public sector organizations, government bodies, academics and the public.

ISO is a non-governmental organization that forms a bridge between the public and private sectors. ISO is a network of the national standards institutes of 162 countries, one member per country, with a Central Secretariat in Geneva, Switzerland, that coordinates the system. ISO published the standard ISO 26000 in November 2010 in which it emphasizes the value of public reporting on social responsibility performance to internal and external stakeholders, such as employees, local communities, investors and regulators. This represents an important new level of international attention to the issue of reporting that disclosure on economic, environmental, social and governance performance becomes as commonplace and comparable as financial reporting. Other standards, such as ISO 14001 for Environmental Management Systems have had a significant impact globally on business sustainability. When in the 1990s a large producer of cars required all first tier suppliers to have an environmental management system in place certified to the ISO 14001 standard, there was an almost doubling of the number of management systems in place globally and the auditors required to verify them.

## *Discussion*

One difficulty in assessing the sustainability performance of a business is how to compare across different activities, priorities and performance levels. Business A might focus on reducing carbon emissions whilst Business B might focus on labour standards and community support. Which business is more sustainable? What if Business C has reduced its energy consumption and waste generation but its most senior management salary is more than 100 times that of their lowest paid worker? Is Business C still performing sustainably if inequitably? Should a consumer buy from Business A or Business B? If they are part of a supply chain, how can a business upstream (i.e. buying their input from other suppliers to make their output products or services) understand the sustainability impacts that are inherent in their purchases? How does an investor understand the risk associated with businesses in relation to sustainability performance?

Investors have led the way in developing evaluation models and methods that take a sustainability point of view, and similar models have been rolled out by major retailers. The models and methods require financial and non-financial data like environmental, governance and social (ESG) performance information which are used for the evaluation. *Environmental* evaluation criteria can include policy around key environmental issues like greenhouse gases, water and bio diversity. *Social* evaluation criteria can include the company's social contribution to job creation, workers' rights to association and human rights; and lastly *Governance* can mean the board's practice, the percentage of independent directors and the independence of the audit committee. These are only some of the evaluation criteria. Some methodologies and their applications are discussed below.

*Case study of sustainability evaluation in business*

Two of the indexes that are used to assess business sustainability, particularly with respect to investment, are the SAM (Sustainable Assets Management) Dow Jones Sustainable Index (DJSI); and FTSE4Good Index.

These two indexes are among the most popular indexes with which to evaluate corporate sustainability. However, there are big differences in their evaluation methodology. SAM DJSI takes a 'best-in-class' approach whilst FTSE4Good relies on negative screening. The explanation is given below.

SAM Dow Jones Sustainability Index

The Dow Jones Sustainability Indexes are based on SAM's internationally recognized leading Corporate Sustainability Assessment (CSA) methodology. The Dow Jones Sustainability Indexes launched in 1999 were the first global indexes tracking the financial performance of the leading sustainability-driven companies worldwide. The results of the annual SAM Corporate Sustainability Assessment form the research backbone for the construction of the Dow Jones Sustainability Indexes. This family of indexes takes a 'best-in-class' approach to selecting sustainability leaders from all industry sectors on the basis of defined sustainability criteria embedded in the SAM Corporate Sustainability Assessment. This means that they include only companies that fulfil certain sustainability criteria better than the majority of their peers.

SAM also provides the opportunity to conduct a dialogue with companies from all sectors and thereby influence incremental improvements in companies' sustainability practices. To be included or remain in the index, companies have to continually intensify their sustainability initiatives. SAM believes this approach will benefit all stakeholders: investors, employees, customers and, ultimately, society and the environment.

FTSE4Good Index

FTSE is an independent company jointly owned by The Financial Times and the London Stock Exchange. FTSE4GOOD criteria have been set at a level that represents good practice standards, thus screening out businesses that do not meet the criteria. In addition, the negative screening also excludes specific sectors for their sustainability impacts, such as alcohol producers, arms makers and sellers, companies with breaches in the human rights of employees or local residents, gambling, nuclear power, polluters, supporters of oppressive regimes, pornography and tobacco.

FTSE develops a dialogue with business, providing directions on how to meet the standard. This proactive engagement process has contributed to sustainable changes in corporate practices. Independent committees of senior fund managers, derivatives experts, actuaries and other experienced practitioners review and approve all changes to the indexes to ensure that they are made objectively and without bias.

### Sustainability in the Supply Chain

Gathering information and enforcing standards through the supply chain by retailers is also having an impact on business sustainability. Many UK supermarkets, including Tesco, Waitrose and Marks & Spencer require their suppliers to meet extensive sustainability performance guidelines. In the USA, Walmart has introduced a Sustainability Index that aims to impact suppliers around the globe and provide the sustainability information to consumers at point of sale (i.e. in the shop) so that they can make an informed decision about the impacts that are associated with what they are buying. These programs have much further reach than government legislation and are often more binding as it directly relates to what is being bought and sold. For example, the standards set by Tesco for food and beverages sold in the UK have an impact on how growers and producers hire labour in countries as far away as Australia and South Africa. When compared to the time taken for international agreements, such as to the Kyoto Protocol, to take effect and for member countries to commit to and implement these protocols, businesses enforcing high sustainability standards on other businesses can deliver fast, specific and measurable results.

### Conclusion

Business and industry have a role in creating a sustainable future. As significant users of resources, employers, neighbours, polluters, innovators and members of every community, the way a business operates is intricately connected to people and the planet. As consumers we all have an influence on how businesses operate through what we buy. If we give preference to consuming less, equity and purchasing goods and services with positive ESG outcomes we can support businesses in their drive for sustainability. We all know people employed by businesses and people who own businesses and many students will one day work in a business. People and businesses are interconnected.

Our methods for evaluating business performance are becoming more sophisticated as we start to consider sustainability issues. Indexes provide companies with crucial insights into their sustainability performance, making them aware of key sustainability issues to be considered in their corporate agenda. Standardized data on sustainability issues is needed to enable investors and consumers to compare the activities of companies. There are initiatives to standardise data which will make it easier for stakeholders to evaluate companies on sustainability alongside financial performance in near future.

Driving sustainability in business is crucial for sustainability in society and can be for the mutual benefit of companies, investors and individuals. As this benefit circle strengthens, it will have a positive effect on societies and economies.

---

***Thinking it through: where do I stand?***

Who are some of the big businesses you support through what you buy? Do you know what they do on sustainability?

Are there any indexes that give you more information on what you buy? Have a look at the electronics industry and see how different companies are rated on sustainability. Greenpeace International publishes an annual guide on greening the electronics industry. Have a look at who makes your computers, mobile phones and games consoles and see how they rate for sustainability performance. Would you choose to buy from another brand based on sustainability performance?

Choose one of your utility providers and see if they publish a sustainability report. Does their report make reference to the GRI? Do they publish any information on their sustainability performance in their Annual Report?

Where do members of the local community work? Ask students to ask their parents if they know what their employer is doing to make their organization more sustainable.

What is happening in your country on emissions trading or carbon taxes? Do you think it will encourage business to be more sustainable?

---

***Action: what can I do?***

Your school will buy lots of things, including desks, paper, food and buildings. Think about how your school takes into account sustainability when it buys something. Contact some of the suppliers to your school and ask if they participate in the CDP or write a sustainability report. Ask them to come and talk to your class about sustainability and what it means to them.

Try to research different options next time you want to buy something and see if you can support a business that is trying to be sustainable.

---

### Further reading

Sullivan, R. & Mackenzie, C. (2006). *Responsible Investment*. Greenleaf Publishing Limited.

Krechowicz, D., Venugopal, S. & Sauer, A. (2010). *Weeding Risk*. World Resources Institute.

Mackay, D. (1998). *Sustainable Energy - Without Hot Air* (available as a free download from www.withouthotair.com )

McDonough, W. & Braungart, M. (2002). *Cradle to Cradle: Remaking the Way We Make Things*. New York: North Point Press.

Klein, N. (2000). *No Logo*. Toronto: Knopf Canada.

## *Viewing*

### *The Story of Stuff* by Annie Leonard

This 20 minute animated feature shows the environmental, social and economic cost of the things we buy and how they are made. Shorter features, such as the Story of Bottled Water, are also very informative. There are also educational resources and further readings available on the website.
http://www.storyofstuff.com/

### *Our Story* by Cadbury

An interactive website takes you through Cadbury's history, including a story line on their philanthropy. You can also look at their current commitments to sustainability.
http://www.cadbury.co.uk/cadburyandchocolate/ourstory/Pages/ourstoryFlash.aspx

## *Resources*

Carbon Disclosure Project https://www.cdproject.net/en-US/Pages/HomePage.aspx
Climate Disclosure Standards Board (CDSB) http://www.cdsb-global.org/
Energy Conservation Centre Japan http://www.asiaeec-col.eccj.or.jp/index.html
European Commission Climate Action: Emissions Trading Scheme http://ec.europa.eu/clima/policies/ets/index_en.htm
Eurosif SRI resources http://www.eurosif.org/sri-resources/sri-country-resources/united-kingdom
FTSE 4 Good Index. http://www.ftse.com/Indices/FTSE4Good_Index_Series/index.jsp
Greenpeace International Guide to Greener Electronics http://www.greenpeace.org/international/en/campaigns/toxics/electronics/how-the-companies-line-up/
International Integrated Reporting Committee (IIRC) http://www.theiirc.org/
International Organization for Standardization (ISO) http://www.iso.org/iso/home.html
Marks & Spencer Sustainability http://plana.marksandspencer.com/
OECD Guidelines for Multinational Enterprises http://www.oecd.org/department/0,3355,en_2649_34889_1_1_1_1_1,00.html
Sustainable Assets Management (SAM) http://www.sam-group.com/htmle/about/portrait.cfm
SAM Dow Jones Sustainable Index http://www.sustainability-index.com/
The Global Reporting Initiative http://www.globalreporting.org/Home
United Nation finance Initiative http://www.unepfi.org/
United Nations Global Compact http://www.unglobalcompact.org/

United Nations Principles for Responsible Investment Initiative
        http://www.unpri.org/about/
World Business Council for Sustainable Development (WBCSD)
        http://www.wbcsd.org/templates/TemplateWBCSD5/lay-
        out.asp?MenuID=1
World Bank Market Capitalisation of Listed Companies http://data.world-
        bank.org/indicator/CM.MKT.LCAP.GD.ZS
Walmart Sustainability Index http://walmartstores.com/Sustainability/

# Chapter 7
## Sharing Responsibility Between Consumers and Producers

*Thomas Wiedmann*
*CSIRO Ecosystem Sciences, Canberra, Australia*
*Integrated Sustainability Analysis, University of Sydney*
*Centre for Sustainability Accounting, York, UK*

*Christopher Dey*
*Manfred Lenzen*
*Integrated Sustainability Analysis, University of Sydney*

## *The issue*

### *How to share responsibility between consumers and producers?*

Who is responsible for what? In modern economies, both production and consumption have consequences, often detrimental, for the natural environment, the climate or for ecosystems. In short, both producers and consumers are responsible for sustainability impacts. But how should the responsibility be shared, if at all? For example, should a company have to improve the eco-friendliness of its products, or is it up to the consumer to buy or not to buy? We introduce the concept of shared responsibility, which was developed to address a lack of accurate quantification and comparability of impacts in corporate sustainability reporting. We demonstrate the applicability of the concept with a practical example.

## Context

### Corporate Sustainability Reporting and the responsibility question

Companies are beginning to apply the concept of sustainability at a practical level in terms of environmental and sustainability accounting and reporting. These accounts and reports must contain qualitative and quantitative information on economic, environmental and social performance, and integrate these into sustainability management. Such Triple Bottom Line (TBL) accounting enables decision-makers to quantify trade-offs between different aspects of sustainability.

Even though there are some guidelines for TBL accounting, e.g. the Global Reporting Initiative, there are no strict standards as there are in financial accounting. Quantitative TBL accounting is therefore often confronted with inconsistencies and boundary problems, leading to under- or overcounting and making it difficult to compare the performance of different companies.

It is also important to address the question of how to assign responsibility for environmental and social impacts along production and supply chains.

In this Chapter we illustrate the concept of 'shared responsibility' and explain with a simplified supply chain example how it can be applied in practical circumstances

## Discussion

### The concept of shared responsibility

#### Assigning responsibility along supply chains

When thinking about environmental and wider sustainability impacts of production and consumption, crucial questions arise such as: who is responsible for what, or: how is the responsibility to be shared, if at all? For example, should a company have to improve the eco-friendliness of its products, or is it up to the consumer to buy or not to buy? And further, should a business be held responsible for only the consequences of the use of its products (e.g. fuel economy of a car), or should it also be aware of impacts caused by its suppliers and therefore be responsible for its procurement decisions? If so, how far should the 'downstream' and 'upstream' spheres of responsibility extend? Similar questions can be phrased for the problem of deciding who takes the credits for job creation or successful abatement measures that involve producers and consumers: who has the best knowledge of, or the most influence over, how to increase social benefits or reduce adverse impacts associated with the transfer of a product from producer to consumer?

*Full producer and consumer responsibility*

Traditional company environmental reports are based on a 'producer responsibility' perspective (so are, by the way, all national environmental statistics). This means that companies usually report their 'own' impacts, such as on-site emissions to air and water, and other direct impacts such as noise, waste, direct use of energy and resources etc.

In the following example we compare this production-based approach with a consumption-based perspective. We are looking at a simple, fictitious supply chain. A supply chain is a system of organisations, people, technology, activities, information and resources involved in moving a product or service from supplier to customer. Supply chain activities transform natural resources, raw materials and components into a finished product that is delivered to the end customer. Sometimes supply chains are referred to as production chains or economic chains.

In the 'consumer responsibility' approach all impacts that occur along the supply chain of a product are added up and attributed to the consumer. This approach follows the notion, expressed by Adam Smith in 1776, that consumption is "the sole end and purpose of all production". Therefore the consumer is to bear all the indirect consequences of his or her action. Such a consumption-based perspective is also taken in Life Cycle Assessment (LCA) studies – the 'life-cycle inventory' or 'footprint' of a product is the sum of all impacts associated with its existence.

Consider the carbon dioxide emissions caused by one particular economic chain: the production and consumption of glass containers and their food content. This is a purely illustrative example with fictitious numbers, and for the sake of simplicity we assume that the participants of this economic chain do not supply anyone other than the next actor in the chain. According to the traditional perspective of producer responsibility accounting, we note the direct (on-site) emissions of each member of the supply chain (Figure 1 and Table 1 ). The final consumer does not emit $CO_2$ in this particular process and therefore no emissions are attributed to them.

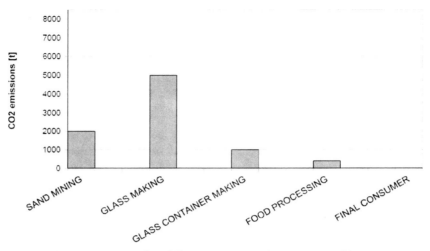

Figure 1: Example for a full producer responsibility account of direct
$CO_2$ emissions along a supply chain

Note that there would be double-counting if the producers of glass, glass-containers and food used traditional LCA or carbon footprinting to calculate and publicise their $CO_2$ emissions. This is because the 'life cycle' perspective of LCA requires that all contributions from previous members of the supply chain be added up and reported. The emissions caused by the sand miner, the glassmaker and the glass container maker would appear in the food company's $CO_2$ emissions account because they are all suppliers. Hence the 'embodied' $CO_2$ emissions of this final production stage, derived by traditional LCA / carbon footprinting, would be 8400 t (the total of all actors' emissions). However each organisation along the way might have already reported its own full upstream footprint. Therefore when the life-cycle emissions reported by all actors in the chain are taken as a whole multiple-counting would have taken place.

Let us now look at full consumer responsibility. In life-cycle or footprint thinking, the consumer of products is placed at the very end of the supply chain and all impacts incurred during production are attributed to them. Therefore if double-counting is to be avoided, LCA and footprinting can strictly only be used for the final consumers in an economy: the impacts of any producer must be zero. This is a full consumer responsibility account as depicted in Figure 2 .

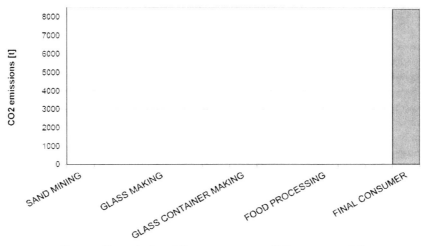

Figure 2: Example for a full consumer responsibility account of all
$CO_2$ emissions along a supply chain

A particular disadvantage of either full producer or consumer responsibility is that neither allows for both producers and consumers to evaluate their TBL impacts simultaneously without double-counting. Full producer and consumer responsibility therefore appear somewhat unrealistic in their extremeness. Both producers and consumers wish to report their respective part of the impact, and it is intuitively clear that responsibility is somehow to be shared between the supplier and the recipient of a commodity, because the supplier has directly caused the impacts, but the recipient has demanded that the supplier do so.

*Quantifying shares of responsibility*

As with many other allocation problems, an acceptable consensus probably lies somewhere between producer and consumer responsibility. In order to assign responsibility to actors participating in these transactions, one has to know the respective supply chains or inter-industry relations. Hence, a problem poses itself in the form of the question: "How can one devise an accounting method that allows environmental (or other TBL) impacts to be apportioned to both producers and consumers whilst avoiding double-counting?".

In reality, both the final consumers and their upstream suppliers play some role in causing environmental impacts. The suppliers use resources and energy in order to produce, and make decisions on how much and what type of resources and energy they use. Consumers decide to spend their money on products coming from those upstream suppliers. The concept of shared responsibility recognises that there are always two persons, or groups of people, who play a role in commodities produced and impacts caused, and two perspectives involved in every transaction: the supplier's and the recipient's. Hence, responsibility for impacts can be shared between them. Naturally, this applies to both benefits and burdens, and therefore to all positive and negative TBL indicators.

Sharing impacts between each pair of subsequent supply chain stages gets rid of the double-counting problem described above. The immediate question that arises is in which *proportion* impacts should be shared between supplier and recipient in an economic chain. One possibility could be a 50%-50% split, where 50% of an on-site impact is retained by the producer and 50% is passed on to the producer's downstream client. However, a 50%-50% share leads to a methodological inconsistency: the part of the impact that is passed on and eventually reaches the final consumer is dependent on the number of participants in a supply chain. In other words, the more businesses are involved in the production of a product the more 'diluted' will be the consumer's share of responsibility. This characteristic, however, is inconsistent and undesirable because it encourages organisations to de-merge in order to put more steps in the chain and so dilute their impacts.

As a solution to this problem, researchers have suggested to use the economic parameter Value Added to determine the percentage split of responsibility between supplier and recipient.[1] No matter whether a production / supply chain is represented as many or few stages, the total value added is always the same at the end of the chain. The share of responsibility retained by any supplier in the production chain can then be calculated with a simple equation:

Retained Responsibility (RR) = Value Added (VA) / Net Output (NO)

Using the supply chain from above, we apply this equation with examples of values for Value Added (VA) and Net Output (NO) for each supplier as shown in Table 1.

---

1. See reference to Lenzen et al. (2007) under Further Reading.

Table 1: Quantitative example of allocating $CO_2$ emissions in a (hypothetical) supply chain by applying the shared responsibility approach (compare to Figure 3)

|  | Sand mining | Glass making | Glass container making | Food processing | Final consumer |
|---|---|---|---|---|---|
| Value added (VA) [$m] | 0.4 | 1.6 | 2.1 | 16.0 |  |
| Net output (NO) [$m] | 1.6 | 3.2 | 5.3 | 21.3 |  |
| RR = VA/NO | 0.25 | 0.50 | 0.40 | 0.75 |  |
| *These values define the proportion of 'retained responsibility', i.e.:* | | | | | |
| Responsibility share | 25% retained, 75% passed on | 50% retained, 50% passed on | 40% retained, 60% passed on | 75% retained, 25% passed on |  |
| On-site $CO_2$ emissions [t] | 2000 | 5000 | 1000 | 400 |  |
| $CO_2$ received [t] |  | 1500 | 3250 | 2550 | 738 |
| *On-site plus received emissions are then split up according to the proportions above:* | | | | | |
| $CO_2$ retained [t] | 500 | 3250 | 1700 | 2213 | 738 |
| $CO_2$ passed on [t] | 1500 | 3250 | 2550 | 738 |  |

Assume the sand mine supplies $1.6million worth of sand to the glass maker, to which the latter adds $1.6m of value to produce $3.2m worth of glass net output. To this, the glass container manufacturer adds $2.1m of value, producing $5.3m worth of glass containers. To this, the food manufacturer adds $16m of value, producing $21.3m worth of food.

The sand mine adds 25% of value to sandstone by turning it into sand. It will hence retain a shared responsibility of 25% of their $CO_2$ emissions (500 t out of 2000 t) and send the remaining 75% (1500 t) down the supply chain to the glass manufacturer. The glass maker will add 50% of value to sand by turning it into glass. The glass maker is hence assigned 50% of 1500 tonnes of $CO_2$ passed down from sand, plus 50% of 5000 tonnes used while manufacturing glass. The remainder (3250 t) is passed on to glass containers. The glass container manufacturer will add 40% of value to glass, and is thus assigned 40% of the emissions embodied in glass containers, and so on. Finally, the food manufacturer adds 75% of value to glass containers, and is therefore assigned 75% of emissions embodied in packed food. Final consumers (households, the government) are at the end of the supply chain, and receive the remainder (738 t of $CO_2$). This process of sharing responsibility by using a VA/NO allocation is depicted in Figure 3; the final results are shown in Figure 4.

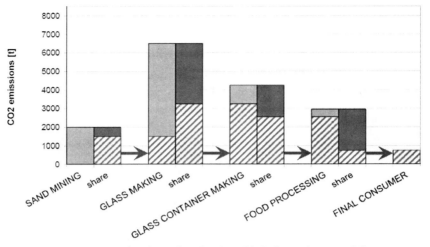

Figure 3: Process of applying shared, value-added-allocated responsibility to CO2 emissions in one particular supply chain (blue/grey columns = on-site impact; patterned columns = share that is passed on from one supplier to the next; purple/dark columns = retained impact)

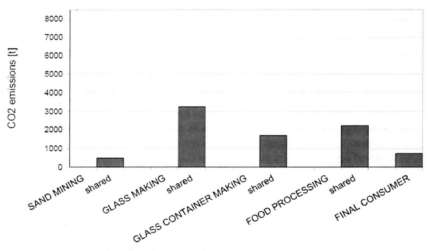

Figure 4: Results of applying shared, value-added-allocated responsibility to CO2 emissions in one particular supply chain (identical to the purple/dark grey columns in Figure 3)

The logic of this allocation scheme (as opposed to a 50%-50% split) is that an organisation that controls its production to a high extent retains a high share of the responsibility for the emissions. High control, or influence over the product, can be approximated by high value added: production processes that add a high percentage of value onto inputs usually transform these to a high extent, while low-value adding entities operate more as an "agent" of their inputs.

*Case study*

*Shared TBL account of an example company*

In the following we show the results of a hypothetical TBL analysis of the glass container making factory from the previous section. Instead of only looking at $CO_2$ emissions, we now expand the scope and include a range of economic, social and environmental indicators.

Figure 5 shows impacts of eight selected indicators and how they have been attributed to the supply chain entity.

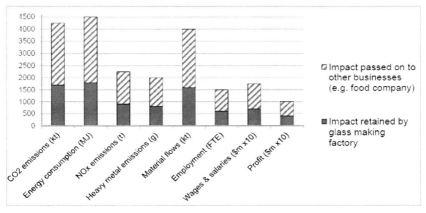

Figure 5: Responsibility shares of TBL impacts of an example company (glass container factory). For each indicator the impacts are split into 40% retained and 60% passed on, according to the values shown in Table 1

TBL impacts of the company can be compared in a meaningful way with other enterprises in the same sector if they are normalised to the business size. This can be done by dividing the absolute impact (e.g. tonnes of $CO_2$ emitted) by the company's total expenditure in the same time period (normally one financial year). For benchmarking purposes the resulting impact intensities (e.g. in t $CO_2$ / $) can be directly compared to those from the sector-average.

This can be depicted conveniently in a spider (radar) diagram as shown in Figure 6. The ratios of business-to-sector intensities convey an overview of the business's TBL performance on all indicators. The ratios divide business intensity by sector intensity for indicators that are deemed negative ("less is good", e.g. $CO_2$ emissions), so that better performance leads to lower ratios. For indicators that are deemed positive ("more is good", e.g. employment), these ratios are inversed, so that better performance leads to lower ratios. The TBL spider diagram can therefore – within limits – be interpreted as "dents are good, spikes are bad".

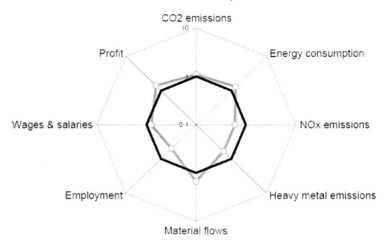

**TBL Benchmark Spider**

⊸○⊸TBL performanc of glass container maker     ▬▬TBL performance of glass industry

Figure 6: A spider diagram presentation of the Triple Bottom Line performance of key financial, social and environmental indicators of a (fictitious) glass container factory (red/grey line). The regular polygon in the centre of the diagram (thick black line) shows the average TBL performance of the glass industry as a whole, allowing a benchmark comparison between the company and its sector. Indicators with above-average performance are closer to the centre, while below-average indicators are positioned closer to the outside boundary

The first-level evaluation example presented in Figure 6 indicates that the glass container factory has slightly higher $CO_2$ emissions, energy consumption and material flows than the industry average but performs better in terms of pollutant emissions. The employment generated by the activities of the glass container maker and the wages and salaries paid exceed those of the sector, respectively, while profits in the sector are higher.

It should be borne in mind that the impact performance refers to the *retained* share of the *total, life-cycle wide* impact, not only to the direct impact of the company. Similar to the procedure explained in the previous section, the total impact (which is the sum of on-site plus indirect impacts embodied in upstream production) is divided into one part that is retained by the company and another part that is passed on further down the supply chain.

---

*Thinking it through: Sharing Responsibility*

Who is responsible for the impacts of production - the producer or the consumer? In this section we argue that both should burden a share of responsibility and make suggestions as to how this could be done. With the concept of 'shared responsibility' it is possible to allocate TBL impacts amongst the participants of an economic chain, including all producers and consumers of commodities. The main differences between the principle of shared responsibility and that of either full producer or full consumer responsibility are:

---

- Under shared responsibility every member of the supply chain is affected by their upstream supplier and in turn affects their downstream recipient, hence it is in all actors' interest to enter into a dialogue about what to do to improve supply chain performance. There is no incentive for such a dialogue in full producer responsibility. In shared responsibility, producers are not alone in addressing the issue of TBL impacts, because their downstream customers play a role, too.

- Shared responsibility provides an incentive for producers and consumers to enter into a dialogue about what to do to improve the profile of consumer products. It gives consumers information about where the impacts occur that are embodied in the products they buy.

---

### *Action: what can I do?*

1. Play the responsibility game!
   An insightful game was developed that playfully addresses the problem of responsibility sharing. It uses the carbon footprint of a jar of jam as an example. The game has been played with around 200 participants from business and industry, government and non-government organisations. It has proved to be an effective teaching tool in conveying the concepts of double counting and shared responsibility (the game is described in 'The Sustainability Practitioner's Guide to Input-Output Analysis', see Further Reading)

2. Ask your suppliers:
   Contact suppliers of your school or organisation and ask them about their carbon emissions and whether they have ever thought about sharing these with their clients (whilst at the same time accepting responsibility for some of the emissions from their own suppliers). Ask them whether they participate in initiatives such as the Carbon Disclosure Project (which allows for the reporting of own emissions and those from suppliers)

---

## *Further reading*

Foran, B., Lenzen, M., & Dey, C. (2005). *Balancing Act: A Triple Bottom Line Analysis of the Australian Economy.* Canberra, Australia: Commonwealth Scientific and Industrial Research Organisation (CSIRO).

Lenzen, M., Murray, J., Sack, F. & Wiedmann, T. (2007). Shared producer and consumer responsibility - Theory and practice. *Ecological Economics, 61*(1), 27-42.

Murray, J. & Lenzen, M. (2010). Chapter 16: We're all in this [Supply Chain] Together - Is it a Blame Game or a Responsibility Game? In: J. Murray & R. Wood (Eds.), *The Sustainability Practitioner's Guide to Input-Output Analysis* (189-196). Champaign, USA: Common Ground Publishing LLC.

Wiedmann, T. & Lenzen, M. (2008). Unravelling the Impacts of Supply Chains - A New Triple-Bottom-Line Accounting Approach and Software Tool. In: S. Schaltegger, M. Bennett, R. L. Burritt & C. Jasch (Eds.), *Environmental Management Accounting for Cleaner Production* (Chapter 4: 65-90). New York: Springer.

# Chapter 8

## What Role for Government in Sustainability?

*Frank Stilwell*
*Department of Political Economy, University of Sydney*

### Introduction

People commonly look to governments to solve social problems. So, faced with a threat such as climate change, it is reasonable to ask what governments should do. Posing that question leads into quite complex considerations of economics, politics and ethics. It takes us into the controversial territory known as 'the political economy of the environment'.

Let us start by considering the tasks that governments generally perform. Why do we have governments? We do so, most simply, because people, acting individually, cannot adequately address and resolve social challenges that require a collective response. Dealing with external threats is a classic example. Historically, a primary function of governments has been to defend national populations against aggressors. Governments have financed these military activities through taxation and sometimes conscripted selected citizens into the armed forces. Is the challenge of climate change similar to the prospect of war, requiring a comparable response? Perhaps so, although there are two obvious differences: the threat of climate change is *internally* generated, and it requires nations to cooperate worldwide to meet the common threat, not to be at war with each other. These differences require us to think carefully about what is involved in developing government policies to enhance sustainability.

Governments already undertake numerous activities that shape how societies use their resources and capacities. The traditional role of organizing national defence is only one part of the story. Other elements include the provision of infrastructure, such as railways, roads, hospitals, schools, sewerage facilities and water, gas and electricity supply systems. Governments also provide services, usually including health, education, housing, welfare, urban planning and police. They manage the overall level of incomes, employment and economic output through monetary and fiscal policies, supplemented by trade and industry policies. They redistribute incomes between rich and poor people through their taxing and spending. By policing borders, governments also determine who is allowed to enter the country and who can become citizens. They regulate what the citizens and businesses are permitted to do – determining the maximum speed at which motorists are allowed to drive, where new urban developments can occur, how industrial wastes may be disposed of, and a host of other matters. All these governmental activities influence the distribution of wealth and economic opportunities in the society.

Such considerations, when adapted to current concerns about sustainability, lead to the obvious inference that governments should add managing environmental quality to their list of responsibilities. Faced with the threats of climate change or resource depletion, governments should act decisively to create more sustainable economic and social arrangements that enable us to 'tread more lightly' on the planet. It is an apparently simple inference yet it generates some profound questions. *How* should governments seek to constrain or prevent environmentally degrading activities? What impediments limit the effectiveness of their policies? Are there trade-offs to be considered, for example, between environmental quality and economic prosperity or between the impacts of environmental restrictions on rich and poor people? Can governments work in unison for a common purpose? And, if governments do take the lead in promoting sustainability, does that relieve the rest of the society, especially business interests, from taking responsibility for doing 'the right thing'?

This chapter explores these political economic concerns with particular emphasis on the range of policy instruments that governments may use when trying to create more sustainable outcomes. As we will see, the policy possibilities are numerous but so too are their respective pros and cons. Indeed, governments *can* steer the way towards sustainability but deciding on the right 'policy mix' for this purpose requires sophisticated political economic judgements. Getting governments to act also requires political organization and social pressure.

*Developing Market Mechanisms*

Governments grappling with the question of how to formulate responses to environmental problems commonly seek advice from economists. The UK government did so when it appointed Nicholas Stern to head its major environmental policy review, while the Australian government also did so when it asked Ross Garnaut to advise it on responding to the threat of climate change. Predictably, such economists emphasise the application of economic policy instruments. 'Putting a price on carbon' has become their mantra.

The climate change reviews prepared by these economists have had three positive features. First, they recognize that the scientists' warnings about climate change have to be taken seriously, requiring major restructuring of economies and societies to produce more sustainable arrangements. Second, they emphasize that the economic costs of inaction would eventually be greater than the costs of taking remedial steps, so there is an economic as well as an ecological case for seeking sustainability. Third, they put a spotlight on government policy as the avenue through which a change of direction may be driven. Although government policy initiatives are not the be all and end all of the drive towards sustainability, even market-oriented economists recognize that governments are crucial in setting and changing 'the rules of the game'. But what policy approach should governments take?

Emissions trading, sometimes called a 'cap and trade' policy, has been at the top of government policy agendas since the international environmental summit held in Kyoto in 1997. The policy has a strong basis in mainstream economic theory, so it is not surprising that economists like Stern and Garnaut advocate it. According to the theory, a limit (or cap) should be set on the total amount of carbon emissions. If permits to pollute up to that limit are then issued by the government and traded in the market, they will be acquired by those with the greatest need to pollute and the greatest ability to pay for doing so. A market logic prevails. In practice, the effectiveness of an emissions trading policy depends upon how strictly the limit on acceptable pollution is defined, how vigorously it is policed, whether the initial allocation of permits gives preferential treatment to existing polluters, and the conditions under which the market operates. All these practical considerations can result in the policy producing a much less effective outcome in the real world than the mainstream economic theory would imply. Experience with the policy in Europe has not been encouraging for those who had been committed to emissions trading as the principle driver of change towards a sustainable economy.

An alternative market-based mechanism that has been advocated by environmentalists for many years is a carbon tax. This directly penalises activities that use fossil fuels and thereby compound the problem of climate change. It would have a differential impact on the price of different goods and services according to the amount of fossil fuel consumed in their production. Products whose manufacture and supply requires the burning of much fossil fuel would become more expensive. Aluminium products are a case in point. Their manufacture involves the use of enormous amounts of electricity, typically produced by burning coal or oil. Proponents of carbon taxes argue that once aluminium products become heavily taxed consumers will seek to switch to cheaper less environmentally degrading products.

Like emissions trading, the case for a carbon tax has its roots in mainstream economic theory. The theory assumes that the array of goods and services that we produce and consume will adjust to changes in the market price signals. On this reasoning, 'putting a price on carbon'– either through emissions trading or a carbon tax – would discourage activities that cause climate change. It would generate more ecologically responsible and sustainable patterns of production and consumption. An incentive would also be created for businesses and households to develop technological changes that reduce their reliance on non-renewable materials, energy sources and products. Price changes would drive behavioural changes, leading to more sustainable patterns of production and consumption.

So is the policy choice for governments simply whether to implement an emissions trading scheme or a carbon tax? Indeed, this choice has been widely discussed by economic policy advisors. It has sometimes led to the advocacy of policies that combine elements of both, such as the hybrid scheme that was introduced by the Australian government in 2011. In principle, either emissions trading or a carbon tax can achieve a similar outcome. An emissions trading scheme sets the permitted level of output of pollutants and allows the market price of pollution permits to vary. A carbon tax policy, on the other hand, determines the price to be paid by the persons or businesses creating the pollution and allows the output of pollutants to vary. In the former case, changes in the level of the 'cap' will tend to drive changes in the market price of the pollution permits. For the carbon tax alternative the rate of tax can be adjusted up or down in order to achieve the acceptable level of carbon emissions.

All of this sounds deceptively neat. In practice, both policies have some substantial drawbacks that stem from their underlying assumptions about the actual and potential role of markets. Adopting a broader political economic perspective, we can see that 'pricing the environment in order to save it' is indeed a rather strange principle. Seeking sustainability through extending private property rights to environmental access and/or by using a new tax to change the prices of goods and services has a narrow 'market logic'. It does not adequately recognize the more fundamental problems associated with capitalism as an economic system, and how economic growth and the extension of markets have created the environmental stresses in the first place. As environmentalists like Ted Trainer have emphasised, the more fundamental problem is the unsustainable relationship between economic growth and the finite character of non-renewable natural resources. Attempts at environmental 'fine-tuning' through creating new markets or modifying market prices do not address the problems that are inherent in a system based on capital accumulation, profit-seeking and consumerist behaviours. Nor does it deal directly with the exercise of corporate power by big businesses that have vested interest in maintaining the existing political economic system.

'Putting a price on carbon' also has predictably adverse outcomes from a social equity perspective. Raising the price of environmental resources makes them less accessible to the poor. In the extreme, access to good environmental quality – even to the requirements for life itself – becomes a matter of ability to pay. So the question of compensation has to be addressed. Indeed, it recurs regularly in debates about emissions trading and carbon taxes because governments have to be sensitive to the needs (and votes) of lower-income groups. However, if everyone who has to pay more as a result of 'putting a price on carbon' is directly compensated for that extra expense, then the policy won't work. By its very nature, the policy has to 'hit people in the pocket' to create the direct financial incentive to adopt more environmentally sensitive behaviour.

Pragmatically, the other big concern is whether the economic policy instruments are effective anyway. This depends substantially on how people respond to the changed market signals. Ethical as well as narrow monetary considerations are relevant in this context. Consider the complex relationship between market prices and social responsibility, for example. Does buying a permit to pollute or paying a carbon tax effectively absolve the polluter from the personal responsibility to act in a more ecologically responsible manner? If so, then the extent of pollution abatement that results from 'putting a price on carbon' may be disappointingly small. Indeed, that seems to have been the case so far in countries where this type of policy has been implemented. Perhaps we should not be surprised. Having paid the market price, polluters may be seen to have established the right – and the incentive – to continue polluting.

Critics of using market-based economic policy instruments to achieve environment goals commonly note this tension between the economic and ethical implications of the policies and the uncertain outcomes that result. A carbon tax is better than emissions trading in this respect because at least it aligns the price signal more directly with the ethical concern. Like a tax on cigarettes, there is little ambiguity about a carbon tax being an impost on undesirable and anti-social behaviours.

Nor is a carbon tax likely to promote new 'carbon futures' markets, as tend to result from having an emissions trading system. Because the latter policy establishes new tradeable property rights in the use of environmental resources, it predictably leads to the development of trading in derivatives. These derivatives, like 'carbon futures', are financial instruments whose market value depends on predictions of future changes in the market price of pollution permits. An emissions trading system thereby introduces a pronounced speculative element into the operation of environmental policy. Indeed, it would be an awesome prospect if the unstable and speculative market that was evident during the recent global financial crisis were now to be extended into the field of environmental policy.

The Australian environmental scientist Sharon Beder has explored some of the general consequences of the use of market-based policy instruments in an excellent book, called Environmental Principles and Policies. She discusses three environmental protection principles – a sustainability principle, a polluter pays principle, and a precautionary principle. She then identifies three social principles – an equity principle, a human rights principle and a participation principle – that are also relevant in evaluating public policies. Assessing economic instruments for pollution control according to these six general principles produces consistently negative conclusions. Beder shows that market-based environmental policies do not measure up against what is needed. So, if we, as a society, are to go beyond tinkering with the current political economic arrangements, we have to engage in yet more fundamental thinking about new directions in environmental policy.

### Policies Beyond the Market

*Regulation* is an alternative to the market-oriented economic policy instruments that governments need to consider when seeking to prevent further environmental degradation. Regulation relies on the capacity of government to make laws and to enforce them. It sends strong signals to producers and consumers and generally produces predictable outcomes. It is implied to some extent in 'cap and trade' emissions trading, in that the 'cap' is set by a government regulator. More firmly though, regulation may be extended to the prohibition of particular environmentally degrading and hazardous activities.

Mainstream economists are usually reluctant to embrace direct regulation by governments because they regard it as less sensitive than market arrangements. Regulation in the form of prohibition implies, in effect, an infinite market price – precluding activities that are not to be allowed at any price. The mainstream economists say that this uncompromising position tends to have major social costs. For example, prohibiting particular activities may instantly drive some firms out of business. Well, you might say, perhaps they should go out of business if they have been causing climate change. But the mainstream economists prefer to use a policy of 'putting a price on carbon' because that creates an incentive for firms and their customers to adjust their behaviours in their own time, taking account of the changed market signals. This objection to regulation reflects a particular value judgement – that the 'freedom of the marketplace' is a goal in itself. In effect, the mainstream economists place more weight on 'process' than 'outcome', emphasising the case for maintaining individual choice rather than the necessity of getting a particular social result. The problem is that, faced with a major threat such as climate change, it is the outcome of the policies that ultimately matters.

Stricter regulations can make a direct contribution to driving the changes needed for sustainability. Actually, the public policy choice in practice is not usually between pricing policies or regulation, because governments commonly engage in both to achieve diverse social goals. Consider land markets for example. Governments influence the prevailing market prices of land through the imposition of land taxes and stamp duties on property transfers, but they also prohibit environmentally degrading land uses or restrict them to particular localities where the ecological damage can be contained. Regulations and controls exist in other fields too, even under the auspices of market-oriented neoliberal governments. Some forms of pesticides have been banned because they are injurious to health, as have asbestos building materials. Domestic appliances that do not meet stipulated energy-efficiency standards could be given similar treatment. Mandatory 'green building' standards can be implemented, requiring construction practices to conform to specific ecological goals. Indeed, this is already starting to happen in some countries. In these various ways, regulation can directly produce behavioural changes that reduce environmental damage.

Government *expenditures and subsidies*, designed to create more environmentally sensitive and sustainable economic outcomes, also warrant more attention. Government expenditures that encourage the development and use of more ecologically sustainable *transport* technologies are a case in point. If the proportion of trips taken on public rather than private transport were to rise as a consequence of improved public transport services that would lower emissions and fuel consumption *per capita*. Indeed, there is no point making private motoring more expensive by 'putting a price on carbon' (or introducing congestion taxes on car travel in city centres) if there are not readily available public transport alternatives to which people can switch. Government expenditure on the necessary infrastructure and services can ensure that those more ecologically responsible alternatives actually exist in the right places and at the right times. Planning more integrated patterns of urban development, so that people have less need to make long trips between homes, workplaces and shops, could also contribute mightily to creating cities with smaller 'ecological footprints'.

By similar reasoning, governments can also contribute directly to ecological sustainability by subsidising the installation of solar power and wind power and by supporting the development of other renewable energy technologies. Using industry policies to achieve environmental goals is the name of the game. The targeted expenditures may take the form of subsidies to private sector businesses producing the alternative technologies or they may go directly into the development of government-owned businesses. Conservative economists stress that these expenditures must be properly funded, but that is not a substantial problem for governments in practice. Revenue generated by carbon tax is one obvious source of additional funds (at least until the tax achieves its eventual goal of eliminating the burning of fossil fuels). The required revenue can also come from income tax, land tax, or company profit tax, for example. There is no necessary reason why environmental expenditures need be funded only from explicitly environmental taxes: they can draw from any government revenue source. Governments should not be obsessed with balancing the budget anyway. As political economists commonly note, at a time when not all productive capacity is fully employed, increased government spending is largely self-funding. Government spending on industries developing renewable energy and other sustainable technologies creates jobs and incomes, which then generate more government tax revenues.

Public ownership of key industries, such as those providing electricity, gas and water, also needs careful consideration in this context. Public sector enterprises can directly provide valuable public revenue sources. More importantly from an environmental perspective, publicly owned enterprises need not be so directly geared to the pursuit of short-term profits as is the case with private sector businesses. Consider the electricity generation and distribution industry, for example. Privately owned energy providers have a direct stake in increasing the demand for their product because that increases their profitability. From an environmental perspective, what is needed is the opposite. We need electricity to be provided by institutions that will work with customers in order to reduce their power consumption. From this perspective, public ownership, linked to ecologically responsible managerial practices, keeps open the possibilities of suppliers and consumers working together to achieve more sustainable outcomes. The neoliberal penchant for privatisation sits awkwardly, to say the least, with this long-term environmental concern.

### *Promoting Profound Changes*

The process of shifting to more ecologically sustainable arrangements needs to embrace a yet broader array of social changes. 'Top down' government policies will not suffice. First and foremost, there must be good public *information* about the nature of environmental problems such as climate change and the impact of different forms of production and consumption. Awareness is a precondition for purposeful action. Education is also crucial – a recurring theme in this book. From early schooling onwards – and through the media – education about sustainability needs to show the nature of the problems and the avenues through which solutions may be achieved. Unless people of all ages understand what needs to be done and feel involved in the process of formulating responses, even well-intentioned government policies are likely to founder. An educated and aware society is conducive to more socially responsible behaviours. The sustainability of the government policies themselves depends on it.

Education can also be an integral element in the broader *challenge to consumerism* as the dominant socio-economic ideology. As political economists emphasise, it is the prevailing social norms that shape people's behaviour. So, if a more sustainable economy and society is to be achieved, we need to go beyond environmental pricing and regulation: we need to change what is socially valued. This is something to which all educated citizens can personally contribute, challenging the prevailing tendency to equate social worth with affluent lifestyles rather than civic responsibility. It often takes personal courage to go 'against the crowd'. However, when a critical mass develops, social norms can change. The currently dominant consumerist ideologies and practices can give way to ideologies and practices centred on beliefs about sustainability. 'Bottom-up' social change must always accompany 'top down' policies.

Coordination is crucial, particularly between the different tiers of government – national, state and local. Cooperation enhances effective policy development and implementation. Consistent with the case for a 'bottom up' approach, it is often appropriate to start at a local level. Indeed, local governments can do a lot in relation to creating more ecologically responsible patterns of resource use. They can build bikeways, expand public transport, encourage recycling and implement more effective waste disposal systems, for example. But they need to operate within a broader, supportive legislative and fiscal context that only state and national governments have the capacity to provide. It is these higher levels of government that have the greater resources because of their broader taxation base and, usually, stronger constitutional power. They have to be active participants in implementing sustainability policies.

Governments represent nation states. However, as noted at the start of this chapter, the environmental challenge – particularly the threat of climate change – is being acted out on a *global* scale. In the absence of a single world government, progress depends on inter-governmental cooperation. That is difficult to achieve in practice. Notwithstanding some slow progress through international agreements during the last two decades, major impediments to cooperation and commitment persist. These impediments are structural in character and therefore not easily overcome, even with the goodwill of all participants. Particularly fundamental are the problems that result from *uneven development* between rich and poor nations. The more wealthy nations need to take a lead in reducing environmental stresses because that is a precondition for gaining the cooperation of the poorer countries. The latter are understandably more reluctant to embrace policies that may slow their rates of economic growth, unless they see yet more vigorous sustainability initiatives from the richer nations themselves.

*Local production for local consumption* is a principle that also needs more attention in these circumstances. A prodigious amount of energy and transport resources is currently used in moving products around the world in order to increase the range and variety available at particular locations in 'the global supermarket'. This is not sustainable. Some aware and responsible consumers are already starting to give priority to the advantages – including the freshness of food – of consuming products that are relatively local in origin. Herein lays the potential to marry concerns about personal health, good living and wellbeing with broader environmental concerns. Changed local consumer practices can have global ramifications.

The embrace of this principle of local production for local consumption, while thoroughly in tune with the adage 'think global, act local', would have quite radical implications. It flies in the face of the neoliberal policies that have promoted more international commerce and the growth of international trade agreements. Neoliberal globalism is fundamentally anti-ecological. Civic organisations can contribute to the development of alternative practices through encouraging cooperatives and local exchange trading schemes. But the broader challenge to neoliberal globalism entails confronting the power and influence of transnational corporations, and supra-national economic institutions such as the World Trade Organisation and the International Monetary Fund. These key actors on the political economic stage have shown themselves to be deeply wedded to economic theories and practices that prioritise global profit-seeking and capital accumulation over ecological concerns.

### *Driving Political Actions*

What do these explorations into the political economy of the environment lead us to conclude about the role of government? First, they suggest that governments can be important drivers of change. Second, they indicate that governments themselves need to change – shifting from neoliberal practices underpinned by mainstream economic ideas to a more ecological economic approach. Third, and most fundamentally, they lead us to the understanding that developing policies promoting sustainability is also inevitably a political challenge to those who have a direct stake in unsustainable economic practices.

Consider, for example, the coal industry in Australia. It is the nation's largest export industry, generating enormous profits. Australia is a relatively small economy by world standards and its energy use is a correspondingly small part of the global drivers of carbon emissions causing climate change. However, as the world's largest coal-exporting nation, it has a particular responsibility to change its economic orientation. A 'dig it up, sell it off' economic approach provides an easy means of achieving prosperity for the time being. Other nations also welcome the easy access they currently have to Australian resources through international trade. Huge mining companies and their shareholders – including Australian workers whose superannuation funds hold shares in those companies – have a strong stake in the *status quo*. But the arrangement is not sustainable, either nationally or internationally. So there is a striking tension between the short-term economic gains from an environmentally rapacious form of production and the moral imperative to embrace the principle of global ecological sustainability.

'Down on the farm' a similar story can be told. From the early days of European settlement in Australia there has been widespread clearing of native forests in order to convert the land to agricultural uses. The unwise application of chemical fertilisers has sometimes degraded the land. In the world's driest continent, irrigation systems have also extended the areas capable of agricultural use, but at the expense of causing major stresses on river systems, particularly in the huge Murray-Darling basin. Salination of soils and threats to the riparian environment are common problems. Shifting to more sustainable practices is difficult because farmers have developed a stake in an economic system that is out of kilter with ecological realities.

So even as governments come to understand the need for remedial actions
– as they have in the Murray Darling basin – they tend to back away from
consistent implementation of the policies that would actually create a more
ecologically sustainable economy. But, of course, farmers are citizens too
and have a shared interest in ensuring sustainability: their future profits depend on it. Moreover, their close connection with the land gives them an
intrinsic advantage in understanding the connection between economic viability and environmental issues like soil quality and water availability.

So what social forces are most likely to drive the processes of restructuring for sustainability? Governments do not formulate their policies in a vacuum: they respond to political pressure. That pressure is typically strongest
where it is broadly-based. No one group within the community has a monopoly of concern or the independent capacity to drive the necessary changes.
*Coalition building* is politically necessary in this context. Thankfully, there
are good prospects for the green and environmental movement, the labour
movement and participants in social welfare organisations being able and
willing to work together. These groups all have strong traditions of opposition to the politics of extreme neoliberalism and have cooperated periodically in pushing for more progressive public policies. There are tensions
between them, of course, because they have distinctive histories, interests
and political cultures. Yet they have a common interest in opposing further
environmental degradation and seeking sustainability.

The role of the trade unions and the labour movement is particularly important in emphasising the link between environmental policies and employment creation. Phasing out ecologically unsustainable industries causes
job losses. That has led some unions to be understandably wary of policies
that they regard as undermining the livelihood of their members. But 'jobs
versus the environment' is not a helpful way of seeing the issue. Rather,
a strategy must be developed for at least partially reconciling these concerns. The creation of 'green jobs' is needed. The prospective job losses in
industries such as coal mining, aluminium manufacturing and rice-growing
need to be matched with job growth in industries such as these concerned
with conservation, recycling, permaculture and renewable energy production. This needs planning and broad public participation, not simple reliance on market principles.

There are significant precedents for coalitions of social groups cooperating in support of progressive environmental and economic goals. An important foundation was laid, for example, by the 'green bans' movement that
originated in Australia in the 1970s. It brought trade unions into alliances
with community groups in order to defend the quality of the urban environment when faced with the threat of commercial developments, particularly in Sydney. Since then an assertive environmental politics has become
an established theme throughout civic action and public policy in many
countries. Green parties now drive the processes forward in the twenty-first
century.

## *Conclusion*

Thinking in terms of sustainability requires quite a different mindset. It involves a shift from individualism and competition towards more co-operative and collectivist outlooks and behaviours. Governments have a central role to play in this context. As we have seen, there are many potentially potent policy possibilities. The choice between these policies, and how vigorously to implement them, is essentially political. Ideological orientations, particularly those related to economic issues, shape the judgements. Neoliberals favour policies that extend or augment the market principles of a capitalist economy, whereas environmentalists of a more social democratic inclination prefer government interventions that directly restructure the economy on sustainability principles. Views on what is the best 'policy mix' are not just a matter of political philosophy though. The ultimate determinant is what *works* in practice – what is actually timely and effective in averting potentially catastrophic ecological change.

The enormity of the sustainability challenge makes it wise for governments to embrace a combination of policies to drive the necessary processes of economic and social restructuring. Carbon tax, as a direct material disincentive to activities that contribute to climate change, can be a potent part of the mix, notwithstanding the limitations of market-based mechanisms when applied to environmental policy. Concurrently, new forms of regulation, government expenditure and subsidies, industry and trade policies are all essential for steering a path to sustainability. Given the complexity of the challenge we face, it is neither necessary nor desirable to put all the environmental policy 'eggs into one basket'.

Emphasising the centrality of governments in the process of creating a more sustainable economy and society does not let us as individuals 'off the hook'. On the contrary, governments are unlikely to act adequately unless informed and active individuals and politically progressive social groups show the way forward. As an educated citizenry, we have a collective responsibility to create the 'political climate' necessary to avert the looming crisis of the physical climate.

Action for sustainability, particularly if it also embraces concerns with social justice, challenges the dominant political and economic institutions of the current era. Economic and environmental 'fine-tuning' will not suffice. Progressive environmental policies require managed transitions; and strongly committed governments need to be driving those socio-economic transformations. The processes of change cannot avoid conflict because vested interests in the economy and society are threatened. Certainly, we all ultimately have a common interest, as citizens, in pursuing the goal of sustainability but conflicts will inevitably arise in getting to that goal. That means the process is inescapably political. Making the changes necessary for sustainability challenges the prevailing ideology, power structures and practices of corporate capitalism. Simultaneously, it also opens up opportunities for political action, based on the coalition of forces that the pervasive environmental problems make possible and necessary.

The heat is on, and we have not got that long...

*Further reading*

*Journal of Australian Political Economy*, No. 66, Summer 2011.
A special issue on 'challenging climate change'.
Beder, S. (2006). *Environmental Principles and Policies: an Interdisciplinary Approach*. Sydney: UNSW Press.
A critique of the neoliberal approaches to 'environmental fine tuning'.
Diesendorf, M. (2009). *Climate Action: a Campaign Manual for Greenhouse Solutions*. Sydney: UNSW Press.
Analysis of the problem of climate change and alternative political responses.
Australian Conservation Foundation & Australian Council of Trade Unions (2008). *Green Gold Rush*.
Analysis of the prospects for developing green jobs.
Spash, C. (2009). The Brave New World of Carbon Trading. *New Political Economy*, *15*(2), 169 – 195
Afuller exposition of some arguments and analysis introduced in this paper.
Hamilton, C. (2007). *Scorcher: The Dirty Politics of Climate Change*. Melbourne: Black Inc. Agenda
An expose of the corporate interests that have frustrated policies for sustainability.

# Part III

## Sharing in a Sustainable Future

*somebody's dream*
watercolour
12cm by 8cm

# Chapter 9
## Ethics of Sustainability

### A Summary

*Harriet Nalukenge*
*Senior State Attorney, Ministry of Justice and Constitutional Affairs,*
*Uganda*

## *The issues*

### *Economic Growth*

Science and technology have not provided adequate solutions to environmental degradation. States in developing countries are pressured to achieve economic development through industrialisation, so although people may be willing to preserve natural species through traditional practices, their efforts are shattered by developmental policies promoting economic growth. It is now recognised that the effort to promote economic growth has caused great inequalities and injustice. Humans therefore must do something different in order to sustain the environment for present and future generations.

## Law

The law can be used to regulate use of the environment and thereby protect resources. However, dealing with issues of who has to pay for environmental degradation and who has rights is complicated. For example, whether the poor should pay for the pollution of the environment caused by the rich or whether plants or future generations should have rights is often debated. Also, national laws are not very effective in protecting the earth from degradation across national borders. This has led to the growth of international environmental law, but international environmental law lacks sanctions to control the unreasonable exploitation of national resources. States can chose whether or not to ratify an international environmental law and sometimes are not committed to monitoring and reporting their observance of these laws. National and international law are therefore limited in addressing sustainability dilemmas. We need to do something different. We need a new model of sustainability.

## Finding Solutions

Whatever answer we arrive at will be decided by human attitudes. Humans use the environment for subsistence, commodity production, aesthetic pleasure and indirectly for ecosystem services. These uses benefit human life and enhance our standard of living. A challenge is that some members of present generations, especially in developing countries, do not enjoy a good quality of life – so how can they preserve the environment for future generations? Another problem is that people are trying to enrich themselves as much as possible, but resources are limited. In order to change this behaviour, humans need to change their attitude towards nature.

### Traditional Knowledge

Traditional knowledge embedded in community practices, institutions, relationships and rituals has long been used as a basis for decision making in agriculture, health care, food preparation, education, natural resources management and other activities. In traditional communities certain places are given spiritual significance, including sacred groves, caves, mountains, trees and rivers. Activities like hunting or collecting medicinal plants are regulated by confining them to a particular period of time like festivals, or left to particular people. This ensures that nature is preserved. Finding solutions to environmental problems would benefit from greater interaction with traditional knowledge. Governments could use traditional knowledge in the law to regulate use of the environment.

### Environmental Ethics

Western traditions understand that humans can voluntarily choose to do right in a situation where there are alternatives: They have the capacity to make moral judgments. However, traditional western ethics assign greater value to human beings than to any non-human and assume that the protection or promotion of human interests is more important. Environmental ethics propose nature should be preserved because it has intrinsic value. Environmental ethics therefore opposes many of the traditional ethical theories. Such an ethic could go a long way in addressing some of the sustainability dilemmas of this century. The ethics of sustainability complement the conventional tools of sustainability – law and technology.

# Chapter 10

## Natural Capital

### Harmonizing People and Nature [1]

*Gretchen C. Daily*
*Bing Professor of Environmental Science and*
*Director of the Center for Conservation Biology;*
*Department of Biology, 371 Serra Mall, Stanford University,*
*Stanford, CA 94305 USA*
*Heather Tallis*
*Lead Scientist, The Natural Capital Project;*
*Department of Biology and Woods Institute;*
*Stanford University, Stanford, CA 94305 USA*
*Anne Guerry*
*Lead Scientist, The Natural Capital Project;*
*Department of Biology and Woods Institute;*
*Stanford University, Stanford, CA 94305 USA The issue*

### *The issue*

The world's ecosystems – including forests, farms, plains, deep ocean and coral reefs – can be seen as natural capital assets. If properly managed, they

---

1. Based in part on an article that includes references: Tallis, H, A Guerry and GC Daily. In press. Ecosystem services. In *The Encyclopedia of Biodiversity*, Academic Press, San Diego.

yield a stream of vital "ecosystem services". These include the production of goods, such as seafood, timber and industrial products; life support processes, such as water purification and coastal protection; and life fulfilling conditions like serenity and beauty. Ecosystem services also include the preservation of options, such as genetic diversity for future use. Yet, relative to other forms of capital, natural capital is poorly understood, scarcely monitored, and – in many important cases – undergoing rapid degradation and depletion. Often its importance is widely appreciated only upon loss, such as in the wake of Hurricane Katrina or the Asian Tsunami.

Recently, however, great momentum has built around efforts to reveal the values of natural capital and mainstream them into decisions. For example, China has invested over USD 100 billion in restoring natural capital over the past decade. The investment is focused on forests and grasslands, to help secure people from flooding, improve drinking and irrigation water supply, maintain efficient hydropower production and foster more sustainable farming and other aspects of human wellbeing. Other inspiring models of success are emerging in all major regions of the world and the challenge now is to replicate and scale them up

## Context

### Framing and defining natural capital and the ecosystem services that flow from it

Ecosystem services refer to the conditions and processes through which ecosystems, and the species that make them up, sustain and fulfil human life. They maintain biodiversity and the production of ecosystem goods. These include seafood, crops, forage, timber, biomass fuels, natural fiber and many pharmaceuticals, industrial products and their precursors. The harvest and trade of these goods represent an important and familiar part of the human economy. In addition to the production of goods, ecosystem services include actual life support functions such as cleansing, recycling and renewal and the conferring of many intangible aesthetic and cultural benefits.

One way to appreciate the nature and value of ecosystem services is to imagine trying to set up a happy, day-to-day life on the moon. Assume for the sake of argument that the moon miraculously already had some of the basic conditions for supporting human life such as an atmosphere and climate similar to those on Earth. After inviting your best friends and packing your prized possessions, a barbeque grill and some do-it-yourself books, the big question would be, which of Earth's millions of species do you need to take with you?

Tackling the problem systematically you could first choose from among all the species exploited directly for food, drink, spice, fiber and timber, pharmaceuticals, industrial products (such as waxes, lac, rubber and oils) and so on. Even being selective this list could amount to hundreds or even several thousand species. The space ship would be filling up before you'd even begun adding the species crucial to *supporting* those at the top of your list.

Which are these unsung heroes? No one knows which – nor even approximately how many – species are required to sustain human life. This means that rather than listing species directly, you would have to list instead the life-support functions required by your lunar colony; then you could guess at the types and numbers of species required to perform each. At a bare minimum, other companions on the spaceship would have to include species capable of supplying a whole suite of ecosystemservices that Earthlings take for granted.

The inner workings of ecosystems are so tightly interconnected that any classification of services is inherently somewhat arbitrary. The most widely used classification was developed through the Millennium Ecosystem Assessment and identifies four classes of services based on their types of benefits to society:

1. *provisioning services* including the production of goods such as food, water, timber and fiber;
2. *regulating services* stabilize climate, moderate risk of flooding and disease, generate and renew soil fertility and protect or enhance water quality;
3. *cultural services* provide recreational, aesthetic, educational, community and spiritual opportunities; and
4. *supporting services* underlie provision of the other three classes of benefits, including soilformation, photosynthesis, nutrient cycling and the preservation of options.

Armed with this preliminary list of services, you could begin to determine which types and numbers of species are required to perform each. This is no simple task! Let's take soil fertility as an example. Soil organisms play important and often unique roles in the circulation of matter in every ecosystem on Earth; they are crucial to the chemical conversion and physical transfer of essential nutrients to higher plants and all larger organisms, including humans, depend on them. The abundance of soil organisms is absolutely staggering: under a square-yard of pasture in Denmark, for instance, the soil was found to be inhabited by roughly 50,000 small earthworms and their relatives, 50,000 insects and mites and nearly 12 million roundworms. And that is not all. A single gram (a pinch) of soil has yielded an estimated 30,000 protozoa, 50,000 algae, 400,000 fungi and billions of individual bacteria. Which to take to the moon? Most of these species have never been subjected to even cursory inspection. Yet the sobering fact of the matter is, as Ed Wilson put it: they don't need us but we need them.

Rather than listing species to take to the moon, you could focus on the whole ecosystem level and hope to capture the requisite parts. Forests stand out as important, for example, in regulating fresh water flows; in their strong influence on local, regional and global climate; and because of the multiple, interacting threats to their future. They also provide natural products for subsistence use or sale including timber, firewood, mushrooms, fruits and seeds, medicinal plants, rubber, cork and bushmeat. Forest and woodland habitats harbor species that provide pollination and pest control to commercial or subsistence crops.

Other terrestrial ecosystems are important too: grasslands play the same critical roles as forests in addition to supporting vast livestock populations. Wetlands occupy a small fraction of Earth's surface but dominate the landscape where they are concentrated and provide a wide array of water quality, flood mitigation, coastal protection and fish nursery services. Freshwater ecosystems provide a suite of highly visible and widely appreciated ecosystem services ranging from provision of drinking water to serving as pathways for human transportation and recreational or cultural activities.

Marine ecosystems define Earth as the blue planet. Marine fisheries and aquaculture provide nutrition, feed for animals, livelihoods and important recreational and cultural opportunities. Harvests of other species for food additives, cosmetics and pharmaceuticals also support health, nutrition and livelihoods. Marine biogenic habitats (such as coral reefs, oyster reefs and kelp forests) regulate natural hazards including storm surges and may play a critical role in helping coastal communities adapt to sea level rise. Marine systems also transform, detoxify and sequester wastes. In addition, oceans are the center of the global water cycle; they hold 96.5% of Earth's water and are a primary driver of the atmosphere's temperature, moisture content and stability. Oceans are also key players in the global cycles that generate approximately 40% of global net plant production, driving the food chain. Finally, coastal communities reap many benefits from tourism (one of the world's most profitable industries) and numerous coastal communities define their very identities in relation to the sea and all it brings.

All of these ecosystem services are generated by a complex of natural cycles, driven by solar energy, that constitute the workings of the biosphere – the thin layer near Earth's surface that contains all known life. These cycles are ancient, the product of billions of years of evolution, and have existed in forms very similar to those seen today for at least hundreds of millions of years. They are absolutely pervasive, but unnoticed by most human beings going about their daily lives. Who, for example, gives a thought to the part of the carbon cycle that connects him or her to the plants in the garden outside, to plankton in the Indian Ocean or to Julius Caesar? Noticed or not, human beings depend utterly on the continuation of natural cycles for their very existence.

For millennia, humanity has drawn benefits from these cycles without causing global disruption. Yet today, human influence can be discerned in the most remote reaches of the biosphere: deep below Earth's surface in ancient aquifers, far out to sea on tiny tropical islands and up in the cold, thin air high above Antarctica. Virtually no place remains untouched – chemically, physically or biologically – by the curious and determined hand of humanity. Although much more by accident than by design, humanity now controls conditions over the entire biosphere.

## History

It is primarily through disruption and loss that the nature and value of ecosystem services has been illuminated. For instance, deforestation has demonstrated the critical role of forests in the hydrological cycle – in particular, in mitigating floods, droughts, the erosive forces of wind and rain and the silting of dams and irrigation canals. Release of toxic substances, whether accidental or deliberate, has revealed the nature and value of physical and chemical processes, governed in part by a diversity of microorganisms that disperse and break down hazardous materials. Thinning of the stratospheric ozone layer sharpened awareness of the value of its service in screening out harmful ultraviolet radiation. The loss of coastal wetlands has brought into relief their importance in regulating coastal hazards such as hurricanes and tsunamis.

A cognizance of ecosystem services, expressed in terms of their loss, dates back at least to Plato and probably much earlier:

> "*What now remains of the formerly rich land is like the skeleton of a sick man with all the fat and soft earth having wasted away and only the bare framework remaining. Formerly, many of the mountains were arable. The plains that were full of rich soil are now marshes. Hills that were once covered with forests and produced abundant pasture now produce only food for bees. Once the land was enriched by yearly rains, which were not lost, as they are now, by flowing from the bare land into the sea. The soil was deep, it absorbed and kept the water... and the water that soaked into the hills fed springs and running streams everywhere. Now the abandoned shrines at spots where formerly there were springs attest that our description of the land is true.*" (Plato)

Modern concern for ecosystem services traces to George Perkins Marsh, a lawyer, politician and scholar. Indeed, his 1864 book *Man and Nature* describes a wide array of services, again, often expressed in terms of their loss. Remarking on the terrain of the former Roman Empire, he notes that it "is either deserted by civilized man and surrendered to hopeless desolation, or at least greatly reduced in both productiveness and population" (p 9). He continues, describing the reduction of hydrological services: "Vast forests have disappeared from mountain spurs and ridges, the vegetable earth... [is] washed away; meadows, once fertilized by irrigation, are waste and unproductive, because... the springs that fed them dried up; rivers famous in history and song have shrunk to humble brooklets" (p 9). He also draws connections between deforestation and climate: "With the disappearance of the forest, all is changed. At one season, the earth parts with its warmth by radiation to an open sky – receives, at another, an immoderate heat from the unobstructed rays of the sun. Hence the climate becomes excessive, and the soil is alternately parched by the fervors of summer, and seared by the rigors of winter. Bleak winds sweep unresisted over its surface, drift away the snow that sheltered it from the frost, and dry up its scanty moisture" (p 186). Finally, he even wrote of decomposition services: "The carnivorous, and often the herbivorous insects render an important service to man by consuming dead and decaying animal and vegetable matter, the decomposition of which would otherwise fill the air with effluvia noxious to health" (p 95).

Other eloquent writers on the environment emerged following World War II, including Fairfield Osborn (*Our Plundered Planet*, 1948), William Vogt (*Road to Survival*, 1948) and Aldo Leopold (*A Sand County Almanac and Sketches from Here and There*, 1949). Each discusses ecosystem services without using the term explicitly. In *The Population Bomb* (1968), Paul Ehrlich describes anthropogenic disruption of ecosystems and the societal consequences of doing so, addressing the need to maintain important aspects of ecosystem functioning. Meanwhile, in the 1960s and 70s, economists set out to measure "the value of services that natural areas provide", with efforts focused on agricultural production, renewable resources, non-renewable resources and environmental amenities.

Fast-forwarding to the past decade, three major advances have ignited research on ecosystem services and brought them into the public eye. First, the Millennium Assessment represented a visionary and seminal step in global science – it was the first comprehensive global assessment of the status and trends of all of the world's major ecosystem services. It was requested by United Nations Secretary General Kofi Annan in 2000 and carried out between 2001-2005 with contributions from over 1360 experts worldwide. The key finding of this assessment was that two-thirds of the world's ecosystem services were declining. This captured the attention of world leaders and emphasized the connections between human decisions and the natural environment that feed back to the human condition via changes in the flow of ecosystem services.

Second, ecosystem service science has advanced greatly, along each part of the framework in Figure 1. And this understanding is being packaged into useful tools for a wide range of decision-makers. For example, the Natural Capital Project, an international effort, has developed InVEST, a family of tools for Integrated Valuation of Ecosystem Services and Tradeoffs (www.naturalcapitalproject.org). InVEST helps decision makers visualize the impacts of potential policies – identifying tradeoffs and compatibilities between environmental, economic, and social benefits – by modeling and mapping the delivery, distribution and economic value of ecosystem services under alternative scenarios.

Lastly, major experiments in new policy and finance mechanisms for securing ecosystem services and integrating their value into decisions are now well underway all over the world. The following section describes some of these efforts in more detail.

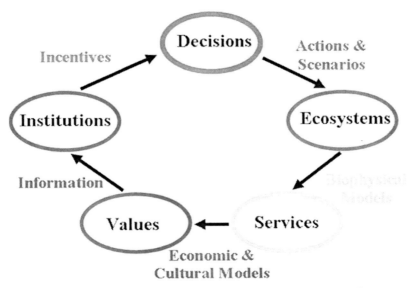

Figure 1: A framework showing key elements for integrating Ecosystem Services
into decision-making. One could link any two ovals,
in any direction, in different decision contexts

## *Integrating natural capital into decisions*

The urgent challenge today is to move from theory to practical implementation of ecosystem service tools and approaches in resource decisions taken
by individuals, communities, corporations and governments. The framework in Figure 1 connects the science of quantifying services with valuation
and policy to devise payment schemes and management actions that take
account of ecosystem services. This connection is expressed in the real
world in a variety of ways across scales from local to global.

A great number and diversity of efforts to implement the ecosystem
services framework have emerged worldwide over the past decade. Individually, most of these efforts are small and idiosyncratic. But collectively,
they represent a powerful shift in the focus of conservation organizations
and governments (primarily) toward a more inclusive, integrated and effective set of strategies. Taken together, these efforts span the globe and target a full suite of ecosystem services, including principally forest-generated
services of carbon sequestration, water supply, flood control, biodiversity
conservation and enhancement of scenic beauty (and associated recreation/
tourism values).

Many local or regional efforts focus on a single service that stands out as
sufficiently important, from economic and political perspectives, to protect
it. Under the institutional umbrella created for the focal service it is possible
that other services may be at least partially protected. Beginning in the late

1990s, larger-scale investment in natural capital for water flow regulation in China – and for a broad suite of ecosystem services in Costa Rica – set pioneering examples that are now being adapted elsewhere and scaled up

Next, we briefly describe some contrasting models of success, at different scales and in different kinds of social-ecological systems. In each case, there is an acute or looming crisis, innovative leadership and pursuit of dual goals: improving both human and ecosystem service condition.

## A. *Local Scale: Water Funds*

In the mid-1990's, New York City made one of the first and most famous investments in ecosystem service provision in recent history. The city invested about USD 1.5 billion in a variety of watershed protection activities to improve drinking water quality for 10 million users rather than spending the estimated USD 6-8 billion needed (excluding annual operating and maintenance costs) for building a new filtration plant. This seminal example is widely cited as evidence of the business case for investing in natural capital instead of built capital. Yet the effort remains very much an experiment in the science and policy of investing in natural capital and one on which there is international focus.

Globally, watersheds are now emerging as the target of a range of creative policy and finance mechanisms that link beneficiaries to suppliers through a payment system. In these "water funds," water users voluntarily pay into a pool that is collectively managed by contributors and invested in watershed management improvements. The Nature Conservancy has now established more than ten water funds in Latin America, has plans to create 22 more by 2015 and is exploring the possibility of establishing the first funds in Africa.

Agua por la Vida y la Sostenibilidad, one of the recently established water funds, demonstrates the diversity of water users that are becoming engaged in these funds and the kinds of watershed management changes these funds motivate. Formally established in the Cauca Valley, Colombia in 2009, this water fund is supported by the region's sugar cane grower's association (PROCAÑA), the sugar producers' association (ASOCAÑA), 11 local watershed management groups, The Nature Conservancy and a Colombian peace and justice non-government organization. Each member of the water fund voluntarily pays a self-determined amount into the fund that is then jointly managed by the members to improve landscape management in 11 watersheds covering over 3,900 square kilometers.

Members in this fund have currently committed to contributing USD 10 million over five years to be invested in five kinds of management changes: protection of native vegetation, restoration of denuded lands, enrichment of degraded forests, fencing of rangelands and implementation of best practices combining trees, pasture and livestock. The fund is starting a monitoring program that will ensure that these investments lead to measurable improvements in water quality for approximately 1 million water users downstream and significant improvements in terrestrial and freshwater biodiversity.

B. *Local Scale: Coastal and Marine Spatial Planning*

People commonly think of oceans as relatively featureless expanses that defy the drawing of lines on maps. However, recent political and scientific advances have highlighted the need for a comprehensive approach to planning marine and coastal uses and the need for practical tools to make this more comprehensive approach a reality on the ground and in the water. In a marine spatial plan, many of uses of the marine environment are put on one map. But an understanding of how such plans are likely to yield changes in the delivery of the broad range of services people receive from the system has, until recently, remained elusive.

Along the west coast of Vancouver Island Canada, multiple, often competing interests are struggling to define the future character of the place. Existing extractive, industrial and commercial uses; traditional First Nations subsistence and ceremonial uses; recreation and tourism; and emerging ocean uses such as the extraction of wave energy are all in the mix.

The West Coast Aquatic Management Board (WCA) is charged with creating a marine spatial plan for the region. WCA is a public-private partnership with participation from four levels of government (Federal, Provincial, local and First Nations) and diverse stakeholders. Ultimately, WCA's vision is to manage resources for the benefit of current and future generations of people and non-human species and communities.

WCA has partnered with the Natural Capital Project to explore how alternative spatial plans might affect a wide range of ecosystem services and to provide information about trade-offs among ecosystem services. Key considerations include balancing important industrial and commercial activities (such as shipping, mining, logging, aquaculture and fisheries); increased development of tourism and recreation; renewable energy generation; and a strong cultural desire for sustaining the remote, wild feeling of the place.

WCA is exploring the suitability of alternative regions for these different activities. For example, maps of coastal vulnerability to erosion and flooding from storm surge are helping to direct coastal development permits to low-risk areas. Similar maps of the value of captured wave energy are being overlaid with existing ocean uses (e.g. fishing and recreational activities) to highlight regions of high wave energy value, where wave energy generation facilities might be constructed while having minimal impacts on other activities. Examinations of trade-offs among aquaculture (finfish, shellfish), wild salmon fisheries, recreation (e.g. kayaking, whale watching and diving), coastal development (on coastal land as well as float homes) and habitat and water quality are underway.

The general framework and modeling of ecosystem services are helping to articulate connections between human activities that are often considered in isolation, to align diverse stakeholders around common goals and to make implicit decisions explicit. Ecosystem service modeling has informed early iterations of the marine spatial plan and will inform the creation of the final plan in 2012.

C. *National Scale: Land-Use Planning and Human Development in China*

The ecosystem service investments being made in China today are impressive in their goals, scale, duration and innovation. Following massive droughts and flooding in 1997-98, China implemented several national forestry and conservation initiatives, into which investments exceeded 700 billion yuan (about USD 100 billion) over 2000-2010. The larger and older of these initiatives, the Sloping Land Conversion Program (SLCP), involves 120 million farmers directly and is being rigorously evaluated to improve its design and efficacy.

These initiatives all have dual goals: to secure critical natural capital through targeted investments across landscapes and to alleviate poverty through targeted wealth transfers from coastal provinces to inland regions where many ecosystem services originate. The Chinese government aims to reduce the loss of soil, improve water retention, reduce desertification and generally protect biodiversity and ecosystems in the west of the country for flood control, hydropower production efficiency, irrigation supply, more productive agriculture and ecotourism. In addition, it wants to change the economic structure in rural areas to increase local household income while simultaneously making local households' patterns of land utilization and agricultural production more sustainable.

Evaluation of the programs shows significant achievement of the biophysical goals, with remarkably rapid land conversion in the desired directions. For example, by the end of 2006, the SLCP had converted approximately 9 million ha of cropland into forest or natural grassland and had afforested around 12 million ha of barren land. Village-level field measurements have shown not only that the payments for ecosystem services have altered land use patterns but in turn soil erosion has been decreased in some areas by as much as 68%.

Overall social impacts of the programs are mixed. In some places, payment levels and types are leading to improvements in economic measures of well-being, whereas in others payments were not sufficient to compensate for loss of income from shifting livelihoods. In addition, in some places where participation in the SLCP has significant positive impacts upon household income, it has not yet transferred labor towards non-farming activities as the government wished. Payments are now being adjusted to improve success in achieving goals of poverty alleviation and growth of new economic sectors in rural areas.

Future ecosystem service investments in China are potentially enormous, certainly within the country. For example, a new set of reserves is being planned that will span 25% of the country. The investments also promise to be significant globally, in the form of enhanced carbon sequestration and reduced dust export, and perhaps most importantly in lessons on making the investments needed in natural capital and human wellbeing everywhere.

D. *International Scale: Global Policy and Research Efforts*

As described above, the Millennium Assessment was the first major effort to establish ecosystem services in the international policy arena. Activities stemming from that effort are now aimed at bringing countries together in making tangible commitments to safeguard ecosystem services and to assess national and international progress towards those commitments.

Several new international research efforts aim to feed into these international processes including the Natural Capital Project. As one example of many burgeoning international efforts, we describe this effort in greater detail.

The Natural Capital Project (NatCap) (www.naturalcapitalproject.org) is an international partnership working to harmonize people and nature by developing tools that make incorporating natural capital into decisions easy and replicable; by demonstrating the power of these tools in important, contrasting places; and by engaging leaders globally. NatCap is developing InVEST, a family of tools for Integrated Valuation of Ecosystem Services and Tradeoffs.

InVEST helps decision makers visualize the impacts of potential policies by modeling and mapping the delivery, distribution and economic value of ecosystem services under alternative scenarios. The outputs identify tradeoffs and compatibilities between environmental, economic and social benefits. InVEST is designed for use as part of an active decision-making process (Figure 2) and can be applied at local, regional or global scales.

The first phase of the approach involves working with stakeholders to identify critical management decisions and to develop scenarios that project how the provision of services might change in response to those decisions as well as to changing climate, population, etc. Based on these scenarios, a modular set of models quantifies and maps ecosystem services. The outputs of these models provide decision makers with information about costs, benefits, tradeoffs and synergies of alternative investments in service provision.

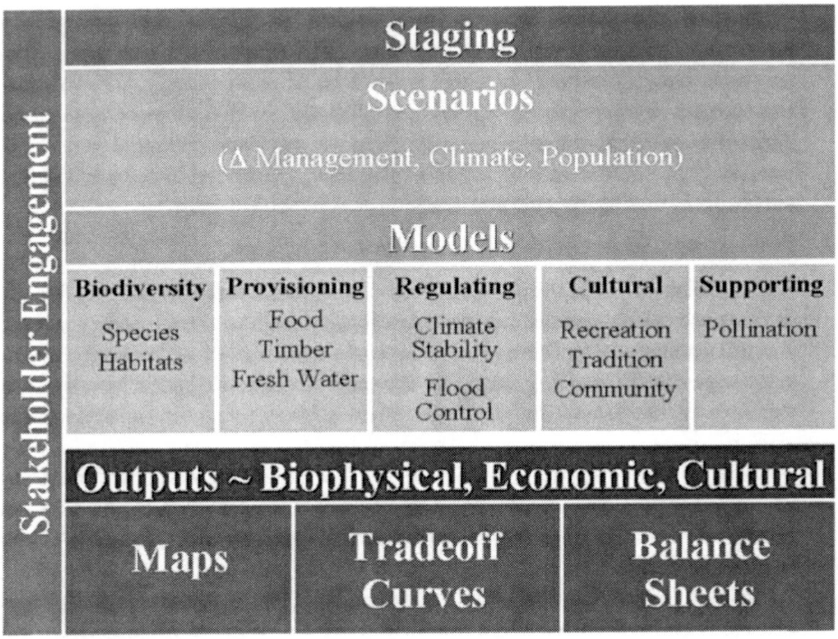

Figure 2: An iterative process for integrating ecosystem services into decisions. The process begins with stakeholder engagement around impending decisions with a focus on realistic, alternative scenarios for the future. The modeling is shaped by stakeholders and typically focused on the services and scenarios deemed most important. Outputs are displayed in accordance with stakeholder preferences, in the form of maps, tradeoff curves and/or balance sheets. These can be expressed in biophysical (e.g. tons of carbon), economic (e.g. dollars) or cultural (e.g. visitor-days) terms

NatCap is using InVEST in major natural resource decisions in diverse contexts around the world, including in the three examples given above (water funds, coastal and marine spatial planning, and land-use planning and human development in China). The aim is to demonstrate the power of these approaches and to learn how to replicate and scale up models of success. The Project is engaged in a suite of international efforts to offer a common, unifying platform for regional and national efforts that are spawned by these initiatives.

### Future directions

With the rapid rate of development of ecosystem service mapping, from the biophysical and economic modeling through to policy application in diverse socioeconomic contexts, it is likely that great advances will be made in coming years. What we report here is only a beginning. Yet there are key arenas in which further learning is crucial to understand what drives variation in the provision of ecosystem services, how they percolate through various arms of society and how social reaction leads to sustainable or unsustainable change in provision.

A. *Relating Ecosystem Services and Human Health*

The relationships between biophysical attributes of ecosystems and human health are complex. Destruction of natural ecosystems can at times improve aspects of public health. Draining swamps, for example, can reduce habitat for the mosquito vector that transmits the parasite that causes malaria. On the other hand, destruction of other systems can have sharp negative consequences for human health. There is emerging evidence that loss of tropical forests, for example, leads to an increase in transmission of malaria. Similarly, fragmentation of, and biodiversity loss from, eastern North American forests is associated with an increase in Lyme disease. There is a great need for research illuminating the links between biodiversity, ecosystem conditions and processes and human health, including mental health.

B. *Distributional Effects*

Much of the science of mapping ecosystem services has focused on identifying where they are generated and where they are delivered. However, less work has focused on identifying to whom services actually flow. This connection is essential if policies addressing ecosystem service delivery are to be equitable and either improve the well-being of the poor or avoid unintended distributional consequences. Past work in this arena has focused on overlaying maps of ecosystem services provision with an array of poverty indicators. Missing from this spatial analysis is information on access to and ability to control the delivery of ecosystem services. In many cases (e.g. for services such as clean drinking water, hydropower production, agriculture, water for irrigation, wave power generation) the actual delivery of services to specific people is affected by the location of infrastructure or institutions regulating access to resources. New science is needed that allows the ready mapping of these connections and the prediction of how they will change under future conditions.

C. *Dynamic Effects – and Shocks and Uncertainty*

Dynamic changes, such as in climate and in the nitrogen cycle are very important – as are changes arising through economic development and evolving human preferences over time. The possibility of feedbacks within ecosystems, and between their services and human behavior, is a key area for further development. Feedback effects can give rise to thresholds and rapid changes in systems that can fundamentally alter system outcomes. The ability to incorporate shocks and the possibility of surprises is another area where further development is needed. Fires, droughts and disease all can have major influences on ecosystems and affect the services produced. Changes in economic conditions or fads in human behavior can similarly cause major changes in systems (e.g. financial crises). The occurrence of each of these and other potential disturbances is difficult to predict but virtually certain to come about. Understanding their likely impacts on ecological and social systems will help us prepare for them.

D. *Valuation in Monetary and Non-Monetary Terms for Decision-Making*

Monetary valuation of ecosystem services is not nearly as prevalent as sometimes assumed. More typically, real-world applications of the ecosystem services framework rely on measures such as water quality or flood risk to inform policy design.

Value is not always easily characterized or fully captured in monetary terms, so it is important to characterize value in multiple dimensions, including health, livelihood support, and cultural significance. This will help ensure that valuation and broader decision-making approaches include the range of benefits and people concerned. Interdisciplinary efforts are presently underway to create a conceptual framework that is useful both in theory and in practice for a broad suite of cultural ecosystem services.

E. *Institutional Design*

However ecosystem services are measured, there is a need for political and social science research to design institutions and policy mechanisms that better capture externalities. Efforts such as national accounts are blossoming now, but it is unclear how they will evolve and how successful governments will be at incorporating natural capital into national measures of wealth. There is great work to be done in determining the merits and limitations of alternative policy and finance mechanisms in different economic, governance and other social contexts. There is also great work to be done in developing institutions that achieve stakeholder representation and participation as part of adaptive governance systems.

---

*Thinking it through: where do I stand?*

Which parts of the landscape or seascape around you provide important ecosystem services?

Who owns or governs the places providing ecosystem services?

Who consumes the services?

---

*Action: what can I do?*

Can you create a game to highlight the connections between people and ecosystems? Maybe a game outside, or a video-based game challenging participants to manage ecosystems well or face serious consequences.

Could you begin discussion of a water fund, or similar program, to secure vital services around you? Who are the primary stakeholders for such a discussion?

---

Could you use InVEST to research the implications of alternative futures in your community? (InVEST is now freely downloadable from www.naturalcapitalproject.org for use in ArcGIS and will soon be freely available and more accessible on Google's new Earth Engine platform.)

What are the spin-off effects of your action? How will it impinge on other aspects of sustainability?

### *Further reading*

Daily, G.C. & Ellison, K. (2002). *The New Economy of Nature*. Washington DC: Island Press.

Heal, G. (2000). *Nature and the Marketplace: Capturing the Value of Ecosystem Services*. Washington, DC: Island Press.

Kareiva, PK., Tallis, H., Ricketts, T.H., Daily, G.C., & Polasky, S. (Eds.). (2011). *Natural Capital: Theory & Practice of Mapping Ecosystem Services*. Oxford: Oxford University Press.

Millennium Ecosystem Assessment. (2005). *Ecosystems and Human Well-being: The Assessment Series* (Four Volumes and Summary). Washington, DC: Island Press.

Ruhl, J.B., Kraft, S.E., & Lant, C.L. (2007). *The Law and Policy of Ecosystem Services*. Washington, DC: Island Press.

# Chapter 11

## A Fair Share of the Information Commons

*Ida Kubiszewski*
*Robert Costanza*
*Institute for Sustainable Solutions, Portland State University*

### The issue

Human culture is based on information, as is all economic production, making information essential in attaining virtually all desirable ends. What types of new information would generate the greatest improvements in human welfare at the lowest cost? While this is inevitably a somewhat subjective question, certain issues that dominate the global headlines seem to suggest some likely answers, especially those that are necessary for basic well-being: energy, food, biological diversity, water, shelter, sanitation, and medical treatment, to name a few.

Information has some unique characteristics. Unlike most other goods and services, it is neither rival (use by one prevents use by others) nor non-rival (use by one does not affect use by others), but is 'additive' (enhanced with increased use). Therefore a unique allocation system for both the production and consumption of information is needed. Under the current market-based allocation system, production of information is often limited through the exclusive rights produced by patents and copyrights. This limits scientists' ability to share and build on each other's knowledge.

In this chapter we discuss the special characteristics of information as a type of *commons* that needs special institutions to manage its production and use effectively and create greater overall economic efficiency, social justice and ecological sustainability. These methods include monetary prizes, publicly funded research from which the produced information is released into the public domain, and status driven incentive structures like those in academia and the *open-source* community.

## *Distribution of Information*

Markets privatize knowledge through intellectual property rights (IPRs) in the form of patents and copyrights. As a resource, information has unique characteristics that affect its allocation. Conventional market resources are rival, or subtractive: one person's use leaves everyone else less to use. For example, if one person cuts down a tree to build furniture, it is no longer available for someone else to build a house. Information is a different type of resource. If one person uses information, it does not leave less for anyone else to use. No matter how many people read this paragraph, there will be no less information left for anybody else. Economists refer to such resources as *non-rival*. However, the resource of information is not just non-rival, but actually improves through use. The term *additive* can be used to describe a resource that improves through use. After reading this chapter you may develop new and better ideas from which we may all benefit in the future. Hence, IPRs provide incentives for the production of information, but in exchange create artificial scarcity and inefficiencies in consumption for the duration of the patent or copyright.

Most economists assume that markets reveal the desired ends through market demand as manifested in purchase decisions, then efficiently allocate the scarce resources necessary to achieve those ends. But what is economic demand? Economic demand is preferences weighted by income, implying that those with no income have no demand. For example, this implication states that very little demand exists for life saving cures for contagious diseases that affect poor people since they do not have the income to pay high prices for those cures. Economic markets also only reveal demand for marketed goods and services. Only privately owned goods and services can be marketed, making private property rights a pre-requisite for conventional markets to function. However, many important goods and services are, in practice, *non-excludable* and cannot be effectively privately owned. For example, if a technology to restore the ozone layer is developed, the use of the restored ozone layer cannot be restricted to individuals who pay for its restoration. Within such a system, no market incentives exist to pay for the services, therefore no market demand is created for such services. Conventional economic markets therefore lack the incentives to create information required to cure contagious diseases affecting the poor or to preserve ecosystem services.

An example can clarify how markets are the primary decider on which information to produce and how to allocate it. Some exceptions exist around the production of information by non-profits or non-governmental organizations when they put that information into the public domain. In the 1970s, Aventis, a pharmaceutical company, began developing a compound called eflornithine as a potential anti-cancer drug. During the development process the drug was also found to remove hair and treat human African trypanosomiasis (HAT), or African sleeping sickness, a contagious and debilitating disease endemic in Africa. However, when in 1995, the drug was found to have no affect on cancer, Aventis halted production including the forms of the drug that cured sleeping sickness. At the time, much of central Africa was war-torn, the population requiring the drug was unable to pay for it, meaning that no economic demand existed, so Aventis had no interest in producing it. A few years later another pharmaceutical company, Bristol-Myers Squibb (BMS), began producing a form of this same compound as a facial hair removal cream for women. This again created an economic demand because now rich women were willing to pay large sums for this cream. Once the production resumed, the World Health Organization (WHO) and Doctors Without Borders were able to convince BMS to donate 5 years of the drug to patients in Africa, this move also persuaded Aventis and Bayer to donate $5 million a year for monitoring, treatment, and research and development. Patents on drugs and surgery related techniques and technologies have become increasingly popular in the past two decades. Since 1988, over 145,000 patents have been granted in the United States alone on drugs and bio-affecting and body treating compositions. Net sales and expenditures by the companies have also increased in the past decade. In 2007 alone, net sales from pharmaceuticals and medicines were over $350 billion.

This example shows how economic market forces can allocate scientists' efforts towards producing luxury goods instead of basic necessities for the poor. Scientists, unlike information, are a rival resource, if one is hired to develop cosmetics for the rich, that person is no longer available to work on life saving cures for the poor. Although economic markets are accepted as the deciding mechanism for society's desired ends, if asked directly, most of the population would presumably rank developing life saving cures as a more desirable end for society than removing women's facial hair.

So why is the allocation of information important and why is it a tragedy if not allocated correctly? When the current economic paradigm was originally created, with its assumptions and conventions, material wealth was the limiting factor to improving well-being. That has now changed in many countries, where there is an excess of material goods, but a poor distribution of those goods and a dearth of social and natural capital. This has become a global problem that requires global information exchange to solve. And yet this paradigm has persisted due to a lack of alternative options and the benefits it provides to a key minority. We are now using the market to deal with completely different problems, and need information that is no longer revolving around material production and consumption, but around solving global public goods problems on the social and natural level, such as climate change, biodiversity, and water scarcity. The development and the allocation of this type of information for a greater social good has a different level of responsibility associated with it. It requires that the focus be placed on the social good instead of the private gain.

Society increasingly relies on markets to produce and allocate information; at the same time, society also faces a number of serious problems that may be unsolvable without new information to generate new technologies. For example, many experts believe that if we fail to reduce $CO_2$ emissions by less than 80%, atmospheric carbon stocks will continue to climb, resulting in runaway climate change and ecological catastrophe. However, our society is currently so dependent on fossil fuels that reducing emissions by 80% could result in mass starvation and economic collapse.

Unfortunately, intellectual property rights (IPRs) are unable to solve these types of problems. The changing nature of the problems that the global society faces has increased the disadvantages of using conventional markets to produce and allocate information. The value that is placed on patented technology disregards whether that technology destroys half of the world's forests, kills thousands of people, or pollutes our air and water. It has no way to encourage technologies that generate more human wellbeing by using fewer resources, conserving ecosystem services, and generating less waste. The market is unable to meet society's desirable ends and creates a system that encourages competition instead of collaboration, decreasing the opportunity for innovation. Alternative institutions may be better equipped for managing the flow of information, ones that focus on the social good instead of the private gain. Information should therefore be managed as a global public good, or a *commons*.

Information is also not the only resource that is in jeopardy because of the use of the economic market for its allocation. Another such resource is the services that ecosystems provide that are essential to all life on Earth. When dealing with ecosystem services, the market assumes that they are just another good that can be traded. Private property rights establish a scheme in which buyers and sellers can exchange parts of an ecosystem through changes in land ownership. However, because of the nature of ecosystem services, they benefit not just the owners but the surrounding, if not the global, population. The owners are free to utilize the ecosystem in any way they see fit, with no regard to the social good. Hence, many use those ecosystems to enhance their own personal economic welfare. For example, privately owned forests are often cut down, sold for the timber, and made into agricultural land. This takes away from the social good as it eliminates a key aspect of global carbon sequestration. Landowners receive no compensation, nor any other incentives, to continue providing the ecosystem services. Hence they tend to be underprovided.

## *Alternative allocation mechanisms*

Because the market is unable to properly allocate resources towards public goods that are most likely to be the desirable ends in today's world of climate change, fossil fuels, water scarcity, etc, alternative incentive and allocation mechanisms are required. Throughout history, various incentive schemes have been used to successfully encourage development of specific technologies or solutions to specific scientific problems. Here we review some of these systems and proposed some new ones.

### *Prizes*

One of the most popular alternative allocation methods has been rewarding innovations with monetary prizes and then releasing the information into the public domain. Examples of these include: France offering a prize for the development of the workable water turbine in the seventeenth century; a century long reward, around the same time, for the development of a method to calculate longitude while at sea; or more recently, a prize for creating the 100 mpg car. The use of monetary prizes as an incentive to develop specific information has certain advantages over the use of intellectual property rights. It allows society, and not just the market to decide on which innovations would be most beneficial. Because corporations would be rewarded monetarily through the prize, patents would no longer be necessary on the innovations, allowing the information to be released to the public domain and utilized by more researchers. However, this approach does fail to address the issue of firms competing for a prize instead of collaboratively working together during the production process, thus creating some inefficiency during the process.

### *Non-monetary incentives*

Certain industries do not use monetary incentives as a reward structure. Open source software has recently re-emerged as a strong competitor to patented software and in certain circumstances significantly exceeds its quality (e.g. Firefox vs Internet Explorer). Within this open source community and many academic fields, a type of incentive structure exists based on an individual's reputation amongst his or her colleagues for contributions to the field. This system rewards participants based on how quickly discoveries are made and how quickly they are published within the community. It is typically protected by a Creative Common (CC) license or copyleft. This means that anyone can use and alter the work, however, the original creator has to be given attribution and all subsequent work has to remain protected under the same license, and can never by patented or placed under conventional copyright.

In academia, mathematical theorems cannot be patented, and yet many mathematicians continue to work on their development. The extent of the reward given to an academic working within this system is determined by the community as a whole. The community assesses the quality of the discovery, after its publication, on the criteria of how much it benefits that community and how much it furthers that community's knowledge. The rewards may be monetary in the form of a promotion but commonly consist of such things as honorific awards, positions at more prestigious universities, tenure, large citation numbers, colleagues' esteem, and overall status. The size of the reward is dependent on how much the discovery benefits the community, or in other words, how much it advances the community's efforts towards a single goal or vision. This communal vision is established not by the market but by the community as to what the most desirable ends are.

Besides advancing knowledge in the entire community, the act of publication also serves two other purposes. First, it ensures that the discovery does not remain within the confines of a group which may not have the resources or ability to utilize that discovery to its fullest. Second, it allows for peers to evaluate the discovery, significantly minimizing the opportunity for errors. However, once a discovery is completely disclosed to the community through publication, it becomes simple for others to copy portions of the published work and claim to have also independently done the research. Consequently, academia does not reward second place discoveries, encouraging academics to collaborate instead of competing to discover and publish first.

*Capping salaries*

Historically, inventors worked independently in either the pursuit of profit (e.g. Thomas Edison) or to contribute to the public good (e.g. Nikola Tesla). Today, the majority of scientists work within the private or public sectors, with defined salaries. The rights to any patents they procure are assigned to the organizations that they work for, eliminating much of the incentives for the individual scientists to research one type of information over another. By capping salaries amongst the different sectors, scientists would have no incentive to work for corporations such as Bristol Meyers Squibb over the National Institute of Health. A natural cap could be forced by taking away the right of major corporations to patent drugs that are beneficial to society. Through their choice of organizations, scientists would have the discretion of deciding on how the results of their research were to be utilized. By offering competitive salaries, the government would have the opportunity to promote the type of research most beneficial to society.

*Research consortium*

A global research consortium should determine appropriate technologies for alternative energy, agroecology, green chemistry, industrial ecology, and so on in collaboration with those who would use them. These new technologies could be *copylefted* (as opposed to *copyrighted*), meaning that they are freely available for anyone to use as long as derivative products are available on the same terms. This would allow the consortium to determine that the research priority included finding an alternative, clean source of energy, protecting the ecosystem services, managing fresh water efficiently, or feeding the world's hungry. This institution would consider the global wellbeing of the population instead of purely economic demand.

The US Department of Energy, which oversees the US's energy sector, is beginning to move towards this form of research with the establishment of what they are calling Energy Innovation Hubs. The hubs will "foster unique, cross-disciplinary collaborations by bringing together leading scientists to focus on a high priority technology." The one downfall of these hubs is that when a new technology is ready to be released to the public, it will be handed over to private industry to patent and market. Although the innovation out of these hubs has the potential to solve many of our global problems, placing it into corporate hands only allows this technology to be distributed to the rich.

*Publically funded research*

Potential also exists to move away from the market in funding certain types of research. In the 1950s and 1960s the US government funded much more than half of all research and development, but by 2006, it funded only 28%. By increasing the proportion of publicly funded research and placing all information obtained through publicly funded research into the public domain, monopoly pricing on this technology would no longer be an option, creating both open information and competition for further advancements, two critical aspects to the proper functioning of the market. It would also eliminate 'me too' research, using resources more efficiently. Taxpayers would still be required to fund further advancements in research through the price of goods, however, that price would be set by a market instead of by a single corporation. Patents also create a strong incentive to research information that can be potentially commercialized instead of basic research or applied research that provides and protects public goods, which has historically been an important resource for other researchers in both the public and private sectors. Placing information into the public domain would take the focus away from items that can be commercialized and refocus research on areas most necessary for solving society's problems.

Large governmental grants can also be used to bring together top researchers in specific fields from multiple corporations, universities, and governmental agencies to work together toward common goals. Besides placing the smartest people on a certain topic together to exchange ideas, it would also create collaboration between different institutions and avoid the competition that usually occurs. The information produced would be released into the public domain, allowing the entire world, including developing countries, to benefit. Such systems were used to spur both the Green Revolution[1] and to get humans to the moon, creating remarkable scientific advancements in short periods of times, and in one case deterring a mass famine.

---

1. The Green Revolution occurred between the 1940s and late 1970s. It was a series of research, development and technologies developed to improve agriculture production internationally.

Additional public funding for R&D could be made available through the taxing of certain excludable goods within specific industries. As an example, the computer industry has been having significant difficulties in stopping the pirating of software. Software, due to its nature, should not be an excludable good because after it is developed, the creation of an additional copy has insignificant marginal costs associated with it. This creates a significant social inefficiency. If a system were established in which the hardware was taxed and the revenues used to fund software development that was provided freely to the users, this would eliminate the social inefficiency. Similar taxes can be placed on the energy industry. Technologies based on fossil fuels and use of the fuels themselves could be taxed (or permits auctioned) and that money could be directed towards the development of alternative energy technologies. Such a tax would have multiple advantages, including the reduction of greenhouse gas emissions.

## Conclusion

Goods and services that improve with use, such as information, require alternative incentive structures. Although market-based allocation systems have the advantage of providing incentives to create new information, they fail to correctly determine what information needs to be produced to reach society's desired ends or how that information should be allocated once it is produced. With consumptive goods no longer necessary to improve wellbeing, but information that improves and protects global public goods, such as climate, oceans, etc, being a requirement, a different allocation system is required for both the production and consumption side of information. Since information is the basis of economic production, common ownership of information would significantly increase information transfer and produce a greater rate of innovation. It will also provide a means of allocating information towards the desirable ends of society and the common good by allowing a larger number of scientists and researchers access to the information.

---

*Thinking it through: where do I stand?*

What types of licenses exist for information? What is the difference between copyrighting and copylefting? What are the most popular licenses?

When you download information from the Internet do you know what kind of license it is under? What kind of license is Wikipedia under? What about some of your other favorite websites?

---

*Action: what can I do?*

Find out what information license your school and city websites are using. Does this license all the audience you are targeting to access it? Which license would work best for the information's intended purposes?

---

*Further reading*

Kubiszewski, I., Farley, J. & Costanza. R. (2010). The production and alloc-
ation of information as a good that is enhanced with increased
use. *Ecological Economics, 69,* 1344 – 1354.
Costanza, R., d'Arge, R., de Groot, R., Farber, S., Grasso, M., Hannon, B.,
Naeem, S., Limburg, K., Paruelo, J., O'Neill, R.V., Raskin, R.,
Sutton, P. & van den Belt. M. (1997). The value of the world's eco-
system services and natural capital. *Nature, 387,* 253 – 260.
Hardin, G. (1968). The tragedy of the commons, *Science 162,* 1243 –1248.

*Resources*

The Economics of Ecosystems and Biodiversity (TEEB) -
http://www.teebweb.org/
Creative Commons - http://creativecommons.org/

# Chapter 12

## Responsibility and Intergenerational Equity

*Sharon Beder*
*University of Wollongong*

### *The issue*

Intergenerational equity refers to the need for a just distribution of rewards and burdens between generations and fair and impartial treatment towards future generations. It is based on the idea that a person's value shouldn't depend on when they are born anymore than it should depend on place of birth, nationality or gender.

However, unless substantial change occurs, the present generation is unlikely to pass on a healthy and diverse environment to future generations due to harm that current generations are doing to the environment, including climate change as well as loss of animals and plant species, water quality, and habitat including forests.

Achieving intergenerational equity, therefore, requires significant changes. But why care about the future? As cynics have said: "What has posterity ever done for me?" After all the people of the far off future are strangers, they are only potential people who do not yet exist and may not exist. They will be in no position to reward us for what we do for them, to punish us for our lack of care or responsibility, nor to demand compensation. We don't know what their needs, desires or values will be. How can people who haven't even been born yet demand rights? And if they cannot claim rights do they have any?

Although future generations do not yet exist we can be reasonably sure they will exist and they will require clean air and water and other basic physical requirements for life. And although we don't know who the individuals of the future will be – they are not individually identifiable – they can have rights as a group or class of people, rather than individually, and we can have obligations and duties towards them.

What is more, morality is not dependent on identity. Murder of an innocent person is morally wrong, whoever the victim is. Justice is something that needs to be applied to everyone, whoever they are. Their identity is irrelevant.

Future people may not be able to claim their rights today, but others can on their behalf, for example as members of human rights or environmental organizations or as government representatives. Various national and international laws protect the rights of future generations. Where future generations do not have formal legal representation, people are able to make claims on their behalf using reasoning based on moral principles, such as those outlined below.

### Why worry about future generations?

#### Relating to Others

It is part of being human to be able to relate to others and care about the long-term wellbeing of the larger society, its values, institutions and assets. It is this desire to be part of something that is larger than one's self and will endure beyond one's lifetime that motivates careers in public service, education and scientific research, as well as works of art and literature. Most people would be demoralised and saddened by the thought that the Earth was to be destroyed in 200 years, even though they will be long dead.

The idea of contributing to and being part of an ongoing enterprise enables people to cope with the knowledge of their own mortality. It gives people a sense of purpose and identity. These feelings enable people to transcend concerns about self, and people who do not have them are worse off as a consequence. Ernest Partridge argues it is only those who are alienated from the society around them, or who have some sort of personality disorder, who do not have such feelings.

#### Self Interest

Morality can often be rationalised as being in one's own self interest. It is far more pleasant and desirable to live in a moral community. Because humans can either make each other's lives miserable or help each other through cooperation, it makes sense to encourage mutual respect and moral obligations. A society where citizens are concerned for the welfare of others is one where individual welfare is best secured. In this view there is an implicit social contract between members of a community that requires everyone to treat everyone else in a moral way. The question is, who are members of this moral community? Does it go beyond the current generation to include all generations?

Philosopher John Rawls claims that most people would prefer a more egalitarian and just society if they didn't know where in the society they were to be placed – at the top or the bottom, rich or poor. In a similar way people would opt for intergenerational justice if put in a similar position of not knowing which generation they were to be born into.

This 'do unto others as you would have them do unto you' creed is exemplified by the scenario of the campsite. Most people will feel morally obliged to clean up a campsite they have been using so that it is at least in as good a condition for the next person as it was when they arrived. This is even though they don't know who the next campers will be or when they will come (time and identity are irrelevant). Part of the rationale behind honouring such an obligation is the knowledge that if everyone honours this obligation then everyone benefits. The campers that are now leaving clean up the campsite in the hope that others will do so for them and with gratitude that others have done so before. When applied to generations this creed is that each generation should leave sufficient natural resources and an unspoilt environment for the generations to follow.

*Common Heritage and Public Trust*

The idea of a public trust or common heritage across generations means that environmental resources/values should not be destroyed merely because the majority of a current generation decides that it has better uses for them.

The idea that environmental resources are a common heritage of humanity has ancient roots. The Roman emperor, Justinian, proclaimed: "By the law of nature these things are common to mankind – the air, running water, the sea, and consequently the shores of the sea." The idea of common heritage was incorporated in the 1982 UN Convention on the Law of the Sea, which states that the seabed and ocean floor, apart from a narrow region near national coastlines, are "beyond the limits of national jurisdiction" and all rights in the resources associated with them "are vested in mankind as a whole" and activities in this area shall "be carried out for the benefit of mankind as a whole".

The doctrine of public trust similarly says that some environmental resources are so valuable to humanity that they belong to everyone and should not be privately owned or controlled. This doctrine has been incorporated into various environmental laws and has been reinforced by the courts. For example, in 1983 a US court affirmed 'a duty of the state to protect the people's common heritage of streams, lakes, etc'.

*Responsibility*

Responsibility arises from having power and ability to impact and affect. Increasingly the activities of modern industrialised nations have impacts that are felt not only globally but well into the future. If we know that our actions may harm future generations, and we have a choice about whether to take those actions, then we are morally responsible for those actions. This is particularly pertinent to the environment as many environmental impacts, such as radioactive waste disposal, climate change and the spread of chemical toxins, have long-term implications.

Because current generations can undermine the welfare of future generations they have a measure of responsibility for that welfare. Inaction can also have consequences and so inaction can be just as irresponsible as any action, particularly if it entails allowing existing trends to continue in the knowledge that these will be harmful. The fact that the consequences of our actions or inactions occur some time into the future does not diminish our responsibility.

Because a healthy environment is a shared interest that benefits whole communities, and is often threatened by the cumulative effects of many different human activities, there is a collective responsibility to protect it. Individual efforts to protect the environment can only offer limited solutions and there is a need for government regulation and international cooperation.

### Avoid Actions that will Harm Future Generations

Some philosophers argue that the more distant future generations are from us the less our obligations to them because we cannot know what their needs and wants will be and what is good for them. Others argue that even if we do not know what will be *good* for future generations we do know what will be *bad* for them. We do know that they are unlikely to want skin cancer, soil erosion or frequent catastrophic weather events. Humans have fundamental needs that can be projected into the future, including healthy, uncontaminated ecosystems.

Therefore we may not have positive obligations to provide for the future but negative obligations to avoid actions that will harm the future. We can fairly safely assume that future generations would want a safe and diverse environment. We cannot just assume that future generations will have better technological and scientific means to solve the problems we leave them. For this reason we should endeavour to pass on the planet to future generations in no worse shape than past generations passed it on to us.

### International Agreements

The responsibility of current generations for intergenerational equity has been recognised in various international agreements including the:

- Convention for the Protection of the World Cultural and Natural Heritage, 1972
- United Nations Framework Convention on Climate Change, 1992

- Convention on Biological Diversity, 1992
- Rio Declaration on Environment and Development, 1992
- Vienna Declaration and Programme of Action, 1993

These agreements led up to the UNESCO Declaration on the Responsibilities of the Present Generations towards Future Generations, 1997. The text of the declaration was adapted from a Bill of Rights for Future Generations presented to the UN in 1993 by the Cousteau Society together with over 9 million signatures of support from people in 106 countries. The UNESCO Declaration states that "present generations have the responsibility of ensuring that the needs and interests of present and future generations are fully safeguarded" and that to ensure this they must ensure that the Earth is not irreversibly damaged and ecosystems not harmfully modified by human activity. Article 5 on Protection of the Environment says:

1. "In order to ensure that future generations benefit from the richness of the Earth's ecosystems, the present generations should strive for sustainable development and preserve living conditions, particularly the quality and integrity of the environment.

2. The present generations should ensure that future generations are not exposed to pollution which may endanger their health or their existence itself.

3. The present generations should preserve for future generations natural resources necessary for sustaining human life and for its development.

4. The present generations should take into account possible consequences for future generations of major projects before these are carried out."

Today the principle of intergenerational equity is a principle of international law. A number of national laws and agreements also include intergenerational equity such as Australia's 1992 Intergovernmental Agreement on the Environment, which states that "the present generation should ensure that the health, diversity and productivity of the environment is maintained or enhanced for the benefit of future generations". Such sentiments go back as far as 1916 with the National Park Act in the US, which charges the National Park Service with the duty of protecting the land 'unimpaired for the enjoyment of future generations'. In general the idea of national parks in all countries have the same intergenerational goals.

### *What should be sustained?*

Even if it is agreed that we have an obligation to future generations, the nature of that obligation is controversial. Do we merely need to protect those aspects of the environment necessary for survival and health, such as a minimal standard of clean air and water? And what standard would that be? Which risks from hazardous and radioactive substances do we need to prevent?

The problem is that protecting the interests of the future may conflict with the interests of current generations. How do we balance our obligations to current generations with our obligations to future generations when these conflict? At one extreme is the *preservationist model*, which requires that present generations do not deplete any resources or destroy or alter any part of the environment. In this case an industrialised lifestyle would not be possible and the present generations would make significant sacrifices, living subsistence lifestyles so to benefit future generations.

At the other extreme is the *opulence model*, where present generations consume all they want and assume that future generations will be able to cope with the impoverished environment that remains because they will be technologically better off. Or alternatively advocates of this model assume that future generations will have the technological expertise to find new sources or substitutes for exhausted resources and extinct species. However this model seems to be overly optimistic about the ability for wealth and technology to deal with environmental catastrophe and losses.

*Substitutability of Nature and Wealth*

Many economists and businesspeople tend to argue that what is important is to maintain human welfare over time. By this they mean that a community can use up natural resources and degrade the natural environment so long as they compensate future generations for the loss with 'human capital' (skills, knowledge and technology) and 'human-made capital' (buildings, machinery, etc).

They point out that a depleted resource, say oil, could be compensated for by other investments that generate the same income. If the money obtained from exploiting an exhaustible resource, such as oil, is invested so that it yields a continuous flow of income this is equivalent to maintaining the amount of oil for future generations. In other words, they claim that using significant amounts of minerals or oil is not contrary to intergenerational equity so long as the money earned from using the minerals or oil is invested so that it provides an ongoing income for future generations that would be equivalent to the value of having the oil and minerals. This means that the Amazon forest could be removed so long as the proceeds from removing it were reinvested properly.

Such arguments provide a rationale for continuing to use non-renewable resources at ever-increasing rates. Economists argue that although this might cause temporary shortages, those shortages will cause prices to rise and this will provide the motivation to find new reserves, discover substitutes and encourage more efficient use of remaining resources.

*Non-substitutability of Nature*

However, whilst the economic value of natural resources can be easily replaced, their functions are less easily replaced. Most people, even economists, agree that there are limits on the extent to which natural resources can be replaced without changing some biological processes and putting ecological sustainability at risk. They recognise that some environmental assets could not be 'traded-off' because they are essential for life-support systems and they cannot be replaced.

For example, there are parts of the environment for which there are no substitutes such as, the ozone layer, the climate-regulating functions of ocean phytoplankton, the watershed protection functions of tropical forests, the pollution-cleaning and nutrient-trap functions of wetlands. For those people who believe that animals and plants have an intrinsic value, there can be no substitute for them.

There are other parts of the environment for which we cannot be certain whether or not we will be able to substitute in the future and what the consequences of continually degrading them will be. For example, scientists do not know enough about the functions of natural ecosystems and the possible consequences of depleting and degrading the environment. Therefore it is not wise to assume that all will be well in the end because of some faith in economics and technological ingenuity. The precautionary principle requires that we do not assume that natural resources can be replaced without good evidence.

Environmental degradation can lead to irreversible losses such as the loss of species and habitats, which once lost cannot be recreated. Other losses are not irreversible but repair may take centuries – for example, the ozone layer and soil degradation.

For these reasons environmentalists argue that a loss of environmental quality cannot be substituted with a gain in human or human made capital without loss of welfare. Therefore they argue that future generations should not inherit a degraded environment, no matter how many extra sources of wealth are available to them.

*Access*

The principle of 'conservation of access' implies that not only should current generations ensure equitable access to that which they have inherited from previous generations, but they should also ensure that future generations can also enjoy this access.

Is it fair to replace natural resources and environmental assets – that are currently freely available to everyone – with human-made resources that have to be bought and in future may only be accessible to people who can afford them? Poor people are often affected by unhealthy environments more than wealthier people. A substitution of wealth for natural resources does not mean that those who suffer are the same people as those who will benefit from the additional wealth. For example, if an area of forest is cut down in Brazil to provide wealth for the shareholders, taxes for the government and even perhaps economic growth for the nation, this does not compensate for the loss of access to the forest for future generations of indigenous people whose way of life, sense of identity and livelihoods depend on the forests.

## Options

When resources are depleted and species extinct, the options available to future generations are narrowed. Once plants and animals are extinct, or habitats destroyed, future generations no longer have the option to enjoy or utilise them, for example to produce new medicines. Therefore intergenerational equity demands that the current generation conserve the diversity of nature so as not to restrict the options available to future generations to solve problems and develop in ways that they choose.

We do not know what the safe limits of environmental degradation are; yet if those safe limits are crossed, the options for future generations would be severely limited. Overdevelopment reduces diversity and therefore reduces future options.

## Discussion

Retaining environmental quality for future generations means passing on the environment in as good a condition as we found it. It does not preclude some trade-offs and compromises but it requires that those tradeoffs do not endanger the overall quality of the environment so that environmental functions are reduced and ecosystems are unable to recover.

A minimal environment may be all that is needed for human survival but people have come to expect a lot more than a subsistence lifestyle. Should that be denied to future generations? Justice would seem to require that future generations not only be able to subsist but that they have the same level of opportunities to thrive and be comfortable as current generations. Opportunities require more than mere survival level environmental resources.

---

*Thinking it through: where do I stand?*

Do we have any responsibilities towards people who haven't even been born yet? What might those responsibilities be? How do we decide what to do when there is a conflict between improving living conditions for current generations and maintaining environmental quality for future generations.

---

## Further reading

Beder, S. (2006). *Environmental Principles and Policies*. Sydney: UNSW Press and London: Earthscan.

Partridge, E. (1981). *Responsibilities to Future Generations*. Buffalo: Prometheus Books.

Shrader-Frechette, K. (2002). *Environmental Justice: Creating Equality, Reclaiming Democracy*. Oxford: Oxford University Press.

Visser 't Hooft, H. P. (1999). *Justice to Future Generations and the Environment*. Dordrecht: Kluwer Academic.

Weiss, E. B. (1989). *In Fairness to Future Generations: International Law, Common Patrimony, and Intergenerational Equity*. Dobbs Ferry, New York: Transnational Publishers.

## Resources

Partridge, E. (2011) Topics in Environmental Ethics. http://gadfly.igc.org/e-ethics/ee-topic.htm.
UNESCO (1997). Declaration on the Responsibilities of the Present Generations Towards Future Generations http://portal.unesco.org/en/ev.php-URL_ID=13178&URL_DO=DO_TOPIC&-URL_SECTION=201.html

## Acknowledgement

I would like to thank John Drummond for reading and commenting on this chapter

# Part IV

## Living Healthy, Fulfilling Sustainable Lives

*billen cliffs*
oil on canvass
40cm by 32cm

# Chapter 13

## The Relationship Between Lifestyle and the Environment

*Shigemi Kagawa*
*Yuko Oshita*
Faculty of Economics, Kyushu University
*Keisuke Nansai*
Research Center for Material Cycles and Waste Management,
National Institute for Environmental Studies
*Sangwon Suh*
Bren School of Environmental Science and Management,
University of California, Santa Barbara

### Introduction

The Intergovernmental Panel on Climate Change (IPCC) published its second report in December 1995. The report described a rapid increase in the concentrations of the greenhouse gas, carbon dioxide ($CO_2$), since the industrial revolution in the late 18th and early 19th centuries. In addition, the serious effects of a sharp rise in the amount of greenhouse gases on the natural environment and human society were also clarified (see Figure 1). After publication of the report, countries around the world started focusing on what is now referred to as global warming issue, and many have made specific efforts to reduce $CO_2$ emissions and mitigate the problem of global warming.

The most obvious difference between global warming and instances of environmental pollution (e.g. Minamata disease in Japan[1]), both of which have increased during periods of high economic growth, is the identity of the offenders and victims. In the case of environmental pollution, the offenders have traditionally been businesses and industries and the victims have been local residents. However, in the case of global warming, in addition to businesses and industries, general consumers are also offenders. In cases of cross-border pollution, the offenders and victims are sometimes difficult to identify.

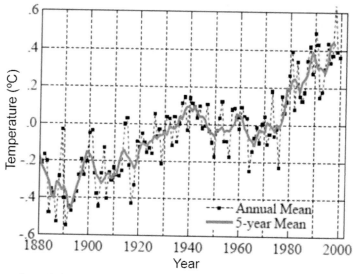

Figure 1: Annual change in global average temperature (°C) for the period 1880 to 2000
Source: Hansen, J.E. et al., 2001: A closer look at the United States and global
surface temperature change. *J. Geophys. Res.*, 106, 23947-23963

Consisting primarily of local residents, the household sector is a major emitter of $CO_2$. The sector contributes to global warming primarily through daily activities that involve energy consumption (gasoline and electricity) for driving, cooking, watching TV and the use of air-conditioners. In fact, several researchers have argued strongly that the increased rate of $CO_2$ emissions is actually due to energy consumption by these local residents (hereafter referred to the household sector) who emit more $CO_2$ than the industrial sector. In response to this increased awareness of the global

---

1.Environmental pollution was caused by mercury emissions from chemical plants near the Minamata Bay in Kumamoto Prefecture. This case is widely regarded as the first Japanese pollution incident.

warming issue, a growing number of studies investigating "sustainable consumption" have been conducted (e.g. the Winter/Spring 2005 issue of the *Journal of Industrial Ecology*).

As a familiar example of an increase in energy consumption by the household sector, the effects of our dietary habits on the environment are discussed below; specifically, we consider the consumption of fried Pacific saury. The process might start by using a gas stove to fry the fish, resulting in the direct emission of $CO_2$. If we consider only the direct $CO_2$ emissions from households, then purchasing and using an electric cooking heater for cooking would reduce direct emissions from the kitchen completely. However, this straightforward measure would totally ignore the $CO_2$ emitted from the thermal power plant that produced the electricity required for operating the electrical stove. Similarly, the total emissions from of the many economic activities that occurred between the time when the saury was initially caught and the point when they are consumed as fried fish would also not be considered. For example, the emissions associated with the combustion of fuel by the saury fishing boats and the emissions associated with the electricity used by seafood processing companies to process the landed fish. The total value of these emissions that accrue throughout the entire supply chain are collectively referred to as Lifecycle $CO_2$ Emissions, or the Carbon Footprint.

An important research theme related to sustainable consumption is how an environmentally friendly form of consumption can be achieved after making the functional units for measuring the consumption of goods consistent. Regarding dietary habits, assuming that the functional units (e.g. caloric intake) of the food being consumed are the same, then the difference between direct emissions from kitchens (gas stoves) frying Pacific saury or cooking breaded pork will not be significantly different. Consequently, assessing the difference in the impact on the environment between fried saury and breaded pork using direct emissions as an assessment criterion is inappropriate. When considering forms of consumption with low associated environmental loads, the assessment criteria should include the carbon footprint. Rather than setting direct emissions as the assessment criteria, such an indicator should show the total $CO_2$ emissions for the entire production process i.e. from harvesting the foodstuffs, through to food processing, distribution, sales and cooking. This would also help to conserve energy, not only within households, but also by foodstuff procurement companies, processing companies, distributors, and retailers to reduce $CO_2$ emissions.

A Japanese beer company declares how much carbon was emitted in the production of its beer products by printing 295 grams per 350 ml can on the sides of the container (see Figure 2). While experts may question the calculation method and various other aspects of the process, the voluntary act of presenting this information on products to raise awareness among consumers should be commended. However, a comparative assessment of products produced by other companies would require the development of methods for standardizing the calculation methods used to derive these values. Clearly, such comparisons would provide a very useful indicator for the environmental assessment of the company's own carbon footprint. This would likely facilitate holistic improvements in energy efficiency through modifications of the production process and/or logistics, reducing the carbon footprint and promote the functional improvement of the products themselves, and facilitate research and development.

In terms of the household sector, the size of the carbon footprint could be factored into market prices and become an important factor in consumer selection, possibly stimulating consumer awareness to a certain degree. In addition, consumers could monitor and compare product manufacturers based on the size of their carbon footprint, which would likely increase environmental awareness among companies. Indeed, the social experiment of carbon footprint presentation has just begun.

This label shows the total amount of $CO_2$ that was emitted to produce this beer; from cultivation of the raw materials to recycling of the can.

Copyright: Y. Oshita

Figure 2: Eco-labelling by a Japanese beer company

### *Thinking about how your food consumption affects your carbon footprint*

In order to understand the environmental impacts associated with food consumption, we consider a simple question in this section. Let us suppose that a homemaker has five ¥1000 bills (¥5000 in total) and that this homemaker then spends ¥1000 on five different types of food (see Figure 3). Let us consider two cases in which this homemaker buys different items of food, noting that these cases are arbitrary.

Case A (Shopping list A):

Bread (¥1000), ham (¥1000), frozen croquettes (¥1000), fruit (¥1000) and milk (¥1000)

Case B (shopping list B):

Rice (¥1000), fish (¥1000), instant noodles (¥1000), packaged food (¥1000) and beer (¥1000)

Figure 3: Simple example of food consumption

An interesting question is 'from the point of view of the carbon footprint, which of the two shopping trips was more environmentally friendly?' Although space limitations in this chapter prevent us from explaining how the carbon footprints were calculated in this study, economic input-output models for environmental life-cycle assessment (EIO-LCA) can be used to estimate the size of the carbon footprint for the shopping list in question (see Lave et al., 1995; Hendrickson et al., 1998; Nansai et al., 2003). We used the carbon footprint estimates contained in the Japanese environmental input-output tables (see Nansai et al., 2003) and developed a simple carbon footprint calculator using Microsoft Excel VBA (see Figure 4). For example, if we press the "Milk" button on the calculator, then the carbon footprint for milk, that is the total amount of $CO_2$ emitted directly and indirectly for a ¥1000 quantity of milk, could be calculated. This means that the carbon footprint for milk will include the indirect emissions associated with milk production, such as electricity consumption in the milk processing plant, the fuel consumed to transport the milk from the processing plant to shops, the fuel required to operate the farm equipment for cultivating the feedstock for milk cows, and so forth (see Chapter 16 in Murray and Wood (2010) for methods on elucidating the emissions in a supply chain). Using these methods, we estimated the carbon footprint of milk to be 2.2 kg.

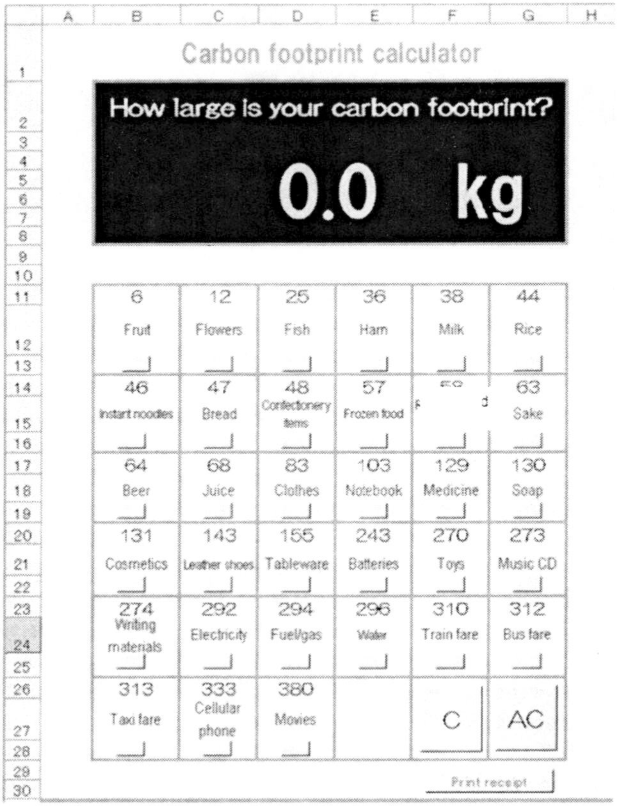

Figure 4: Carbon footprint calculator

Figure 5 shows the carbon footprints associated with shopping lists A and B. The carbon footprint of shopping list A was 9.2 kg, while that of shopping list B was 12.4 kg, implying that shopping trip A was more environmentally friendly than shopping trip B. If we compare the carbon footprints of both cases, it is clear that the inclusion of ham or fish has a marked effect on the size of the footprints; the value for list A is 1.8 kg-C, while the value for list B is 4.8 kg-C. This means that if the consumer buys ham instead of fish, $CO_2$ emissions can be reduced by 3.0 kg-C per ¥1000. These findings show that fishing is considerably more energy intensive (carbon-intensive) than producing livestock. In 2008, Japan's $CO_2$ emissions totaled 331 million ton-C. The consumption shift associated with changing from ¥1000-worth of ham to fish would be equivalent to a reduction in $CO_2$ of $9.1 \times 10\text{-}10\%$, and its contribution to total emissions would be extremely small. However, if we consider that there are about 50 million households (families) in Japan and suppose that all of these households spend ¥1000 on ham instead of fish, then a saving of 150,000 ton-C could be achieved as a result of such a consumption shifts. This substitution effect is equivalent to a 0.4% reduction in $CO_2$ emissions from the most carbon-intensive sector in Japan (Pig Iron production).

| Receipt A | | | | Receipt B | | |
|---|---|---|---|---|---|---|
| Commodity | Price (¥) | $CO_2$ emitted to produce these products (kg-C) | | Commodity | Price (¥) | $CO_2$ emitted to produce these products (kg-C) |
| 1 Bread | 1000 | 1.8 | | 1 Rice | 1000 | 1.6 |
| 2 Ham | 1000 | 1.8 | | 2 Fish | 1000 | 4.8 |
| 3 Frozen croquette | 1000 | 2.2 | | 3 Instant noodles | 1000 | 2.3 |
| 4 Fruit | 1000 | 1.3 | | 4 Retort-packed food | 1000 | 2.2 |
| 5 Milk | 1000 | 2.2 | | 5 Beer | 1000 | 1.4 |
| Total | 5000 | 9.2 | | Total | 5000 | 12.4 |

This shopping causes 9.2 kg-C of $CO_2$ emissions.

This shopping causes 12.4 kg-C of $CO_2$ emissions.

Figure.5: Carbon footprint associated with shopping

## Conclusion

This chapter shows that aspects of our lifestyle, such as food consumption, have a marked effect on the environment. Fortunately, it is possible to quantitatively assess the relationship between our lifestyles and the impact that our lifestyle has on the environment using the carbon footprint principle. A footprint calculator can be built with relative ease using a reliable environmental database (e.g. Embodied Energy and Emission Intensity Data in Japan, http://www.cger.nies.go.jp/publications/report/d031/eng/index_e.htm and the Comprehensive Environmental Data Archive in the US, http://www.eiolca.net/) and software such as Microsoft Excel. Since these environmental databases are both publicly accessible and free, teachers at elementary schools and/or (junior) high schools can construct a calculator similar to ours (see Fig. 4), and ask students to calculate the environmental impact of their shopping trips (consumption choices). We believe that this type of demonstration is very important for making students think more about our daily lives and the environment.

## Further reading

Lave, L.B., Cobas-Flores, E. & McMichael, F.C. (1995). Using input–output analysis to estimate economy-wide discharge, *Environmental Science & Technology*, *29*(9), 420 – 426.

Hendrickson, C., Horvath, A., Joshi, S. & Lave, L.B. (1998). Economic input-output models for environmental life-cycle assessment, *Environmental Science & Technology*, *32*(4), 184A – 191A.

Nansai, K., Moriguchi, Y. & Tohno, S. (2003), Compilation and application
    of Japanese inventories for energy consumption and air pollutant
    emissions using input-output tables, *Environmental Science & Tech-
    nology*, 37(9), 2005 – 2015.
Murray, J. & Wood, R. (Eds.). (2010). *The sustainability practitioner's guide to
    input-output analysis*, Champaign Illinois: Common Ground Pub-
    lishing LLC.

# Chapter 14
## Obesity

### Growth without Limits

*Garry Egger*
*School of Health and Human Sciences,*
*Southern Cross University, Lismore, NSW*

*The issue*

With the adverse consequences of unbalanced ecosystems (e.g. environmental pollution, climate disruption) apparently moving towards reality in the 21$^{st}$ century, a significant concern is the influence this may have on human health. Ecosystem sustainability is obviously not dependent on the health of humans, as 'Gaia', the living earth, will survive and ultimately correct itself irrespective of the state or existence of its human inhabitants. Human health on the other hand is intimately dependant on environmental sustainability. A depletion of resources as well as the build-up of atmospheric pollutants can have dire consequences on public and individual health, not all of which are equitably spread between the rich and poor. The connection between sustainability and health may not have been the case in the past. But as humans have strived to achieve a comfortable standard of living through increased economic growth, the dynamic nature of a growth system, and particularly exponential growth of population and resource usage, means it is inevitable that a 'sweet spot' is reached and ultimately passed. Beyond this the returns from future growth begin to diminish and are reflected in decreasing health gains.

> *A close up: Bill Blogg's parents, born in the 1920s were poor but hard working. Having grown up in a rural region they spent their days physically active in growing and cultivating food for themselves and for sale at the local markets. Such food was 'natural' and healthy as humans had evolved eating this type of unprocessed product for thousands of years. As a result, Bill Snr and his wife Mary were lean and healthy (although the effects of smoking taken up since WWII were starting to take its effects on Bill and it was a constant battle to avoid serious infections such as polio and diphtheria). They lived into their late 60s, with a short period of illness before death. Bill Snr and Mary's offspring, Bill Jnr and Barbara, achieved much greater wealth in their lifetime than Bill and Mary could ever have dreamed of. As a result they had energy-rich, processed food on the table every day without much (physical) effort. And technology that meant they hardly had to lift a finger to enjoy the good life. But around 1980 they started to get fat. As a result, Bill developed Type 2 diabetes and Barbara polycystic ovaries. They're still alive in their 70s but Bill Jnr has now had a stroke and is confined to a wheelchair. Barbara is also feeling the side-effects of the good life and both have had to 'down-size' their living conditions which, they are told, is not good for the economy. And there's the rub! Can we be economically as well as physically healthy in the current growth system? Or is exponential economic growth unsustainable beyond a point and likely to be reflected in diminishing returns in human health?*

## *Context*

*"What is lacking is not sufficient knowledge of the solution but universal consciousness of the gravity of the problem and education of the billions who are its victims."* Rev Martin Luther King

Those with set agendas often misuse the word 'sustainability' – usually for personal justification. 'Sustainable growth' for example, is a term often used by developers and apologists for expansion. The implication here is that physical growth through the exploitation of finite resources can continue indefinitely and that somehow the effects of this, in terms of waste emissions for example, can be contained.

A more apt description of growth is 'expansion to maturity', in which case the meaning of the term becomes dynamic. Given that sustainable means 'able to be maintained indefinitely', the use of the term 'sustainable' in the context of unlimited growth becomes an oxymoron.

In the short term this may only apply to developed countries. However in the long term it is inevitable that it will apply worldwide. The big question is at what point of growth is this liaison between growth, and sustainability breached?

Human health may be a bellwether way of measuring this.

## A (very) short history of disease

*"In order to see where we are, it is important to understand where we have been."*

About 5 million years ago, a form of ape emerged from the jungles of central Africa. Not much is known about these antecedents of *Homo Sapiens* – literally our ancestors – although we might hazard a few guesses:

First, it's highly unlikely that they were obese – or even overweight. Although they probably had the genetic capacity for storing fat (something which evolved with mammals as a means of getting through the inevitable lean times when food was scarce) the prospects of this ever happening were almost certainly limited by a harsh environment and competition for scarce resources.

Contrast this with the 21$^{st}$ century, where an estimated 15% of the world's population (and up to 60% in rich countries like Australia) are now classed as 'overweight or obese' – the reasons for which will become more obvious below.

Second, our early ancestors were exposed to all manner of diseases with little but their evolving immune systems to protect them. Over the coming thousands of years, life would revolve around getting enough to eat, not being eaten or killed in warfare, and battling the countless co-evolving disease micro-organisms, some of which still bother humanity today.

Third, the world in which our predecessors lived was dynamic and rapidly changeable – in the macro, as well as the micro sense. Ice ages and global warming came and went and life survived and evolved, albeit in different forms, throughout it all. Only since the development of Earth System Science based on the initially controversial and revolutionary Gaia hypothesis of English planetary scientist James Lovelock, have we realised just what this has to do with sustainability, why it is so, and how much it continues to be so.

## The Gaia Theory

*"I see the Earth's declining health as our most important concern, our very lives depending upon a healthy Earth. Our concern for it must come first, because the welfare of the burgeoning masses of humanity demands a healthy planet"*: James Lovelock (The Revenge of Gaia)

Gaia was the Greek goddess of the Earth. Although big in ancient Greek mythology, she led a relatively quiet life over the next 3,000+ years usually making her presence felt only in mythological history.

This changed in the early 1970s however, when a confident young English scientist names James Lovelock noticed that, in contrast to other 'dead' planets, like Mars and Jupiter, the Earth is more like a 'living' being. It is responsive to the organisms and changes that occur within its 'shell' to maintain its temperature and composition so as to always be 'comfortable' to some forms of life.

Lovelock made it clear that although it has suffered huge changes throughout time, Gaia the living Earth, has always corrected itself to an equilibrium level (or homeostasis[1]) that is suitable for some forms of life and will do so if pushed by making even *Homo Sapiens* 'no longer welcome'. According to Lovelock, sustainability, on which Gaia is predicated, is not an abstract possibility to be arbitrarily considered, but an absolute certainty to be obeyed in one form or another given the finite limitations of the planet.

Serious Earth scientists regarded lovelock's Gaia hypothesis as just that – a simple hypothesis, or proposal, until the turn of the millennium when it was taken up in the form of Earth System Science in universities throughout the world. Gaia became no longer an hypothesis, but a genuine theory to be tested.

The vision of Lovelock's thesis is in understanding the big picture view of sustainability; that if this is not obtained at the global level, Gaia will take action to return herself to equilibrium. She will do this irrespective of who or what she needs to demolish, just as she did after the death of the dinosaurs and other great extinctions that occurred over earth time.

The modern debate on environmental pollution and climate change has given great impetus to the Gaia theory. In essence this suggests that climate disruption is a reactive response to over-production of waste in the atmosphere. The 'Revenge of Gaia' in Lovelock's terms can be envisaged in deteriorations in human wellbeing, including health. Gaia, says Lovelock, will ensure that the planet will survive in one form or another, although may be brutal to its occupants in ensuring this is so. Seen this way there is no need to save the planet as is often proposed by environmentalists, *as it will save itself*. The question is whether we, as humans can survive and to what extent our health and wellbeing will be affected as a result of defying Gaia.

### *Evolution, sustainability and health*

*"All we have to do to destroy the planet's climate and biota and leave a ruined world to our children and grandchildren is to keep doing exactly what we are doing today, with no growth in the human population or world economy."* James Gustav Speth (The Bridge at the Edge of the World)

How are evolution, sustainability and health connected? What does Gaia have to do with this? And how are all these factors inter-related?

Until the late 20th century this was not clear. Humans have progressively survived the 'four horses of the apocalypse' to increase exponentially as a result of developments in disease prevention. Changes in public health and hygiene amongst richer countries around the time of the industrial revolution of the late 19th century and the development of medical marvels such as vaccination and antibiotics, resulted in a massive reduction in infectious

---

1.Literally '... a physiological equilibrium within living creatures involving a balance of functions and chemical composition' - a term we will come back to when talking about human health.

diseases. In the euphoria of the 1960s it appeared that the battle against disease had been all but won. Few would have predicted that the (apparent) demise of infectious diseases in the modern world would be accompanied by a rise in diseases largely caused by the factors underlying this decrease in infections namely, industrial development, 'modernisation' and economic growth. Lucretius may have been an exception when he wrote in 50 BC, *"In primitive times, lack of food gave languishing bodies to death; now, on the other hand, it is abundance that buries them."* Trans. Latham, 1994.

Meanwhile, in developing countries that lack the luxuries of such growth, 'spill-over' from growth in the western world (e.g. of low nutritional quality, high energy-dense processed foods and the effort-saving effect of transport technology) has meant a paradoxical effect of modern western diseases and traditional problems. Malnutrition and obesity, particularly in children, currently co-exist for example within many of the developing countries of Africa and South America.

Since the beginnings of time, the biggest changes that have occurred in the Earth have been due to physical factors – earthquakes, sunspots, volcanoes, etc. More recently, human factors have played a part. We are currently living in a world transformed by humans, as much as by nature. Irrespective of any argument about the causes of potential changes in climate in future years, there is little doubt that humans have played a significant role in pollution of the atmosphere through increasing emissions of greenhouse gases. This has come largely through industrial production since the beginnings of the industrial revolution beginning in the late 18$^{th}$ century. However it has been compounded by the huge increase in the human population since that time, largely as a result of the improvements of living standards (at least in the developed world), which have come through the industrial revolution itself.

---

*Thinking it through: where do I stand?*

Is it possible to have perpetual growth in material consumption?

How can a rapidly increasing world population afford to increase its per capita material wealth?

Does over-consumption affect an individual's or population health?

How is the modern obesity epidemic related to the current system of continual economic growth?

Can humans have too much of a good thing? Are prosperity and growth the same thing? And how can prosperity continue without growth?

---

### Population growth and sustainability

*"We only have one planet, not two, and can only sustain our growth by depleting the natural capital of the planet – it's like running down our inherited fortune instead of living prudently off the interest."* Dick Smith (Dick Smith's Population Crisis)

World population has risen from around 1 billion in 1800, a figure which took all of recorded history to reach, to ~7 billion in 2011. Predictions for the future are a peak of around 10 billion by the middle of the current century. Whilst it would seem obvious that exponential population growth must tax the sustainability of any finite system, in theory at least, this is not the main limit to sustainability.

Taking a more concrete example of this, and looking only at emissions, the estimated sustainable carbon footprint for a world of 7 million people (as in 2011) is ~5 tonnes per person per year. At this rate, sequestration of carbon equals emissions, therefore not allowing a build-up in the atmosphere. If either the population numbers or carbon emissions per person increase, this will throw the system into unsustainability – more carbon will be emitted than is able to be soaked up in the oceans, forests and soil, and hence there will be a build-up in the atmosphere - with potential consequences.

An analogy can be drawn in the human body with Type 2 diabetes, the 21$^{st}$ century lifestyle-related plague. Diabetes occurs when blood sugars from food, which are normally metabolised as energy, are not 'sequestered' or 'soaked up' by the body's cells for energy. This occurs as a result of too much sugar production through food, or too little sequestration as a result of the breakdown of insulin (which helps blood sugars enter the cells), or both. The build-up is then unsustainable causing diabetes, which can then lead on to heart disease and death.

It may not be drawing too much of a long bow to suggest a similar thing can happen to the planet as a result of a build-up of carbon in the atmosphere. Although in this case, Gaia would guarantee that the planet survives but under different circumstances e.g. without any or with many fewer humans.

As can be seen from this however, population *per se* is not the cause of calamitous unsustainability – at least to a point. It is the per capita *consumption* of humans that needs to be considered and the current drive for continued unfettered consumption for an improved standard of living. It is here where we have to go back to the industrial revolution to find the nexus between human health and sustainability. To do this we need take a short excursion into the human immune system and the changes that have occurred in this over time.

### *Economic Growth and Immunity*

We are herd animals and as such over time gain advantage of adaptations of the body with changing circumstances. The immune system has evolved in mammals to defend the body against injury or foreign invaders, which throughout history have been largely microbial organisms – bacteria, viruses, fungi, etc.

Without going into the complications of the system, it is designed like an army, with sentinels, foot soldiers, killer patrols and officers to direct operations against invaders that are seen as a threat to existence or wellbeing.

Some of these are antigens that the immune system is innately able to recognise as foreign. Other forms of immunity are 'acquired' through experiences over time.

Until the time of the industrial revolution, both components of the immune system were fully occupied defending against the microbial organisms (germs) causing infectious diseases, which made up the vast majority of deaths and disease throughout history. With the industrial revolution came changes to the nature of living: air pollution was more predominant and although reduced from its earlier disastrous levels, such as in the great London smog, took on a different form as microscopic particulate matter. More importantly, lifestyle habits changed. Without the need to move so much for food, humans became inactive, leading to a build-up of body fat and associated hormonal signals.

The production of processed foods, particularly in the last 50 years, led to a food system with which the immune system is not familiar. Hence a different form of immune response to the classical form of inflammation (first identified by the Greek doctor Aurelius Celsius over 2,000 years ago) developed.

This type of inflammation, called 'metaflammation' because of its link with the metabolic system, is much milder and more chronic than that associated with infectious diseases. It is also more likely to lead to ongoing disease, because, unlike the microbial invaders of the earlier diseases, it is not overcome by an extremely heightened and alarmed immune system.

On the other hand the industrial revolution improved quality of life, mainly through improvements in hygiene, but also through medical developments, resulting in a dramatic decrease in infectious diseases and consequent increase in longevity. Instead of living to an average of 50 years as around 1800, people in the developed world now live well into their 80s. But chronic diseases have taken over from infectious diseases, with about 70% of all disease now being made up of these lifestyle-related causes of disease. Hence the question has to become 'are we likely to continue living better, rather than just longer with increases in technology?' Also, what is it that has driven the improvements in industrialisation and technology and consequent growth in population that has caused a greater human footprint on the planet? There are lots of answers, including science and human ingenuity. But one thing that is often overlooked is economics.

---

*Action: what can I do?*
- Organise forums to discuss the limitations to growth.
- Read some of the early comments about exponential growth such as from the Club of Rome, Paul Ehrlich (The Population Bomb) etc.
- Walk the talk: live an environmentally sustainable life and notice how this impacts on your health.

- Eat a plant-based diet – at least for a couple of extra days a week. It will help the environment – and your health.
- Think of movement as an opportunity, not an inconvenience: it will also help the environment and your health.

## *Economic Growth and sustainability*

*"Anyone who believes that exponential economic growth can continue forever is either a fool or an economist."* Kenneth Boulding

Economic growth, which drove, but also followed the industrial revolution, required increases in everything to feed the economic engine. More people buying more products meant more money going back into the system. The discovery of new lands enabled expansion of food sources and greater food security. The 'green revolution' of the 1950s, generated by advances in agriculture, allowed the further development of population to feed the system. And finally advances in technology meant more could be produced to perpetuate the growth cycle.

There's little doubt that this combination of technological advancement, population growth and economic growth worked. For the first 150 years of the industrial revolution at least, humans improved their quality of life, infant mortality, health and longevity. But like any exponential system, the limits must be reached at some point. Just when this is or may be, is unclear and probably diffuse at best. However the big rise in chronic diseases in developed countries since the late 1970s and early 80s means we may have passed a 'sweet spot' in growth, beyond which the returns have begun to diminish. This is indicated in particular by rises in obesity.

We have begun to breach the nexus between sustainability and health. And while technological discovery and medical advances continue to chase the growing complexity of disease cause, the increasing burden of such disease within developed countries suggests the laws of ecology may have been surpassed already.

And so we are heading inevitably, if humans are to survive the wrath of Gaia, towards a steady state economy where health is no longer sacrificed for the sake of growth in the current measure of economic throughput or Gross Domestic Product (GDP). In the words of US ecologist James Gustav Speth, this will be where *"the illusory promises of ever-more growth no longer provide an excuse for neglecting to deal generously with our country's compelling social needs; and where true citizen democracy is no longer held hostage to the growth imperative."*

Of course it's clear that some things still need to grow, particularly in the developing world if people there are to attain a standard of living anywhere near that of the developed world. This does not mean idolatry of GDP as the prime measure of success however as it has been in the past. More appropriately it suggests a shift to human progress that can be achieved without the increasing marginal returns of an exponential, financially dominated, economic growth system.

### *Where to from here?*

There is nothing surer than that humanity must, at some stage, reach a steady state if it is to survive at a level of acceptable health. This implies a steady state of population, resource use and economic growth. It doesn't imply however a stagnation of progress. Indeed JS Mill, one of the early architects of the growth system said:

"...*a stationary condition of capital and population implies no stationary state of human improvement. There would be as much scope as ever for all kinds of mental culture, and moral and social progress; as much and much more likelihood of it being improved, when minds cease to be engrossed by the art of getting on.*" (Principles of Political Economy, 1848).

To get to this point however, and return to a point where health is increased within a sustainable framework, the following are needed:

1.  A recognition by politicians and economists that economic growth, particularly as measured by Gross Domestic Product, cannot continue indefinitely and that an alternative system needs to be discussed and initiated in the near future;

2.  An acceptance that the real driver behind lifestyles and environments leading to chronic disease is much less the behaviour of individuals than the failure of economists and politicians to recognise the limitations of a closed environment;

3.  A break between the supposed link between population growth and human well-being, which has been implicit during the 200 odd years of the modern growth era;

4.  Humans learning to live within the limitations of a finite world while enjoying the benefits of technological advancement. If they don't, the price they'll pay is likely, at best, to be deterioration in human health, and at worst, a war with Gaia, which they are unlikely to win.

Various ages have been named in geological time – Pliocene, Miocene, Holocene, etc. There's little doubt that the industrial era, since the beginnings of the industrial revolution has had it greatest influence caused by humanity. The 'Anthropocene' age has been condensed to miniscule geological time compared to other ages. As with all exponential growth, it must reach its limits. As stated by one commentator, "*growth beyond maturity is either obesity or cancer.*" Neither is healthy and neither is sustainable.

*Further reading*

Delpuch, F., Mair, B., Monnier, E., & Holdsworth, M. (2009). *Globesity: A Planet out of control*. London: Earthscan.

Egger, G., Swinburn, B., (2010). *Planet Obesity: How we are eating ourselves and the planet to death*. Sydney: Allen and Unwin.

Egger, G. (2009). Health, 'illth' and economic growth: Medicine, environment and economics at the cross-roads. *American Journal of Preventive Medicine, 37*(1), 78 – 83.

Jackson, T. (2009). *Prosperity Without Growth: Economics for a finite planet* London: Earthscan.

Gittens, R. (2010). *The Happy Economist: Happiness for the Hard Headed*. Sydney: Allen and Unwin.

Meadows, D., Randers, J. & Meadows, D. (2004). *Limits to Growth: The 30 year update*. Vermont: Chelsea Green Publishing Co.

Lovelock, J. (2007). *The Revenge of Gaia*. London: Penguin.

*Resources*

CASSE (Centre for the Advancement of the Steady State Economy). 5101 S, 11<sup>th</sup> St. Arlington, Virginia 22204 USA. www.steadystate.org

# Chapter 15
## What does Sustainable Agriculture Really Mean?

*Richard Stirzaker*
*CSIRO Land and Water, Canberra, Australia*

Each day the world's farmers must feed seven billion people and each day an extra two hundred thousand mouths join those needing to be fed. Uncertainty over global food supplies in 2007 precipitated a sudden rise in the price of food, pushing it beyond the means of the very poor. In a short time, the 825 million undernourished citizens of the world swelled to over one billion. Riots followed in over 20 countries. It has been said that it only takes nine missed meals to turn an orderly society into anarchy.

In 2011, another famine unfolded in east Africa. The rains had failed and the population, already weakened by years of civil war, simply walked away from their homes and farms, leaving everything in the hope of getting to a place with international food aid. These two examples give us both sides of the food crisis – hunger caused by poverty and hunger caused by scarcity. My reflection about the sustainability of agriculture will therefore be framed within a context of human need. "Can we feed the world a nutritious diet at a price they can afford both now and into the foreseeable future?"

There are, of course, other ways to frame the sustainable agriculture debate. One way is to say that the fundamental resource base needed to support agriculture is being degraded. Examples are soil being eroded, soil turning acid or salty, over-use of toxic chemicals and the pollution of water resources. Another angle is that the inputs needed to sustain modern agriculture are running low, such as good quality water and the essential plant nutrient phosphorus. Moreover agriculture is very dependent on fossil fuels, not only for running tractors and pumps but also for making nitrogen fertiliser.

Degradation of the resource base and depletion of non-renewable resources are serious concerns, which I will return to later. For now we need to delve into the roots of agriculture, to see how and why it started, and how it got to be the way it is. This will give us a platform from which to speculate about sustainability into the future.

Agriculture started around 10 000 years ago in the part of south west Asia known as the Fertile Crescent. Before agriculture, people lived by gathering wild foods and hunting. Hunter-gatherers were often nomadic, constantly moving in search of food, so they lived a very simple life. It was pointless having a lot of material possessions if you had to carry them around with you.

It is likely that seeds discarded from food brought back from foraging expeditions grew up around the temporary dwelling places. Gatherers would search far and wide for a grass with largest possible seeds and would recognise these grasses sprouting from split seed around the home. These would have been cared for and the largest seeds selected and re-sown. The gradual process of plant domestication had begun. Similarly, baby animals orphaned from a hunt may have been raised around the home and the most docile would have been kept and produced offspring, starting the slow domestication of animals.

The reason why agriculture started in the Fertile Crescent was because the wild ancestors of wheat and peas, and the ancestor of the modern sheep and goats, were native to this region. Wheat is mainly a starch or energy food, peas are a legume containing a lot of protein and the animals produced meat, milk and clothing. The human diet is based on a tiny proportion of the diversity of plants and animals, and having three of this small subset in one region was rare. Nevertheless the early farming life was not very secure. Archaeological remains showed that Hunter-gatherers were often in better physical shape than the pioneer farmers.

Eventually, as domestication progressed, agriculture became more productive and not everyone needed to farm. Villages sprang up in Mesopotamia between the Tigris and Euphrates rivers from around 7000 BC and flourished into large cities over the next few thousand years, sustained by the fertile farmlands watered from the mighty rivers and enriched by the silt they carried. These cities have since vanished, almost certainly due to the failure of agriculture, caused by erosion from the tree-cleared mountain slopes and salt left behind from irrigation.

The processes of erosion and salinisation may go largely unnoticed for a while, so there is no urgent signal for the community to change course. Heavy rains wash soil from ploughed fields into coffee-coloured rivers, but the few millimetres of soil lost each year does not translate into declining crop yields for quite some time. Eventually, as the fertility continues to decline with the annual loss of topsoil, so does the lush plant growth which shelters and binds the soil. Then a series of intense storms on unprotected soil carve gullies through the fields, after which they are abandoned by the farmer.

Salinity is particularly insidious, as the problem grows underground and out of sight. All rivers carry some salt dissolved in their waters and this salt gets added to the soil with the irrigation water. The plants only transpire fresh water, excluding the salt at their roots, so salt slowly accumulates season after season in the soil. As more water is applied each year, the salt gets pushed deeper into the soil, usually below the root zone. Down there it is not a problem to the crops – until the water table starts to rise.

Soil needs to be a meter or two deep for crops to grow well. Often soils are many meters deep, but, if you dig deep enough, you eventually hit rock at the bottom. If we think of a wide valley with low mountains on either side, the rock beneath forms a basin. When irrigators apply more water than crops need, as invariably happens, the extra water percolates down until it hits the rock. At this point the water cannot go down any further, so the watertable starts to rise, like the filling of a giant bath tub.

Salt accumulated from many irrigation seasons past is carried upwards by the rising watertable. When the watertable is two meters below the soil surface, there is little impact on the crops, because few roots get that deep. But within a few years it creeps up further and then suddenly the salt hits the root zone and the crop yield quickly declines. This type of problem has been described as a 'long fuse with a big bang.' By the time we realise there is a problem it's too late to do anything about it.

The problem of salinity neatly captures the sustainability issue. A farmer wants to be as productive as possible, so it is better to err on the side of applying too much water than too little, and this does not present a problem in the short term. Thinking decades ahead, and limiting irrigation because the bathtub deep below is filling, could be risky if crop yields are reduced. Or one farmer may be working hard to apply exactly the right amount of water to the crops but the other farmers in the valley are not. The filling bathtub does not respect property boundaries and eventually the prudent and careless farmers of the valley suffer alike.

Unsustainable practices have accompanied agriculture from the very start, as the demise of ancient Mesopotamia attests. Yet farmers have long been aware of the need for more sustainable practices that will ensure yields over the longer term. In the Middle Ages a three course rotation was developed, involving a grain crop, a legume crop and a fallow, and this helped maintain soil fertility. By the late 1800s, it had developed into a four field rotation involving wheat, turnips, barley and clover. The turnips were fed to animals which provided manure for the barley crop and clover is a legume which provided nitrogen for the wheat crop. The pasture phase also rested the land.

It may be that the small farms of Western Europe in the early 1900s, employing the four field rotation and using animal drawn ploughs on fertile soils in a gentle climate, was about as sustainable as agriculture gets. But huge changes were ahead that have transformed the countryside.

During the First World War a chemist named Fritz Haber developed a process to make nitrogen fertiliser by combining the hydrogen from natural gas with nitrogen from air. Haber was actually trying to make nitrates for German bombs but his invention also started the chemical fertiliser industry. It has been said that 40% of all humans on earth are only here because they can be fed through the food produced as a consequence of the fertiliser from Haber's invention. Haber also invented the toxic gas subsequently used in the gas chambers to exterminate the Jews.

If fertilizer was a spin-off of the First World War, then agricultural chemicals, especially pesticides had their beginnings in the Second World War. It is agricultural chemicals that are most commonly seen as the root of what is unsustainable. Even today, fertilisers are often referred to as 'artificial fertiliser' to distinguish from the way fertility was naturally maintained though animal manure and compost. The 'artificial' versus natural debate still permeates discussion on sustainable agriculture. The plant nutrients released from manure for example, are exactly the same chemicals found in the bag of fertiliser, so there is no fundamental difference. What is different, however, is the speed with which highly soluble nutrients could be delivered to the plants. There was no question about the ability of fertilisers to promote high crop yields – what was debated was whether fertilisers and chemicals allowed agriculture to break free of the natural constraints of the resource base and cross thresholds that fundamentally change the way natural ecosystems function.

The artificial vs natural debate is at its sharpest over the use of pesticides. For hundreds of years, compounds based on arsenic, mercury and lead were used as the basis of pesticides – all natural compounds but highly toxic. Such pesticides have now been replaced by synthetic pyrethroids, made in a factory but far less toxic. One of the villains of the pesticide world, the man-made chemical DDT was spectacularly effective in killing pests, particularly malaria-carrying mosquitoes. It had low toxicity to mammals, but the effect in the food chain was catastrophic, especially for birds. The experience showed us that agriculture would always be part of a complex web of interactions, and 'solutions' applied to one part of the system could have unforeseen and disastrous consequences in another.

The twentieth century saw massive change to agriculture as innovation came from all directions. It is important to understand the relentless power with which innovation shapes the global food production system. Since there is a finite amount of food each of us can eat each day, farmers are essentially all in competition with each other. The price of a staple food is set by the lowest price that allows the farmers collectively to stay in business. Consider the situation where a farmer adopts an innovation, such as one of the first tractors, that allows him to produce more food for a year's work. This farmer makes a bigger profit than everyone else because the price is set by the vast majority of farmers who can only farm a much smaller area.

Over time, more farmers realise that they could also produce grain more cheaply if they bought a tractor. After a larger number of tractors have been bought, more food is being grown than is needed, and the price drops. Farmers without tractors now find that their farms are not viable against this new lower price. They are forced to purchase tractors, just to stay in business. Not all farmers can afford tractors and those that cannot, go out of farming altogether.

This example shows innovation as a two-edged sword. The top one third (say) of farmers who could adopt the innovation reap a windfall. The price they get for their produce is set by the less efficient technology of the majority. The next one third had to adopt the innovation but reap no benefit because the price has now fallen. They have to adopt the new practice just to stay in business. The last third, for one reason or another, cannot adopt the new technology and they flock to the ever expanding cities in search of a new job. The winners are the consumers. Because of innovation, food prices have fallen relative to the cost of most other things. Because of innovation, the percentage of undernourished citizens of developing countries halved between 1970 and 2005.

The history of the Australian wheat industry provides a fascinating case study of innovation, and a platform with which to explore the sustainability debate. Virgin bush was cleared in the 1850s and farmers were able to reap wheat yields of about one ton to the hectare. Over the next 50 years these yields fell to about one half of that obtained from virgin land, largely due to depletion of soil nutrients.

The situation started to turn around after 1900 when new wheat varieties were bred that were more resistant to disease and matured before the onset of the hot dry summer. Farmers were getting tractors and could plough the land and leave it fallow, allowing the soil to release nutrients and store water for the subsequent wheat crop. These innovations together restored yields almost to those obtained from the virgin land.

In the 1940s phosphorus fertiliser became available. Clover, which needed high levels of soil phosphorus, now became the dominant pasture species. The nitrogen accumulated by the leguminous clover was released as the pastures were rotated with wheat. Average yields quickly jumped to higher than those obtained from virgin land, and stayed higher for several decades. Yet signs of degradation were appearing and not showing up in the yield statistics. The most obvious was that some land had to be abandoned because of salinity, caused by the clearing of too many trees. The second sign was soil acidity, largely a consequence of the legume based pastures.

The next innovation was as surprising as all those that had gone before. Most people thought that yields in the semi-arid Australian wheat belt were being limited by water, but this proved not to be so. A new oilseed crop, canola, was developed in the 1980s, and soon became profitable to grow in rotation with wheat. Wheat crops often grew better after canola than just about any other crop. It turned out that canola inhibited the growth of some soil bacteria and fungi that had been nibbling away unseen on wheat roots. The canola acted as a mild form of soil fumigant, allowing the wheat roots to grow deeper in search of water. With more water available, farmers found that their crops started to respond better to nitrogen fertiliser. By the time this innovation was widely adopted, average wheat yields were double that obtained after clearing the virgin bush.

What does this tell us about sustainability? Some commentators have labelled the first 50 years post clearing as the 'organic agriculture phase', as no artificial inputs were used. But this period was clearly unsustainable. The advent of new varieties and fallowing increased yields, but the accelerated erosion from ploughed fields earns a failure status on sustainability grounds. The pasture revolution based on phosphorus and clover dramatically increased yields but did nothing to address the emerging salinity and acidity problems. The most recent innovation of disease controlling rotations increased yields again. Wheat production became profitable enough for farmers to purchase lime which addresses the acidity problem. Effective herbicides meant that farmers could control weeds without the plough, leaving the wheat stubble on the ground to protect it from erosion.

In this case study innovation, sustainability and increasing yields all appear to be positively correlated. But this is not the whole picture and global statistics are more sobering. In the period that the world's farmers doubled food production, nitrogen fertiliser use increased seven fold. Much of the excess nitrogen finds its way to lakes and rivers, where it becomes a pollutant, or escapes to the atmosphere where it acts as a greenhouse gas. Moreover the expansion of agriculture has contributed massively to loss of biodiversity with unknown consequences for future food production.

Notwithstanding all the innovation and new technology that has gone into the irrigation industry, it is estimated that over a million hectares of irrigated land world-wide is seriously degraded by waterlogging and salinity each year. Countries such as India and China are over-exploiting their groundwater reserves for food production. India produces 15% of its grain crop by pumping up groundwater reserved that are not being replenished.

The impacts of innovation also reach far into the social fabric of the rural areas. More and more large farms mean that small country towns are disappearing as the number of people needed to sustain banks, schools and hospitals falls below a critical level. Social capital in the countryside is declining as farming families feel more isolated and more exposed to the vagaries of global markets and variable climates.

In the end, sustainability may not be the most useful framework for thinking about agriculture. For a farm family to remain financially sustainable they may have to employ farming practices which a soil scientist would deem unsustainable. They will probably have to expand and buy out the neighbours, which the small country town mayor experiences as making the town services unsustainable. Whether we deem something as sustainable or not depends largely on the spatial and temporal scales that frame our concerns.

Sustainability also carries within it the notion of being able to keep doing things in a similar way into the future. A better framework may be that of maximising resilience. The resilience viewpoint anticipates that there will be all kinds of shocks and surprises. We have to develop systems that respond and recover from these shocks, not be overwhelmed by them. We are well aware of some of the shocks to the global food supply system, such as the almost doubling of food demand in the next 50 years in a situation where there is not much more suitable land or water than can be appropriated for agriculture. Other shocks are harder to predict. For example billions of people rely on the snowmelt from the Himalayas for irrigated crops, and the reliability of this supply is threatened by climate change and shifting rainfall patterns. Even harder to predict is the impact of new diseases that attack staple crops. Recently a new strain of rust fungus originated in Uganda, with the potential to decimate the 85% of the world's wheat crop, should it not be stopped in time.

The innovation that has so shaped agriculture operates at a global scale and selects primarily for economic efficiency, not sustainability. Economic efficiency tends to select against a diverse way of doing things and for long integrated industrial supply chains. In the same way that the home loan crisis in the USA snowballed into a global financial crisis, small disruptions to the global food system have quickly destabilised Developing Country governments. The problem is an over-connected system in which we do not detect and respond to the signals that things are going wrong until it's too late. Such a system fails the resilience test.

A resilient agriculture will have to rediscover a diverse way of doing things, even if this comes at a cost of economic efficiency. Diversity gives flexibility and helps to buffer against the inevitable and unexpected shocks of the future. We need the kind of innovation that doubled food production in the last forty years, but we need much more than that. We will need ways of farming that recycle nutrients from the cities; ways of farming that use less energy and water; ways of farming that are less susceptible to pests and disease. We will also have to ask ourselves how healthy our food system really is, as the number of obese in the world rival those who are undernourished and national health bills become overwhelmed by diet-related disease.

A sustainable or resilient agriculture will need a wave of innovation that surpasses the innovation ushered in through the Green Revolution from the 1960s. At this time it's by no means clear where this kind of innovation will come from.

---

*Thinking it through: where do I stand?*

Reflect on ways in which you are separated from the production of the food you eat. What technologies and innovations allow for this separation?

*How are traditional conceptions of sustainability inadequate for thinking about how the world feeds itself? (Think about scale, resilience etc).

*What are some of the key pressures on agriculture?

---

*Would you change what you ate if you there was evidence that the food you were eating was produced in ways that may be unsustainable or unethical?

* What will it take to stop obesity becoming the number one health problem in Developed Countries?

*Action: what can I do?*
Try producing some of your own food, for example by starting a school or community garden.

* Do an analysis of the industrial food chain that produces a fast food meal (see 'The Omnivores Dilemma' in Further reading below).

*Visit a local farm and see first hand how food is produced.

*Do an analysis of the amount of land it takes to feed yourself (you can also think about water and fertilizer). Does this change if you are a vegetarian?

## *Further reading*

Cribb, J. (2010). *The coming famine: The global food crisis and what we can do to avoid it.* Melbourne: CSIRO Publishing.
Pollan, M. (2006). *The omnivores dilemma: a natural history of four meals.* New York: Penguin Press.
Stirzaker, R. (2010). *Out of the Scientist's Garden: A story of water and food.* Melbourne: CSIRO Publishing.
Walker, B. & Salt, D. (2006). *Resilience thinking: sustaining ecosystems and people in a changing world.* Washington DC: Island Press.

# Chapter 16
## Water Security

*Sergey Volotovsky*
*Water Corporation of Western Australia, Perth, Australia*

### Introduction

The issue of water security[1] has become one of the most important challenges for humanity. Water is absolutely essential for all life, and most people know it. However, few people think about it in day-to-day life. Fewer still act and make decisions accordingly.

In this context the task of bringing up future generations of "water aware" leaders and decision makers becomes critical for sustainable development, regardless of the country. And it is hard to underestimate the crucial role that teachers play in performing this task.

This chapter will help you refresh and extend your knowledge of the key issues related to water security. It will also assist you with design of interesting lessons that will hopefully inspire your students to turn on the tap or walk to the water well with new awareness.

---

1. Water security is the capacity of a population to have a continuous access to potable water.

## *The issue*

Out of all the water on Earth, more than 97% is salt water and less than 3% is fresh. Furthermore, most of the fresh water is in ice caps and glaciers (which are rapidly melting), leaving only about 0.8% of the total water on Earth relatively easily available for everyday human use. In other words, if all the water on Earth fit in a 3.8 litres jug, relatively easily available fresh water would equal just over a tablespoonful.

Even though today desalination[2] technology makes it possible to tap into the ocean water supply and saline ground water for potable[3] purposes, it is still a relatively expensive and energy intensive strategy providing only a very small fraction of potable water globally, mainly in developed countries[4].

The tablespoonful out of a jug may not sound like a lot, but it provides for most of humanity's needs, including water for drinking, cooking, bathing, washing, agriculture and recreation. An average human in temperate climate conditions needs to consume about 2.6 litres of water a day (including water in food and beverages) to stay healthy, with another 15 or so litres a day required for basic needs such as cooking, washing and sanitation.

This spoonful also sustains all ecosystems and supports plants and animals on which we in turn intimately depend. For example, green plants produce vital oxygen we breathe and most of the food we eat, and they in turn ultimately depend on water. This is particularly obvious when a drought strikes a country where most of the population depends on water thirsty crops such as rice.

The issue of water security mostly revolves around this tablespoon. The problem is not only how much water is available in a particular country or community, but also what the quality of this water is, who owns and controls this water, how much it costs and how it is used.

The following facts may help to grasp the extent and complexity of the water security issue:

- Everyday millions of people (mostly women and young girls) spend hours walking to collect water from distant locations. Even when they get water, they often cannot be sure that it is safe to drink;

- Around 16% of the Earth's population (over a billion people) lack clean, safe drinking water. This number is predicted to double by 2025;

- Around 2.5 billion people don't have water for sanitation purposes;

- 88% of all waterborne diseases around the world are caused by unsafe drinking water, inadequate sanitation and poor hygiene;

---

2. Process of removing salt from ocean water and saline groundwater, also known as desalinisation.

3. Potable water – water that is safe to drink

4. Some countries, such as UAE, Saudi Arabia and Israel rely on desalination heavily for potable water supply

- These diseases kill over 1.6 million people every year, most of whom are children in developing countries;
- Most of these deaths are preventable and over 1 million lives could be saved every year through improved access to safe water and improved sanitation and hygiene, such as washing one's hands with soap or boiling water before drinking;
- An average family in the developed world uses about 1,900 litres of drinking quality water every day, which is about 50 times more than an average African family. Most of this water does not need to have been treated to the drinking quality standard.
- Many toilets use more water in one flush than many rural families in Africa have for one day of cleaning, cooking, drinking, and bathing;
- Climate change is expected to be responsible for about 20% of the global increase in water scarcity this century. The Intergovernmental Panel on Climate Change (IPCC) predicts that global warming will continue altering precipitation patterns around the world, melting mountain glaciers, and worsening the extremes of droughts and floods;
- More than half of the world's rivers and lakes are badly polluted.

The factors contributing to the water security issue around the world are numerous and vary greatly depending on the region. The most significant of these include:

- Population growth
- Water pollution (sewage, pesticides, fertilisers, industrial waste dumping, etc)
- Climate change
- Inadequate sanitation
- Lack of appropriate infrastructure
- Excessive abstraction and increasing salinity of ground water and soil
- Inefficient water use
- Urbanisation
- Terrorism (specifically targeting the critical water infrastructure)

It is also important to understand the historical, environmental, geographical and political aspects of the water security issue.

### *Historical context and future outlook*

The concept of water scarcity is relatively young. As can be seen from the Figure 1, fifty years ago, when the Earth's population was roughly half of what it is today, our relatives required on average a third of the volume of water we presently consume.

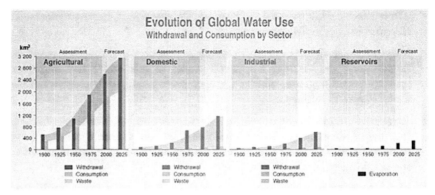

Figure 1: Evolution of Global Water Use[5]

Today, the pressure on water resources is much higher and competition for water is much more intense. Both are predicted to worsen significantly in the coming decades. According to estimates by the United Nations, by 2025 two out of three people in the world could be living under conditions of water scarcity (of which 1.8 billion people could be living in regions with severe water scarcity).

The figure also shows that there is a growing gap between water withdrawal and consumption. In other words, the proportion of wasted water has been increasing across the agricultural, domestic and industrial sectors.

## *Environmental*

The total amount of water on Earth is approximately 1,360,000,000 km³ and remains relatively stable. This amount is distributed on, under and above the surface of the planet and is collectively referred to as the hydrosphere. All this water is interconnected through the continuous water cycle shown on Figure 2.

---

5.Source: Igor A. Shiklomanov, State Hydrological Institute (SHI, St Petersburg, Russia) and UNESCO (Paris), 1999.

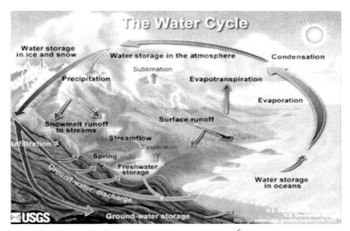

Figure 2: The Water Cycle[6]

Water is not only in the clouds, rivers and oceans, it is also within us and all other living organisms on the planet. An average adult human's body is about 60% water, and in a newborn baby water can account for as much as 75% body weight.

Within the water cycle, one particular molecule of water from today's morning coffee could have been drunk by a dinosaur millions of years ago, and washed the hands of an Egyptian pharaoh much later. Now you drink it and it may soon end up in your body cell, then leave the body with the exhaled water vapour or evaporated sweat and join billions of other water molecules in the air to form clouds that will eventually precipitate.

Your little molecule may then become a part of a river or the ocean and end up in the body of a fish that your future relative will consume in a hundred years' time, and so the cycle continues again and again.

The water cycle helps to understand how even a slight change in precipitation patterns floods one region, while causing a severe draught in another[7], or how dumping toxic waste in the river in one country could compromise the potable water resources and essential ecosystems (i.e. fisheries) in another country downstream of the same river.

It is crucial to remember that humans are a part of nature and that flow of water for human use is intrinsically entwined into the water cycle. Therefore the key is for the humans' consumption of water to be in harmony with the water needs of the ecosystems on which we in turn depend.

This means, amongst other things, not over-abstracting the groundwater resources at a faster rate than they get replenished, not polluting the waterways and minimising the human contribution to climate change.

---

6.Source: John M. Evans, US Department of the Interior, US Geological Survey, 2011

7.Climate change has been shown to severely affect the rainfall patterns around the world

## *Geographical*

Even though the water cycle does not recognise country borders, the issue of water scarcity has very different faces in different parts of the world. In some countries children and women have to walk miles every day for fresh water, while in others obtaining drinking water is as simple as turning on the water tap.

Examples from such places as Australia, where severe droughts may be devastating crops on one side of the continent while the other side is suffering from unprecedented floods, also show that even within the same country water security may have very different meanings.

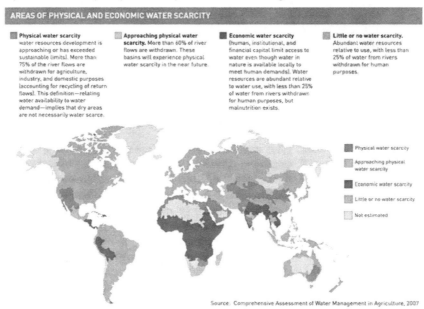

AREAS OF PHYSICAL AND ECONOMIC WATER SCARCITY

■ **Physical water scarcity** water resources development is approaching or has exceeded sustainable limits). More than 75% of the river flows are withdrawn for agriculture, industry, and domestic purposes (accounting for recycling of return flows). This definition—relating water availability to water demand—implies that dry areas are not necessarily water scarce.

■ **Approaching physical water scarcity.** More than 60% of river flows are withdrawn. These basins will experience physical water scarcity in the near future.

■ **Economic water scarcity** (human, institutional, and financial capital limit access to water even though water in nature is available locally to meet human demands). Water resources are abundant relative to water use, with less than 25% of water from rivers withdrawn for human purposes, but malnutrition exists.

■ **Little or no water scarcity.** Abundant water resources relative to use, with less than 25% of water from rivers withdrawn for human purposes.

■ Physical water scarcity
■ Approaching physical water scarcity
■ Economic water scarcity
■ Little or no water scarcity
□ Not estimated

Source: Comprehensive Assessment of Water Management in Agriculture, 2007

Figure 3: The World Water Scarcity in 2007[8]

Figure 3 demonstrates an important distinction between the physical and economic water scarcity. Physical water scarcity occurs when development of water resources is approaching or has exceeded sustainable limits, while economic water scarcity is characterised by human, institutional and financial capital limitations even though water in nature is locally available.

Regions that are most affected by water scarcity, as seen from Figure 3, include The Middle East, Africa, parts of the Americas, Australia and Asia. Because these countries sell goods (such as clothes, food etc) to the other

---

8. Source: Comprehensive Assessment of Water Management in Agriculture, IWMI 2007.

countries, and production of these goods requires water, the issue of water scarcity has flow-on effects far beyond the borders of the worst affected countries[9].

For example, it takes about 11,000 litres of water to manufacture a pair of blue jeans. If these jeans are coming from northern China, one of the world's hotspots in terms of physical water scarcity, all the embedded water "flows" to the other countries further increasing pressure on northern China's water resources.

## *Political*

In November 2002, the United Nations Committee on Economic, Cultural and Social Rights (CECSR) declared access to water a basic human right, reflecting the importance of water to human life and the ongoing challenges societies face in providing water for all their citizens.

Successful execution of this right by country leaders around the world remains one of the key challenges in humanity's quest for water security. Because of the absolute value water has for human life and development, and because of its increasing scarcity, it is becoming one of the central topics for regional and international policy development.

Addressing this issue adequately on a global level will also likely be one of the key conditions to sustaining world peace.

Overall, the political aspects of water are very complex and country specific, and will not be further discussed in this chapter[10].

## *Links with other aspects of sustainability*

The water security issue is intrinsically linked with other global challenges, such as climate change, food shortage, global poverty, ecosystems degradation and so on. It is also a very good example of how the economical,

---

9. This concept is known as virtual water (also referred to as embedded, embodied or hidden water) – the total amount of water used and polluted in a production of a particular good or service. It is often used in the context of water footprint – total volume of fresh water used to produce all goods and services consumed by the individual or community or produced by the business. Virtual water is often broken down into three components: green, blue and grey. Green virtual water refers to the volume of rainwater that evaporated during the production process (mainly relevant to agricultural products). Blue virtual water is the volume of surface water that evaporated as a result of the production. In case of industrial production it is equal to the water withdrawn from ground or surface water that evaporates. Grey virtual water is the water that gets polluted as a result of production.

10. Please refer to the Useful Resources in the end of this chapter for more information. Murray-Darling Basin case study is also a good example of the political aspects significance.

environmental and social aspects of sustainability are all interconnected. These links are further explored in the following scenarios and Case Study 1: Murray-Darling Basin in the end of this chapter.

## Scenario 1

Consider a developing country in Africa, where children and women have to travel miles every day to collect water for basic needs, which takes time they could be spending on education. This in turn undermines their ability to contribute to the country's economy and development in the future. In the same country the lack of education about adequate hygiene and basic water disinfection contributes to thousands of people getting sick and unable to work, which again affects the country's overall progress. At the same time companies and individuals may be selling drinking water at unregulated prices, often worsening the population's financial burden.

## Scenario 2

Imagine a clothes factory which takes thousands of litres of fresh water a day from a nearby river and dumps toxic liquid waste right back. This factory provides jobs and brings money into the country's economy on one hand, but on the other hand it kills the river dependent ecosystems, undermines the city's fresh water supply which is likely to drive the price of potable water up. It is also likely to directly affect the health of the people (including the factory workers).

Or imagine a massive dam which may be providing important flood protection services, serving as drinking water reservoir and possibly generating cheap electricity by utilising the energy of cascading water. However, the construction of this dam could have displaced millions of people, destroyed thousands of hectares of pristine forests, drained the downstream waterways thereby affecting the local ecosystems, disrupted fish migration patterns and increased the risk to downstream communities in case of infrastructure failure (such as dam wall collapse due to terrorist attack or earthquake).

In this context it becomes imperative to understand how a particular entity (business, dam, town, country) affects the natural water cycle in terms of both quantity and quality, how economic, social and environmental costs and benefits stack up and what can be done to minimise or neutralise the negative impacts.

## Scenario 3

Consider a global company which donates 10c from every bottle of water sold to the projects aimed at addressing water security in developing world.

The intention of this company is honourable and potential positive financial impact could be considerable, looking at the size of the market. At the same time, there is a great irony in such a campaign, as there is much more to bottled water than meets the eye.

To put this in the context, in 2006 the global bottled water market was estimated to be worth $60 billion US dollars, with the total volume of over 190 billion litres distributed in around 200 billion bottles. Production and delivery of bottled water uses 17 million barrels of oil every year, which is enough to fuel about one million cars for a year.

Producing and delivering a litre of bottled water can emit hundreds of times more greenhouse gases[11] than a litre of tap water, and be up to 10,000 times more expensive (about US$2.64/litre of bottled water against roughly $0.0004/litre of tap water).

Drinking bottled water could definitely be justified in an emergency relief situation when centralised supply is disrupted and no other sources are available. However, under normal circumstances when tap water is available and is of reasonable drinking quality (and potential residual taste concerns could often be easily solved with a simple sand and carbon filter), its environmental impacts should be considered.

## Scenario 4

Consider a city in the developed world which relies mostly on nuclear power to produce energy. Most people know that it takes energy to collect, treat and deliver drinking water and manage wastewater. For example, as much as one-quarter to one-half of the electricity used by most US cities is consumed at municipal water and wastewater treatment facilities.

The links between energy and water are often referred to as *water-energy nexus*. What is often forgotten or overlooked is that these links are bilateral – it takes energy to produce water, but it also takes water to produce energy. An average nuclear power plant may require about 2.7 billion litres of water per day of operation for cooling, while a typical coal powered plant may require about 46.5 million litres of water per day[12].

Then there are nuclear safety concerns, potential environmental issues associated with altered chemical and physical characteristics of cooling water that is returned to the environment, potential power shortages if reduced rainfall does not adequately replenish bodies of water used for nuclear power plant cooling and many other factors which emphasise the importance of adequately considering the water-energy nexus[13].

---

11. Gases which block the sunlight reflected off the Earth surface, thereby contributing to the "greenhouse effect", such as carbon dioxide, methane, water vapour, nitrous oxide, ozone etc.

12. These figures are for indicative purposes only. Real water consumption would largely depend on the size and type of the plant, cooling technology and other factors. Most of this water would be returned to the environment.

13. The concept of water-energy nexus is not limited to nuclear power plants and refers to general links between water and energy, including such examples as high electricity consumption by desalination plants, usage of water to grow crops that could be used as bio-fuels, using the energy of flowing water to generate electricity in hydro-power plants and so on.

These scenarios are very general and represent only a scratch on the surface of an iceberg of the global water security issue. However, they
serve as a reminder that water flows through everything, both literally
and figuratively.

### *What is being done and what needs to happen?*

As is usually the case, global issues mean global solutions and opportunities.
The issue of global water scarcity today is largely in the spotlight of international, regional and local decision making. Thousands of projects are operating all around the world at all levels, aimed at addressing this issue one way
or another[14]. Countries are also sobering up to the need for radical water efficiency, sustainable agriculture, Water Sensitive Urban Design[15] and water
recycling.

However, there is much more that can and should be done, and as Ma-
hatma Ghandi brilliantly put it, we personally should be the change we want
to see in the world. Local individual solutions will vary, however there are
some basic actions that will be more or less applicable to most people in developed countries. The below list[16] can serve as a basic guide for individual
action on water scarcity.

- Choose outdoor landscaping appropriate for your climate. Native plants
  and grasses that thrive on natural rainfall only are the best choice.

- Install water efficient showerheads. By saving hot water you will also reduce your energy bill.

- If you are after a new toilet, buy a low-volume, ultra low-volume, or dual-
  flush model.

- Fix leaking taps. All those wasted drops add up – sometimes to 70-80
  litres a day.

- Run your dishwasher and washing machine only when full. When it is
  time to replace them, buy a water and energy efficient model. Remember, saving water saves energy, and saving energy saves water.

- Eat less meat, especially beef. A typical hamburger can take about 2,384
  litres of water to produce.

- Don't buy stuff you don't really need. Everything takes water to make. So
  if we buy less, we shrink our water footprint.

---

14. For example, refer to the Water for People and National Geographic Atlas for Actions in the Useful Resources in the end of this chapter.

15. Water Sensitive Urban Design (WSUD) is a holistic approach to the planning and
design of urban development that aims to minimise impacts on natural water cycle
and protect the health of aquatic ecosystems.

16. Adopted from National Geographic.

- Recycle plastics, glass, metals, and paper. Buy re-usable products rather than throw-aways, as it takes water to make almost everything.

- Turn off the tap while brushing your teeth and washing the dishes. Shave a minute or two off your shower time. Millions of people doing even the little things make a whole lot of difference on the global scale.

- Know and enjoy the source of your drinking water – the river, lake, or aquifer that supplies your home. Once you know and enjoy it, you will care about it.

- Participate in local or international projects[17] related to water security through donations or volunteering.

### Case study 1 – Murray-Darling Basin, Australia

Figure 4: The Murray-Darling Basin

The Murray-Darling Basin (Basin) is a large geographical area in the south-eastern corner of Australia, sprawling across the parts of the states of New South Wales, Queensland, Victoria and South Australia (Figure 4[18]). It drains approximately 14% of the Australian land mass and represents the most significant agricultural area in Australia.

In the last decades the Basin has been under enormous stress mainly from excessive allocation of water for irrigation purposes and prolonged droughts. As a result the wetlands, rivers, forests, floodplains and other

---

17. Refer to the Useful Resources in the end of this chapter.

18. Source: Wikipedia

ecosystems in the Basin have been severely affected. Scientific evidence has raised serious concerns about the Basin survival under the current management model.

To address these challenges, the Murray-Darling Basin Authority was formed in 2008 with the main responsibility for planning and integrated management of water resources of the Murray-Darling Basin. In 2010 the Authority released a major document called the *Guide to the Proposed Murray-Darling Basin Plan* which outlined a draft pathway to secure the long-term ecological health of the Basin, with water allocation cuts being one of the main strategies.

The Plan was welcomed by the environmental groups but heavily criticised by many irrigators, farmers and local governments. The main concern voiced by these groups related to the potential negative impacts that the proposed water allocation cuts would have on the local economies. A subsequent legal advice from the Australian government emphasised that the plan would need to give "equal weight" to the environmental, social and economic impacts of proposed strategies. The controversial discussion continues and the release of the final plan has been delayed until 2012.

This case study is a great example of the interconnectedness between the social, economic and environmental aspects of sustainability. It is also a good reminder that while indeed all these aspects need to be weighted and balanced, in the longer term local communities and economies ultimately depend on the ecological health of the Basin. If it collapses under the weight of over-allocation and climate change, the social and economic impacts are likely to be far greater than those associated with water allocation cuts to ensure adequate environmental flows.

### Case study 2 – Play Pumps

A South African company Roundabout Outdoor developed a very simple and effective way of providing water to communities, which is literally fun to operate (Figure 5). As the merry-go-round spins, the groundwater gets pumped seven metres up into the storage tank (Figure 6). Two sides of the tank contain posters with educational messages, such as reminders to wash hands or talk to children about sex, while the other two house advertisements which partially help to pay for the pumps.

The whole system costs around US$14,000 and there are currently over 800 of those installed in four African countries, providing water for almost two million people.

Figure 5: Play Pumps in action[19]

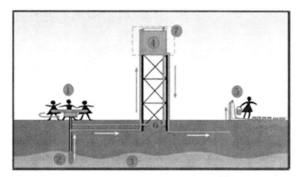

Figure 6: how play pumps work[20]

This is a good example of how multiple objectives (water source, education and activity for children) are achieved simultaneously and how the local communities can be directly involved in addressing the water security issues.

## Teaching Water Security

A good lesson on water security would look very differently depending on the country, student's age and level of knowledge, available materials and equipment, objectives and duration of the class and other factors.

However, there are a few suggestions that could be applicable in most situations.

---

19. Source: http://www.aidforafrica.org
20. Source: http://azsustainability.com

- Be clear on what knowledge or skills specifically you would like the students to walk away with.

- Geographical, political and cultural specifics of the water security issue should be considered when designing the lesson.

- Audio/visual materials, such as short movies or cartoons, online video-games, pictures, handouts, jugs of water, contour maps etc are usually very helpful in delivering messages[21].

- Key concepts such as importance of water for all life, natural water cycle, quantity and quality aspects of water security will help the students to put things into perspective.

## *Conclusion*

The issue of water security is extremely complex and has many different faces depending on the geographical, political, social, economic, environmental and other factors in a particular region at a particular point in time. It is also intrinsically connected with most other global challenges.

While different aspects could be in focus of a particular lesson, it is important to keep the big picture in mind and bring up appropriate links where relevant. Finally, it is crucial to evoke the sense of individual participation in the solution to local and global water security issues.

---

*Thinking in through: where do I stand? Pointers for further discussion*

Do I feel the water crisis? Why/why not?

Where do I spend water? Where could I spend less water?

Where does the water I drink come from? Do I know anyone who doesn't have adequate access to drinking water and sanitation?

How would my life change if I had to walk for four hours every day to collect fresh water?

What else could I do to address the global water security issue?

---

*Action: what can I do?*

*Activity 1 - Breathing on a mirror*

Get students in the class to gently breathe on a mirror and observe "misting" caused by condensation of the warmer water vapour in the exhaled air on the cooler smooth surface of a mirror. This could serve as a visual demonstration that water is within us, and that it can be in the form of a gas (water vapour), not only liquid. Equally, a piece of ice could demonstrate the solid state of water.

---

21. Refer to the Useful Resources in the end of this chapter.

*Activity 2 - Water Efficiency*

Ask the students to pair up or form a few larger groups and discuss where they use water at home. The results could be written on the class board or pieces of paper and presented back to the class. Ask the students which activities require most water. Depending on the audience and objectives of the class, this could be limited to direct water use (i.e. shower, irrigation etc) or be expanded to include virtual water as well (i.e. how much water it took to produce the t-shirt they wear).

Then ask what students would do differently to use less water at home. Be ready to give some examples.

*Activity 3 - The Journey of Water*

Get a glass of water from the local tap (if applicable) or another source from which children would generally get their water, and explore with them where this water came from (both physically and historically).

*Activity 4 - Analysing the case study*

Get your students to analyse a case study, such as Murray-Darling Basin mentioned in this chapter or something relevant locally. Potential questions could include:

What is the issue? Who is affected by it and who is in a position to address the issue?

What are their interests and concerns?

What is most important for the community as a whole?

What are the economic, environmental and social aspects of this issue?

How can these aspects be balanced? What was done about this issue and what are the strengths and weaknesses of these actions?

If you were the decision maker, what would you do differently?

Make sure there is enough information in the case study to develop solutions, but not so much that the answers would be obvious. A good technique is to mix relevant and irrelevant bits of information to stretch your students' thinking.

**Add to your grid**

What are the spin off effects of your action? How will it impinge on other aspects of sustainability?

## Further reading

Black M. & King J. (2009). *The Atlas of Water, Second Edition – Mapping The World's Most Critical Source*. California: University of California Press.

Pearce, F. (2006). *When the Rivers Run Dry. Water – The Defining Crisis of the Twenty-first Century*. Boston: Beacon Press.

Solomon, S. (2011). *Water: The Epic Struggle for Wealth, Power and Civilization*. New York: Harper Collins.

## *Useful Resources*

Murray-Darling Basin Authority Website http://www.mdba.gov.au/

National Geographic Interactive online video game on river protection
http://www.nationalgeographic.com/bluewaterproject/game.html

National Geographic Global Atlas of Action - freshwater and other issues
http://www.actionatlas.org/conservation/freshwater/uid/
plaB6365564D03FDC339

National Geographic online videos on water scarcity http://environ-
ment.nationalgeographic.com.au/environment/freshwater/
?source=NavEnvFresh

National Geographic Green Guide – practical sustainability advice for
every day http://environment.nationalgeographic.com/environ-
ment/green-guide/?source=NavEnvGG

Diary of Jay-Z: Water For Life. The documentary about hip-hop impres-
ario and President and CEO of Def Jam Records, Shawn "Jay-Z"
Carter, teaming up with the UN to explore the water crisis in
Africa. http://www.un.org/works/sub3.asp?lang=en&id=49

UNICEF and Water (Children and Water) http://www.unicef.org/wes/in-
dex.html

PlayPumps International http://www.playpumps.org

UN Water website http://www.unwater.org/index.html

UNESCO: Evolution of Water Use http://www.unesco.org/water/wwap/
wwdr/wwdr3/pdf/18_WWDR3_ch_7.pdf

Water for People – Charity organisation founded by the American Water
Works Association http://www.waterforpeople.org


## *Acknowledgements*

The author would like to acknowledge William Varey, Irina Volotovskaya,
Cilla De Lacy, Sharon Dignard, Margaret Toohey and Mark Handyside for
their comments.

# Chapter 17
## Sustainable Transport

### How City Form Shapes our Choices, a city that builds elements of Walking centres around Transit corridors –

*Peter Newman*
*Curtin University Sustainability Policy (CUSP) Institute,*
*Curtin University, Australia*

### *The issue*

Sustainable transport is about reducing cars and trucks and reducing the carbon and air quality pollutants in vehicle fuels; this means addressing a range of measures like carbon taxes and how much we invest in sustainable transport infrastructure. In this chapter I want to look at something more fundamental: how our cities need to change so that sustainable transport becomes viable and effective.

### *Urban form and transport*

Cities are shaped by many historical and geographical features, but at any stage in a city's history the patterns of land use can be changed by altering its transportation priorities. Italian physicist Cesare Marchetti has argued that there is a universal travel time budget of around 1 hour on average per person per day. This *Marchetti Constant* has been found to apply in every city in our Global Cities Data Base as well as in data on UK cities for the last 600 years. The biological or psychological basis of this Marchetti Constant seems to be a need for a more reflective or restorative period between home and work, but it cannot go for too long before people become very frustrated due to the need to be more occupied rather than just 'wasting' time between activities.

The Marchetti Constant therefore helps us to see how cities are shaped. Cities grow to being 'one hour wide' based on the speed with which people can move in them. So far we have had three city types emerge:

**Walking Cities** have existed for the past 8000 years as no other form of transport was available to enable people to get across their cities other than at walking speed of around 5-8km/h. Thus Walking Cities were and remain dense, mixed-use areas that are no more than 5-8 kilometers across. These were the major urban form for 8,000 years, but substantial parts of cities like Ho Chi Minh City, Mumbai, and Hong Kong, for example, retain the character of a walking city. Kraców is mostly a walking city. In wealthy cities like New York, London, Vancouver, Melbourne and Sydney, the central areas are predominantly walking cities in character. Many cities worldwide are trying to reclaim the walkability of their city centre and they find that they can't do this unless they have the form of ancient walking cities. Melbourne has done some remarkable rejuvenation of its central city to make it more walkable.

**Transit Cities** from 1850-1950 were based on trams and trains which could travel at around 20-30km/h; this meant they could spread out 20-30 kilometers, with dense centers and corridors following the rail lines and stations. Most European and wealthy Asian cities retain this form, as do the old inner cores in US, Australian, and Canadian cities. Many developing cities in Asia, Africa, and Latin America have the dense corridor form of a transit city, but they do not always have the transit systems to support them, so they become car-saturated. Most of these emerging cities are now building the transit systems that suit their urban form, e.g. China is building 82 metro rail systems and India is building 14. Cities without reasonable densities around train stations are finding that they need to build up the numbers of people and jobs near stations otherwise not enough activity is there to support such sustainable transport.

**Automobile Cities** from the 1950s onward could spread 50-80 kilometers in all directions and at low density because cars could average 50-80 km/h while traffic levels are low. These cities spread out in every direction due to the flexibility of cars and were given a few buses to support these sprawling suburbs. Canadian, Australian, US and New Zealand cities that were developed in this way are now reaching the limits of the Marchetti Constant of a half-hour car commute as they sprawl outwards. The freeways that service such areas are full at peak times and commuters are unable to keep within a reasonable travel time budget. This is now a serious political issue as outer suburban residents are demanding fast rail links that can beat the traffic. As well many people are leaving these areas and moving to better locations where they can live within their travel time budget. The first evidence is now appearing that these Automobile Cities are coming back in and reducing their car use.

Cities, like growing megacities or rapidly sprawling ones, are constantly facing the need to adapt their land use or infrastructure to the travel time budget. They may not realize that is what they are doing but if the Marchetti Constant is exceeded then markets and politics invariably ensure people adapt by moving closer to their work or finding a better transportation option. The search for better options can form the basis of social movements that seek to provide greener transportation.

### *Land use for sustainable transport*

Figure 1 from the Global Cities Database shows the huge range in per capita fuel use that characterises cities across the world. They all have a combination of these three city types – Walking, Transit and Automobile Cities.

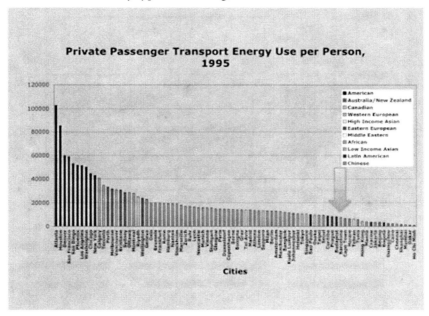

Figure 1: Fuel use per person in cities across the world. Source:
Kenworthy and Laube et al, 1999

The city arrowed – Barcelona – uses just 8 GJ per person compared to 103 GJ at Atlanta and around 35 GJ per person in Australian cities; huge variation and yet they all have similar per capita levels of wealth. The difference seems to be that Barcelona is substantially a Walking City with some elements of a Transit City and almost no Automobile City whereas Atlanta is almost completely an Automobile City; the Australian cities are somewhere in the middle with a mixture of all three city types.

The broader picture is expressed in Figure 2 where travel patterns (as reflected by either per capita car use or passenger transport energy use) is exponentially related to density of urban activity. Atlanta is six people per hectare and Barcelona is 200 per hectare.

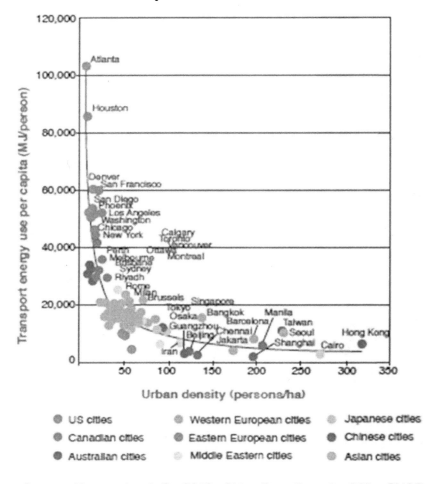

Source: Kenworthy, J. R., 2010, *Cities Data Base for 2005*, CUSP,

Figure 2: Transport fuel per person and Urban Density (people per hectare)

The same patterns can be seen across cities where often the centres are Walking Cities, the middle suburbs are Transit Cities and the outer suburbs are Automobile Cities. This can be seen in Figure 3 where Melbourne and Sydney data are shown covering transport greenhouse gases per person by suburb versus the density of residents and jobs.

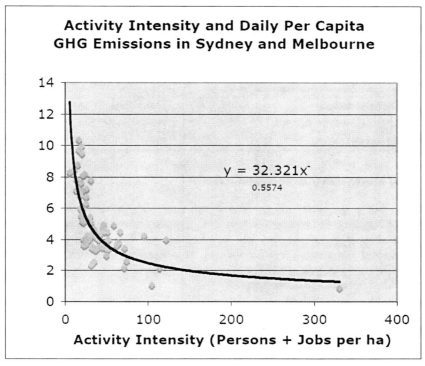

Figure 3: Transport fuel (expressed as greenhouse gas per person) vs Density (people and jobs per hectare) in suburbs of Melbourne and Sydney

Questions of wealth do not appear to be driving this phenomenon, as there is an inverse relationship between urban intensity and household income in Australian cities – outer suburbs are poorer and yet households in these areas can drive from 3 to 10 times as much as households in the city centre. As the data on Melbourne below (Table 1) indicate, the poorer households are driving more, using public transport less and walking less.

There are obviously other factors than the intensity of activity affecting transport, otherwise there would be an even stronger relationship within cities between activity intensity and transport patterns; such factors include the network of services provided, income, fuel prices, cultural factors etc, but all of these can also be linked back to the intensity of activity in various ways. Thus although many discussions have tried to explain transport in non-land use terms, the data suggest that the physical layout of a city does have a fundamental impact on movement patterns. This chapter will now try to take the next step and explain how the relationship between transport and activity intensity works.

Table 1: Differences in wealth and travel patterns from
the urban core to the fringe in Melbourne.
Source: (Kenworthy and Newman, (2001)

| | Core | Inner | Middle | Fringe |
|---|---|---|---|---|
| Percentage of Households earning >$70,000 pa | 12 | 11 | 10 | 6 |
| Car Use (trips/day/cap) | 2.12 | 2.52 | 2.86 | 3.92 |
| Public Transport (trips/day/cap | 0.66 | 0.46 | 0.29 | 0.21 |
| Walk/bike (trips/day/cap | 2.62 | 1.61 | 1.08 | 0.81 |

## *What densities help walking and transit?*

From the two density graphs above and from data in areas where viable transit happens and where viable walking happens, there seems to be a density at around 35 people and jobs per hectare for transit and around 100 people and jobs per hectare for walking. How can these numbers be understood in terms of guidelines for development to ensure transit and walking are viable options for more people?

A pedestrian catchment area or "Ped Shed", based on a 10 minute walk, creates an area of approximately 220 to 550 hectares for walking speeds of 5 to 8 km/h. Thus for an area of around 300 hectare developed at 35 people and jobs per hectare, there is a threshold requirement of approximately 10,000 residents and jobs within this 10 minute walking area. The range would be from about 8,000 to 19,000 based on the 5 to 8 km/h speeds. Some centres will have a lot more jobs than others, but the important physical planning guideline is to have a combined minimum activity intensity of residents and jobs necessary for a reasonable local centre and a public transport service to support it. The number of residents or jobs can be increased to the full 10,000, or any combination of these, as residents and jobs are similar in terms of transport demand. Either way, the number suggests a threshold below which transit services become non-competitive without relying primarily on car access to extend the catchment area.

Many new car dependent suburbs have densities more like 12 per hectare and hence have only 1/3 of the population and jobs required for a viable centre. When a centre is built for such suburbs it tends to just have shops with job densities little higher than the surrounding population densities. Hence the Ped Shed never reaches the kind of intensity that enables a walkable environment to be created which can ensure viable transit. Many new developments are primarily emphasising changes to improve the legibility and permeability of street networks, with less attention to the density of activity. As important as such changes are to the physical layout of streets, we should not be surprised when the resulting centres aren't able to attract viable commercial arrangements and have only weak public transport.

However, centres can be built in stages with much lower numbers to begin with, provided the goal is to reach a density of at least 35 per hectare through enabling infill at higher intensities.

If a Walking City centre is required then a density of 100 per hectare is needed. This gives an idea of the kind of activity that a Town Centre would need approximately 100,000 residents and jobs within this 10 minute walking area. The range again is from around 70,000 to 175,000 people and jobs. This number could provide for a viable Town Centre based on standard servicing levels for a range of activities. Fewer numbers than this means services in a Town Centre are non-viable and it becomes necessary to increase the centre's catchment through widespread dependence on driving from much farther afield. This also means that the human design qualities of the centre are compromised because of the need for excessive amounts of parking. Of course, many driving trips within a walking Ped Shed still occur. However, if sufficient amenities and services are provided then only short car trips are needed, which is still part of making the centre less car dependent. 'Footloose jobs', particularly those related to the global economy, can theoretically go anywhere in a city and can make the difference between a viable centre or not. However, there is considerable evidence that such jobs are locating in dense centres of activity due to the need for networking and quick 'face to face' meetings between professionals. High amenity, walking scale environments are better able to attract such jobs because they offer the kind of environmental quality, liveability and diversity that these professionals are seeking.

*Politics of sustainable transport*

Developing more sustainable transport and land use patterns has been made difficult over recent decades, as car dependent suburbs have been facilitated by the construction of fast roads. Until recently it has been hard to do anything for either public transport infrastructure (especially rail) or walking/cycling in centres. Mostly, such changes have been demanded by the public and have been achieved through political intervention.

The reason for this seems to be a professional reticence to push sustainable modes and in particular a deep seated anti-rail sentiment. The idea that 'anything a train can do a bus can do better and cheaper' has remained dominant; this has meant that in cities where bus systems are stuck in traffic that the ideology of car dependence has been meekly acceded to. This is seen in organisations such as the International Energy Agency and World Bank. Such analyses accept second best for transit systems and, in essence, car traffic is seen as inevitable and requiring higher priority. Car dependence has been the major outcome. This is highly problematic as it is simply not sustainable from either a local or global perspective.

Most citizens who experience car dependence, and have long commutes stuck in traffic, can understand the phenomenon, since they directly feel and bear its economic, social and environmental consequences. They want other options provided for them. As cities continue to evolve, the politics of sustainable transport will demand both more liveable and less car dependent options for the future.

The key to this move towards sustainability is better provision of access to transit that is faster than cars along corridors, and better provision for walking and cycling in local areas, associated with a supportive land use structure of intensive centres with minimum land use activity intensity of at least 35 people and jobs per hectare. This is due to a fundamental need to ensure that the more sustainable transport modes have a competitive speed advantage for long trips (transit) and for short trips (bike/walk) within centres.

Such change is evolutionary but it will always require political leadership.

## The demise of the automobile city?

In 2009 the Brookings Institution were the first to recognize a new phenomenon in the world's developed cities – declines in car use. The data below confirm this trend and now much internet traffic is discussing the phenomenon of 'peak car use'. Peak car use suggests that we are witnessing the end of building cities around cars – at least in the developed world. The peak car use phenomenon suggests we may now be witnessing the demise of further Automobile City building.

## The data on car use trends.

The trend in per capita car use decline started in 2004 in US cities. They were able to show that this trend was occurring in most US cities and by 2010 was evident in absolute declines in car use. The data are summarized in Figure 4 along with the rising fuel price which must be one of the causes of this phenomenon.

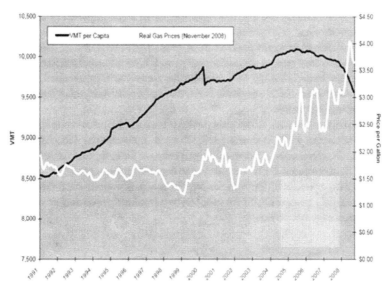

Source: Traffic Volume Trends and Energy Information Administration

Figure 4: Peaking of US vehicle miles of travel (VMT)

A similar trend is now clear in European and Australian cities and the peak came at a similar time – 2004. The data are shown in Figure 5.

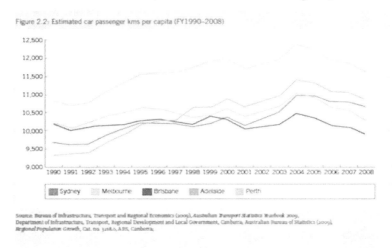

Figure 5: Peaking of car use in Australian cities

Millard-Ball and Schipper examined the trends in eight industrialized countries that demonstrate what they call 'peak travel'. They conclude that:

*"Despite the substantial cross national differences, one striking commonality emerges: travel activity has reached a plateau in all eight countries in this analysis. The plateau is even more pronounced when considering only private vehicle use, which has declined in recent years in most of the eight countries. ... Most aggregate energy forecasts and many regional travel demand models are based on the core assumption that travel demand will continue to rise in line with income. As we have shown in the paper, this assumption is one that planners and policy makers should treat with extreme caution."*

European cities that show this pattern include London that has declined 1.2%, Stockholm 3.7%, Vienna 7.6%, Zurich 4.7%. In the US, Atlanta went down 10.1%, Houston 15.2% (both from extraordinarily high levels of car use in 1995), Los Angeles declined 2.0% and San Francisco 4.8%.
Peak car use appears to be happening. It is a major historical discontinuity that was largely unpredicted by most urban professionals and academics. So what is causing this to occur?

### *The possible causes of 'Peak Car Use'*

The following six factors are examined and then their overlaps and interdependencies are explored afterwards:

1. *Hitting the Marchetti Wall*

   As outlined above, the travel time budget matters. Freeways designed to get people quickly around cities have become car parks at peak hours. Travel times have grown to the point where cities based around cars are becoming dysfunctional. As cities have filled with cars the limit to the spread of the city has become more and more apparent with the politics of road rage becoming a bigger part of everyday life and many people just choosing to live closer in.

   The travel time budget limit is observable in most Australian and US cities where the politics of transport has been based on the inability of getting sufficient road capacity to enable the travel time budget to be maintained under one hour. Thus there has been a shift to providing faster and higher capacity public transport based on the growing demand to go around traffic-filled corridors or to service growing inner area districts. At the same time the politics of planning in the past decade has turned irrevocably to enabling greater redevelopment and regeneration of suburbs at higher densities closer in to where most destinations are located. The Automobile City seems to have hit the wall.

2. *The Growth of Public Transport*

   The extraordinary revival of public transport in Australian and American cities is demonstrated in Figures 6 and 7.

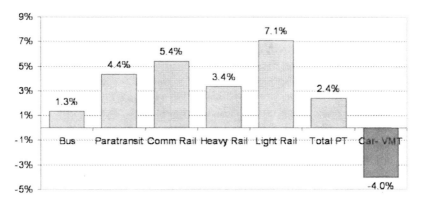

Figure 6: Recent strong growth in US transit use and declining car use

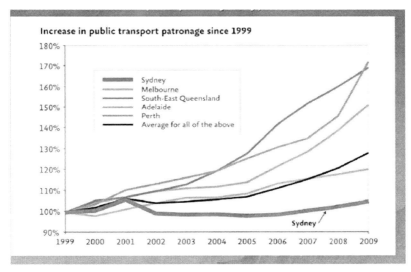

Figure 7: Growth in transit use in Australian cities since 1999

The global cities data currently being updated show that in ten major US cities from 1995 to 2005 transit boardings grew 12% from 60 to 67 per capita, five Canadian cities grew 8% from 140 to 151, four Australian capital cities rose 6% from 90 to 96 boardings per capita, while four major European cities grew from 380 to 447 boardings per capita or 18%. The growth in transit was always seen by transport planners as a small part of the transport task and car use growth would continue unabated. However, there is an exponential relationship between car use and public transport use that indicates how significant the impact of transit can be. By increasing transit per capita the use of cars per capita is predicted to go down exponentially. This is the so-called 'transit leverage' effect. Thus even small increases in transit can begin to put a large dent in car use growth and eventually will cause it to peak and decline.

3. *The Reversal of Urban Sprawl*

The turning back in of cities leads to increases in density rather than the continuing declines that have characterized the growth phase of Automobile Cities in the past 50 years. The data on density suggest that the peak in decline has occurred and cities are now coming back in faster than they are going out. Table 2 contains data on a sample of cities in Australia, the USA, Canada and Europe showing urban densities from 1960 to 2005 that clearly demonstrate this turning point in the more highly automobile-dependent cities. In the small sample of European cities, densities are still declining due to *shrinkage* or absolute reductions in population, but the data clearly show the rate of decline in urban density slowing down and almost stabilizing as re-urbanisation occurs.

Table 2: Trends in urban density in some US, Canadian,
Australian and European cities, 1960-2005

| Cities | 1960 Urban density persons/ha | 1970 Urban density persons/ha | 1980 Urban density persons/ha | 1990 Urban density persons/ha | 1995 Urban density persons/ha | 2005 Urban density persons/ha |
|---|---|---|---|---|---|---|
| Brisbane | 21.0 | 11.3 | 10.2 | 9.8 | 9.6 | 9.7 |
| Melbourne | 20.3 | 18.1 | 16.4 | 14.9 | 13.7 | 15.6 |
| Perth | 15.6 | 12.2 | 10.8 | 10.6 | 10.9 | 11.3 |
| Sydney | 21.3 | 19.2 | 17.6 | 16.8 | 18.9 | 19.5 |
| Chicago | 24.0 | 20.3 | 17.5 | 16.6 | 16.8 | 16.9 |
| Denver | 18.6 | 13.8 | 11.9 | 12.8 | 15.1 | 14.7 |
| Houston | 10.2 | 12.0 | 8.9 | 9.5 | 8.8 | 9.6 |
| Los Angeles | 22.3 | 25.0 | 24.4 | 23.9 | 24.1 | 27.6 |
| New York | 22.5 | 22.6 | 19.8 | 19.2 | 18.0 | 19.2 |
| Phoenix | 8.6 | 8.6 | 8.5 | 10.5 | 10.4 | 10.9 |
| San Diego | 11.7 | 12.1 | 10.8 | 13.1 | 14.5 | 14.6 |
| San Francisco | 16.5 | 16.9 | 15.5 | 16.0 | 20.5 | 19.8 |
| Vancouver | 24.9 | 21.6 | 18.4 | 20.8 | 21.6 | 25.2 |
| Frankfurt | 87.2 | 74.6 | 54.0 | 47.6 | 47.6 | 45.9 |
| Hamburg | 68.3 | 57.5 | 41.7 | 39.8 | 38.4 | 38.0 |
| Munich | 56.6 | 68.2 | 56.9 | 53.6 | 55.7 | 55.0 |
| Zurich | 60.0 | 58.3 | 53.7 | 47.1 | 44.3 | 43.0 |

The relationship between density and car use is also exponential as shown above. If a city begins to slowly increase its density then the impact can be more extensive on car use than expected. Density is a multiplier on the use of transit and walking/cycling, as well as reducing the length of travel. Increases in density can result in greater mixing of land uses to meet peoples' needs nearby. This is seen, for example, in the return of small supermarkets to the central business districts of cities as residential populations increase and demand local shopping opportunities within an easy walk. Overall, this reversal of urban sprawl will undermine the growth in car use.

4. *The Aging of Cities*

Cities in the developed world are all aging in the sense that the average age of people living in the cities has been getting older. People who are older tend to drive less. Cities therefore that are aging are likely to show less car use. This is likely to be a factor but the fact that all American and Australian cities began declining around 2004 suggests there were other factors at work than just aging as not all cities in these places are aging at similar rates. The younger cities of Brisbane and Perth in Australia still peaked in 2004.

5. *The Growth of a Culture of Urbanism*

One of the reasons that older aged cities drive less is that older people move back into cities from the suburbs – the so-called 'empty nester' syndrome. This was largely not predicted at the height of the Automobile City growth phase nor was it seen that the children growing up in the suburbs would begin flocking back into the cities rather than continuing the life of car dependence. This has now been underway for over a decade and the data presented by the Brookings Institution suggest that it is a major contributor to the peak car use phenomenon. They suggest this is not a fashion but a structural change based on the opportunities that are provided by greater urbanism. The cultural change associated with this urbanism is reflected in the Friends TV series compared to the Father Knows Best suburban TV series of the earlier generation. The shift in attitudes to car dependence is also apparent in Australia. The patterns of change in cities are more dramatically seen in younger people where the decline in car use and growth in use of sustainable transport modes is very evident. One possible cultural reason for this is the growth in social media devices like mobile phones, tablets and computers which means younger people are free and connected through these devices and indeed car driving interferes with the ability to use such technology.

6. *The Rise in Fuel Prices*

The vulnerability of outer suburbs to increasing fuel prices was noted in the first fuel crisis in 1973-4 and in all subsequent fuel crisis periods when fuel price volatility was clearly reflected in real estate values. The return to 'normal' after each crisis led many commentators to believe that the link between fuel and urban form may not be as dramatic as first presented by people like us. However the impact of $140 a barrel oil on real estate in the US dramatically led to the GFC (sub-prime mortgagees were unable to pay their mortgages when fuel prices tripled).

Despite global recession the 21$^{st}$ century has been faced by a consolidation of fuel prices at the upper end of those experienced in the last 50 years of Automobile City growth. Most oil commentators including oil companies now admit to the end of the era of cheap oil, even if not fully accepting the peak oil phenomenon. The fuel price is obviously going to contribute to reducing car use growth though few economists would have suggested these price increases were enough to cause peak car use that set in well before the 2008 peak of $140 a barrel.

### Implications for Future City Planning

The urban planning profession has been developing alternative plans for Automobile Cities in the past few decades, cities that build elements of Walking centres around Transit corridors – often called the Polycentric City as in Figure 8 – with the rationale of reducing car dependence involving all of the above factors. Few however would have thought they would be quite so successful, perhaps because each of the factors had such interactivity and reinforcing effects.

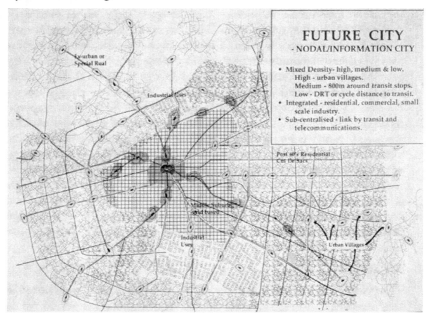

Figure 8: The Polycentric City

The need for the Polycentric City has emerged as the solution to reducing car dependence and creating a new city form that enables people to keep within the Marchetti travel time budget and create a more sustainable transport system. The Polycentric City is demonstrated in Figure 8 showing the need for good public transport across and into the centre of cities as well as the need for density to be increased in a range of centres across the city. These centres would be the key destinations for the upgraded transit system. In these centres walking and cycling would be the main priority.

## Conclusions

Sustainable transport needs support from land use planning. It needs more of the Transit City and the Walking City to be made part of the Automobile City. This will be the only way that the Marchetti travel time budget will be enabled in heavily car dependent areas. It will also significantly decrease car use and as the phenomenon of peak car use appears to have begun there are clear signs that sustainable transport is going to grow much further in the future. Sustainable transport seems to be mainstreaming.

---

*Thinking it through: where do I stand?*

How long does it take students and their families to travel to work and school. Is there an average around the Marchetti travel time budget? Relate this to the modes used and the distances travelled. Can this be improved by changes in land use? How?

---

*Action: what can I do?*

What are the travel patterns of people in different urban communities? How do these relate to the land use of the area? Can changes to transport infrastructure help make this more sustainable? What else can be done?

---

## Further reading

Newman, P. & Kenworthy, J. (1999). *Sustainability and Cities: Overcoming Automobile Dependence.* Washington DC: Island Press.

Newman, C.E. & Newman P.W.G. (2006). The Car and Culture. In P. Beilhartz & T. Hogan (Eds.), *Sociology: Place, Time and Division.* Oxford: Oxford University Press.

Newman, P. & Kenworthy, J. (2011). Peak Car Use: Understanding the Demise of Automobile Dependence. *World Transport Policy and Practice, 17*(2), 32 – 42

Schiller, P.L., Bruun, E.C. & Kenworthy, J.R. (2010). *An Introduction to Sustainable Transportation: Policy, Planning and Implementation.* London: Earthscan.

## *Resources*

www.ecoplan.org/**wtpp**/
www.**itdp**.org/
www.sustainability.curtin.edu.au
www.ecoplan.org/wtpp/wt_index.htm
http://worldstreets.wordpress.com/

# Chapter 18
## Ecocities and Sustainable Urban Environments

*Phil McManus*
*The University of Sydney*

## *The issue*

Most people in the world live in urban areas, with this proportion predicted to rise to about 70% of the world's population by 2030. The built environment comprises residential, commercial and industrial buildings, transport infrastructure such as roads, railways and airports and all of the other facilities that make up our towns and cities. While cities occupy only about 2% of the planet, the construction and maintenance of urban infrastructure has major environmental impacts both within and beyond the boundaries of cities. Buildings are said to consume 32% of the world's resources, including 12% of its water and up to 40% of its energy, while producing 40% of waste going to landfill and 40% of air emissions.

Former British Prime Minister Winston Churchill observed, initially in a speech in 1943 to the House of Commons, that "we shape our dwellings, and afterwards they shape us". The built environment shapes us and 'hardens' environmental impacts because roads and buildings last for many years and once open space or agricultural land is built over, it is very unlikely to return to its former state. The planning and design of the built environment creates opportunities or barriers for sustainable living and generates associated environmental impacts such as greenhouse gas emissions, water use and energy use. Improvements in planning and design can influence, but not determine, other actions to reduce negative environmental impacts.

To achieve sustainability we must make our built environment more sustainable. A number of similar ideas have been proposed, including "green urbanism" (often associated with denser European cities), sustainable cities and more recently "ecocities". Achieving sustainability means both retrofitting our existing built environment and the creation of new built environments, either as extensions of the existing cities or as separate new ecocities that are specifically designed, constructed and operated to achieve sustainability. This raises questions of not only how it will be achieved, who is going to achieve it, who will fund the costs and reap the benefits, but of the meaning of sustainability in relation to cities.

Should the end-point be making cities more sustainable, or is this a vital step in making our planet sustainable? If cities contribute to the sustainability of the planet, how do we conserve resources within cities, limit the negative ecological impacts of cities beyond their boundaries and encourage new sustainability initiatives that result in changing the physical structure of cities, the behaviour of urban inhabitants and the ecological impacts of cities on the planet?

Cities are therefore more sustainable if they minimise negative ecological impacts within their boundaries (in terms of energy, water, waste), limit the export of negative impacts beyond their boundaries now and into the future, and by conserving habitats so that species other than humans can share the cities with us. Ideally, residents of these cities would have a greater ecological literacy about sustainability issues locally and at other scales and be living lifestyles consistent with the ecological values embodied in the city planning, design and construction. The quest for sustainable cities is the latest in a long line of ideas to improve our cities. This makes it both new and exciting but also part of a tradition of trying to improve cities and the lives of people living in the cities.

In this chapter we explore some of the issues to achieving sustainability and some of the initiatives that have been developed at various scales. The chapter includes two case studies. One is of a new ecocity in northern China (the Sino-Singapore Tianjin Ecocity Project) and the other is of a slightly older commercially viable green building in Melbourne, Australia (the 60L Building) that set new benchmarks for sustainability in the built environment and is continuing to achieve remarkable sustainability outcomes.

## Context

### Historical

Humans have survived as a species because we have built structures to provide us with shelter, water storage, food processing and distribution and other necessities of life. These structures have used materials obtained from nature. Initially these materials embodied little transformation. For example, trees were cut down and the wood was used to make houses. Over time these structures have tended to become more sophisticated and we have often forgotten that the materials for these structures are obtained from the environment. Today our cities include high-rise office structures of steel, glass and cables that are often only possible given sophisticated technology and the transformation of raw materials such as iron ore and coal into new materials such as steel.

Historically cities have developed at the sites of abundant raw materials, the intersections of major trade routes, or at strategic military positions. Compact urban areas (such as London and Edinburgh), constrained by defensive city walls and walking as the main means of transportation, existed prior to the Industrial Revolution in the late eighteenth century. The expansion of cities during the Industrial Revolution was uninhibited by defensive walls but still primarily relied on walking as a means of transport. Workers often lived close to their site of employment, unlike today when in many cities workers may commute across the city, or from outside of the city.

In these rapidly growing industrial cities of the nineteenth century, not unlike fast-growing cities in some developing countries today, workers were often housed in buildings that were poorly designed, poorly built, poorly maintained and overcrowded. This led to calls for reform and some wealthier industrialists built new factory towns in places such as New Lanark (near Glasgow) and Saltaire, near Bradford, (see Figure 1) to provide good quality housing, access to sunlight and recreational opportunities (usually involving the absence of alcohol) for their workers. These towns and cities are the forerunners of many planning attempts to improve the built environment for social, economic and environmental reasons. The notions of sustainable cities and ecocities are contemporary examples of similar thinking, to improve the urban environment to address the main economic, social and environmental issues as they are understood at a particular time in a particular place. In many older European towns and cities, some of the housing built during the Industrial Revolution survives today, albeit retrofitted with double-glazed glass, insulation, and modern telecommunications so that it is suitable for contemporary living.

Figure 1: 19<sup>th</sup> Century housing retrofitted for 21<sup>st</sup> Century living in the new town of Saltaire, near Bradford, in the north of England. Photo credit: Phil McManus

While cities expanded in size when walking was the main mode of transport for most people, this expansion was further facilitated by forms of transport that used energy sources derived from nature. Steam trains, electric trams, diesel buses all led to the city expanding further, often leaving gaps of un-developed land between the various railway lines or main roads. During the twentieth century, cities in many developed countries were shaped largely by the automobile, which has allowed the infill of these wedges of land between radial rail lines converging on the city centre and the spread of the city beyond the rail terminus. Older cities in countries such as the USA tend to have a denser urban core, surrounded by low density suburbs. This sub-urban expansion has generally been low-rise, low density development with spaces for gardens, children to play and sunlight. In countries such as Aus-tralia, low density cities were associated with physical and moral health, and were contrasted with the older, denser cities in England, Scotland and main-land Europe.

After the end of the Second World War, and with the increasing access-ibility of the automobile, inner city areas in many Australian cities became rundown as wealthier residents moved to new, spacious suburbs. This trend was somewhat countered by the gentrification of preferred inner city sub-urbs from the late 1960s onwards, but suburban expansion continued sim-ultaneously. In recent years these expansive cities have become associated with fossil fuel dependency, greenhouse gas emissions, loss of remnant bush and agricultural land, and inefficient provision of urban infrastructure. In summary, rather than being seen as good cities because they allow residents adequate space for living, they are increasingly understood as cities that are unsustainable because they have significant ecological impacts and they export these impacts to other parts of the planet. The need for cities to be made more sustainable is now recognized throughout the world, but what it means and how it will be achieved differs greatly depending on the context.

*Political*

Cities are shaped by political decisions at multiple levels. International organizations, such as the United Nations (UN), influence sustainability issues in cities. In 1991 The Sustainable Cities Program was initiated to promote environmentally sustainable urban development. The emphasis has changed during the different phases of this program but it is an example of international organizations (partly funded by wealthier countries such as the United Kingdom, the Netherlands, Japan, Denmark and so on) working through an internationally recognized organization to enable developing countries (such as Zambia, Morocco, Cuba, Ecuador and so on) to improve the environments of their often fast-growing cities.

In some countries, particularly developing countries, institutions such as the World Bank and International Monetary Fund, influence urban development by funding infrastructure projects or by limiting a national government's ability to spend on infrastructure. The World Bank links long-term economic growth in cities with the reduction of poverty in developing countries, but recognizes that rapid urbanization results in poor quality urban environments (slum housing, poor sanitation, unhealthy environments and premature death). In late 2009 the World Bank released its Urban and Local Government Strategy (System of Cities) that highlights the connections between cities, and the links between cities and issues such as climate change. The role of Singapore, in encouraging private and state investment in urban infrastructure and managing urban environments, was considered crucial by the World Bank as a leading example of what other countries could be doing. The expansion of this model was encouraged by World Bank-Singapore government partnerships to promote investment in countries such as Vietnam and China (see ecocities below).

Within many countries, the political structures vary and the responsibility for making cities more sustainable may be different depending on the division of responsibilities between different levels of government. This generally relates to the country's constitution. For example, in Australia state governments have significant constitutional responsibility for urban planning and environmental management. On occasion, the Australian Labor Party (ALP) has attempted to have a more pronounced and higher profile role at the national level. Local government is very important in promoting, or inhibiting, sustainability in the built environment. The influence of local government relative to state government varies between countries. In the USA, metropolitan-level governments are often strong, whereas in Australia the cities are generally fragmented in their governance structures and therefore relatively weak in relation to the states. On the issue of climate change when the US Federal Government under then President George W Bush was seen as lagging, mayors of cities used their influence to create change at a different scale. Led by the Mayor of Seattle, the US Conference of Mayors Climate Protection Agreement was initiated and has now been signed by over 1000 mayors, representing cities and towns in all fifty US states and over 88 million residents. Even where such collaboration is not possible, local governments can still demonstrate leadership through their own planning and building programs, through purchasing policies and through education initiatives with local residents.

*Geographical*

Over half of the 7 billion people in the world now live in urban areas. The absolute number of urban dwellers, and the proportion of urban dwellers as part of the world's population, are both increasing. Cities are, however, very different throughout the world. The issues relevant to each city vary, as does the capacity of each city to deal with sustainability issues. Cities in developing countries are often experiencing rapid population growth (both due to rural-urban migration and natural population increase within the urban area) alongside inadequate urban infrastructure. In many cases, in developing countries the population is increasing but the infrastructure is dated, or deteriorates rapidly due to poor quality construction and/or harsh environmental conditions. In some cases where there is rapid economic growth, new cities are planned as ecocities. There are similarities between the planning of a number of ecocities of the 21st century in China and the planning of "new towns" in the UK from 1944 onwards and the development of nine new cities in France in the 1960s. The major difference appears to be the emphasis in contemporary planning on sustainability, as opposed to improved environmental amenity for residents. One example of an ecocity in China is the planned Sino-Singapore Tianjin Ecocity near Tianjin in northern China (see case study below).

The population of many developed countries is stabilizing, or declining in countries such as Japan. Many cities in developed countries are well-positioned to move towards sustainability. A combination of political stability, technical expertise, available funds and/or access to credit facilities, and in many cases a willing population, mean that these cities can, and should, be leaders in this endeavour. The major constraint appears to be a lack of political vision and commitment to achieving sustainable cities as part of a more sustainable planet.

## Discussion

The built environment encompasses many different fields that could potentially, and must, contribute to sustainability. While they are too numerous to cover in this chapter, it is important to note the links between the built environment and issues such as climate change (through the burning of fossil fuels for electricity generation, or the emission of greenhouse gases from transport) and health (ranging from clean drinking water in developing countries through to the provision of local organic food and the construction of footpaths and cycleways in some wealthier countries to encourage healthy diets and exercise through the use of more active and less damaging modes of transport). It is possible to consider some of the more important individual issues by looking at different scales, ranging from a comparative sustainable city approach to the scale of new cities and then to making individual buildings "green".

## Comparative Sustainability Indicators

One of the major developments in making cities more sustainable is the rise in comparative indicator approaches. These approaches vary significantly in the number of cities and the number of variables chosen. For example, Mercer's global scale approach measures 221 cities, using six criteria that were non-weighted: water availability, water potability, waste removal, sewage, air pollution and traffic congestion. By way of contrast, the European Green Cities Index, released in December 2009 by the Economist Intelligence Unit ranked 30 European cities in 30 countries using 30 indicators. The indicators were grouped into 8 categories; carbon emissions, energy, buildings, transport, water, waste and land use, air quality and environmental governance. In this study Copenhagen performed best, ahead of Stockholm, Oslo, Vienna, Amsterdam and Zurich.

Within individual countries, US City Rankings were produced in 2005 by SustainLane, and repeated in 2006 and 2008 and cover the 50 most-populous cities. Each city's performance is benchmarked in 16 areas of urban sustainability, including the preparedness for an energy crisis and the risk of natural disaster, the growth of renewable energy and green building technology. A weighting system was used. Eleven of the 16 data categories receiving a weighting of 1, while maintaining a stable water supply and commuting to work were both weighted 1.5. The impacts that are of a secondary nature (such as congestion, housing affordability and the risk of natural disasters) were each weighted 0.5. In 2008, Portland (Oregon), San Francisco, Seattle, Chicago and New York all performed well. These rankings are generally consistent with other rankings from the USA, including the Natural Resources Defence Council's Smarter Cities, which ranked a total of 655 cities, using nine categories (including air quality, water quality, green building, environmental participation, but not water supply). Amongst the larger cities, Seattle ranked first, followed by San Francisco, Portland, Oakland and San Jose.

In the United Kingdom, the Forum for the Future's annual Sustainable Cities Index tracks the progress on sustainability by assessing 13 indicators, which are weighted, in Britain's 20 largest cities. Bristol and Brighton have been among the top three cities in each of the three years. Similar rankings have been done in Canada since 2007 by Corporate Knights, ranking 17 Canadian cities using the five equally weighted parameters of ecological integrity, economic security, governance and empowerment, infrastructure and built environment and social well-being. In Australia, the Sustainable Cities Index released in 2010 by the Australian Conservation Foundation ranked the 20 largest cities in Australia using 15 criteria. These were air quality, ecological footprint, green buildings, water, biodiversity, health, density, well-being, transport, employment, climate change readiness, education, food production, public participation and household debt. Drawing on the Forum for the Future's Sustainable Cities Index in the UK, it was intended to attract media attention, promote friendly competition between cities and raise awareness of what it means to be a sustainable city.

These urban sustainability indices highlight the issues that experts believe cities must address to become sustainable. The different weightings in some systems highlight the perceived importance of some issues relative to other issues. The differences between the ranking systems both reflect varying situations in countries, and disagreement between the developers of these indices as to what is important. Rather than seeking a single correct answer, the commonality between many indicators in the indices and the existence of some differences can be useful in encouraging debate about what really makes a city sustainable. These ideas can then be used to improve other existing cities, or form the basis for the planning of new ecocities.

*Ecocities*

Ecocities may be existing cities, although the term is often used to indicate new cities. The new cities may seem more exciting because they appear to offer the opportunity to start from nothing and to build an entire new city that includes all the latest eco-technology, design and materials, while avoiding the need to engage with the problems of the existing built environment. This so-called "greenfields site" overlooks the importance of existing environmental conditions, hence the importance of the site selection process in the Sino-Singapore Tianjin Ecocity (see case study below).

One of the earliest uses of the term "ecocities" was by Richard Register, in relation to Berkeley (Oakland, California). This idea included the notion of "bulldozing suburbia" to start again, a process advocated by the architect Le Corbusier in the early 20th century for the Right Bank of Paris, and implemented in the mid-19th century in Paris under the direction of Baron von Haussmann, when the medieval city was demolished to make way for a city of boulevards (for military control of the city) and to let light into what had been a dense, dark city. Again, we note the similarities between thinking about ecocities and earlier ideas and movements to improve the city of the time.

A number of exciting new ecocities have been proposed, including Masdar in the United Arab Emirates (UAE), Dongtan in China (currently on hold) and the Sino-Singapore Tianjin ecocity near Tianjin in China. Masdar, located near Abu Dhabi, is the collaboration between the government and the British architectural firm Foster + Partners. Masdar is important because, similar to the 60L Green Building (see case study below) it emphasizes commercial viability as part of ecological sustainability and a high quality of life. The architecture often invokes tradition Arabian architectural themes, but the emphasis is on clean technology, energy reduction and reducing the environmental impact of the city. The existence of new ecocities

## Further reading

Dittmar, H. (2009). The Human Habitat. *The Ecologist*, June, 14.
This is the lead article in a special issue on Sustainable Cities. Other articles
include climate change, food, transport and green building
themes.
Lehmann, S. (2010). *The Principles of Green Urbanism. Transforming the City
for Sustainability*. London: Earthscan.
A recent publication that explores the European-oriented idea of "green
urbanism" as a way of promoting zero-carbon emissions in 64 cities, with a case study of the Australian city of Newcastle.
Madlener, R. & Sunak, Y. (2011). Impacts of urbanization on urban structures and energy demand: What can we learn for urban energy
planning and urbanization management? *Sustainable Cities and Society*, *1*(1), 45 – 53.
A research article on energy and the built environment, in the first issue of
a new journal that in the future is likely to have many interesting
and important articles about sustainable cities.
McManus, P. (2005). *Vortex Cities to Sustainable Cities: Australia's urban challenge*. Sydney: UNSW Press.
A book that covers many important themes and challenges in sustainable
cities, including a history of urban development that explains how
the present situation of unsustainable cities arose.
Pearce, F. (2006). *New Scientist*, 17 June, 2006. Special Issue - Ecopolis now,
36-44.
A series of articles about making cities sustainable, with discussion about
London, food production in cities, the rise of megacity regions
and the proposed ecocity of Dongtan in Shanghai.

## Resources

Australian Conservation Foundation – 60L Building. Available at
http://www.acfonline.org.au/articles/news.asp?news_id=3100
A website that provides detail on the 60L Building, including the innovative green leasing arrangements and updates of its performance.
Huffington Post, The. http://www.huffingtonpost.com/2011/01/13/tianjin-
eco-city_n_806972.html#s221883
This site contains a brief overview of the Sino-Singapore Tianjin Ecocity
plus 13 images of plans and what the proposed city will look like
when it is built. There are over 1000 comments on this website –
you can add your thoughts.

International Centre for Sustainable Cities (2008) Youth led development in sustainable cities: From idea, to policy to practice. Discussion Paper for World Urban Forum, Nanjing, China, November 2008. Available at http://sustainablecities.net/docman-resources/cat_view/110-resources/189-youth
A discussion document specifically aimed to involve young people in the development of sustainable cities.
U.S. Green Building Council - Elements of a Green School. Available at http://centerforgreenschools.org/main-nav/k-12/greenschool/-interactive
Information about what makes a school "green" – useful for teachers, parents and students.
World Bank, The, http://web.worldbank.org/WBSITE/EXTERNAL/COUNTRIES/EASTASIAPACIFICEXT/CHINAEXTN/0, contentMDK:2281007
A website that includes updates on developments in China and links to a large report released in January, 2011, called Sino-Singapore Tianjin Eco-city: A Case Study of an Emerging Eco-City in China.

# Chapter 19

## Art and Sustainability

*Maja Fowkes*
*Reuben Fowkes*
*Translocal, Budapest*

### *Introduction*

The relevance of sustainability for contemporary art can be approached from two distinct angles. On the one hand, we may consider the role of art in highlighting environmental issues, expressing criticism towards unsustainable factors in society, and offering imaginative ideas for how to achieve sustainability. The other approach is to turn eco-criticism back towards the art world itself, to examine the environmental impact of the production of art works, the functioning of art institutions, or, for example, the phenomenon of international art biennials that have mushroomed around the world in recent decades.

In addition to traditional media of painting and sculpture, contemporary artists as part of their artistic practice make use of a wide range of new technologies such as videos, films and internet, or choose to combine them in complex installations in order to best convey ideas about the issues they are addressing. Furthermore, some artists opt for non-object based practices such as performances, ephemeral actions and interventions in public space, which despite their minimal form may have strong resonances among the art public. The issue of sustainability in contemporary art, which is founded on the propositions of freedom of subject matter as well as freedom of artistic form, implies the opportunity for artists to question the role of art in society and express environmental concern in their works, while at the same time it makes them aware of ecological, social and ethical dimensions of their practice.

## Historical context

Painting beautiful landscapes and depicting the wonders of the natural world has always been a favoured subject for artists, while art was traditionally praised for its power to mirror nature. Artistic engagement with environmental issues is however a relatively recent phenomenon, although notably it was the Fontainebleau School of painters centred around the artist Theodor Rousseau who in 1848 initiated one of the first environmental campaigns in France. They started a petition for the legal protection of the Fontainebleau Forest near Paris, which was threatened by urbanisation and industrial development.

During the course of the twentieth century, modernist art was oriented towards extracting natural features from their context and dwelling on their formal properties, such as colour, shape and rhythm, with the radical separation of the artwork from everyday life. Artistic practice here corresponds to industrial society's experience of nature in terms of alienation, separation and distance. In parallel with the development of modern ecology in the 1960s and 70s, art also underwent transformations, from the modernist ideal of abstract art envisaged for the purified atmosphere of a white cube gallery to a new questioning of the role of art and its position in society. As a consequence, artists began to look outwards to the public sphere, experiment with art designed for natural settings, consider the political implications of art, and in some cases also respond through their work to the endangered state of the natural environment.

### Land Art and Conceptual Art

Among the new art movements that emerged in the 1960s, Land Art and Conceptual Art both have a strong relevance to sustainability and have been influential for recent contemporary approaches to ecology in art. Land Art was instrumental in bringing art out of the gallery and placing it in a natural setting, with pioneers such as American artist Robert Smithson choosing deserts and other remote locations for their large scale interventions in the natural environment. However, those artists typically saw the landscape as a huge canvas, on which they used 'a bulldozer instead of a paintbrush' to create Earth Works that regularly showed no concern for the environmental impact on the chosen location. For example, to create his famous *Spiral Jetty* in 1970, Smithson employed two trucks, a tractor and a large bulldozer to shift 6,783 tonnes of earth to create a spiral shape in the Great Salt Lake. The little concern he showed for ecology in his work even led to environmental protests, which successfully prevented him from carrying out another of his earth works by blocking the border crossing of trucks carrying broken glass destined for a remote Canadian island.

Moving beyond the confines of the gallery setting did not of course always mean heading out into nature, and many influential art works from the period engaged with the urban environment. One such public art project with a strong ecological dimension was Alan Sonfist's *Time Landscape*, which took place in the heart of New York and was conceived as a living monument to the forest that once covered Manhattan Island. After extensive research into the native plants, geology and history of the area, Sonfist created a small park with native trees, shrubs, wild grasses and flowers to represent the Manhattan landscape as was enjoyed by Native Americans before the arrival of European settlers. From this it is clear that when considering issues of sustainability in art, it is not so much a matter of the creation of artworks outdoors, which was the main preoccupation of Land Art, but art's ability to express powerful ideas about, for example, the loss of biodiversity through urbanisation.

Emerging in the same period of the late 1960s and early 1970s, Conceptual Art abandoned art objects and sought dematerialised ways to express artistic ideas. Conceptual artists often used a text or an ephemeral action that very often left no trace in the world except for its documentation, but nevertheless had the potential to make a strong artistic impression. Many of today's practising artists recycle the strategies of the early conceptual artists to stress the centrality of the concept or idea that their project aims to transmit. They often conduct in depth artistic research into a certain subject or issue, and in that way gather alternative knowledge which distinguishes itself from the knowledge that field experts or scientists offer. In terms of sustainability, the following artistic projects illustrate the potential of contemporary art to generate innovative perspectives on environmental questions.

## Case studies

### Ursula Biemann: The Black Sea Files

Swiss artist Ursula Biemann's ten-part video work, the *Black Sea Files*, tells the story of the giant pipeline that connects the oilfields of Azerbaijan to the global oil market, passing through the mountainous Caucuses before ending up at a Turkish seaport.

Ursula Biemann, Black Sea Files, video 2005

Based on in depth artistic research into the politics of the oil industry in the region and combining information gathered using the methods of anthropologists, embedded journalists and even secret intelligence agents, the work gives voice to the ordinary people whose lives have been transformed by the construction of the pipeline in 2005. Through interviews with the Azeri and Georgian farmers who live along its route, the artist reflects on the urban and rural transformations brought by the oil industry to the region and the connection between local development and trends in the global economy.

Ursula Biemann, Black Sea Files, video 2005

## Helen and Newton Meyer Harrison: Endangered Meadows

Among the first artists to directly tackle environmental issues in their work, over a long artistic career American artists Helen and Newton Meyer Harrison have kept their promise 'only to do work that benefits the ecosystem.' Their project *Endangered Meadows* involved transplanting a 400 year old meadow, which was due to be destroyed through urban development, to the roof garden of an art museum in Bonn, Germany. The exhibition lasted for two years from June 1996, after which their meadow was transplanted to the Great Rhine Park of Bonn, with seeds from the 'Mother Meadow' used to generate other bio-diverse green areas throughout the city's parks, adding a further dimension of self-sustainability to the work. Europe's traditional meadows are for the artists an example of sustainable collaboration between humans and the rest of the ecosystem, while their work draws attention to the threat posed to them by over-grazing and mechanized agriculture. By taking the example of an ordinary meadow, rather than choosing a protected site of natural beauty, the Harrisons draw attention to the fact that we are allowing these equally amazing and biologically-diverse environments to quietly disappear from our everyday lives.

## Krisztina Leko: Cheese and Cream

Croatian artist Kristina Leko has explored the issue of the survival of traditional methods of making and selling cheese and cream in a wide-ranging and influential community art project. The focus of her work is on the traditional occupation of the milkmaid, who sells her own homemade cheese and cream at the market, seen as the meeting point of rural and urban culture. Her artistic research involved interviewing more than 500 milkmaids, filming and photographing them, and collecting their stories, recipes and opinions, which are documented on the sirivrhnje.org website.

KRISTINA LEKO, SIR I VRHNJE / CHEESE AND CREAM, 2002/03, THREE-CHANNEL VIDEO INSTALLATION HERE: STILLS FROM THE VIDEO CHANNEL 1 DOLAC MARKET PLACE

Dolac Market Place, stills from *Cheese and Cream* 2002/03

Along with an exhibition, the project also developed into a campaign to protect cheese and cream as an 'indigenous product and custom' from new regulations and competition from multi-nationals. Thanks to her artistic project, the issue of the future of Croatia's traditional 'cheese and cream' become a touchstone of the debate over globalisation and the costs and benefits of European integration in the country.

KRISTINA LEKO, SIR I VRHNJE / CHEESE AND CREAM, 2002/03, THREE-CHANNEL VIDEO INSTALLATION HERE, STILLS FROM THE VIDEO CHANNEL 1 DOLAC MARKET PLACE)

Dolac Market Place, stills from *Cheese and Cream* 2002/03

## *Janek Simon: Make Your Own Digital Watch*

While the preceding works had wider social implications, the work of Polish artist Janek Simon is concerned more with individual well being. His work has a strong DIY ethic that empowers us to understand and take personal responsibility for the technological world that surrounds our everyday lives. His artistic practice is often based on internet research into, for example, how to build a digital watch, bringing a skill that is usually confined to industrial machines back into the sphere of individual human activity.

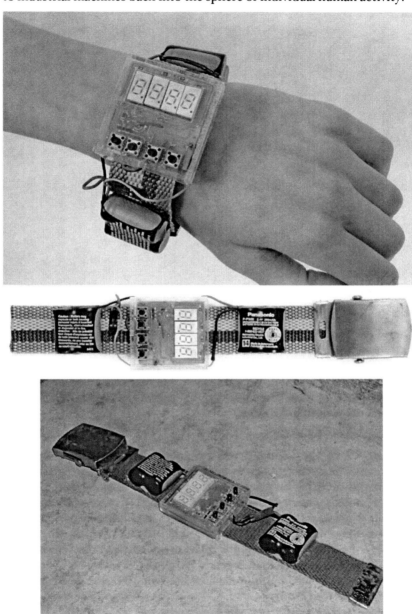

Janek Simon, Home Made Electronic Watch, 2005

Making an implicit statement about the need for diversity, he also once took apart a Volkswagen camper van and completely rebuilt it using parts of different colours.

Janek Simon, Volkswagen Transporter T2, installation, 2008

Another of his works that points to the loss of the ability to make our own things and dependence on buying finished products is a series of homemade toys made from cheap and recycled everyday materials. The designs for these remade toys were based on the DIY toys of the artist's childhood in socialist Poland during the 1980s.

*Tomas Saraceno: Airport City*

Also dealing with the possibilities of technology, but from a more high tech and futuristic perspective, Argentinean artist Tomas Saraceno is fascinated with the possibility of human life in the skies. His work Airport City is a vision of an airborne platform made up of floating cells that would be environmentally friendly, solar powered, and designed to improve our quality of life. His utopian floating world would ignore international boundaries and be equipped with flying gardens and make use of cutting edge technologies such as 'Aerogel', an ultra-light gas used in spacecraft to enable them to fly on solar energy. Straddling the boundary between the real and the imaginary, his work pushes the limits of utopian architecture and scientific experimentation for the solution of human problems.

As can be seen from the preceding examples, contemporary artists approach issues of sustainability in a variety of ways. Art projects may act as a source of information about environmental problems and initiate the search for enduring solutions, while in other cases the autonomous position of art enables artists to criticise government policies and the behaviour of big business. Artists are often finely tuned to the problem of 'green wash' and show awareness of the danger that environmentalism can become a new form of consumerism, criticising the persistence of a growth model in the economy and society. The imaginative solutions proposed by artists often involve creating one's own means to achieve goals and inventing what is needed rather than depending on readymade products. Furthermore, artist projects sometimes face forwards, looking in innovative ways at the future forms of the lived environment, or alternatively gaze back into the past to uncover old knowledge and traditional skills that are relevant to achieving sustainable lifestyles.

### Sustainability of the art world

The topic of sustainability and contemporary art can also be approached from the alternative perspective of considering the impact of artworks on the environment, rather than simply asking whether or not they carry an ecological message. What is decisive in considering an artwork's relation to sustainability turns out not to be its content in terms of ideas, but rather its form, or physical presence in the world.

In order to consider the environmental impact of an artwork, a logical first step would be to establish criteria to measure it. Environmental science provides a number of tools and techniques with relevance to the contemporary artwork, from the ecological footprint to life-cycle analysis, measures that are designed to indicate the sustainability of an action, object, community, or state. In common with other public projects, the construction of new art museums, artistic interventions in the urban or rural environment and even the organisation of art fairs and biennials, are also subject to regular environmental impact assessment by government agencies.

The starting point of any attempt to calculate, for example, the environmental impact of a major artwork such as a museum installation is to consider the ecological footprint of the materials in its production. Art institutions could if they wished carry out a life cycle analysis of all the elements that make up the artwork, including the impact of its production, transport, installation and disposal after the exhibition closes. Additional factors to be considered include energy use through lighting, heating or cooling, or other mechanical elements of the work, with calculations based on the length of the exhibition and the daily consumption of power. The net could even be widened to include for example the carbon footprint of any travel by the artist or curator in the months leading up to the exhibition, or the environmental impact of the catalogue, publicity materials, or even branded merchandise created for the museum shop. It is though not always a simple matter to decide where the ecological footprint of the individual artwork stops and that of the art institution begins, or where to draw the line in the inclusion of ever more extended environmental impacts that can be ultimately traced back to a particular artwork.

Further complications in calculating the environmental impact of art-works follow from the specific characteristics of contemporary art that make it different from other products and human activities. While tradi-tionally we are used to perceiving an artwork through certain numbers, such as its dimensions, date of production or monetary value, there would surely be resistance to any attempt to add an extra numerical tag to express its environmental impact. Contemporary art is in any case frequently hard to measure, as even an artwork's size can be fluid, with 'dimensions variable' a standard description on exhibition labels. Contemporary art is a slippery territory with artists constantly finding ways to outwit attempts to categor-ise or pin down their work so that any attempt to measure an artwork's so-cial or ecological impact is likely to be seen as endangering the precious autonomy of art.

It may, in practice, be more useful to focus on the ecological footprint of art institutions than of individual artworks. Artists themselves have taken the lead in drawing attention to the negative environmental impact that museums can have and the large amount of energy they consume in order to maintain perfect conditions for the viewing and preservation of precious artworks. Danish artist Tue Greenfort's project for the 2007 Sharjah Bien-nial, for example, involved the host museum agreeing to turn down the air-conditioning in the building by 2 degrees for the duration of the show, mak-ing a point about both the ecological footprint of art institutions and the wider need to reduce carbon emissions to reverse global warming. In addi-tion to their direct environmental impact, more philosophical questions can also be raised about the problem of the stockpiling of artworks for eternity in ever-growing museum collections.

Considering the sustainability of an artwork may also mean looking at the social and ethical dimensions of art projects rather than just their nar-row environmental impact. This is especially the case with public art pro-jects in which the artist works with a specific community where care needs to be taken over issues of, for example, collective authorship and respect for privacy, as well as more general questions about how human subjects are used in an artwork. The issue of the treatment of animals may also be of rel-evance in particular cases, with an expanded notion of ecological citizenship also inferring respect for the rights of other species.

The ecological dimension of the artwork was until recently rarely con-sidered by mainstream artists or museums, although today the issue of the environmental impact of artworks and the art institutions that house them is increasingly hard to ignore. Where artists deal in their work with issues of sustainability, they are often implicitly or explicitly critical of our collective addiction to the idea of inexorable growth. Artistic engagement with sus-tainability on the one hand reaffirms the observation that ecology is a sub-versive science because it has implications for all aspects of human activity. On the other, the deep ecology credo of 'making do with enough' turns out to be useful advice for discovering sustainable forms of artistic practice.

*Thinking it through: where do I stand?*

Does art have the power to change human opinions and behaviour regarding sustainability?

Art is often said to be autonomous, so should it also be free from questions of ecology and the environmental impact of the artwork? Or should artists, despite their philosophical freedom to do whatever they like, also consider the sustainability of their work?

*Action: what can I do?*

Go to a gallery or museum and look at the art works. Think about what kind of materials are used, how they are installed and how much energy is used to store them.

Which artworks show concern for the natural environment or alternatively a complete disregard for the fate of nature and animals?

## Further reading

Kastner, J. (Ed.). (2005). *Land And Environmental Art*. London: Phaidon.
Gablik, S. (1997). *Conversations before the End of Time*. London: Thames & Hudson.
Andrews, M. (Ed.). (2006). *Land, Art: A Cultural Ecology Handbook*. London:RSA.

## Resources

www.translocal.org

# Chapter 20
## Sustainable Happiness

*Catherine O'Brien*
*Cape Breton University*

*Introduction*

If you ask a teacher about one of his/her happiest moments in teaching, there's a good chance that the answer will be, "that moment when I see the light go on," or, "those times when I see a student make a new connection, discovering something about the world around them or mastering a challenging skill." Our passion for learning has taught us that these are precious moments of growth. We feel deep satisfaction when we help our students to thrive.

What does thriving mean for students in the 21<sup>st</sup> century? There isn't a one-size-fits-all answer to this question. However, there are some fascinating developments in the last decade that provide some guideposts. Sustainability, of course, is essential and every section in this book provides a view into its relevance for educators. This chapter invites you to explore the possibilities that arise when we combine sustainability with happiness – creating a new concept, sustainable happiness. In a nutshell, sustainable happiness is about everyone thriving – but not at the expense of other people, other species or the natural environment. Let's start by looking at happiness.

## Happiness and education

If you haven't been thinking about the relevance of happiness to education, you're not alone. Education texts and curricula don't tend to discuss happiness. Yet, we all know that when students are happy and engaged they learn well. We know that stress inhibits learning. We also know that a toxic learning environment is soul crushing for teachers and students. Until recently, however, there has been little written about happiness and education. With the introduction of positive psychology, this is starting to change. Positive psychology is a relatively new branch of psychology that emerged around the turn of this century. Psychologists recognized that, for decades, considerable attention has been given to studying mental illness but researchers had been overlooking what could be gained by studying people and institutions that flourish. The kinds of questions that are now being asked are: What can we learn from happy people? What are the benefits of happiness? Can happiness skills be taught? For example, if you were to rate yourself on a scale from 1-10 at 6 in terms of your happiness or life satisfaction, are there skills or interventions that could shift you to a 7, 8 or higher? If so, can that new level of life satisfaction be sustained?

We'll take a look at each of these questions and then consider how we can 'take happiness to the next level' by linking it with sustainability.

Some of the truly significant things that we can learn from happy people are that they tend to be resilient, generous, appreciative, empathetic, have healthy relationships, are honest, and may also be inclined to engage in environmentally friendly behaviours. They aren't happy all the time. Their resilience comes, in part, from having the capacity to experience a full range of emotions. They meet challenges in their life, even severe trauma, and move through these events without becoming stuck. One of the skills that assists them with this is their capacity to creatively generate options when faced with a problem. Furthermore, they know what makes their heart sing, and they incorporate their passions into their lifestyle and work whenever possible.

The benefits of happiness are underscored by happiness and health research studies. These demonstrate that positive experiences of subjective well-being (happiness) correspond with numerous positive health outcomes including lower blood pressure, the inclination to seek out and act on health information, reduced risk of heart disease and more robust immune systems than those of less happy people. Happy people tend to live longer and studies indicate that feeling connected to nature is associated with happiness.

Positive psychologists who study children and youth have found that character strengths such as love, gratitude, and hope are predictors of life satisfaction. Prosocial behaviours such as empathy and sympathy have been associated with positive social functioning and some studies have also found a positive correlation between prosocial behaviour and student academic achievement.

The great news for educators is that happiness skills can be taught. Effective interventions can range from fostering gratitude and appreciation, teaching learned optimism, focusing on healthy relationships, learning to be mindful, practicing meditation, and engaging in healthful behaviours such as healthy eating and physical activity. I have had the most success through teaching the Foster and Hicks happiness model. It provides a clear roadmap for individuals, communities and organizations to thrive.

At this point in the chapter, perhaps you are experiencing some of the same questions that arose for me as I began to read about happiness. What kind of happiness are we talking about? As an educator, I wonder "who, or what is teaching us about happiness?" and "what are we learning?" These questions create the bridge between happiness and sustainability. The type of happiness that leads to the positive health outcomes described above has been referred to as 'authentic happiness' and it isn't achieved through the overconsumption of material things. We aren't happier because we have a bigger house or car than our neighbour. In fact, comparing ourselves to others, getting caught in these external measures of success is likely to lead to dissatisfaction with our lives rather than the enduring experience of life satisfaction that is associated with happiness. Instead, intrinsic values seem to be more important – valuing relationships, being engaged in our community or work, feeling that our life has meaning and purpose.

The evidence is also clear that money doesn't buy happiness. Once we meet our basic needs and a little more for financial security, earning additional income does not necessarily lead to greater life satisfaction. People in the wealthiest sector of society are not significantly happier than people who have a modest income who are living within their means.

In summary, this growing body of research suggests that applications of positive psychology to schools and classrooms will contribute to curriculum and practices that foster student well-being and build skills that assist students (and teachers) to flourish. As a result, we are starting to see books and educational resources that offer recommendations for positive schools and positive classrooms. These initiatives are invaluable for fostering health and wellness. With the increase in youth depression and anxiety, as well as rising levels of physical inactivity, the need for health promotion and disease prevention is critical. Introducing happiness curricula and resources to students and teachers will be an important step toward promoting individual health and well-being.

Incorporating happiness studies into the education sector will also provide a counterpoint to the media messages that associate happiness with consumption. One of the outcomes could be developing "happiness literacy" so that students can recognize messages that are selling happiness though material consumption. Teachers have noticed that current generations of students seem to feel more entitled to possess luxuries. Cell phones, computers, iPods, designer clothes, etc. are experienced as a 'need' that is expected to be satisfied. Educators describe a lack of appreciation and gratitude in their students. Since we know that these tendencies are not associated with authentic happiness, nor sustainability, we can incorporate lessons in happiness to address some of these trends.

## *Sustainable happiness – taking happiness to the next level*

Our individual happiness does not exist in isolation from other people and the natural environment. Every day, our life touches and is touched by other people, other species and the natural environment through our daily encounters, the clothes we wear, the food we eat, how we transport ourselves, the materials that provide shelter, and so on. Sustainable happiness captures this interdependence.

> *Sustainable happiness is happiness that contributes to individual, community, and/or global well-being and does not exploit other people, the environment or future generations.*

I created the concept of sustainable happiness in order to draw attention to the consequences, both positive and adverse, of how individuals, communities and nations pursue happiness. In a globalized world, everyone's actions have repercussions on distant lands and people. Some impacts are immediate and short term while others have enduring effects.

Sustainable happiness is a concept that can be used by individuals to guide their actions and decisions on a daily basis; at the community level, it reinforces the need to genuinely consider social, environmental and economic indicators of well-being so that community happiness and well-being are sustainable; at the national and international level it highlights the significance of individual and community actions for the well-being of all – now and into the future. Therefore, even if a nation's economic indicators or well-being indicators suggest that it is thriving, but that success is based on the overconsumption of non-renewable resources, or the exploitation of labour from other countries, then the life satisfaction or happiness indicators for that nation are not reflecting sustainable happiness.

To demonstrate how this applies for individuals, consider the momentary pleasure of drinking a cup of coffee. Being mindful of our sensory experience can be relaxing and reduce stress. Viewed through the lens of sustainable happiness, this momentary pleasure can be placed in a wider context because we can also attend to whether that cup of coffee is Fair Trade coffee, which means that workers in the coffee plantation have been paid fairly and the coffee was grown with regard for the environment. It is important to reflect on whether the positive emotion derived from the coffee, has come at the expense of other people or the natural environment. The conditions under which clothes are manufactured, how far our food is transported, the pesticides that are sprayed on the local golf course, all have some impact on, and connection to, how individuals pursue happiness. On a daily basis, there are countless choices that individuals, organizations, and governments make which could contribute to sustainable happiness, whether we look at an individual's commute to work, an organization's procurement policies or a nation's foreign trade policies.

Sustainable happiness reinforces the fact that we are interconnected and interdependent with all life on the planet, even life that is yet to be born. It can also be used to foster sustainable behaviour. Our natural desire for happiness can become the entry point for discovering that our well-being is inextricably linked to the well-being of others and the natural environment. It can also dispute a common misconception that living sustainably will lower our quality of life. Sustainable happiness offers a fresh approach that invites reflection on sustainability issues coupled with opportunities to enhance our quality of life and contribute to individual, community, and global well-being. It also may be used to motivate behaviour change through compassion for others and the environment that sustains us.

For example, there are many daily activities that bring an experience of pleasure, but are not contributing to our overall well-being, or are detrimental to the well-being of others or the environment – this would include the consumption of products that have been made in a sweat shop or that have severely degraded the environment. Additionally, there are socially acceptable behaviours for dealing with stress. One of these is "retail therapy" which involves shopping to make oneself feel better, regardless of the potential adverse impact this consumption may have beyond the shopper. Through an exploration of sustainable happiness we can "decouple" happiness from consumption and discover ongoing opportunities to enhance well-being and sustainability.

### *Exploring sustainable happiness, personally and professionally*

Applying sustainable happiness to your own lifestyle may inspire you to apply this to your classroom and school. You could start by creating your list of 'Natural Highs'. These come from moments of shear delight and are generally not related to material possessions. Examples of Natural Highs could be: feeling the sun on your face, hearing the laughter of children, watching your son or daughter sleep, the smell of lilacs, walking in the rain, the smell of freshly cut grass, the fragrance of your favourite spice, the cold side of a pillow, the sound of ocean waves, and so on. Appreciating these simple pleasures fosters mindfulness, appreciation and positive well-being. One suggestion is to post your list of Natural Highs on your fridge and add to the list from time to time.

Making the connection between daily choices and our happiness footprint can also be accomplished by completing a Baseline Chart. Choose at least one day to chart your activities and the potential impact of those activities on your well-being, the well-being of other people, and the natural environment. Then generate options for enhancing your well-being, the well-being of someone else, your community, or the natural environment. That may require you to do more of something, to consume less of something, or to consume differently. Students in my sustainable happiness course often find that the Baseline Chart motivates them to make healthier lifestyle choices, to consider purchasing local products, to reduce unnecessary consumption, to seek out fair trade products, spend more time with family and friends, to walk for short trips, or organize carpools.

Gratitude and appreciation are such cornerstones of enduring life satisfaction that this is an attitude worth cultivating. Some people find that keeping a Gratitude Journal works for them. Others make a point of thanking people more often or even writing a Gratitude Letter to someone, expressing their appreciation beyond the usual verbal interactions. Those who are artistically inclined enjoy creating songs or art works that reflect their appreciation. In my experience, taking a few moments each day, to consider aspects of my life that bring genuine wealth tends to enhance my well-being. For example, I try to remind myself about things that could easily be taken for granted – breathing, the ability to walk, my senses, easy access to clean water, a beautiful environment, a high trust neighbourhood, wonderful friends and family – and the list goes on!

## Sustainable happiness and health

Sustainable happiness can be applied to health education to foster healthy attitudes and behaviours – healthy for students, the community and the natural environment.

Health curricula around the world address many similar outcomes related to active, healthy living, nutrition, personal wellness, healthy relationships and media awareness. We also share common concerns regarding physical activity levels of young people, rising levels of overweight and obesity, increasing incidences of depression, and risk-taking behaviour. If you read through the *Sustainable happiness and health education – Teacher's guide* (available at http://www.sustainablehappiness.ca/for-educators/) you'll find further activities that you could undertake for yourself and then bring the lessons to your students and colleagues. A teacher in Manitoba, Canada read through this resource and then decided to organize a staff development day. All of the school staff were involved in considering how it applied to their home life, their classrooms and their school. He wrote,

> This resource is exactly what we have been looking for as it effectively and efficiently ties together a variety of sustainability concepts under one common theme.

## Thriving in the 21st century

Progress in Education for Sustainable Development (ESD) has not kept pace with the need to mobilize the global community towards actions that will substantially shift our unsustainable trajectory. In a survey of current practice, a United Nations report questioned whether education is the problem or the solution. We would be deluding ourselves if we were to assume that current efforts to integrate sustainability into elementary and high school curricula is adequate in an era of climate change, massive environmental deterioration, and escalating loss of non-renewable resources.

The global challenges that threaten life on the planet and wreak untold human suffering can at face value seem unrelated to happiness. However, despite decades of environmental education that have attempted to shift policy and behaviour, we have not sufficiently shifted our unsustainable trajectory. Sustainable happiness has the capacity to attract the attention of individuals who might never consider themselves to be environmentalists or who feel weary of being prodded toward environmentally friendly behaviour through guilt. It also has the capacity to forge a transformational shift for students who internalize the realization that we are interdependent.

Education in the 21$^{st}$ century can continue to evolve at a comfortable pace that is entirely out of step with the leadership that is needed to embrace sustainability education. Or we can shake off the dusty, obsolete practices that are barriers to individual, community and global well-being. Sustainable happiness provides a concept and process for doing the latter.

Happiness is at the heart of who we are. Incorporating sustainable happiness into our lifestyle, classroom and school can inspire us to leave a legacy of sustainable happiness- a happiness footprint that contributes to the well-being of other people, other species and the natural environment.

---

*Action: what can I do?*

*Gratitude*

*Objectives:*

1. Students will understand that expressing gratitude contributes to their well-being and the well-being of others
2. Students will express gratitude to someone or about something.

Invite students to suggest how people show that they are grateful or appreciative. Ask what it feels like to express gratitude and to experience it. Assist students to realize that this is a readily accessible source of positive well-being that they can choose to experience.

Ask students to think of someone they appreciate or something they appreciate. This may be done best with their eyes closed. Guide them to think about all the reasons why they are grateful to that person or appreciate the thing (or animal) they have in mind. Ask them to consider how they would like to express their gratitude or appreciation. It may be a card, a song, a poem, a picture, a sculpture, etc. They may also want to do something for that person/pet or spend time with them. This could be encouraged as an addition to making something that expresses their gratitude or appreciation.

*Happiness Interview*
*Objectives:*

1. Students will explore the concept of happiness and what it means to different people
2. Students will discover that for most people happiness comes from relationships with family and friends, being involved in the community, meaningful work, feeling connected to other people or the natural environment, spiritual beliefs (and is associated less often with material possessions).

Explain to the class that this activity is about discovering what contributes to lasting happiness and well-being. Instruct them to interview someone from home, school or the community whom they know well (not a stranger). They should probably pick the happiest person they know and ask the following questions (they may add some of their own questions too):

1. What contributes most to your experience of happiness?
2. What lessons have you learned about happiness through the tough times in your life?
3. What advice do you have for my generation about having a happy life?

Once the interviews are complete, prepare four large pieces of paper (or four columns on a white/black board). Each page should include one of the above questions. The fourth page is for other questions that the students asked. Students can use point form to summarize the answers they received for each question.

Once the chart is completed by each student, review the answers with the class. Ask the class to point out similarities and differences. What are some of the key lessons from this? Do they agree with the advice that has been given? How does the interview information compare with the information that the media gives us about happiness?

*Excerpts from: Sustainable Happiness and Health Education- Teacher's Guide, O'Brien, C. 2010. Available at no cost: www.sustainablehappiness.ca*

## Further reading

Foster, R. & Hicks, G. (1999). *How we choose to be happy.* New York: Perigree.

Gilman, R., Huebner, E.S., & Furlong, M. (Eds.). (2009). *Handbook of positive psychology in schools.* New York: Routledge.

O'Brien, C. (2010). Sustainable happiness and health education – Teacher's guide. Available at www.sustainablehappiness.ca.

O'Brien, C. (2010). Sustainability, happiness and education. *Journal of Sustainability Education, 1.*

Seligman, M. (2002). *Authentic happiness.* Toronto: Free Press.

## Resources

### Baseline Chart

Choose one day this week to create your own log of activities. Fill in as much detail as you can. The chart on this page gives you a sample of what you might write. You may complete more than one day if you wish. Remember to answer the question below as well.

### Sample Chart

| TIME | ACTIVITY | EMOTIONAL EXPERIENCE | IMPACT ON SELF | IMPACT ON OTHERS | IMPACT ON NATURAL ENVIRONMENT |
|---|---|---|---|---|---|
| 8:00 | Breakfast – coffee, toast, cereal | Rushed, distracted, thinking about day | Didn't taste the food, fairly healthy meal, could have chosen whole wheat bread | Coffee was fair trade coffee so positive for coffee workers; bread from farmers market, good for local producers; cereal, not sure | Fair trade coffee, care taken for environment Bread – made locally so not transported very far Cereal – highly processed and transported a long way |
| 8:30 | Carpooled to class/work | Enjoyed talking with friends | Less expensive; Less stress than driving alone; Feel good about it | Pretty good re air quality but would be better to be able to cycle or walk | Better than driving alone but still my best option given where I live |

### Baseline Chart

| TIME | ACTIVITY | EMOTIONAL EXPERIENCE | IMPACT ON SELF | IMPACT ON OTHERS | IMPACT ON NATURAL ENVIRONMENT |
|---|---|---|---|---|---|
|  |  |  |  |  |  |
|  |  |  |  |  |  |
|  |  |  |  |  |  |
|  |  |  |  |  |  |
|  |  |  |  |  |  |
|  |  |  |  |  |  |

Areas where I could improve my own well-being, or the well-being of others and/or the natural environment.

# Part V
## Sustainability:
## A Whole-system View

*like a whirlwind or a school of fish*
oil, ink and charcoal on canvas
150cm by 150cm

# Chapter 21
## Sustainability Through the Lens of Resilience Thinking

*David Salt*
*ARC Centre of Excellence for Environmental Decisions (CEED),*
*The Fenner School of Environment and Society, College of Medicine,*
*Biology & Environment, Australian National University*

*Introduction*

Does the emerging science of ecological resilience have anything to offer to the field of sustainability? Without doubt it does, but to appreciate why you need to understand a few of the building blocks that go into resilience thinking.

Indeed, I'd go further to say that a real engagement with the ideas that underpin ecological resilience can literally transform a person's ideas on what sustainability actually is; and I speak from personal experience. I've been writing about science for 25 years and involved in many debates on sustainability, often wondering what it is we were hoping to achieve. It seemed that most of the research I was covering, science that purported to deliver 'sustainability', was simply a new process or piece of technology that did things more efficiently – more outputs for less inputs (or less waste). Is that it? Is efficiency the ultimate solution to the challenge of sustainable development?

Then I was asked to write a book on ecological resilience, and I remember thinking it was going to be a text on how to build systems that would more *efficiently* cope with anything we could throw at them. Resilience is just about recovery, right? Actually, that's wrong. It is about recovery but it's so much more.

Ecological resilience is really about understanding the complexity of the systems we depend on (catchments, agricultural industries, forests and fisheries etc) and what allows them to continue to provide us with the goods and services we rely upon for our survival.

In any event, by the time I'd completed the book my understanding of sustainability was transformed. And my ideas on the connections between efficiency and sustainability had also gone through a significant change. The book was called *Resilience Thinking*, and I wrote it with Dr Brian Walker, one of the world's experts on ecological resilience.

In this chapter I don't have space to take you on the journey I went through but maybe I can give you enough information to excite you to begin your own enquiry into resilience thinking. I'll begin with some notes on the concept and definition of the term resilience, and then I'll attempt to explain the building blocks that make up the backbone of resilience thinking. I'll conclude by connecting this back to sustainability and efficiency.

Before I begin I need to qualify my opening question. Ecological resilience is not an emerging science. It's been around now for over forty years and these days there are hundreds of ecologists, economists and social scientists actively engaged in it around the world (see the website of the Resilience Alliance, http://www.resalliance.org/). What is new, and what allows me to describe it as emerging, is the growing use of the concept in policy and management. Indeed, anyone following the national debate on sustainability and natural resource management will have observed how frequently the word resilience is now appearing in policy statements and political rhetoric.

### Concepts of resilience

There's more than one take on resilience. Concepts of resilience are used in all sorts of disciplines and, on top of this, there are many informal ideas of what it means. Its formal usage has four main origins – psycho-social, ecological, disaster relief (and military) and engineering. Psychologists have long recognised marked differences in the resilience of individuals confronted with trauma and disaster. Ecologists have tended to describe resilience in two ways; one focused on the speed of return following a disturbance, the other focused on whether or not the system *can* recover (how much it can be disturbed and still manage to recover). People working in disaster relief incorporate both aspects (i.e. speed and ability to recover). Indeed, there is a lot in common in the understanding of resilience in the areas of psychology, ecology and disaster relief.

In engineering ideas on resilience are somewhat different. Engineers more commonly use the term *robustness* with an understanding of *designed resilience*. It differs from the other three uses in that it assumes bounded uncertainty – that is, the kinds and ranges of disturbances and shocks are known and the system being built is designed to be robust in the face of these shocks. Engineering concepts of resilience focus on a designed amount of resilience while in ecological, psycho-social and defence arenas what is important is how resilience can change – how it can be gained or lost.

The definition that forms the base of resilience thinking (known as ecological resilience) is: "the capacity of a system to absorb disturbance and re-organise so as to retain essentially the same function, structure and feedbacks – to have the same identity". In other words, resilience is the ability to cope with shocks and keep functioning in much the same kind of way.

A key word here is *identity*. It emerged independently in ecological and psycho-social studies, and it imparts the idea that a person, a society, an eco-system or a social-ecological system can all exhibit quite a lot of variation, be subjected to disturbance and cope, without changing their *identity* – without becoming something else. It should be noted that keeping the same identity does not mean staying identical.

Resilience thinking is based on appreciating the complexity of the systems being considered. Its building blocks are the concepts of thresholds, interconnected domains, cycles and scale.

### Self-organising systems

At its heart, resilience thinking is all about understanding the systems we depend upon as self-organising systems (often referred to as complex adaptive systems).

All the things that most resource managers are interested in (for example, farms, landscapes and catchments) but also things like your bodies, brains and businesses, are self-organising systems. You can control bits of the system but the system will then self organise around this change. Other bits will change in response to your control. Sometimes you have a good idea how the system will respond to your actions, sometimes it's difficult to predict.

Most of the time the system can deal with the changes it experiences, be it some form of management or some shock like a disease outbreak. The system absorbs the disturbance, re-organises and keeps performing in the way it did – it retains its identity.

But sometimes, despite our best efforts, the system can't absorb the change and begins behaving in some other (often undesirable) way. Sometimes a fishery crashes and doesn't come back when fishing pressure is removed. Sometimes a national park loses the very biodiversity it was set up to protect. Sometimes, even with the best intentions, our management turns our most precious landscapes from valuable assets to expensive liabilities.

This often happens because our traditional approach to managing resources, which usually focuses on narrowly optimising a part of the system (e.g. fish or timber or grain), fails to acknowledge the limits to predictability inherent in a self-organising system.

### *Thresholds*

There are *limits* to how much a self-organising system can change or be changed and still recover. Beyond those limits it functions differently because some critical feedback process has changed. These limits are known as thresholds. When a self-organising system crosses a threshold it is said to have crossed into another *regime* (also called a *stability domain*) of the system and now behaves in a different way – it has a different identity.

On coral reefs, for example, there is a threshold associated with nutrient levels in the water. Plant nutrients find their way to coral reefs from fertilisers being used on the land. The nutrients stimulate the growth of algae. When the concentration of nutrients goes over a certain level, algae outcompete coral for bare spaces on the reef. There is a critical level of nutrient concentration where this takes place and this is a threshold.

Below the nutrient-load threshold, corals predominate when bare space is created by some disturbance. But if the reef crosses the nutrient threshold, algal growth overwhelms the young corals. It might be a storm or a bleaching event that creates the bare space but suddenly the system is behaving in a dramatically different way (a new regime – the system has a new identity). This change has major consequences for the all the organisms (and people) that depend on that reef.

In self-organising systems you need to put the emphasis on thresholds because crossing them can come with huge costs. Resilience thinking is very much about thresholds – understanding them, determining where they might lie and what determines this, and appreciating how you might deal with them.

Thresholds occur in ecosystems and in social systems. In social systems they are more often referred to as *tipping points*. Tipping points might be changes in fashion, voting patterns, riot behaviour or markets.

Thresholds are often difficult to identify. Many variables in a system don't even have them; that is, they show a simple linear response to the change in underlying controlling variables and at no point exhibit a dramatic change in behaviour (see Figure 1a.). For the variables that do have thresholds, however, it's really important to know about them.

It's also important to appreciate that not all thresholds are the same. Sometimes you can cross a threshold but it's a relatively easy thing to cross back again. Water changes to ice when it crosses a temperature threshold (of zero degrees Celsius) but it changes back to water when you raise the temperature above this threshold.

Sometimes there's a large step change when you cross a threshold and then a similar large reverse when you recross back, at the same point. A common example of this is when landscapes lose more than about 90% cover of native vegetation. Below this threshold there is a loss of a suite of native animal species from the landscape. However, provided they haven't been lost entirely from the whole region, restoring the landscape to more than 10% cover results in their re-establishment.

All too often, however, crossing back over a threshold is difficult, involving a hysteresis effect. A hysteresis effect is where the threshold you need to cross to return to the regime you've left is different from the threshold you crossed when you moved out of that regime in the first place.

Productive rangelands, for example, can trend towards a degraded state if the level of grass is allowed to fall under a certain threshold level allowing woody shrubs to take over (they take over because there is not enough grass to carry a fire, and regular burning is what controls the shrubs). This can happen if too many cattle are grazed. However, simply reducing grazing pressure (by removing cattle) won't reverse the situation once the threshold has been crossed because the system is now behaving in a different manner – shrubs dominate and it will take time for the shrubs to die off to allow sufficient amounts of grass back into the system. The pathway back to a grassy rangeland is different to the pathway to the shrub-dominated rangeland. This is shown in Figure 1b.

Sometimes, thresholds are irreversible; once you've crossed a threshold you can never return. When saline ground water rises it crosses a threshold when it reaches 2m below the surface. At this point soil capillarity draws the salty water to the surface. This affects the chemical and physical structure of the surface layer of soil such that even if the level of ground water drops, salt stays in the surface layers. It would take a long time for the salt levels to drop or multiple episode of heavy flushing rain. For the landholder, however, once the saline groundwater rises to within 2m of the surface, the land effectively becomes unproductive and the change is irreversible. This is depicted in Figure 1c. It doesn't matter how much the saline groundwater drops, the salt levels in the soil surface stay high.

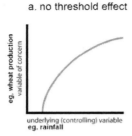
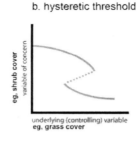
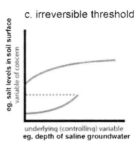

a. no threshold effect    b. hysteretic threshold    c. irreversible threshold

Figure 1: Different kinds of thresholds

*Many variables in your system may not have thresholds on them (1a). However many do; some involve return paths that differ once you cross them (1b) and some are irreversible (1c). (Adapted from Walker and Salt in press.)*

Thresholds are important, yet they're difficult to manage. They come in different forms, can be difficult to detect (until you cross them) and they can move (an example of this in Figure 2). They can occur along biophysical variables like nutrient levels and plant cover, but they also exist in the social and economic domains of your system. What's more, crossing a threshold in one domain can cause the system to cross other thresholds in other domains.

### Linkages between domains

Many of the problems associated with managing natural resources come down to the fact that our approaches don't acknowledge that we're dealing with systems that have linkages between the social, economic and biophysical domains that make them up. Fisheries, for example, are often based on models of how many fish can be harvested over time, but the models focus only on our understanding of the biophysical domain – the dynamics of the fish population under various levels of harvesting - and quotas are set accordingly.

History has shown that these models based on expectations of optimum sustainable yield often lead to the collapse of a fishery, firstly because they fail to acknowledge thresholds. But these failures are then exacerbated by the effects of linkages to the economic domain that were not included in the model. For example, commercial fishers often carry large amounts of debt in the purchase of their boats and fishing equipment, and their need to service this debt leads to overharvesting of the fish resource.

Changes in one domain (e.g. debt levels in the economic domain) will often lead to changes in another (e.g. overharvesting in the biophysical domain, or stress in the social domain) and these then feed back to cause further changes in the first domain. This is one of the hallmarks of complexity; in self-organising systems you can't understand one domain without understanding the connections with other domains and their feedback effects.

And those linkages are possibly most important when they involve the crossing of thresholds. That's because the crossing of one threshold can cause the crossing of other thresholds in other domains forcing the system into a new (undesirable) regime. What's more, experience has shown that going over a series (or cascade) of thresholds (a debt threshold in the economic domain causing the crossing of a biophysical threshold, like a collapsed fishery) leads your system into a highly resilient alternate regime. In other words, a cascading collapse is very hard to return from and resilience isn't a desirable condition when it means you can't escape a bad situation.

Figure 2 depicts two interacting thresholds in two domains of a grazing enterprise on a rangeland (it's based on Fernandez et al, 2002). It plots grass cover against the landowner's debt levels (i.e. it shows us a variable in the biophysical and economic domain of this business).

If the landowner runs too many cows, he or she could cause the operation to drop under a threshold level of grass cover (BT for biophysical threshold) as it moves from state 1 to state 2. System feedbacks change and the rangeland now tracks towards a degraded condition. Productivity drops and the landholder then also crosses an economic threshold (ET) as he or she is forced to borrow more money to keep the enterprise going.

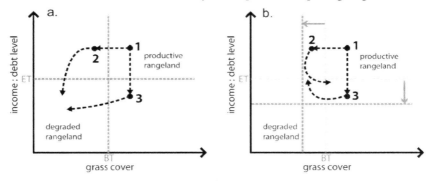

Figure 2: Thresholds in two domains
*The state space of a rangeland plotting two variables: grass cover vs income:debt ratio
(Adapted from Walker and Salt in press, based on Fernandez et al, 2002.)*

But this could happen another way, too. The system might travel from state 1 to state 3 because the landowner might borrow more money (lowering his or her income-to-debt ratio) and cause the enterprise to cross the economic threshold. To service the debt the grazer is forced to run too many cows, which now pushes the enterprise over the biophysical threshold.

This is a simple example but highlights the interactions between two domains and emphasises you can't understand this system without appreciating this interplay. Indeed, in the field of ecological resilience, all these natural resource systems (farms, forests, fisheries etc) are referred to as social-ecological systems.

You can also begin to see in this example how resilience thinking allows us to frame sustainability. Sustainability, in terms of this grazing enterprise, is the ability of this system to continue to grow meat (or maybe fibre if it involved sheep). And that can happen anywhere in the top right hand corner above the economic threshold and to the right of the biophysical threshold. These thresholds mark the borders of the safe operating space for this enterprise.

Figure 2b also demonstrates that this safe operating space can be enlarged if the thresholds can be moved. And this is possible in a number of ways. One way the economic threshold might move is by improving the knowledge behind management decisions. A good example of this is more effective medium-term weather forecasting. If a landowner has greater certainty that the following season will be favourable, he or she can increase stock numbers well in advance and take advantage of the good times and still stay away from the ecological threshold. Likewise, advanced notice of a poor season will enable destocking in time. In the longer term, better forecasting increases average incomes meaning the farmer can service a higher debt. In other words, the economic threshold is lowered thereby increasing the safe operating space of the enterprise.

In regard to the ecological threshold, one way of increasing resilience of the grass cover is to keep as much of it in the form of perennial grasses (as opposed to annual species) as possible. Perennial grasses have much stronger root systems and promote higher infiltration than annual grasses for the same amount of cover. So with perennial grasses the threshold is at a lower level of grass cover, and since the state of the system varies much less there is less chance that it will be pushed across the threshold in a bad year.

However, just as it is possible to increase your safe operating space, it's equally possible for it to shrink. For example, if interest rates are raised, suddenly the debt threshold might shift up (i.e. less debt can be tolerated). Or if there's an invasive plant species, it's possible the amount of grass cover you need might go up. Either way, if the farm is operating close to a threshold it might, without warning, find itself on the wrong side of the threshold because of factors beyond the farmer's control. Which leads to another of the important points about resilience thinking – cross scale interactions and knowing what is happening at other scales.

### *Adaptive cycles*

The next thing to appreciate is that the behaviour of self-organising systems changes over time. The way that the components of the system interact goes through cycles in which the connections between its components tighten, loosen and even break apart. As this happens, the capacity of the system to absorb disturbance (its resilience) also changes, as does the potential for people managing the system to make changes.

Consider a forest recovering after a fire or a new business set up to make and sell a new product. Both are self-organising systems and the components that make up these systems will change over time, as will the manner in which these components interact.

As they establish themselves these systems undergo a period of rapid growth as they exploit new opportunities and available resources. In the business, it's the entrepreneurs that can often do well and get ahead. In the forest, it's the fast growing generalist species that prosper because they can cope well with a bit of variability.

However, over time the capacity and potential for rapid growth diminishes because the system is no longer operating in an *open field*. Availability of resources is reducing as the operating space gets filled; connections between players (or species) are increasing and becoming stronger. The fast growers in the forest are being displaced by the dominant trees (the stronger competitors, but slower growers) that soak up all the available light and nutrients. The entrepreneurs in the business are being displaced by the accountants and the middle managers who have to improve productivity through increasing the scale of the operation and introducing ever more efficiency (often by cutting out perceived redundancies). Risk taking is no longer encouraged, and often not even tolerated, and the system is much more conservative in its approach to business. The system enters a phase of *conservation* in which net production gets very small and size asymptotes; the forest or business is no longer getting bigger.

But just as rapid growth can't go on forever, so too this mature conservative phase inevitably comes to an end. The forest biomass builds to its maximum (climax) level and becomes ever more inflexible, with nutrients locked up in heartwood. It is more and more prone to a disturbance such as fire or a pest outbreak. Or the business has grown so big it can no longer steer its way through a changing economy or seize opportunities (like new technologies) as they arise. It takes a smaller and smaller disturbance to initiate a collapse – which inevitably happens.

All social-ecological systems, be they forests or businesses, go through cycles where they rise and fall. And when they fall things become very uncertain. Connections between components that were once locked tight are torn apart. Economic, social and biophysical capital (e.g. nutrients locked up in trees, and in accumulating dead organic matter in the forest) are released and the equilibrium of the previous conservation phase disappears.

The release can be brutal for some, and it's always an uncertain time. Resources are lost (nutrients are leached out, money and people leave the enterprise) but it also opens the way for renewal in which a new order or new generation can rise up. Often the new order is pretty much the same as the old order but sometimes it is something dramatically different.

As re-organization and renewal proceed, a new order, and perhaps a new *attractor* (potential equilibrium state) emerges, connections begin to grow between the components of the system and before you know it you're back in a phase of rapid growth.

The cycle that has been discussed here for a forest or a business is described by ecologists as an adaptive cycle (Gunderson and Holling, 2002), and is observed throughout a wide range of self-organising systems. Its four phases are rapid growth, conservation, release and reorganisation (or renewal).

There are times in the cycle when there is greater leverage to change things and other times when effecting change is really difficult (like when things are in gridlock in the late conservation phase). And very importantly, the kinds of policy and management interventions appropriate in one phase don't work in others.

Taken as a whole, the adaptive cycle has two opposing modes. A development loop (or 'fore' loop), and a release and reorganization loop (or 'back' loop) (see Figure 3). The fore loop (sometimes called the front loop or forward loop) is characterised by stability, relative predictability and conservation and this enables the accumulation of capital (which is essential in human systems for wellbeing to increase).

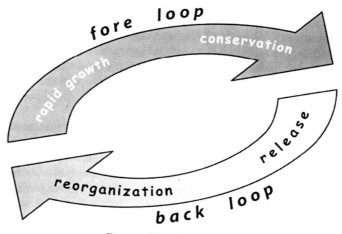

Figure 3: The adaptive cycle
*The system is relatively predictable in the fore loop and this is when there is a slow accumulation of capital and potential through stability and conservation. The back loop is characterised by uncertainty, novelty and experimentation and during which there is a loss (leakage) of all forms of capital. (From Walker and Salt, 2006)*

### Linkages between scales

The adaptive cycle is a useful concept for understanding why a system is behaving in a certain way at a certain time but it's only half the story. Self-organising systems operate over a range of different scales of space and time and each scale is going through its own adaptive cycle. What happens at one scale can have a profound influence on what's happening at scales above and the embedded scales below.

Another key insight arising from resilience thinking is that you can't understand your focal scale (the thing that you're interested in) without appreciating the influence from the scale above and below – and often beyond that to larger and finer scales.

Indeed, it's useful to imagine the system you're interested in as composed of a hierarchy of linked adaptive cycles operating at different scales (in both time and space). The structure and dynamics of the system at each scale is driven by a small set of key processes and, in turn, it is this linked hierarchy of cycles – referred to as a *panarchy* - that governs the behaviour of the whole system.

## *Resilience thinking in action*

Complexity, thresholds, domains, cycles and scales: these are the building blocks of the resilience thinker. Understand the social-ecological system of your interest using these ideas and you're guaranteed to see its behaviour in a new light.

But the framework of resilience thinking encompasses a few other concepts that a resilience practitioner needs to get their head around. The first is that there are two aspects of resilience: specified and general.

**Specified resilience** is the resilience of some specified part of the system to a specified shock; a particular kind of disturbance. A manager of a system would be looking at specific types of shocks they think their system would have to deal with and attempt to ensure the system can absorb them. Specified resilience is about identifying specified thresholds and understanding where your system might lie in relation to those thresholds.

**General resilience** is the system's general capacity to absorb other (non-specified) kinds of disturbances – you can think of it as the system's general coping capacity. Studies of a variety of social-ecological systems suggest **diversity, openness, reserves, tightness of feedbacks, modularity** and **redundancy** are all important characteristics of systems with high levels of general resilience. Another way of thinking about this is that a loss of diversity, openness, reserves etc, can lead to a social-ecological system losing its ability to cope with disturbance.

In understanding your system's resilience you need to deal with both aspects as they are related. There is a trade off between specified and general resilience. Channelling all your efforts into one kind of resilience will reduce resilience in other ways. So it is necessary to consider both.

Once you've assessed your system's resilience you need to consider what's an appropriate response given your understanding. Do you work to keep the system in a safe operating space – do you adapt? Or is the system somewhere that you don't want it to be and there's little prospect of you getting it out of that state. In this case you'll need to transform the system.

**Adaptability (or adaptive capacity)** is the capacity of a social-ecological system to manage resilience – to avoid crossing thresholds, or to engineer a crossing to get back into a desired regime, or to move thresholds to create a larger safe operating space (see the discussion surrounding Figure 2 for an example of this).

Transformability (or transformative capacity) is the capacity to change your system into something else – a new way of making a living, a different kind of system. If the system you're in isn't working and it's unlikely you can adapt to it, transform the system into something else. For example, in Zimbabwe a few decades ago the business of grazing cattle was going nowhere fast. Drought and poor terms of trade was sending pastoralists bankrupt. Many pastoralists acknowledged they couldn't adapt so they transformed their farms into ecotourism parks. They tore down their fences and allowed the wildlife to proliferate. They re-imagined their enterprise.

Towards the beginning of this discussion I made the comment that a system keeping its identity is not about staying identical. It's an important point in relation to understanding resilience and worth reiterating. It's often mistakenly thought that resilience is about keeping a system in exactly the same condition. It's not. A resilience approach is about acknowledging change, embracing it, and working with it. Resilience thinking is structured around the acceptance of disturbance, even the generation of disturbance, to give a system a wide operating space. Indeed, the act of keeping the system the same (say in a state of optimal yield) causes its safe operating space to shrink.

### Sustainability according to resilience thinking

So, what does all this add up to with respect to sustainability? The original definition of 1987 stated that sustainable development meant "development that meets the needs of the present without compromising the ability of future generations to meet their own needs."

A resilience take on this would be something along the lines that management and policy governing the manner in which we exploit natural resources needs to understand how it is possible to extract the goods and services we depend upon from our natural systems without compromising their capacity to deliver these services into the future.

In other words, sustainability is about our natural resource systems being managed in a way that ensures they continue to deliver what we need from them while coping with shocks and disturbances. It's about these systems absorbing disturbance but keeping their identities.

An important insight emerging from resilience thinking is that to be able to do this we need to be able to appreciate the systems that we are specifically interested in (e.g. farms, forests, fisheries, industries, national parks etc) as social-ecological systems. We need to understand them as self-organising systems with thresholds and interconnected domains and scales.

We also need to appreciate that narrowly defined efficiency – that means holding a part of our system in a state that delivers optimal returns (e.g. food or fibre) without considering interactions with other domains or scales – leads to a loss of resilience making it less likely that these systems will continue to deliver into the future. Efficiency is important but by itself it is not *the* solution to the challenge of sustainability.

Sustainability is a many faceted thing (as this book demonstrates). Engage with resilience thinking and you'll discover that much of the challenge and opportunity in the concept of sustainability is inextricably linked with the complexity of the systems we wish to sustain — systems that we depend on, that we are a part of.

### *Further reading*

Bellwood, D. R., Hughes, T. P., Folke C., & Nystrom M. (2004). Confronting the coral reef crisis. *Nature, 429*, 827 – 33.

Carpenter, S. R., Walker, B., Anderies, J. M., & Abel, N. (2001). From metaphor to measurement: resilience of what to what? *Ecosystems, 4,* 765 – 781.

Folke, C., S. R. Carpenter, S. R., Walker B., Scheffer, M., Chapin T., & Rockström J. (2010). Resilience thinking: integrating resilience, adaptability and transformability. *Ecology and Society* [online] URL: http://www.ecologyandsociety.org/vol15/iss4/art20/

Fernandez, R.J., Archer, E.R.M., Ash, A.J., Dowlatabadi, H., Hiernaux, P.H.Y., Reynolds, J.F., Vogel, C.H., Walker, B.H. & Iegand, T.W. (2002). Degradation and Recovery in Socio-ecological Systems A View from the Household/Farm Level. In J.F. Reynolds & D.M. Stafford Smith, (Eds.), *Global Desertification: Do Humans Cause Deserts?* Berlin, Germany: Dahlem University Press.

Gunderson, L. H. & Holling, C.S. (Eds.). (2002). *Panarchy: understanding transformations in human and natural systems.* Washington DC: Island Press.

Holling, C. S. (2004). From complex regions to complex worlds. *Ecology and Society* 9(1), 11. [online] URL: http://www.ecologyandsociety.org/vol9/iss1/art11/

Kinzig, A. P., Ryan, P., Etienne, M., Allison, H., Elmqvist, T. & Walker, B. H. (2006). Resilience and regime shifts: assessing cascading effects. *Ecology and Society 11*(1), 20. [online] URL: http://www.ecologyandsociety.org/vol11/iss1/art20/

Levin, S. (1999). *Fragile dominion.* Cambridge, Massachusetts, USA: Perseus Books Group.

Scheffer, M., Carpenter, S., Foley, J. A., Folke, C., & Walker, B. (2001). Catastrophic shifts in ecosystems. *Nature 413*, 591 – 596.

Walker, B. and Salt, D. (2006). *Resilience Thinking: Sustaining ecosystems and people in a changing world.* Washington, D.C., USA: Island Press.

Walker, B. and Salt, D. (In press). *Resilience Practice.* Washington, D.C., USA: Island Press.

# Chapter 22

## The Cybernetics of Sustainability

### Definition and Underlying Principles

*Michael Ben-Eli*
*The Sustainability Laboratory, New York*

*Sustainability: Has the true meaning been lost?*

For decades now, increasing numbers of thoughtful observers have called attention to disturbing patterns in the current trajectory of human affairs. Accelerating dramatically since the early days of the industrial revolution, powerful forces in development and technology have brought new promises and opened so many new possibilities for humankind. At the same time, driven largely by the impact of human activities, serious threats have emerged to the integrity of whole ecosystems, to other forms of life and to the future well-being of humanity itself.

In response, a growing number of individuals, communities, governments, academic institutions, businesses, faith-based organizations, and others have begun to join forces in actively seeking more harmonious, inclusive, peaceful, and sustainable forms of development. Ensuring a conscious transition of society and the world's economy to a sustainable basis has emerged as the most significant challenge of our time.

The broad-based, worldwide, growing awareness of the sustainability issue is surely a most welcomed development. Popular acceptance, however, seems to have its price. The word sustainability, which was introduced only relatively recently, has quickly become the current buzzword, politically correct and to be used everywhere and in any context. With popularity it seems to have lost some of its essential meaning. In economic development circles, for example, one can hear references made to sustainable projects, the reference is to whether a development project would outlast the period of subsidies. In financial circles, one often hears talk about sustainable financing usually related to the question of whether loans would be profitable in the conventional sense. In business circles, the concept of corporate sustainability consistently puts the well-being of a particular corporation at the fore. Similarly, analysts proclaim that this or that company still has to show sustainable profits, and one hears commentators ask whether the stock market bubble is sustainable, whether a particular domestic or international government policy is sustainable, and so on. All these uses are grammatically correct, implying a sense of continuity, but all miss the essence of our looming global crisis, the crisis of destabilizing the very systems upon which life depends.

Even the prevailing definition of sustainability, the one advanced by the United Nations Commission on Environment and Development, does not help much. This definition, which emphasizes cross generation equity, is vague and deeply flawed on at least three accounts. It is conceptually weak by making one aspect of a desirable end result – the well-being of future generations – the primary condition for attaining itself without specifying what this requirement would actually entail. If instead, for example, we were able to establish the underlying parameters of sustainability as a state and ensure that the values of such parameters were actually secured, vibrant prospects for future generations would follow. Furthermore, the definition is operationally weak since it is difficult to establish economic utility values for future generations, thus allowing for many different interpretations and encouraging the avoidance of clear commitments. Finally, it is flawed with respect to process since no representatives of future generations can participate in critical decisions made on their behalf. Few of us would be happy, I suspect, if Neanderthal humans in their caves had been making decisions on our own behalf, decisions, which would affect directly our lives today.

The seemingly attractive concept of the triple bottom line has its problems as well. It is essentially fragmented and it allows companies who do very well financially, who claim social concerns and donate to environmental causes, claim themselves to be green even when the very essence of their operations – current practices and the depletion of finite resources in the fossil fuels sector, for example – could not be termed sustainable under any stretch of the imagination.

In this chapter the term sustainability will be used in the broad context of our whole planet, the integrity and health of its biosphere and the future well-being of humanity. In addition, a cybernetics perspective on the concept of sustainability will be explored. This particular perspective throws a uniquely useful light, which could bestow rigor and bring operational precision to a term whose meaning has been watered down to the point of trivialization.

## Taking the cybernetics perspective

In the broader context of general system theory, cybernetics puts a specific focus on a consistent theme: the questions of how systems regulate themselves, how do they adapt and evolve, how do they self-organize and, in particular, what are the structures and specific mechanisms which mediate their underlying dynamics. The emphasis is on understanding cause and effect relationships between key variables, or system's components, and how such relationships produce particular outcomes.

The emphasis on underlying system structure is central to the significance of the cybernetic perspective – in our case, related to better understanding the concept of sustainability – since it exposes the very constraints that ultimately shape manifest outcomes. This, in turn, opens the door to a proactive design approach, which involves specification of the particular structures that are most likely to bring about desired results. In other words, taking the cybernetic perspective gives us a direct handle on the operating prerequisites, the essential conditions, the design parameters, the principles, if you will, that cannot be compromised if we are serious about obtaining a particular system state.

The idea, incidentally, goes back to a now classical paper from 1943, *Behavior Purpose and Teleology*, in which Norbert Wiener, the father of *cybernetics* and his colleagues, established the essential connection between a system's output, its observed behavior, and its internal structure. This idea sounds simple and obvious now, but think about how often, in attempting to change a situation, reform an institution, an individual, a country, or the world, efforts are focused on manipulating the outcomes rather than on reconfiguring the structure that is responsible for bringing these about.

The structures in question, it turned out, take the form of networks, in which the now familiar feedback loops, that amplify or dampen conditions, interact to form a recognizable 'something', a particular organization, a system, or a system's state. Invariably, the crux of any organization, any system, is stability of some characteristics, which is preserved intact. That which remains stable can be the system itself or some particular relation of parameters, an equilibrium point, that is essential to its existence in the first place.

From this point of view, sustainability can be regarded as a specific system's state, distinct from a wishful goal or an adjective-like attribute. As such, we would expect for it to be mediated by an internal structure – internal wiring of a particular configuration – anchored in specific variables that can be defined, recognized, destroyed or preserved, even enhanced, by intervention. In this lies the power of the cybernetic perspective. It allows us to operationalize the concept of sustainability. Two points, then, are crucial to this perspective: first, that sustainability is seen as a particular system state born by a particular underlying structure and second, that sustainability can be regarded as a type of stability characterized by some quantity that remains invariant.

## *A definition of sustainability*

What then is the essence, the quantity to be preserved intact, if the condition of sustainability is to hold? The answer is simple: it is a particular kind of equilibrium in the interaction between a population and the carrying capacity of its environment. It could be any population and any environment. It could be amoeba in a Petri dish, algae in a lake, elephants in their habitat, or humans on the planet. As simple as this idea is, it is rarely allowed to drive the sustainability agenda. Both sides of the equation, population on one hand and carrying capacity on the other, are often seen as too sensitive to be tackled head on. Perhaps because they require addressing issues of population dynamics along with issues of consumption patterns and waste, all unpopular subjects requiring a close look at how we humans behave. This would, of course, be uncomfortable since it might throw our whole way of life, our whole civilization into question.

The particular kind of equilibrium referred to earlier as an essential characteristic of the state of sustainability is well familiar to cybernetics. It is embodied in a two-way circular structure, a loop, in which key variables, population and carrying capacity in this case, continuously affect one another. In this kind of circular interaction the two sides of the equation actually define one another; they are involved in a process of co-creation producing a state of dynamic equilibrium whereby, at least for a time, they hold each other in check. A particular environment defines what kind of population is possible in the first place and populations, in turn, modify and remake the environment itself. The long history of the biosphere bears witness to this kind of interaction.

In fact, living organisms and the large complex dynamic systems that comprise the major components of the biosphere, including atmospheric cycles and ecosystems, rain forests, coral reefs, societies, economies, institutions, urban areas, and whole civilizations alike, all display similar characteristics inherent to circular interdependencies. All such systems consist of networks of multiple variables, myriad multi-loops and multiple interactions, all co-accommodating to produce a state of dynamic equilibrium for the whole. It is such equilibrium that makes the recognition of a particular system, a specific identity, possible and it endures largely due to the enormous redundancy of its underlying network. Pathologies in such systems arise when one cluster of loops, one species, begins to aggressively dominate its surroundings destroying the very fabric upon which it depends.

The simple two-way loop of population and carrying capacity is depicted at a higher level of resolution below. Population is indicated at the left of the diagram and carrying capacity at the right. At any given time, population size is determined by net growth rate which is driven, in turn, by a complex interaction of factors including birth and death rates and other variables not all of which is entirely understood today. The carrying capacity exerts its own shaping pressure as can be demonstrated in laboratory experiments with simple organisms in closed environments where the number of individuals in a population and even the actual physical size of individual organisms vary with food distribution patterns.

A population exerts its impact on the carrying capacity of its environment as a function of the rate and intensity of its activity and this impact is driven by two main channels: the demand on resources and the generation of by-products. In a very real sense, populations consume their environments and their activities generate by-products that the environment, in turn, needs to be able to absorb. Sustainability in this context requires that the rates of consumption and generation of resources as well as the rates of generation and absorption of by-products are at equilibrium. This state of equilibrium is dynamic in that it represents a moving target depending on the relative values of the underlying variables at each given time.

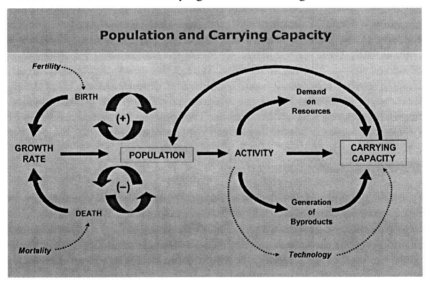

Note, incidentally, that in the case of human society, technology, which can be regarded as an externalized extension of basic metabolic functions, can have a considerable impact on the carrying capacity of an environment. It can expand and deepen it by opening up new and previously entirely unforeseen possibilities. For example, some five hundred years ago, ship building and navigation technologies extended the range and speed of exploration, opening up vast new territories virtually overnight. The discovery of the full range of possible chemical elements – only nine were known in 1250 AD – extended tremendously life support possibilities. Agricultural technologies increase effective yields from given plots of land, other technologies increase the performance obtainable from each pound of resource, and the vast potentials inherent in space exploration are still to be glimpsed, let alone fully realized.

Anchoring the concept of sustainability to the interaction of population and carrying capacity and the state of equilibrium which requires un-hampered regeneration capacity leads to a rigorous definition of sustainability that contains a number of key variables, all potentially measurable. For example: population size, rate of consumption of resources, impacts on absorption capacity of sinks such as forests oceans and soil, rates of regeneration capacities, a measure of well-being, and the like. I would thus like to offer the following definition:

*Sustainability: A dynamic equilibrium in the processes of interaction between a population and the carrying capacity of its environment such, that the population develops to express its full potential without producing irreversible adverse effects on the carrying capacity of the environment upon which it depends.*

It is this equilibrium that has been compromised in our time with the unprecedented explosion of human population and the related rapid intensification in levels of development activities that currently overwhelm the capacity of the planet's sources and sinks. The system is out of balance at present with many components of the biosphere showing relentless signs of severe stress. The list is familiar. It includes ozone depletion; climate change; loss of biodiversity; soil erosion and desertification; diminishing fresh water resources; shrinkage of forest cover; and the growing income disparity between and within nations. This pattern needs to be reversed if systemic collapses of increasing severity are to be averted.

## *What is going on?*

Systemic patterns of stress that characterize our planetary reality can be interpreted by three essentially different perspectives. The first would be largely dismissive. It would argue that all the reported signs of stress might be annoying but they are secondary issues at best. It would insist that things could be fixed as we go along. It would claim that there is no convincing proof to show that circumstances are as bad, that the underlying science is incomplete and that those who sound the alarm have a vested interest at stake. This perspective, which advocates business as usual, still dominates mainstream leadership in business and government and is held by a majority of the general public.

The second perspective, suggested by many thoughtful commentators, concerned scientists, environmentalists and others, holds that humanity has reached absolute limits; that we need to restrain future growth or face major cataclysm. According to this perspective, human activity throughout history was insignificant relative to the size of the planet. It has now grown to dominate the biosphere and the rapidly expanding demand on resources will require more than one planet in order to be satisfied. The advocated response, which inevitably follows, calls for limiting current growth and retreating to a less intensive, perhaps more pastoral way. Except that the genie is well out of the bottle and there seems to be little prospect for peacefully arresting development, especially in all the many parts of the world were the majority of humans are still deprived of the most basic of prospects.

The third perspective is the most intriguing. It would argue that the prevailing signs of stress are real enough but that they largely represent a failure of currently dominant concepts, beliefs and practices to adapt to new possibilities and changing demands. According to this view, prevalent signs of planetary stress are the symptoms of an ongoing conflict between the prerogatives of new possibilities immanent in a next evolutionary step beckoning humanity, and the old ways of perceiving and doing things. They are a result of a tension between a new reality struggling to be born and stubborn, conservative constraints that are blocking its way. This last perspective is compelling because of its proactive, forward-looking characteristics. It lays credence in an evolutionary outlook and puts confidence in the latent potential of life – never completely guaranteed in advance, to be sure – to reconfigure its very structure when the conditions of its context change. This perspective requires that humanity now steps up deliberately, consciously and collectively to shape the next chapter in its own evolution.

One thing is clear. Even by virtue of its numbers alone, humanity has entered a whole new relationship with its home planet. This is well evident even from a quick glance at the exponential curves depicting the growing numbers of the human population. There is no precedence to the current numbers. For thousands of years, humanity fluctuated on both sides of the one billion mark. Within the relatively short period of recent times the number shot up to seven billion and two billion people more are expected to be added by the year 2050. Scientists who study demographic scenarios still argue about the ultimate number but they are really addressing the slope at the very tip of the curve. The big, unprecedented bulge has already occurred. It brings with it entirely new kinds of challenges for which there is no ready-made prescription available. There is simply no experience of managing the world's resources and nine billion people in harmony and in peace.

"Rethink everything!" ought to be the central mantra of our time. Nothing less will suffice. Most existing tools, concepts, institutions, frameworks and mechanisms with which we address the new realities are not going to be adequate to the task. They evolved in the past in a different context and for issues of entirely different nature and magnitude. Most stand now in the way of the necessary change, looming obstacles in the process of reconfiguring our collective reality. The possibility of realizing a sustainable economy of peace and abundance for all calls for a complete reorientation in human affairs. This will require a deep change in our world-view; in the values we hold dear; in the structure of our economy; in our ways of allocating the world's resources; in our priorities for the use of technology; and in our modes of governance. The need is for a second order change, change that will not only affect this or that aspect of our ways of dealing with the world, but will also fundamentally transform the whole underlying system itself.

Anyone who has experienced the difficulties of managing major transformation, in personal, institutional or national life, will appreciate the enormity
of the challenge.

## *The dimensions of sustainability*

A number of key factors shape the equilibrium condition in the interaction
of a population with the carrying capacity of its environment. As already
suggested, these include population size, volume and intensity of activity,
composition of the environment, available technology, and all the physical
quantities that define the channels of metabolic exchanges. As distinct from
other living creatures, human society has evolved to the point whereby a
number of important non-physical factors weigh heavily as well, including
the manifested level of consciousness, the prevailing view of the world and
the abstract framework of explicit assumptions, values and principles by
which society organizes its activities.

Together, all these factors represent the constituent components of the
vector of a population's interaction with its environment. In this sense, they
shape the conditions upon which a state of sustainability ultimately depends
and provide a framework for deriving the principles that define it as a state.
As a system, this framework can be expressed in relation to five essential dimensions representing logically distinct but co-dependent, interacting domains. They include the following:

- *The material domain,* whichconstitutes the basis for regulating the flow
  of materials and energy that underlie existence.
- *The economic domain,* which provides a guiding framework for creating
  and managing wealth.
- *The domain of life,* which provides the basis for appropriate behavior in
  the biosphere.
- *The social domain,* which provides the basis for social interactions, and
- *The spiritual domain,* which identifies the necessary attitudinal, value
  orientation and provides the basis for a universal code of ethics.

From each domain a single sustainability principle is derived, each, with its
own policy and operational implications. The result is a set of five core principles, a set that is fundamentally systemic in nature since each domain affects all the others and is affected by each in return. This systemic aspect
is fundamental. It reflects the interdependent nature of reality itself. It has
far reaching implications for policy and for any competent attempt at bringing about change. It implies that in seeking a transition to sustainability as
a predominant planetary state, no piece-meal approach – emphasizing some
aspects while neglecting others – is likely to yield the desired end state.

## *The five core principles*

The ultimate objective of establishing the concept of sustainability as an organizing principle is to foster a well-functioning alignment between individuals, society, the economy and the regenerative capacity of the planet's life-supporting ecosystems. The five core principles that follow prescribe the necessary conditions for attaining this state.

I. *The material domain*

All the physical processes that provide the basis for human existence are subject to the primary laws of physics, for example: Einstein's law of the inter-changeability of energy and matter; the first law of thermodynamics which addresses the fundamental conservation of energy in universe; and, the second law, which stipulates the direction of energy events. These laws prescribe the ultimate limits of possibilities in physical systems and, therefore, underlie the productive potential in the use of resources.

The Second Law underscores the ultimate increase of entropy, diffusion and disorderliness in all physical systems. At the same time, it does not rule out the possibility of local order increase, at least temporarily, as manifest in the formation of complex organic molecules, organisms, whole eco-systems and at least one currently known whole planet – our own – a precious cosmic region in which energy is compounded to create order of increasing complexity, a prime characteristic of life.

Consciousness itself may turn out to be the ultimate anti-entropic enabler. Consciously disciplined intelligence, applied to the design of universally advantageous configurations of energy and matter – arranging and rearranging components of the physical domain – provides the essential tool for creating the wealth infrastructure of lasting abundance.

The crucial point is that our current industrial infrastructure is highly entropic. It is wasteful, destructive, fragmented and grossly inefficient. Entropy cannot be eliminated entirely, of course, but it can be reduced and managed by superior design employed to deliver lasting, regenerative advantage for all. Hence,

*The first principle: Contain entropy and ensure that the flow of resources, through and within the economy, is as nearly non-declining as is permitted by physical laws.*

II. *The economic domain*

Economies consist of markets where transactions occur and guiding frameworks by which transactions are evaluated and decisions about commitments are made. Often treated as though they reflect an independent, objective reality, such frameworks ultimately represent human constructs, rooted in values, biases and dominant interests and concerns. These latter factors determine adoption of the underlying economic perspective: short-term, narrow, linear focus, or long-term, comprehensive, eco-sensitive cycles of return.

The accounting framework used at present to guide our economy grossly distorts values. It systematically ignores important cost-components, for example, depletion of resources and impacts of pollution and waste. Economists are beginning to reflect on the inadequacies inherent in the narrow concept of growth that dominates measurement of national economies, and some even highlight the basic absurdity of counting consumption as if it were income, a common practice in the way we treat natural resources.

Inadequate measurements, with regulations and subsidies, which often accompany them, drive markets and continue to fuel the destructive effects of the economy as a whole. The prevailing conventions of our accounting framework exacerbate such effects and limit the scope of individual initiatives seeking better practices. This self-reinforcing pattern is clearly one key dimension requiring radical change.

***The second principle:*** *Adopt an appropriate accounting system, fully aligned with the planet's ecological processes and reflecting true, comprehensive biospheric pricing to guide the economy.*

III. *The domain of life*

The adaptive success of the human species and its quick propagation almost everywhere on planet earth comes at the continuous expense of many other forms of life. The destruction of individual animals, species, habitats and whole ecosystems, a trend now reaching ominous proportions, is a deep cause for concern.

Complex, self-organizing, living systems – brains, societies, ecosystems, and industrial economies alike – depend on their very complexity, their internal variety, for long term viability. Lasting stability in all such systems is in fact, science tells us, a direct function of their very complexity, of inherent redundancy, which allows for emergence and re-emergence of different configurations in response to changing context events. Monocultures are brittle in principle, the antithesis, in this context, of vibrant life. With our current practices we are striping biospheric variety away.

On this point contemporary science seems to be joining with many of the world's ancient traditions, which insist on the uniqueness and fundamental sacredness of all forms of life.

***The third principle:*** *Ensure that the essential diversity of all forms of life in the biosphere is maintained.*

IV. *The social domain*

Work of early 20<sup>th</sup> century scientists and philosophers of science brought to the fore the fundamental fallibility of human knowledge pointing out that, with regard to *knowing*, complete certainty is in principle all but impossible. This suggests that, in a true ecological fashion, myriad expressions and species of truth should be allowed to coexist without any particular one seeking to aggressively dominate others.

Societies, like ecologies, depend on diversity and internal redundancy for robustness, long-term viability and health. This alone underscores the importance of encouraging variety and plurality in social forms. At the same time, modern genetics and the sequencing of the human genome indicate that the underlying genetic differences between the many ethnic groups on the planet are insignificantly small, rendering arguments for an inherent superiority of any group, baseless.

All these thoughts reinforce the still fragile idea that open processes, responsive structures, plurality of expression and the equality of all individuals ought to constitute the corner-stones of social life. As we enter the twenty first century however, society continues to operate predominantly by the worn-out assumptions, concepts and structures of yesterday.

***The fourth principle:*** *Maximize degrees of freedom and potential self-realization of all humans without any individual or group, adversely affecting others.*

V. *The spiritual domain*

The human spirit has consistently sought to transcend material, biological, physiological, psychological, conceptual, and technological limitations. This constant drive for touching a 'beyond', for taking progressively more into the field of vision and integrating an increasingly broader 'reality', has a huge practical significance. With its intuitive reach for wholeness and completion, it fuels the development and evolution of individuals and societies alike.

The extent to which this deeply rooted drive is actually allowed to manifest in the daily affairs of society, affects the choices we make and the quality of our actions in the world. Ultimately, it underscores the difference between a greedy, egocentric, predatory orientation and a nurturing, self-restrained, inclusive approach, which honours the larger system of which we are a part and on which we depend for our very existence.

The essential quality of the spiritual domain, recognized, as it is, by all known wisdom traditions, is not easy to pin down. In the English language, the term spiritual carries opposing connotations: sacred, exalted, virtuous, divine, but also, insubstantial and occult. It is meant here to evoke a sense of a deep, underlying essence—a combination of inspiration, meaning, purpose, and a motivating, all-encompassing value. The fundamental imprecision that is involved is manifest in the more elaborate way in which the fifth principle is expressed.

### The fifth principle:

*Recognize the seamless, dynamic continuum*
*Of mystery, wisdom, love, energy, and matter*
*That links the outer reaches of the cosmos*
*With our solar system, our planet and its biosphere*
*Including all humans, with our internal metabolic systems*
*And their externalized technology extensions –*
*Embody this recognition in a universal ethics*
*For guiding human actions*

The five core principle can be summarized in a few simple words: contain entropy; account for externalities; maintain diversity; self-actualize benignly; and, acknowledge the mystery.

### The five sustainability principles as an integrated whole

Deeper reflection on the concept of sustainability and the five core principles, which together prescribe it, reveals that the spiritual dimension, the spiritual principle, is fundamental to the quality and coherence of the whole. It is rarely incorporated however, in the conventional calculus of practical affairs.

As a guiding principle the spiritual dimension does not carry the connotation of conventional religion. Rather, it evokes the soul-focused integration of mind and heart in realization of the essential oneness at the center of being.

By anchoring the essence of human motivation and intention, the spiritual principle acts as the causal root that sets the tone for the whole. It drives the integration of the other four principles, those related to the material, economic, life, and social domains. If integrated in a balanced way, it can infuse a common purpose, provide a common foundation and stimulate common resolve. Lacking the ethical commitment implied by the spiritual principle, considerations of questions related to the four other domains, no matter how elaborately expressed, are reduced to mere technicalities.

---

1.The Five Sustainability Principles were first published by Michael Ben-Eli in 2006, on the web site of the Buckminster Fuller Institute, in New York. The principles are being used as a basis for the work of the Sustainability Laboratory, established in order to develop and demonstrate breakthrough approaches to sustainability practices.
Application of the principles as an integrated, whole framework is demonstrated in the Lab's current flagship project – Project Wadi Attir – an initiative with a Bedouin community in the Negev desert, designed to showcase a model for sustainable agriculture in an arid zone (see www.sustainabilitylabs.org).

By their very nature language, logic and action force separation, discrimination and choice. A balanced, simultaneous and full integration of all five principles is essential however, for conceptualizing and realizing sustainability as a state. The whole set has to be integrated into a single unity in which the five principles come together as one.

As already suggested, the five domains underlying the principles interact and co-define one another. Further, as in a holographic image, each embodies the whole general scheme in its own sphere. When the principles are thus integrated and seamlessly inform choices and actions, a state of sustainability, which otherwise appears as a difficult, distant goal, can be realized spontaneously and completely.

### *Policy and Operational Implications*

For each domain and from each principle, a few primary policy and operational implications follow. Taken together, these combine to sketch out key elements for a comprehensive blue print for the future. Briefly, they include the following, primary demands:

*In relation to the physical domain:* Strive for highest resource productivity; Amplify performance with each cycle of use of resource; Employ *income* rather than *capital* sources for energy and continuously recycle non-regenerative resources; Affect an unbroken, closed-loop flow of matter and energy in a planetary industrial infrastructure conceived as a whole; Control leakages and avoid stagnation, misplaced concentrations or random diffusion of chemical elements during any cycle of use; Establish a predominantly service, performance leasing, rather than ownership orientation for managing durable goods.

*In relation to the economic domain:* Employ a comprehensive concept of wealth related to the simultaneous enhancement of five key forms of capital: natural, human, social, manufactured and financial; Align the world's economy with nature's regeneration capacity and incorporate critical externalities in all cost and benefit accounts; Embody a measure of well-being and human development in economic calculations; Design regulation and taxation policies to accentuate desirable and eliminate adverse outcomes, optimizing the whole; Rely on market mechanisms, calibrated to reflect true costs, for allocation of capital assets.

*In relation to the domain of life:* Assume a responsible stewardship for our planet's web of biological diversity; Harvest species only to regeneration capacity; Conserve the variety of existing gene pool; Shape land use patterns to reduce human encroachment on other forms of life and enhance biological diversity in areas of human habitat.

*In relation to the social domain:* Foster tolerance as a cornerstone of social interactions; Enshrine universal rights within a framework of planetary citizenship; Provide for inclusion and effective democracy in governance; Ensure equitable access to life nurturing resources; Establish cooperation as a basis for managing global issues and planetary commons; Outlaw war and trade in weapon technologies; Promote sustainability literacy through education at all levels; Embody sustainability enhancing measures in an effective planetary framework of legislation.

***In relation to the spiritual domain:*** Acknowledge the transcendent mystery that underlies existence; Seek to understand and fulfil humanity's unique function in Universe; Honour the Earth with its intricate ecology of which humans are an integral part; Foster compassion and an inclusive, comprehensive perspective in the underlying intention, motivation and actual implementation of human endeavours; Link inner transformation of individuals to transformations in the social collective, laying foundations for emergence of a new planetary consciousness

Even a casual review will suggest that every one of the conditions referred to above is being ignored or worse, violated, everyday and everywhere. This is why our current path is not sustainable, why it must be changed. With a long evolutionary process behind it civilization seems now to be poised on the threshold of a possible future of abundance, peace and creative well-being. Will it be wise enough to secure such a future? It could – by employing a higher, more inclusive level of consciousness and by addressing the challenge purposefully, decisively and collectively, with sensitivity, thoughtfulness, and deliberate, comprehensive design.

It can be argued that many of our current global predicaments are the direct results of a fragmented, reductionist view of the world and the associated overspecialization in education and the professions. Systems thinking and cybernetics can provide the conceptual framework and some of the particular tools that are essential for ensuring the required transformation.

# Chapter 23
## A Cybersystemic Framework for Practical Action

*Ray Ison*
*Professor of Systems, Communication & Systems Department,*
*The Open University, UK and Professor, Systems for Sustainability,*
*Monash Sustainability Institute, Clayton, Australia*

*The issue*

The scientific consensus that humans are changing the climate of the Earth is the most compelling, amongst a great many reasons, as to why we humans have to change our ways of thinking and acting. Few now question that we have to be capable of adapting quickly as new and uncertain circumstances emerge and that this capability will need to exist at the personal, group, community, regional, national and international levels all at the same time.

The phenomenon of human-induced climate change is new to human history and it is accompanied by 'peak oil', rising population and consumerism, changing demographics and over exploitation of the natural world, including widespread loss of biodiversity and the over exploitation of water resources. So, climate change *per se* is not the only issue. In the face of such complexity and uncertainty human ingenuity will be tested.

   This chapter frames the issue of concern not as a problem of the so-called natural world but as an issue which at its core is to do with how we humans think and then act in relation to: (i) the biophysical world, (ii) other species and (iii) other human beings. In many ways we are in a trap of our own making. Breaking out of this trap requires ingenuity – the invention of new ways of thinking and acting as well as looking at what has been done in the past that could be mainstreamed in ways that help us now. So, when we look around us what different ways of thinking and acting could be helpful? And how do humans change their ways of thinking and acting? As a response to these questions this chapter argues that development of our capabilities to think and act *systemically* is an urgent priority. Systems thinking and practice are not new but individually and socially our capability to do it is very limited. Unfortunately these are not abilities developed universally through schooling, at university or in the workforce.

   The rise of specialised subject-matter disciplines, the focus on science and technology at the expense of praxis (theory informed practical action) and reductionist research approaches have driven the intellectual and practical fields of Systems and Cybernetics, forms of trans-disciplinary or 'meta' thinking, from the curriculum. Consequently, current generations of students are rarely exposed to what I call cybersystemic ways of thinking and acting. As a result there is limited familiarity with the language and concepts of cybersystemics. For this reason readers are encouraged to actively explore the range of cybersystemic terms and ideas that can be found on some key web pages (see suggested actions at the end of the chapter).

   In this chapter some of the history of cybersystemic thinking is introduced. The concept of a structurally coupled socio-biophysical system is then introduced as a way to think about, and act, in regard to the on-going relationship between humans and the biosphere. Practical examples from the governance of watersheds or river catchments and the invention of eco-systems service institutions are provided.

## Context

### Historical

If one accepts that through human agency aspects of our world are changing in undesirable and unsustainable ways then it follows that only humans can act to change what they do. In other words only we can take responsibility. However, it is not possible to be responsible if, at the same time, we are unable to be response-able. What constrains us from being response-able? The most widespread constraints, I argue, are our lack of awareness of (i) what it means for humans to live in language and how language uses us; (ii) how theories shape what we do and think, and (iii) the rules and norms we humans invent that become part of our cultures, or how we govern ourselves, which I will call 'institutions'. Institutions are pervasive and range from road rules, laws and policies to the conventions families adopt about dinner time. Language, such as the way nouns work in English to suggest that objects exist independently of us, in contrast to some Amero-Indian languages in which there are no nouns, as well as institutions, can constrain our actions in ways that are beyond our awareness. Institutions become the accepted 'ways things are' rather than being subjected to critical scrutiny by asking: are these human inventions still relevant to today's circumstances?

So there is not much point asking, or trying to make people responsible if their circumstances mean they are not response-able. When *response-ability and responsibility* operate together they are said to be recursively related. *Recursion*, a form of circularity, is a key cybersystemic concept. How it operates can be understood from being in a conversation. The word conversation, from the Latin which means 'to turn together', can be understood as a form of dance with one partner responding to another recursively, each taking their cue from the other but retaining their own autonomy as they act. The performance that emerges is different to the parts – it is said to be an *emergent property*, another key cybersystemic concept. When Stephen Talbott asks how we should act to change things for the better he says:

> *"We do not view the sovereign individuality and inscrutability of our fellows as a reason to do nothing that affects them. But neither do we view them as mere objects for a technology of control. How do we deal with them? We engage them in conversation. We converse to become ourselves."*

So what are some of these cybersystemic concepts and where do they come from? Figure 1 has been developed to facilitate a conversation about the lineages and complexities associated with the intellectual field of cybersystemics. Of course there is never any settled or agreed way to depict or describe an academic field. This is no bad thing as it is important to understand and appreciate different perspectives. However, all too often what divides us takes greater precedence over that which we have in common. At this moment we need sufficient agreement to engage in practical action on multiple fronts.

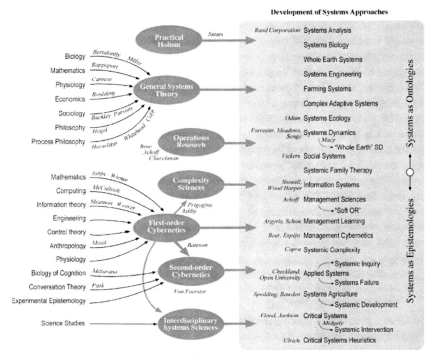

Figure 1: An heuristic model of some of the different influences that have
shaped contemporary cybersystemic approaches and the lineages from
which they have emerged (Source: Ison 2010 p. 29)

Figure 1 is best read from right to left (more or less). Down the right-hand
side is a set of contemporary systems approaches which are written about,
put into practice and sometimes taught. Some names of people (systems
and cybernetic practitioners), associated with particular approaches and lineages, have been added, though the choices are far from comprehensive. If
one does a search, most of the approaches listed in the grey-shaded area of
the figure could be found with a reasonable literature associated with each.
They can be understood as more-or-less contemporary forms of approach to
cybersystemic practice but they are not static, arising in and from particular
lineages, and in their manners of conservation lay down new or conserve ex-
tant lineages.

On the left, seven formative clusters are identified that have given rise
to these contemporary approaches. By following the arrows backwards it
is possible to get a sense of some of the different lineages, though rarely
are they as simple as depicted here. There is a close affinity between cybersystemic thinkers and process thinkers. Some historical accounts of systems lineages start with the concerns of organismic biologists who felt that
the reductionist thinking and practice of other biologists was losing sight of
phenomena associated with whole organisms. For example in the western
world, or in countries that adopt a western lifestyle, the rise of breast cancer

incidence in women seems predominantly to do with a complex of factors in the environment that create affects that operate at the level of the whole person. Organismic or systemic biologists were amongst those who contributed to the interdisciplinary project described as 'general systems theory' or GST (Figure 1). Fortunately 'systemic biology' is undergoing a resurgence. Other historical accounts start earlier – with notions of practical holism or even earlier with process thinkers such as the Greek philosopher, Heraclitus, who is reputed to have said: "You cannot step into the same river twice, for fresh waters are ever flowing in upon you."

Below GST in Figure 1 the next two clusters are associated with cybernetics, from the Greek meaning 'helmsman' or 'steersman'. The term was coined to deal with concerns about feedback as exemplified by the person at the helm responding to wind and currents so as to stay on course. In my own work I understand governance from this cybernetic perspective. A governor on a steam engine for example was a device to monitor (communicate) and control feedback. A key image of first order cybernetics is that of the thermostat controlled radiator – when temperatures deviate from the optimum feedback processes adjust the heat to maintain the desired temperature. First-order cyberneticians are, or were, mainly concerned with communication and control, particularly in 'engineered systems'. Second order cyberneticians concern themselves with second order phenomena such as the cybernetics of cybernetics, or the control of control. Building on the original Greek understanding, second-order cybernetics raises questions such as who charts a course for what purpose in response to feedback? This is clearly the domain of human activity and not engineered processes. Governance is thus concerned with how groups, organisations, teams and societies chart courses in response to feedback, which of course involves learning and adaptive change.

Figure 1 has many limitations and it is not possible to describe all the influences or approaches in detail but it does capture a way of understanding the 'cybersystemic field'. The current approaches on the right are also organised from top to bottom in terms of what are perceived by me to be common commitments, or tendencies, of a majority of practitioners within the given approach. Towards the top of the Figure these 'commitments' relate to seeing systems as 'real entities' (ontologies) that exist in the world independently of us. Towards the bottom the commitment of most practitioners is to see systems as human inventions that help us to better know about complex and uncertain situations (i.e., epistemologies). The latter position, which I prefer, provides a cybersystemic practitioner with more choices to act in complex situations (Figure 2).

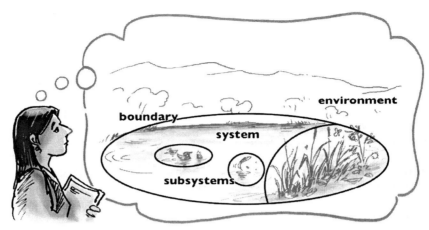

Figure 2: Key elements of systems practice as a process – within a situation a system of interest comprising a system (with subsystems), boundary and environment is 'brought forth', or distinguished, by someone as they engage with the particular situation (Source: Ison 2010a)

As outlined earlier, in everyday situations people either implicitly or explicitly refer to things that are interconnected (exhibit connectivity) when they use the word 'system'. A common example is the use of 'transport system' or 'computer system' in everyday speech. Unfortunately everyday use of the word system, a noun, implies that systems exist before we humans formulate or invent them. This everyday usage seduces us into the systems-as - ontology position, often unknowingly. Reification is the term given when, knowingly or unknowingly, something that is conceptual is made into a thing. Later I will describe how this has happened with the concept 'ecosystem'.

As well as a set of interconnected 'things' (elements) a 'system' can also be seen as a way of thinking about the connections (relationships) between things – hence a process. This process dimension can be understood by working through Figure 2 carefully. Figure 2 depicts one of the key practices associated with cybersystemic practice. It is the act, or practice, of distinguishing or formulating a system, in a situation as a way of thinking about and acting in that situation. The woman in Figure 2 is conceiving of the situation in a particular way known only to her. She could be thinking about fish for dinner, and hence her conception of what her system of interest does (its purpose) is to produce fish. By seeing 'a system to produce fish' she is focusing first on what the pond is for from her perspective. She is creating a 'system of interest'. Equally she may be thinking in terms of protecting endangered species, or of creating a garden pond. Systems of interest are devices related to purpose, so that the boundary and subsystems will be different in each particular system of interest. Systems of interest even in the same situation are also likely to differ somewhat because each is constructed or formulated by one or more people who have different experiences and backgrounds and possibly purposes.

The key systems concepts that are involved in formulating systems of interest are:

- making boundary judgments
- creating the levels of system, subsystem, suprasystem
- distinguishing a system from an environment – that outside the system boundary – which I understand as creating a relational dynamic between system and environment mediated by a boundary, rather than 'a thing' called 'system'
- elements and their relationships
- attribution of purpose to the system
- monitoring and evaluating the performance of the system against named measures such as for efficacy, efficiency, effectiveness, ethicality

A little reflection makes it obvious that the idea of system as a 'thing' is not that helpful because in the same situation what one person will see as a system – the interconnected elements that combine to form a whole – will be different from someone else. Because each individual has a unique experiential history they will 'see' different elements connected in different ways and thus make different boundary judgments.

Of course the primary purpose of engaging with cybersystemic understandings is to act differently in the world and to create innovations and changes that are more systemic (or holistic) rather than just systematic (i.e. linear, step by step thinking about causality and change which currently predominates). Both systemic and systematic approaches are important but at this historical moment we need more development in the systemic domain than the systematic.

My claim is that by developing cybersystemic capabilities and using them explicitly we can improve the overall effectiveness with which we deal with complex situations such as that involved in responding to sustainability. As I said earlier, cybersystemic thinking is not new in human history but unfortunately it is likely to be new to many of those living today.

*Geographical*

Many indigenous societies have had more systemic understandings and practices than those which characterize the western intellectual tradition. For example, in an increasingly urbanized world fewer and fewer people have an understanding of how to 'read' the land and its associated vegetation. Perception and interpretation of land and the nature of change of land, and its associated vegetation, are important issues for the future. If we act before it is too late we can benefit from the rich traditions of understanding in indigenous cultures. The ethnographer, Deborah Bird Rose, articulated four transcendant rules interpreted from the Yarralin Aboriginal Community consistent with cybersystemic thinking:

1. Balance – a system cannot be life enhancing if it is out of kilter, and each part shares in the responsibility of sustaining itself and balancing others.
2. Response – communication is reciprocal. There is here a moral obligation: to learn to understand, to pay attention, and to respond.
3. Symmetry – in opposing and balancing each other, parts must be equivalent because the purpose is not to 'win' or to dominate, but to block thereby producing further balance.
4. Autonomy – no species, no group, or country is 'boss' for another; each adheres to its own Law. Authority and dependence are necessary within parts, but not between parts.

The world-wide loss of indigenous languages is another unfolding tragedy of human origin. Each culture has developed ways of thinking and acting in relation to their world. As we lose the diversity of ways of knowing, so do we limit the variety we might draw on for innovation and change in an uncertain and complex future.

## *Discussion*

Mainstream economics, which dominates the treasuries of the world, and thus most political decision-making, is essentially built upon systematic rather than systemic thinking (Straton, 2006):

> *"The classical conceptualization of value (in economics) is related to supply; it is also objectivist, locating the origin of value in the things from which objects are made, such as land or labour... In contrast, the modern neoclassical conceptualisation of value incorporates a convergence of supply and demand that produces an equilibrium or market clearing price. Value is considered to originate in the minds of individuals, as revealed through their subjective preferences. In short, value is determined by the market-place. Ecological resources complicate the modern neoclassical approach to determining value due to their complex nature, considerable non-market values and the difficulty in assigning property rights. Application of the market model through economic valuation only provides analytical solutions based on virtual markets, and neither the demand nor supply-side techniques of valuation can adequately consider the complex set of biophysical and ecological relations that lead to the provision of ecosystem goods and services (p 402)."*

The particular understanding of human behaviour and rationality that is at the core of the neo-classical paradigm has been shown to be both limiting and flawed as recent Nobel prizes in economics testify. In addition, situations such as climate change are best understood as non-equilibrial yet for decision making we rely on a paradigm that is built on concepts of equilibrium.

With this claim about the nature of mainstream economics as background, I want to develop a case study of where cyberstemic thinking, if applied, would lead us humans down a different pathway to that which we are on. Please note my use of language here – I am trying to avoid the trap of simple cause and effect thinking that implies that if we only did x, then y would happen. For me it is more a governance question – about the relationship between purpose, charting a course, and how the feedback we are receiving, particularly from the biophysical world, is interpreted and acted upon.

## Case study: ecosystems services

As I have intimated already there are many situations to be concerned about at the moment so why single out 'ecosystems services'? Well, in spite of more than four decades of international summits and agreements, mounting evidence has shown that humans are influencing what we have come to call ecosystems more rapidly than at any similar time in human history, drastically altering ecosystem functioning in the form of the degradation of the functions they fulfil, the increased risk of abrupt and irreversible ecosystem changes, and exacerbated poverty for part of the human population. A complex challenge now faces the world: match the rapidly changing demand for food from a larger and more affluent population to its supply; do so in ways that are environmentally and socially sustainable under climate change; and ensure that the world's poorest people are no longer hungry. Together, these challenges are unprecedented in human history. Navigating them will require a revolution in the social and natural sciences concerned with food production, as well as a breaking down of barriers between academic fields.

Serious effort is being invested into halting or reversing ecosystem degradation and the loss of ecosystem services, improving food productivity, and reducing poverty. A central 'innovation' in these responses is the concept of 'ecosystems services'. In simple terms this concept refers to all the goods and services that 'ecosystems' provide to humans such as soil retention; flood or tide mitigation; water filtration; carbon sequestration; pollination etc. It is thus a utilitarian concept in which processes formerly outside the market (externalities) become internalised in a market. The concept is gaining ground in ways that are concerning. I contend that this development needs a forceful cybersystemic critique. In 2010 Brian Czech described how:

> "On November 15, five nations issued a complaint about a UN initiative called the 'Global Green New Deal'. These nations claim that nature is seen (by the UN) as 'capital' for producing tradable environmental goods and services. They express their concern about the 'privatization and the mercantilization of nature through the development of markets for environmental services.' They also declare their 'condemnation of unsustainable models of economic growth'."

In this same article, Brian Czech explores how, in the Green New Deal, ecological microeconomics (such as valuing ecosystem services) has risen from the recesses of academia into the realm of international diplomacy whilst ecological macroeconomics (such as the limits to growth) has not. These developments have a range of implications that from a cybersystemic perspective raise significant concerns. I want to draw attention to three conceptual weaknesses in the emerging discourses that warrant more widespread consideration, otherwise we run the risk of heading off in the wrong direction. These are: (i) the reification of ecosystems; (ii) concern with value rather than valuing and (iii) opportunities and limitations in the conceptualisations of a socio-ecological system.

As outlined earlier there is replete within the academic literature confusion over the concept 'system' and whether 'system' is an epistemological device, a way of knowing about the world and thus a choice to be made in context sensitive ways, or an ontological claim i.e. a claim that systems are 'real' and thus describable objectively. This confusion extends to the concept 'ecosystem' itself. The term ecosystem was coined in 1930 by Roy Clapham to mean the combined physical and biological components of an environment. In 1935 British ecologist Arthur Tansley refined the term, describing it as "the whole system... including not only the organism-complex, but also the whole complex of physical factors forming what we call the environment". Tansley regarded ecosystems not simply as natural units, but as mental isolates. In Tansley's original conception 'ecosystem' was a concept, an invented term, coined to work as a conceptual or epistemological device, and which, like all systems involves boundary judgments. However, over time the concept *ecosystem* has come to be reified, made into a 'thing' that exists independently of those who make the boundary judgments that create any system of interest. This shift has had, and will continue to have, profound implications unless the cybersystemic implications are more widely appreciated. There is also the issue of whether humans are considered part of, or outside, ecosystems or connected in other ways.

Central to the emerging discourse on ecosystems services is a concern with valuing these services. The primary motivation is to be able to internalise these values in markets and national accounts and other forms of economic transaction. Valuing ecosystems services is based on the idea that values can be assigned to, or reified in, certain ecosystems processes. This is a product of the neo-classical economic paradigm and an issue from which even ecological economics, a branch of economics, has not escaped. An alternative is to regard values as the emergent outcome of a process of valuing by stakeholders (i.e. a form of practical action or praxis) informed by, but not restricted to, best available science. As I have argued elsewhere it is dangerous to attribute values to groups or sectors rather than to be concerned with how the process of valuing happens in our daily living. How we relate to each other, other species and the biophysical world in daily life is a manner of living that becomes conserved as part of family, cultural and spiritual lineages.

From a cybersystemic perspective there seem to me to be many dangers in pursuing the current trajectory. However, by taking a 'design-turn', values could become expressed in context sensitive designs for ecosystem services and livelihood security i.e. this would avoid reification beyond context and the universalising of ecosystems services in a globalised trading system. For example, local stakeholders in a river catchment, as part of its ongoing governance, could come together and invent, or design rules and procedures for how managing the river in particular ways might provide more ecosystem services. Flooding across a floodplain is a natural process which replenishes soil fertility, thus allowing this to happen rather than engineering flood defences may be a way to provide, or maintain, ecosystem services. The 'design turn' comes from humans coming together in local contexts to design new rules, or institutions, relevant to the situation and not imposed by the activity of a market or a government department in a distant city. To make this shift it is necessary to invent new ways of understanding river catchments such as that depicted in Figure 3. Traditionally, for governance purposes, rivers have usually been regarded as hydrological or natural systems but these framings are no longer adequate.

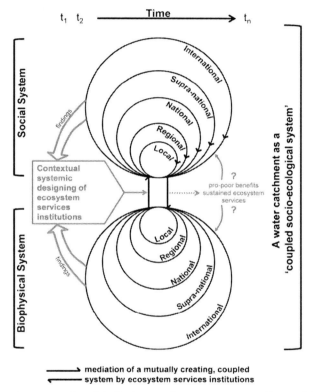

Figure 3: A conceptual model of a river catchment as a structurally coupled socio (or social) – biophysical system. If such a conception were used as a basis for governance then there would be a need to focus on how institutions, such as ecosystems service institutions, are designed in locally relevant ways capable of achieving a purpose, such as to deliver pro-poor benefits as well as maintain ecosystem service provision. Designs have to be part of a nested hierarchy from the local to the international and how we understand these have to be built into designs

In academic discourse it is clear that there is movement away from unhelpful conceptualisations of 'ecological, or natural, systems' and 'social systems' as a dualism. A dualism is a self-negating pair like objective and subjective.

On the other hand there is little appreciation of how the alternative to a dualism, i.e. a duality, functions. A duality exists when a pair is considered as jointly forming a whole, like the concepts predator and prey – these concepts only make sense in relation to each other and together form a unity. The Chinese yin and yang symbols are often used to convey the idea of a duality.

In recent times a new concept has been coined as an attempt to break out of the trap of the social and ecological dualism. Several versions of the same idea exist: some use the term socio-ecological system, some social-ecological system, and others a coupled human-environment system. My own preference is that of a social-biophysical system (Figure 3). Clarifying these conceptions and teasing out the policy and practice, especially governance implications, is an imperative but not easy. Cybersystemic concepts such as feedback, recursion, variety, autopoiesis (self-production) and structural coupling offer opportunities.

As depicted in Figure 3 water catchments or watersheds could be conceptualised as structurally coupled social-biophysical systems thus drawing attention to what relations might best be conserved over time, and what mediating functions are, or could be, carried out by current institutions or institutions still to be invented. Figure 3 breaks out of the dualism trap by thinking of a social system in an ongoing, dynamic, relationship with the biosphere (i.e. a bio-physical system) in which each system is mutually influencing the other (i.e. structurally coupled) much as two people are coupled in some forms of dance. Shifting to this conception changes much, including the need for institutional design and more systemic and adaptive governance. If, over time, the two systems depicted in Figure 3 continue to mutually influence each other in ways that maintain their coupling then they can be described as in a co-evolutionary dynamic which only ceases when the structural coupling fails.

Let me try to unpack Figure 3 some more by using a metaphor associated with walking. Walking, as a form of practice happens because of the recurrent interaction of 'two systems' – an organism, say a person and a medium, say a floor. If you take one of this pair away then walking does not happen. Also, when walking, shoes can be seen to mediate the relationship between humans and the earth (the medium). Shoes become and remain comfortable as part of ongoing recurrent interactions between a foot, the shoe and the medium. Qualities of the shoe that mediate the recurrent interactions will, over time, determine if it is fit for purpose or damages the foot, the medium or both. In this depiction ecosystems service institutions can be understood as the shoe (and other institutions that we invent can be understood as other types of shoe). In water catchments different stakeholders – particularly those at different levels of governance, or in a purchaser-provider supply chain will value different shoe designs.

In the specific case of ecosystem services a challenge for their design is in providing the evidence base that would enable the buyers of the ecosystem services to know what they are getting and thus be willing to pay. Conversely local people who became reliant on the provision, or management, of these services for their livelihoods would need to be confident that their income stream was reliable over time. Thus fit for purpose institutional arrangements need to be situated in a conducive governance framework that is systemic and adaptive i.e. open to change, not rigid.

Governance is not the same as government, although the latter are heavily involved in the former. Governance operates at the level of the team, the project group, the organisation etc but generally it is not something we do well. All too often if we get a good, effective team it is by accident rather than design. Cybersystemic ideas have much to offer and the different methods and techniques associated with these ideas can help 'do governance' more effectively – these are skills and capabilities we all need at this historical moment. Breaking out of the traps associated with our current ways of thinking and acting and inventing new ones is one of the most practical actions we could take.

---

**Thinking it through: where do I stand?**

Think about the example I gave of walking as a relational phenomenon. Consider whether you mainly think in linear cause and effect ways or in systemic, relational terms. Test this walking example out with others. Ask the question: How does walking happen as a form of practice? See what type of answers you get.

Explore some of the resources given below so as to become more familiar with the language of cybersystemics. Pick out some that appeal to you as different and potentially useful. Explain your choices.

Why is cybersystemic thinking so uncommon in the West? Why is it not part of the school curriculum? Perhaps visit some on-line discussions groups such as Systems Thinking Group Members <group-digests@linkedin.com>

---

**Action: what can I do?**

Spend some time developing systems diagramming skills. Some guidelines are available here: http://growingwingsontheway.blogspot.com/2011/05/diagrams.html or here: http://openlearn.open.ac.uk/mod/oucontent/view.php?id=397793&section=1.3.2

Use one of these diagramming techniques to explore a complex issues related to sustainability. An article in the daily press could be a good starting point.

Read one of Simon Caulkin's articles and consider why he is a systemic journalist: http://www.simoncaulkin.com/

Compare his work to other articles on the same topic and see if the author has treated the issue with cybersystemic sensibility.

Put yourself firmly in the sustainability situation. Make how you and others (disciplines, groups, cultures etc) think and act part of the sustainability situation. Does this chapter alter how you now think about, or 'frame' the issue of sustainability?

## *Further reading*

Czech, B. (2010). Ecosystem Services: Pricing to Peddle? *The Daly News*, CASSE (see http://steadystate.org/ecosystem-services-pricing-to-peddle/ accessed 14th February 2011).

Ison, R.L. (1993). Changing community attitudes. *The Rangeland Journal 15*, 154-66.

Fisher, F. (2006). *Response Ability*. Melbourne: Vista Publications.

[1]Ison, R.L. (2010). *Systems Practice: How to Act in a Climate Change World*. London: Springer.

Ison, R.L. (2011). Cybersystemic conviviality: addressing the conundrum of ecosystems services. ASC (American Society for Cybernetics) Column, *Cybernetics & Human Knowing 18* (1, 2), 135-141.

Knudtson, P. & Suzuki, D. (1992). Wisdom of the Elders. Sydney: Allen and Unwin.

Molle, F. (2009). River-basin planning and management: The social life of a concept. *Geoforum 40*, 484-494.

Straton, A. (2006). A complex systems approach to the value of ecological resources, *Ecological Economics 56*, 402– 411.

## *Resources*

American Society for Cybernetics http://www.asc-cybernetics.org/

Open Learn see http://www.open.ac.uk/openlearn/whats-on/ systems-practice

Principia Cybernetica http://pespmc1.vub.ac.be/

Ray Ison's Blog: http://rayison.blogspot.com/

Starting off Systemically in Environmental Decision Making. http://www.ouw.co.uk/store/%28S%283sgvj455xdo3fr55szg3ft-mr%29%29/catalog/productinfo.aspx?id=5145&cid=1130 &AspxAutoDetectCookieSupport=1

Systemic Practice & Action Research http://www.springer.com/business+%26+management/journal/11213

Talbott, S. (2002). Ecological conversation: wildness, anthropocentrism and deep ecology, *Technology and Human Responsibility*, Netfuture 127 [online], http://www.netfuture.org/2002/Jan1002_127.html (Accessed 13th March 2011).

Tansley, Clapham background see http://en.wikipedia.org/wiki/Ecosystem

---

1. I draw heavily on this work for this chapter along with Ison (2011).

# Part VI

## Demonstrating Sustainability:
## Case Studies

***ocean view***
**watercolour**
**45cm by 39cm**

# Chapter 24
## Climate Change Schools Project

### Enabling Young People to Lead on the Challenges of Climate Change

*Krista McKinzey*
*Climate Change Schools Project Manager*
*Science Learning Centre North East (Durham University, UK)*

### Climate Change Schools Project Rationale

The UK's award-winning Climate Change Schools Project (CCSP) aims to:

- help schools to embed climate change throughout the national curriculum; and
- showcase schools as 'beacons' for climate change teaching, learning and positive action in their local communities.

Operating since 2007, the Climate Change Schools Project empowers young people through teachers and schools to become 'everyday experts' on climate change. Creating a solid grounding in the core principles of climate change science in young people of all ages and abilities underpins the Project's aims – this enhanced understanding then enables young people and their schools to inform and inspire positive action in their local communities.

The Project contributes to a wide range of aims and objectives that include:

- To ensure that climate change becomes a core part of education;
- To help schools use the curriculum as a catalyst for positive climate change action in and around their local communities;
- To influence and support others to benefit from the North East of England's expertise (sharing best practice);
- To promote the development and delivery of climate change mitigation and adaptation actions by schools in order to collaborate with their local communities in the long-term (schools as 'centres of excellence' in climate change teaching, learning and positive action).

Integral to the success of the Climate Change Schools Project has been the:

- widespread ownership of the Project via engagement of multiple stakeholders;
- tailoring delivery and content to meet regional needs;
- providing an ongoing and personal support network for schools;
- encouraging school-led 'organic' growth of the Lead Schools network;
- long-term commitment to using climate change as a catalyst for engagement across the school curriculum, campus and local community;
- showcasing the unique role that schools and young people play in inspiring behavioural changes at a local level and raising the adaptive capacity of their local communities in response to a changing climate.

The Climate Change Schools Project is a collaboration between Science Learning Centre North East (where the Project is based and operated via Durham University), the UK's Environment Agency via the Northumbria Regional Flood Defence Committee (core funders), ClimateNE (the regional climate change partnership via the UK's Department for Environment, Food and Rural Affairs, also core funders), the North East Strategic Partnership for Sustainable Schools, One World Network North East and the Association of North East Councils.

### *Climate Change Schools Project Approach*

The Climate Change Schools Project achieves its aims through the *Climate Change Lead Schools* network, first established in 2008-2009, who participate in an ongoing annual process including:

1. making use of the creative, dynamic and cross-curricular resources developed especially for the Lead Schools by the teachers themselves;
2. taking part in a programme of tailored teacher CPD;

3. engaging in regular *Sharing Best Practice* open to all Project stakeholders;
4. participating in monitoring and evaluation processes.

The cross-curricular materials that Lead Schools use are packaged as a set of 6 Modules covering 6 themes of climate change – these include:

1. The science of climate change (*Climate change nuts & bolts*)
2. Climate change and the media (*Don't believe the hype*)
3. Indicators of climate change (*Climate change all around me*)
4. Climate change impacts (*The 'so what?' of climate change*)
5. Climate change mitigation (*Climate change champions*)
6. Climate change adaptation (*Making the most of it*)

The Modules are designed as Curriculum Webs & Schemes of Work, and are provided with much detail around learning outcomes, suggested hands-on activities, possible resources (to complete each activity) and extension activities. The emphasis is to take the Modules and use them as best suits a teacher's style, time available and their learners' abilities. These are key outcomes of the initial CPD course *How to be a Climate Change Lead School*, whereby Lead Schools' teachers are walked through example Module activities and given time to explore the opportunities for teaching climate change in a creative and flexible way. If so desired, the Modules could be used as-is, but the Lead Schools teachers strengthen their own professional development skills by learning to adapt and apply climate change teaching and learning throughout the curriculum in their own unique ways. This has proven to be a very powerful element of the Climate Change Schools Project, whereby empowering teachers is having a direct impact on empowering young people.

Modules are accessed through the Lead Schools site (www.slcne.org.uk/ccspweb/) they can be downloaded and saved to a teacher's own computer in Word format, such that any amendments or additions can easily be made. Lead Schools teachers are also encouraged to submit their own ideas and suggested additional material to be added into the Modules, as the website allows widespread and efficient access for a dynamic set of resources.

Over 200 teachers and 8000 young people, from ages 5 to 18, have been involved in the *Climate Change Lead Schools* network to-date, culminating in over 50,000 hours of climate change related activity, such as:

- integrating climate change as a cross-curricular theme using a variety of teaching methods and strategies relevant to each individual school;
- delivering whole-school *Climate Change Weeks*;
- holding *Climate Change Open Afternoons* for schools and local communities;
- undertaking energy audits, reducing carbon footprints and saving schools money;
- developing allotments on school grounds or in partnership with community groups;

- producing and performing climate change theatre;
- through the CCSP's *Adaptation Challenge,* showcasing the unique role that schools and young people play in inspiring behavioural changes at a local level and raising the adaptive capacity of their local communities in response to a changing climate.

Rose Fletcher, Year 3 teacher of Geography, Religious Education & Able Children Coordinator at Edmondsley Primary School, has been involved in the Climate Change Schools Project since 2008. She states: "The Climate Change Schools Project enables climate change teaching to be delivered through the creative, dynamic, cross-curricular yet user-friendly resources – made *by* teachers *for* teachers. Successful delivery is further supported by tailored teacher CPD and regular *Sharing Best Practice* meetings. The project understands the pressures teachers face to deliver an already full curriculum to children from a wide variety of backgrounds and beliefs, in schools with diverse priorities – it is an invaluable and reassuring tool through which the facts can be delivered in an innovative, manageable, economical, cross-curricular fashion. Many Climate Change Lead Schools teachers have discovered in themselves an unexpected confidence, enthusiasm and level of expertise in climate change delivery. They in turn are empowering an 'eco army' of young people, by educating them with the facts contributing to global warming and resulting from it, then encouraging and establishing in them positive lifestyle habits which they share with their families and carry with them throughout their lives."

The Climate Change Schools Project and its Lead Schools network is also an exemplar under the banner of the Regional Centre of Expertise for North East England within the UN University's Programme on Education for Sustainable Development (ESD). The Project also continues to facilitate closer relationships between schools and Local Authorities in terms of the CRC Energy Efficiency Scheme, European Covenant of Mayors and helping schools to contribute towards climate change risk assessments and action planning.

### *Other Climate Change Schools Project Activities*

Within the wider Climate Change Schools Project portfolio sits a number of additional projects (see Table 1) that are currently being delivered.

Table 1: Additional projects within the CCSP 'umbrella' which
are being delivered in 2010-2011

| Other CCSP activity | Project details & outcomes |
| --- | --- |
| *Adaptation Challenge* | The CCSP's 'Adaptation Challenge, complimenting the 'Big Society' agenda, is helping to foster unique and creative collaborations across local communities via partnership projects engaging schools, local businesses, community groups and councils to strengthen responses in a collective and proactive way to the impacts we face from climate change, e.g. flooding, drought, extreme weather, biodiversity etc. |
| *Community Scientists* | The CCSP is working in collaboration with Northumbrian Water and GLOBE UK, along with the support of regional BBC meteorologists, the Environment Agency, Durham University and ClimateNE, to enable young people to become 'everyday experts' on weather and climate in order to empower their local communities to be ready for the impacts of a changing climate. |
| *Schools' Climate Change Risk Assessments & Adaptation Planning* | The CCSP is working in partnership with Durham County Council to develop and deliver a schools' approach to climate change risk assessment and adaptation planning. Outcomes of this work will help schools consider and plan for the real costs of climate change impacts, and feed into Local Authority risk assessments and action plans, helping to inspire local action on the ground. |
| *UKCIP and UKCP09 projections A-level teaching module* | Newcastle College & Kenton School through the CCSP are leading the development of a school's approach to using the UK Climate Impacts Programme's BACLIAT tool and climate projections as a workshop-based activity to be used in A-level Environmental Sciences teaching (and possibly with some of their business students). They are using a scenario-based approach to look at how businesses are responding to the impacts of a changing climate and what lessons can be learned for others in their local communities. |
| *Global Dimensions of Climate Change* | The CCSP is working in partnership with One World Network North East and the Tees Valley One World Centre to help young people learn from adaptation actions other people around the world are taking to live with the impacts of climate change. |
| *AstraZeneca Science Teaching Trust* | A collaboration between the CCSP, Science Learning Centre Yorkshire & Humber and Sheffield Council to develop creative approaches to using science to inform and inspire climate change adaptation in the UK. |

## *Climate Change Schools Project 'Adaptation Challenge'*

Increased understanding of climate change science and the impacts that climate change may have on local communities has also catalysed some Lead Schools to establish pioneering partnerships through the Climate Change Schools Project *Adaptation Challenge*. These phase 1 projects occurring in 2009-2010 were funded by the Climate Change Schools Project with grants from the Northumbria Regional Flood Defence Committee (via the Environment Agency) and ClimateNE (via the Department for Environment, Food & Rural Affairs) to help Lead Schools initially address the risks they face from the impacts of climate change in creative and innovative ways. The simple though creative measures which the Lead Schools are taking encourage all of us to consider how we should physically prepare our homes, schools and wider communities for increased flood risks, warmer temperatures, droughts and extreme weather, and then, most importantly, to do something about it.

Phase 1 Adaptation Challenge projects involved:

- creating shaded outdoor classrooms to cope with rising summer temperatures;
- management of surface water flooding using plants to reduce run off (to cope with more frequent 'high intensity' rainfall);
- improving resilience to flooding by helping the community to learn more about flood risk and how to prepare for flood events;
- developing climate change 'biodiversity gardens' to provide habitat for struggling species, whilst also providing a shaded community garden which can be used by vulnerable members of the community;
- creating a climate change adaptation information 'drop-in' centre for the wider community to help raise awareness of why it is important and what local action can be taken to cope with the impacts of a changing climate;
- designing and circulating a community leaflet giving helpful hints about preparing homes and businesses for flooding and other climate change impacts.

Jayne Lees, Deputy Headteacher of Bill Quay Primary School, who has been one of the pioneering Lead Schools involved in the Adaptation Challenge since 2009, states: "Bill Quay Primary School has been a Climate Change Lead School since the beginning of the Climate Change Schools Project – the chance to work in partnership with so many schools around the region ensures that we continue to share good practice and support each other as we aim to bring climate change to life, for our young people and the wider community. Being involved in the Adaption Challenge has enabled us to become even more outward-facing, encouraging behavioural changes amongst the local community with our young people leading the way. Better understanding of what climate change adaptation is all about, and how to respond proactively to adapt to climate change impacts, has been enormously helpful."

Phase 2 of the Adaptation Challenge in 2010-2011 is currently underway, whereby initial projects are already expanding their breadth of engagement, sharing best practice with the private and public sector, and importantly, inspiring other Lead Schools to begin new Adaptation Challenge projects.

Phase 3 of the Adaptation Challenge involves schools specifically as community hubs for river or coastal flood risk reduction. The activity, funded by small grants through the Environment Agency via the Northumbria Regional Flood Defence committee, is projected to entail four Climate Change Lead Schools located in specified flood zone areas that may undertake the establishment of:

- a community flood group, sharing of advice and support on what to do before, during or after a flood; or
- minor physical works to reduce actual flooding.

It is anticipated that the schools, supported by the Climate Change Schools Project, will be able to mobilise volunteering and other donations to collaborate on this activity.

Overall, young people leading the way to prepare their communities for climate change impacts is unique – fundamental understanding of the science behind climate change, driven through the Lead Schools activities, is crucial to the success of these projects, in order for young people to research, monitor and assess impacts and tailor appropriate solutions. The Project's long-term commitment to making the curriculum pivotal to the Climate Change Schools Project has allowed Lead Schools to evolve into centres of excellence, promoting behavioural changes in teaching practice, schools and in their local communities.

### *The Climate Change Schools Project through 2012*

The Climate Change Schools Project has truly become embedded within the North East of England, and, as a result, is now more able to help share best practice farther afield. The Project's inherent flexibility and widespread ownership allows its management approach to be dynamic and extends benefits in a variety of ways to all who are involved. Leading on and contributing to other deliverables, such as the widely expanded and highly regarded Adaptation Challenge, provides practical examples of how young people can use science to inform and influence positive climate change action, within their schools, homes and local communities.

The Project also helps to increase exposure of science using creative and engaging methods to teachers that may not ordinarily teach or use science in the classroom on a regular basis – these teachers, with other curricular expertise, have discovered new approaches that allow them to bring science to life for young people by using climate change as a constant theme across different subject areas.

Matthew Coe, Learning Leader for Drama, Bydales School, has helped the school to incorporate climate change creatively through drama. He states: "We have produced a 30 minute drama called 'What a Wonderful World'. My drama group have used Comedy/Drama/Satire/News Reports/Forum Theatre/Physical Theatre/Song and Dance to communicate messages about climate change, that the world is being neglected and gradually being destroyed. We wish to entertain and provoke thought rather than just preach our messages. We hope those who watch our work will be entertained, educated and empowered to make a difference." The student drama group performed their piece to various audiences ranging from other schools, to regional government agencies, and was very well received.

The most noticeable achievement over the last year is the way in which the Climate Change Schools Project has undergone a 'step-change' in development and delivery – moving from focussed school curriculum support, to an ever-more action-oriented support for schools to truly become hubs of climate change activity. Already, these inspiring schools and young-people led 'beacons' are sprouting up across the North East – one of the main aims over the next two years is to connect these beacons into a wider network of activity which showcases the strength of what schools and young people can achieve. This web of Climate Change Schools Project supported activity will further enable a strong and coherent model of practice which can be shared with others as the Project continues to roll-out into other parts of the UK.

### Case study

*Highcliffe Primary School by Alison Smith (PSHEE Lead)*

| Key objectives | We were a school already committed to working within the Sustainable Schools Framework. We were working towards a Green Flag Award as an Eco-School. We considered that becoming a member of the CCSP as a Lead School would help us to achieve our aims. We were also looking to whole school curriculum review and were looking for CPD which would support this both for myself as a coordinator in leading the staff and for direction and resources to support the children's learning. |
|---|---|

| | |
|---|---|
| **What happened during the Lead Schools year?** | Personal highlights were the initial CPD day which I found extremely motivating, relevant and practical and the subsequent opportunities to share information and 'tips' with colleagues. The information passed on by email re events, training and resources has been a very useful sift. As the intention would be for the whole school to work with the materials and modules in 2010/11 it was agreed that I would pilot resources in Year 5 this year in support of our work from module 1. The children also worked with resources from Power Down developing information posters which were placed around the school. Later they presented to the rest of the school a performance developed in conjunction with Konflux Theatre re. Reduce, Recycle, Reuse. We also worked with the Climate Cops Team for a day (late November) to reinforce our learning. At present in literacy we are working on persuasive writing and are using materials from module 6 and also looking at the problems associated with wind turbines. The letters written will be displayed when completed. |
| **What Module(s) did you focus on?** | Module 1: Climate Change Science Module 6: Climate Change Adaptation. Beginning to look at adaptation. Lots of work looking at mitigation as part of our sustainable schools self evaluation. The children have responded to the real life problem solving aspects to their work. A small group of Y6 children working on a sustainable schools project and following up on some of the module 1 information and also mitigation. Spent time devising a questionnaire on regarding recycled materials and subsequently designed a seed planter window box for the elderly to grow herbs, veg etc out of recycled materials. They were interested to find that from their small sample the older people were less interested than the younger in recycling and they felt that there were some issues here for them to address re informing people in the community. |
| **Evidence of success** | For me learning, sharing, and the opportunity to take these issues whole school. Hopefully the evidence will form over the next year. At this time only impressions but it would appear that there has been a significant effect on colleagues. After a second year as a member I would hope that there will be much to comment on. The timing of our curriculum review has been significant. |
| **What did and didn't work** | The cross curricular aspect of the resources has had a huge impact upon the response of the whole staff. The only real issues so far have been re pressures of the present curriculum. |

| Personal and professional development | The CPD was very interesting and stimulating... this together with the guidance (links to relevant sites etc) proved to be important and very helpful in developing my own subject knowledge in an area which is constantly advancing. Professionally the cross curricular aspect of the resources and lesson plans was exactly what I was looking for as that is the way I teach but also what we were looking for as part of our curriculum review. It has been beneficial drawing together all of the diverse ways we have already been covering climate change and mitigation, around the project and the learning resources. Important links with the (UK's) Sustainable Schools Agenda and Eco-Schools |
|---|---|
| The future | Certainly and I very much hope that this will be whole school. |
| Comparison | The CCSP is overarching and other programmes now appear to be more closely co-ordinated and run alongside or dovetail into the project. |
| Other information | Just to say thank you for your dedicated approach and lead, which has been so motivating. Can't wait for next year now. |

*Thinking it through: where do I stand?*

How does my school integrate teaching and learning about climate change? What resources are available to me to enable our school to further our progress? What might the benefits or impacts be on pupils, staff, the school and wider school community if my school took the lead?

*Action: what can I do?*

1) Visit www.climatechangeschools.org.uk and follow the links to the Climate Change Lead Schools site where you can sign up as a 'guest user' and access some of the cross-curricular Module materials.

2) Research the local impacts of climate change that your school may be vulnerable to. In North East England, increased severity and frequency of flooding (both surface water and river) are the main impacts being addressed by schools. However, increased summer temperatures and drought, and impacts on living things (people, plants and animals) are also of concern. Choose an impact local and meaningful to you, and work in partnership with other community groups, local government or businesses to find creative collaborative solutions to become better prepared for this impact.

What are the spin-off effects of your action? How will it impinge on other aspects of sustainability? If you can make your local area more resilient to climate change impacts, and achieve this by working together across your local community, what other benefits might such a partnership approach foster in terms of wider sustainability activity?

## *Further reading*

ClimateNE (2008). *North East England Climate Change Adaptation Study.* Available to download from www.adaptne.org/

Grant, L. & Featherstone, H. (2009). *Climate Change Schools Project – Final Evaluation Report.* Available to download from www.climate-changeschools.org.uk

McKinzey, K. (2010). Climate Change Schools Project – using science to inform and inspire positive action in local communities. *Education in Science, 240,* 18 – 19.

McKinzey, K. (2010). *Climate Change Schools Project – Phase 2 Report (2009-2010).* Available to download from www.climate-changeschools.org.uk

## *Resources*

Climate Change Schools project website (including further Case Studies): www.climatechangeschools.org.uk

Eco-Schools England website (international awards scheme): www.eco-schools.org.uk

The Pod website (supports Eco-Schools activities directly): www.jointhepod.org

UK's 'Sustainability and Environmental Education (SEEd)' website (contains links to teaching resources): www.se-ed.co.uk

## *Acknowledgements*

Thank you to:

- all Climate Change Schools Project partners: Science Learning Centre North East (operated by Durham University), the Environment Agency via the Northumbria Regional Flood Defence Committee, ClimateNE, North East Strategic Partnership for Sustainable Schools, One World Network North East and the Association of North East Councils;
- all Climate Change Lead Schools past and present;
- Rose Fletcher, Jayne Lees and Matthew Coe for their testimonials; and
- Alison Smith, Highcliffe Primary, for allowing inclusion of the school's 2009-2010 Case Study.

# Chapter 25
## Murder Under the Microscope

*Catherine Nielsen*
*Curriculum & Learning Innovation Centre, NSW Department of*
*Education and Training*

### *Motivation for change*

Have you ever heard the 'hmmm... not that again' sound when you're introducing a topic about sustainability in the classroom? Often when students are told they are about to 'learn about sustainability or the environment', they may well think they're about to hear another sad news story. Children, like many adults are beginning to feel that environmental disasters occur often, are complicated and have few, if any, viable solutions.

In 2006 plans were made to develop an environmental educational resource –Murder under the Microscope (MuM) – to offer a different way into the content. Evaluation of MuM over the last few years suggests that the students become engaged in the content through a strong, contemporary narrative and the quest to solve the environmental 'crime' in teams within a limited time period.

## Background

This case study focuses on how students and teachers responded to MuM. Approximately 25,000 students have participated in MuM each year for the last four years i.e. around 100,000 students from around Australia and overseas have experienced MuM. The case study is based on surveys and videos of sample groups of students and teachers working on MuM.

MuM is an annual, online, educational game in which teams of students (typically a class of 30 students) compete against other teams to solve an ecological mystery presented through the metaphor of a 'crime'. Clues to the eco-mystery crime are progressively delivered via a multimedia web interface. The clues are cryptic, needing the students to analyse and compare the information to their researched facts in order to help solve the investigation case. The students take on the role of investigators working within a team and much of their activity is focussed on research and collaboration.

The clues delivered through the website include video excerpts, simulated sms and mms messages and voice mail messages. The website interface also provides online connection with science experts and simulated social media elements to connect students with the characters in the website.

Over the six-week period of the game, the students become immersed in a battle of wits to be the first to correctly identify the specific *victim, villain* and *crime site*. Typical *victims* are endangered animals, typical *villains* are ecological pests or contaminants and typical *crime sites* are ecologically sensitive environments[1].

Figure 1: 'Danno' and 'Zahara', two of the characters from the MuM website

## Target audience

MuM is designed for children in upper primary and lower secondary across Australia, that is Years 5 to 10, typically children aged 9 to 14 years and their teachers. In some cases parents register so that they can participate as a family as well. Notably, the number of home-schooled students registering as teams has significantly increased over the last four years.

---

1. For examples of past games see http://www.microscope.edu.au/public/archive/index.aspx

*What happens when things go wrong? Support for teachers*

There are several videos about implementing the program in the classroom located under the heading, 'How to play' on the main page of the website[2]:

Teachers can obtain information, a step-by-step teachers' guide and downloadable classroom resources before registering and months before game start. There's also a teachers' wiki[3], telephone and email support[4].

To sustain the metaphor, officers answering email and phone calls respond with: 'Catchment Headquarters'. Some students also use the contact email and phone number when working on MuM at home.

The case study showed that over the last four years, there has been a noticeable decline in the number of phone calls from teachers needing technical assistance such as problems with registering or problems with their video players. The enquiries have tended to shift to questions about classroom management and education resources and away from technical problems. Regardless of the subject of the communication, there has been a growth in the reliance on email over the past four years. Is this due to greater access to improved technology in schools or improved technical skills of teachers? Regardless, it is a positive direction.

The great cries for help have come from exasperated teachers whose students have gone above and beyond their usual level of engagement only to be thwarted by lack of time or misadventure. Officers of *Catchment Headquarters* are flexible, fair and experienced in guiding teachers through what can seem catastrophic emotional moments. Reflections of such moments have been captured in the feedback and survey responses from the teachers:

> *Thanks to the guys at Catchment Headquarters, I kept my sanity in meeting tight deadlines and helped to channel the enthusiasm of the kids into learning. Though at times it seemed like chaos, it was organised chaos!*

## Development of Murder under the Microscope 2007-2012

In 2006, the NSW Department of Education and Training's Centre for Learning Innovation undertook an ambitious project to re-design an environmental education program as an interactive and fully online educational experience. The original program was known as 'Murder under the Microscope' (MuM) operational from the early 1990's to 2003 and based on:

- a set of print materials;
- a series of televised broadcasts;
- faxes to environmental experts.

---

2.www.microscope.edu.au

3.http://murderunderthemicroscope.wikispaces.com/

4.catchment.hq@det.nsw.edu.au

The old MuM was discontinued in 2003 after a series of organisational re-structures at state and national levels and personnel changes.

In 2007 the new MuM was launched. While retaining the original name, it was given an updated logo and look and feel in keeping with contemporary investigation crime scene TV shows and interactive games. The core of the game play was retained, that is students working in teams using clues and their own research to solve an environmental crime. The goal of the game is to identify the specific environment (crime site), the effects (victim) and the cause (villain).

Instead of televised broadcasts the new MuM website was fitted with state of the art technology to automatically roll out a series of videos and synchronised messages and clues on a daily, and at times, hourly basis. While innovative for its time the TV broadcasts of the old MuM required teachers to organise the equipment needed to watch television in the classroom. The improvements of web-based video enabled the new MuM to have greater screen resolution and flexibility in viewing and reviewing than the older style TV broadcasts.

The faxes of the old MuM were replaced by a series of web features such as an online 'ask the scientists' forum, simulated sms and mms messages from the various characters, 'CNN-like' ticker tape messages along the bottom of the screen, and other well-placed text, video and graphical assets to deliver clues at various intervals of the game. There's also a virtual space for students to see the profiles of other teams and the local environments. These features and the whole interface of the website are intended to give a sense of purpose, identity and urgency, enticing the student to take responsibility for solving the environmental crime.

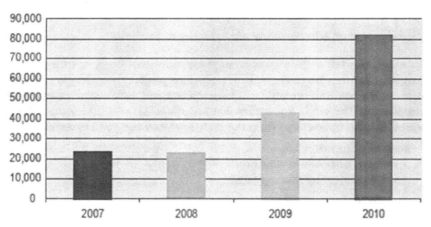

Figure 2: Number of unique visitors to the MuM website over a six week period, in 2007, 2008, 2009 and 2010, from Googlanalytics

### Content of MuM

MuM is now a regular part of the learning program in many schools around Australia. Students can experience it more than once because the environmental themes change each year as listed below.

Each year the theme is based on cause and effect in various ecosystems. This provides a tangled web of clues for the students to unravel and use in their investigation of who or what really 'dunnit'. The drive to solve the case before other teams do so heightens the excitement and is a great motivator to get to the facts about how the environment works and how it can be greatly upset.

While the environmental crime each year is fictitious it is based in scientific fact and may well happen in real life. The authenticity of each year's 'crimes' is usually borne out by subsequent real events.

- 2007 – *CSI Wetlands* focused on weeds, introduced species that look good in landscaped ponds and gardens but can have disastrous effects on native wild life. Weeds are often seen as a benign nuisance and weeding as something that can be put off until tomorrow. But for the native flora and fauna of Australia – weeds are a matter of life or death. In this case the death was the Black Bittern and the weed was the introduced species, Salvinia molesta.

- 2008 – *Heartbreak on the Horizon* looked at soil as a living entity. Soil is formed through the weathering of rocks, the growth and decay of plants and the efforts of millions of small animals and micro-organisms. Grains, vegetables, fruit, meat, in fact everything we grow on the land to eat depends on this process. But unsustainable land management can lead to the destruction of the soil and the demise of the local species such as the Bush Stone-Curlew. Many of us recall that day in September 2009 when Sydney was blanketed in red dust – topsoil from the west.

- 2009 – *Crisis on the Coast* featured buzz pollinators such as the Blue-banded bee. These creatures are specialised pollinators to a variety of native plants. When the habitat of the Blue-banded bee was destroyed by an overzealous cleanup the effects were far reaching. Coincidently, in early 2011 the threat of the European wasp was again in the media.

- 2010 – *Shockwave on the Shoreline* focused on the disastrous effects of small changes in sea temperature. Increases can have a big effect on the lives of organisms living in the sea. Species can move from their normal distribution to new areas. This is what happened to the Weedy seadragon when the spiny sea urchin moved into its area as a result of rising temperatures.

- 2011 – *Horror in the Harvest*. The investigation of this crime started at the time of writing the case study. A full report about the villain, victim and crime is now available on the website.

## How the students learn through MuM

MuM supports several curriculum areas including Years 5 and 6 Science and Technology and Human Society and its Environment and Years 7, 8 and 9 Science and Geography. It also aims to build knowledge of environmental issues and an appreciation of the need for sustainable practices in production, work and life activities.

Rather than presenting environmental issues in an overwhelming light, MuM places students in a position of authority and responsibility. It does this by:

- putting students at the centre of the investigation and challenging them to take responsibility for solving a 'crime against the environment';
- focussing on inquiry skills, knowledge and values in a way that is purposeful, authentic and current;
- working in teams, problem solving and collaboration.

To demonstrate learning experiences gained throughout the game, students are asked to produce a team-based piece of work, such as a website or digital story that provides a long-term solution for the environment, preventing any chance of the villian striking again. The piece of work reinforces and integrates learning.

## Teachers' comments

Over the past four years, evaluations of the MuM program have provided feedback from participating teachers and students. Many of the teachers said they suspected that the engagement in learning during MuM would enable their students to become more ecologically informed and optimistic. In fact changing behaviour as a result of participation in MuM, was reported by the majority of students (66%). Students' comments in included:

*[MuM] made us realise that some of the little things we do have a bad affect on the environment*;

*I have started turning off lights at my house and unused appliances. Thinking about the Weedy seadragon reminds me to turn them off.*

Many teachers claimed that the enthusiasm of their students actually spilled over into other classroom activities and provided a memorable experience.

Sara, a teacher involved in MuM wrote:

*My class is totally addicted to this game, as am I! We are even emailing each other at night to continue to solve the clues.*

Sally, a regular teacher of MuM, said:

*MuM can reveal sides to children you don't otherwise see...kids who are often quite diffident in the classroom about other things come to school bursting with information they've looked up on the Internet the night before and they're so keen to tell you about it. As a teacher, you always hope to find the thing that ignites that interest in the kids you teach.*

Most teachers reported that they could draw on their existing repertoire of teaching practices, such as class and group discussion, students presenting their findings, negotiating, reaching consensus. Amy, a MuM teacher wrote:

*...I love that the kids need to access all kinds of information, listening visual and reading skills are all necessary... I am seeing such wonderful discussions and skills being used... learning so much about Internet researching, skimming and scanning information and summarising facts. They each have an investigation file, which includes a clues note page. It is so neat to see them all taking notes from each other and from the clues and then referring to them when they ask questions and present their ideas. They are like real life mini investigators. There is some really exciting learning happening in our room at the moment. Thanks again for providing such a fun and high quality educational experience.*

### Students' comments[5]

When students were asked to identify the benefits for their own learning, they typically listed 'improved skills for research', 'learning about animals and plants', 'learning how to solve problems', and 'becoming more aware of the environment'. Some students' comments allude to a heightened sense of critical awareness: 'I now look more closely into what people say and do' and the idea of 'cause and effect in ecosystems'.

When students were asked about what they enjoyed the most, the predominant response was 'figuring out the mystery'. The other features that students commented on were grouped into the following list. The list is not hierarchical.

1. interactive video and graphical interface
2. time-released clue drop via video episodes
3. characters based on everyday people
4. a strong episodic narrative
5. presentation of real world issues
6. conflicting evidence and information
7. opportunities for self-directed learning
8. team-based learning
9. 24/7 web presence
10. connection with real expert scientists to answer their questions

---

5. Watch a short video about student perceptions of Murder under the Microscope at *http://www.youtube.com/watch?v=NvWOK5bWUus*

## *Beyond 2011*

The project continues into 2011 and beyond, with a steady increase in participation each year. It is anticipated that the program will become a viable resource for the support the new Australian Curriculum. And each year, new web-based features are incorporated into the website that capitalise on the growing number of computers in schools and young people's growing use of technology and social media.

Unfortunately, world and national environmental problems are plentiful and provide ample 'crimes' for students to solve in MuM.

The new theme for each year is announced by end of the year[6].

Figure 3: Website screen for 2011 Murder under the Microscope

6. For more information and registration: www.microscope.edu.au

# Chapter 26

## Education for Sustainable Development

### Learning from Local and Global Collaborations

*Annukka Alppi*
*Mahnala Environmental School, Hameenkyro Municipality, Finland*

*Mauri Åhlberg*
*University of Helsinki, Finland*

*The questions that motivated change*

What makes it worthwhile to conduct research and develop our own school and its collaboration with its supporting municipality and local community? Why not just do as has always been done or as national or local school administrators suggest? Why collaborate with local and global formal and informal networks and projects? Why is it wise to link the surrounding people and their life and villages into school teaching and education? Why is it wise to collaborate with university professors and other ESD experts?

## Context

### Where and when

Mahnala Environmental School is a rural comprehensive school in the middle of traditional, national landscapes: plenty of boreal forests, lakes, fields, bogs, agricultural and cultural regions, including farm houses and villages. It is located in Hameenkyro Municipality, 30 km from Tampere, the third biggest city in Finland.

Mahnala Environmental School in June when the apple trees are blooming

Mahnala Primary School was founded in 1895 and the 'new' school building was built in 1903. In 1990 one active teacher, a nature lover, Mr Hannu Jarvinen, began to develop the school into a kind of nature school. In 1996 Ms Annukka Alppi was appointed as a classroom teacher. She had the interest, motivation and energy to develop the school into an environmental school. She and the school shared common principles including: purposefully building education and learning on local countryside and the rural life, a pedagogy of work and sustainable everyday practices, including the use of local and organic food. In 1999 the school was awarded WWF's Panda prize for its achievements in environmental education. It was the first time that WWF's Panda prize had been awarded in Finland. In 1999 the school was renamed as Mahnala Environmental School. In 2002 Annukka contacted Professor Mauri Åhlberg and joined the national and international network that was originally supported by the Organisation for Economic Co-operation and Development (OECD) and was called Environment and School Initiatives (ENSI). In this collaboration her thinking became more explicit, she learnt new theories and new methods, her ideas and working theories were continually tested and improved. The permanent right to use the Green Flag, trademark of an Eco School, was achieved in 2003.

Ringing young jackdaws is a tradition of the second grade pupils

## People

Annukka is a classroom teacher, vice principal of Mahnala Environmental School, and a doctoral student in Mauri´s Research & Development Group of Sustainability Education at the University of Helsinki. The Principal of Mahnala Environmental School is Mr Hannu Jarvinen, a classroom teacher and an ornithologist who has a licence to capture, ring and release birds. In Mahnala Environmental School, the whole school, pupils, staff and parents, are involved. In fact, in Mahnala Environmental School there is more than a whole school movement, the whole local Mahnala community is involved, even villagers who have no children at school.

## Governance

According to the constitution of Finland, everyone is responsible for conservation of nature and its diversity and for a healthy environment. In Finland teachers have a considerable degree of autonomy when it comes to school laws and curriculum guidelines. All primary school teachers have achieved university level professional status, all of them are Masters of Education, MSc (Education). There are national curriculum guidelines from which Hameenkyro Municipality has created its own local version. From this the school level curriculum was created and Mahnala Environmental School's own curriculum. The individual subjects in the curriculum facilitate and support the integration of teaching and learning and their interaction with the immediate school environment, which can be utilized in teaching.

## Development

In 2002 Annukka contacted Mauri and joined the national and international OECD ENSI network. From the beginning the school has had a strong spirit of traditional Environmental Education (EE): recycling, energy saving, local organic food, school garden, collaboration with local farmers and fishermen for example. Collaboration with Mauri and the University of Joensuu and the University of Helsinki resulted in many national and international meetings of OECD ENSI (and its projects such as 1) School Development through Environmental Education (SEED) and 2) Partnership and Participation for a Sustainable Tomorrow (SUPPORT) and separate European Union projects like Sustainability Education in European Primary Schools (SEEPS). Annukka learnt new ideas, theories, tools and methods of integrating Environmental Education in Mauri's Research and Development (R&D) Group during the years 2000-2004. In 2004, this R&D Group was renamed the R&D Group for Sustainability Education or Education for Sustainable Development (ESD). She learnt to integrate the best available theories and methods, to test them both theoretically in thinking and empirically in her school practice and to improve them continually. Learning about local species and their sustainability is an integral element of Mahnala Environmental School. Since 2008 the NatureGate Online service[1] has been tested and used at the school.

A pupil is picking wild cranberries on local bog as a part of school education

---

1.http://www.naturegate.net/

## *Promoting local and global EE and ESD in Mahnala Environmental School and in Hameenkyro Municipality*

At the beginning there was teacher learning, thinking and plenty of practical activities with pupils and parents and local villagers. There was the will to promote environmental awareness and actions for conserving and improving the environment and well-being of the local people. The time line is presented in the table below. The necessary extra resources were gathered by pupils and their parents e.g. by arranging bazaars and craft fairs.

| Important dates and years | Description of what happened |
|---|---|
| 1990 | A kind of Nature school was created by Principal Hannu Jarvinen, an ornithologist. He had a licence to ring birds and he started the tradition of ringing birds with third grade pupils. Field studies and gardening were started. Collaboration with local citizens started. |
| 1996 | Annukka brought ideas of modern Environmental Education to Mahnala Environmental School, including Global Learning and Observations to Benefit the Environment (GLOBE). |
| 1999 | WWF's Panda award was given to Mahnala Environmental School. This was the first time that the Panda award had been given to any school in Finland. |
| 2002 | Joined research group and university level collaboration with Mauri, joined national and international school R&D projects such as OECD ENSI, SEED, SEEPS, NatureGate. |
| 2008 | The school was selected to be part of the Development Centre for Environmental Education in Tampere Region, areas of responsibility included early education, teaching and in-service training. |
| 2008 | The Green Year medal, a national award presented to Mahnala Environmental School. The reason for the award: Use of schoolyard as a learning environment. |
| 2008 | Participated in the international ENSI SUPPORT project and its conference in Espoo, Hanasaari. |
| 2009 | A co-authored Poster in the 5th World Environmental Education Congress in Montreal, Canada. |
| 2010 | Environmental Rose Award from National Society of Environmental Education personally to Annukka. |
| 2011 | A co-authored Poster in the 6th World Environmental Education Congress in Brisbane, Australia. |

The immediate surroundings of the school have been the source of inspiration for the operations of Mahnala Environmental School. From the beginning, one of the shared aims of Mahnala schoolteachers was to cooperate with the inhabitants of the school region.

In Mahnala Environmental School Annukka has the following principles and reasoning chains concerning sustainability education:

1.  It has to include intentional, planned use of surrounding environment, including its nature.
2.  This kind of education increases awareness of environmental issues, the surrounding nature and sustainability.
3.  In this way, pupils, their parents and teachers will know and understand better the local environment and nature, and their sustainable use.

One of the main principles of the project is *commonplaceness*, which is defined in The Free online dictionary as: *"Having no remarkable features, characteristics, or traits; ordinary"*. The question is not about individual themes, although they are also integrated into the curriculum as a whole. Commonplaceness is integrated within everyday activities: eating organic and local foods; sorting waste; work education; the everyday presence of nature and environment; and directing our attention to the life around us (sense of community and locality).

The countryside provides activities that will instruct us to take responsibility for our environment by working together with one another. The learning environments are manifold. Activities are focused on the local environment in cooperation with local rural entrepreneurs. Work education (learning by doing) is one of the crucial methods used by Mahnala Environmental School. It constitutes one part of the countryside-orientated approach. Pupils are allowed to take part in harvesting at local farms.

Over the years, together with the pupils and their families, the parents' association has been replenishing the learning environment at the schoolyard with such things as an ice hockey rink, outhouse, playhouse, tipi, a nature trail and bird boxes. Old bicycles have been repaired at the club meetings to be used by school and local villagers. Pupils have the chance to take part in looking after the school garden during the summer with their families. In order to accomplish the more extensive work projects, the school has had to find partnerships and collaborate in close association with local experts.

Pupils are painting self-built storage house using self-made traditional red ochre paint

In Mahnala Environmental School, teaching and educational work emphasizes the promotion of sustainable development through everyday practices following a sustainable lifestyle. For children, the local environment represents a place of growth of ancestral roots. Once the pupils obtain a strong knowledge of their home district and its nature, population community, settlements and means of livelihood as well as the local culture, they will start to understand the environment and the community that lives in it more comprehensively.

All these issues have been continually researched, presented, reflected and discussed in the R&D Group of Sustainability Education, national and international meetings, conferences and congresses of the ENSI program.

Collaborative knowledge building was used and tested in the Knowledge Forum platform 2000-2004.

A recent example is acting as user and tester of the NatureGate Online Service[2]. Mahnala Environmental School is one of the national test beds for this new possibility for schools to promote sustainable use of biodiversity and at the same time to learn to identify local species. The International Union for Conservation of Nature Commission on Education and Communication (IUCN CEC) recommends the use of the NatureGate Online Service approach[3].

2.http://www.naturegate.net/

3.http://www.iucn.org/about/union/commissions/cec/?2614/

## *Results*

For a teacher it is very rewarding to conduct research on her own work, to collaborate with colleagues, administrators and university researchers. It is very rewarding to be an active partner of an informal international network of teachers as researchers and developers of their own work. It is rewarding to develop professionally, to learn what other teachers are doing, what is shared and what is different in various contexts and in different countries. To be an educational innovator and change agent for sustainable development among other educational innovators and change agents is hard, time-consuming and rewarding. The point is to be open, to share what you are doing, learning from what you are doing and learning from others, learning from the best of each field. There are people in education who try to avoid sharing and open dialogue. They do not seem to learn personally and professionally. Only by having honest dialogues teachers may continually develop both personally and professionally

In Finland, children have a duty to learn according to the official school curriculum. It may happen either in schools or at home. Most parents can choose the school education for their children. Initially, every child is offered the nearest comprehensive school. But parents are allowed to choose also a special school for special reasons. Mahnala Environmental School has become popular. Many parents choose it as a preferred school for their children. This is an indicator of success. There is a notable increase in the number of pupils in Mahnala Environmental School. In 1990 there were 49 pupils for school grades 1-6. In 2011 there are 120 pupils in the grades 1-6 of the comprehensive school and 19 Preschool pupils.

Pupils are ice fishing as a part of their school curriculum

## Research and development in Mahnala Environmental School

In school development as well as professional development it is important to join local, national and international networks. Participants of these networks are usually school and university level innovators. For Mahnala Environmental School and Annukka, the most important network has been the ENSI network. ENSI has included many European Union projects like SEED and SUPPORT. Other networks have included being a school partner in SEEPS. ENSI involves both national and international activities and meetings. Annukka and her Mahnala Environmental School have actively participated and collaborated in Mauri's R&D Group's work, for example in the testing of school use of the NatureGate Online Service. There are many shared presentations and publications as evidence of this collaboration.

Mahnala Environmental School is closely linked to life around the school. For many years, the staff has implemented environmental and sustainability education. At the same time they have been creating a conceptual model for sustainability education in everyday comprehensive school education. This model may become a national tool to promote school learning environments and work culture.

In Mahnala Environmental School, education for sustainability uses the same kinds of methods as Environmental Education. For example the use of organic food and local food may influence what kind of food other organizations (kindergartens, schools and other public organizations) will use in future. One of the aims is to work closely with the surrounding community and local organizations. In this way children become more empowered to influence local life. Pupils are also helped to understand how actions of society are linked to local and global environmental and sustainability issues.

Mahnala Environmental School supports regional ESD and EE. In 2008, Mahnala Environmental School was selected to be part of the Development Centre for Environmental Education in Tampere Region: areas of responsibility include early childhood education, teaching and in-service training. Mahnala Environmental School has the expertise to provide advice when an organization wants to develop its own ESD or EE. Contacts are made to Kindergarten and schools from primary level to secondary level. ESD and EE seminars are arranged. They are focused on tools and methods from ESD and EE. Mahnala Environmental School and Annukka produce learning materials. Annukka takes an active part in conferences and seminars as an expert of ESD and EE. Contacts are actively kept with the University of Helsinki, Ministry of Education, Ministry of Environment and National Board of Education. Mahnala Environmental School and Ms Annukka Alppi coordinate the activities of Finnish ENSI Schools.

## *Where to now?*

Future plans include creating a Regional Nature School. A bigger school complex is hoped, in which school from Kindergarten level to upper secondary school will be integrated and also in-service education of teachers.

## The vision of Mahnala Environmental School

Annukka's vision for Mahnala Environmental School in 2020 is that it will be a regional center for ESD and EE:

- *A conceptual model for Sustainability Education will have been created for school education, for everyday living, and it will be continually developed as a working theory. It will be a tool, as concrete as possible. The developed model will be applied at all levels of general education.*

- *The Mahnala conceptual model for Sustainability Education will be a national tool for development of school learning environments and organizational culture.*

- *Organic and local food will be used increasingly in Tampere region schools. It will be part of everyday sustainability.*

- *Mahnala Environmental School will have an established position among regional and national schools.*

- *Small-scale farming will be a part of the school curriculum, e.g. organic potatoes, school garden, hens and sheep.*

- *Mahnala Environmental School will be a regional residential Nature School and there will also be shorter one-day courses for nature studies and sustainability education.*

- *Mahnala Environmental School will be an information center for the surrounding national landscape area and for countryside tourism, during summer months.*

- *Mahnala Environmental School will be an established institute for Tampere region teachers in further education for sustainability. This kind of activity began in 2008. The vision is to continually develop in Kindergarten education, teaching and in-service education for sustainability education, including EE and nature education.*

## *Impacts on other human and ecological systems*

Mahnala Environmental School is a strong central actor in local and regional life. Pupils, their parents and other citizens have common school activities such as festivities, fairs and voluntary work for the school and Mahnala community. Taking an active part in local farming and fishing, composting, worm composting, recycling, energy saving, waste management, traditions and country life in general has positively influenced both human and ecological systems, integrating ecologically, economically and socially sustainable development. Mahnala Environmental School has been successful locally, nationally and internationally in R&D networks for sustainability education. It is understandable that Mahnala Environmental School's influence on local human and ecological systems is clearer and stronger than national and international systems.

---

*Thinking it through*

Could an ordinary teacher become an educational sustainability change agent like Annukka?

What does it require?

Could any school promote sustainability, sustainable development?

What does it require?

What could be done without university collaboration?

What are the benefits of school and university collaboration in sustainability education?

---

*Action: what can I do?*

Think through what you know about sustainable development and sustainability.

Read what the United Nations and UNESCO write about the Decade of Education for Sustainable Development (2005-2014) and the underpinning main documents.

Think about the best way to learn to use the local biodiversity sustainably and to learn to identify local species, because there is no sustainable use of biodiversity without identifying and knowing the main local species.

Test the NatureGate online approach as one option. Check what IUCN CEC writes about possibilities of creating this kind of collaborative service in your region.

Begin a dialogue for truth with those kinds of people who are already actively promoting sustainability and sustainable development.

Search for university collaboration because the chances of making critical friends there are greater than outside universities.

Try to test all your ideas and working theories both theoretically in thinking and dialogue, as well as empirically in your everyday life.

Start using systems thinking in practice, because the world is a system.

Use inquiry-based teaching and learning and collaborative knowledge building when possible because sustainability can be constructed only on truthful and tested grounds and underpinnings, not on any untested dogmas and illusions.

Be as open as possible. Share what you have learnt. Trust creates trust. Only by sharing, by teaching others, learning from the best of each field, you will learn both personally and professionally. It often means becoming a member of informal or formal networks for sustainability. One option is to become a Facebook friend of known researchers and developers in sustainability education such as Mauri. He believes in cumulative collaborative knowledge building and has accepted hundreds of people who share his interest to promote sustainability, good environment and good life.

## *Further reading*

Åhlberg, M. (2008). Concept mapping as an innovation: documents, memories and notes from Finland, Sweden, Estonia and Russia 1984-2008. In A. Cañas, P. Reiska, M. Åhlberg & J. Novak (Eds.). (2008). *Concept Mapping: Connecting Educators. Proceedings of the Third International Conference on Concept Mapping.* Tallinn, Estonia & Helsinki, Finland. http://cmc.ihmc.us/cmc2008papers/cmc2008-p288.pdf

Åhlberg, M., Kaasinen, A., Kaivola, T. & Houtsonen, L. (2001). Collaborative knowledge building to promote in-service teacher training in environmental education. *Journal of Information Technology for Teacher Education 10*(3), 227 – 238. http://faculty.ksu.edu.sa/Alhassan/2503/collaborative%20knowledge%20building%202001.pdf

Åhlberg, M., Lehmuskallio, E. & Lehmuskallio, J. (2009). NatureGate®: Free, rapid, interactive online service for identification of species, promoting biodiversity learning, studying, teaching and understanding. Poster at the *e-Biosphere 09 conference,* June 1-3, 2009, London, UK. In the category: New Tools, Services and Standards for Data Management and Access, http://www.e-biosphere09.org/posters/D1.pdf

Alppi, A., Kaivola, T. & Ahlberg, M. (2009). What can be learnt and generalized from a narrative study of Mahnala Environmental School? Poster presented at the *5^{th} World Environmental Education Congress.* May 10-14, 2009. Montreal, Canada, http://www.mv.helsinki.fi/home/maahlber/Alppi_Kaivola_Ahlberg_POSTERI_5WEEC.pdf

Dillon, P., Kaivola, T., Åhlberg, M. & Mylläri, J. (2009). *ICT Supported Education for Sustainable Development and Global Responsibility.* Report of the Conference at the Hanasaari Swedish-Finnish Cultural Centre, Espoo, Finland, September 1-4, 2008, http://www.mv.helsinki.fi/home/maahlber/Hanasaari FINAL DEFINITIVE, Jan 20.doc

Houtsonen, L., Kaasinen, A. & Ahlberg, M. (2009). The Finnish ENSI R&D program 2000-2008: ICT supported education for sustainable development in the schools. Poster presented at the *5th World Environmental Education Congress.* May 10-14, 2009. Montreal, Canada, http://www.mv.helsinki.fi/home/maahlber/Houtsonen_Kaasinen_Ahlberg_5weec_POSTER.pdf

IUCN CEC. (2009). Easily Identify Species with New Online Service from CEC Member in Finland, http://www.iucn.org/about/union/commissions/cec/?2614/

Lehmuskallio, E., Lehmuskallio, J., Kaasinen, A. & Åhlberg, M. (2008). NatureGate® online service as a resource source for CmapTools. In A. Cañas, P. Reiska, M. Åhlberg & J. Novak ( Eds.). (2008). *Concept Mapping: Connecting Educators. Proceedings of the Third International Conference on Concept Mapping.* Tallinn, Estonia & Helsinki, Finland. http://cmc.ihmc.us/cmc2008papers/cmc2008-p801.pdf

Myllari, J., Ahlberg, M. & Dillon, P. (2010). The dynamics of an on-line knowledge building community. A five-year longitudinal study. *British Journal of Educational Technology 41*(3), 365 – 387.

### *Resources*

Homepage address of Mahnala Environmental School is http://www.hameenkyro.fi/palvelut/kasvatus-ja-opetus/perusopetus/alakoulut/mahnalan-ymparistokoulu/

NatureGate Online Service for sustainable use of biodiversity and rapid, interactive species identification: http://www.naturegate.net

# Chapter 27
## Pigface Point

## A Radical View of Sustainability

*Ted Trainer*
*School of Social Work, University of New South Wales, Australia*

### Why we need to change

Most people think about sustainability in terms of changes and new ways whereby we could solve the big global problems while we go on enjoying much the same lifestyles and economic and political systems that we have today. However for more than fifty years a small number of concerned people have been arguing that this society has become so unsustainable, and the global economy has become so unjust, that global problems cannot be solved without huge and radical change to a very different kind of society.

In other words the argument here is that most people do not understand the seriousness of the sustainability problem. They do not realize that it cannot be fixed within or by consumer society. Some of the basic systems, structures and ways at the core of our society cause the big problems and we cannot solve them without transition to what we refer to as *The*

*Simpler Way*. Although most people do not take this view of the situation, there is a strong case supporting it, and environmental educators should give their students the opportunity to consider it.

This chapter takes the reader on our guided tour of Pigface Point, which introduces visiting groups to this radical perspective, and more importantly, introduces visitors to the nature of *The Simpler Way*.

One of the main points we try to make is that the global situation involves a number of interconnected problems, including environmental destruction, resource depletion, Third World poverty and inappropriate development, armed conflict and war, and the deteriorating cohesion and quality of life in even the richest countries. It is important to see that all these are caused by the quest for levels of production and consumption that are far beyond sustainable.

Another important theme is that far more than personal lifestyle change is required. Unless huge changes in the structures and systems of our society are made, including largely scrapping the economy, the problems can't be solved. So the Pigface Point tour is not just about alternative ways individuals could choose. It is mainly concerned with making clear the new kinds of economies and forms of settlements we must build.

## The site

Pigface Point is a 20 hectares block within 100 hectares of bushland, about 20 kilometres SW of central Sydney. Our family has lived here since the early 1940s. The main house and the caretaker's cottage are the only dwellings in the area. We began taking visitors through in 1985 and in some recent years the numbers have exceeded one thousand. The main guided tour takes about three hours including morning tea, but we also run whole day and overnight experiences for special groups. Visits are free and we receive no funding. We hope to elaborate the venture in the near future, especially by organizing volunteers to take more groups through, and building small cabins to enable weekend events.

## Water and electricity

We are not connected to the city water or electricity mains and we collect all our house water from the roof. Garden water is pumped by windmills from the wetland. We recycle our kitchen and other wastes to the animals and compost heaps. We use some bought bottled gas for cooking and fridges but in winter the house is heated with firewood. All electricity for the two houses, running the lights, workshop machinery, computers etc. comes from four PV panels. Because these systems are technically simple we can do all the maintenance, repairs and extensions ourselves. We have built all the houses and structures on the site. Simple systems mean that handymen will be able to make and fix most things around the new highly self-sufficient neighbourhoods we will need to develop in order to live *The Simpler Way*. There will be much less need for expensive tradesmen and professionals.

## *Let's go for a walk*

The house, workshop, tea house and caretaker's cottage are now set among more than 200 tall trees that we planted long ago on a bare sandy and dry slope. We named the site Pigface Point because for years that tough little succulent was the only plant we could get to grow.

This is where we begin. The sign on the left lists the main global problems, saying they are all due to over-consumption. The one on the right lists the basic principles of *The Simpler Way*, which are: much less affluent lifestyles; highly self-sufficient ways in localized economies; participation and cooperation not competition; and some very different values to those central in consumer society.

Meet Smokey, our lawnmower. He is a good example of the permaculture principle of getting a job done by something that will also do several other useful things. He can carry firewood using saddlebags, kids can ride on him, he has an interesting personality and adds to our leisure resources, and he produces manure for our poor garden soils.

Now we come to the vegetable gardening area. This is a chicken shed made from mud. It opens to three pens that are also vegetable gardens. When the chickens have cleaned one up and fertilized it we plant. They do the work for us.

The garden shed is made from rammed earth bricks. Earth is the best building material and around the site we are slowly adding examples of the many ways to build with it. There are big buildings in China made from earth, 800 years old, and in the Middle East there are multi-storied buildings made from it.

There is a greenhouse in the main vegetable garden area, along with our nursery and fern shade house. We compost kitchen scraps or feed them to the animals. No pesticides or artificial fertilizers are used. There are fruit and nut trees here and there as well as in two small orchards. A family can easily produce most of its own food with a few person-hours work/play a week. A sustainable local economy would have small dairies, grain lands and orchards nearby, eliminating the need for trucks, warehouses, ships, marketing... and experts in suits sitting at computer screens.

Just outside the vegetable garden gate is one of the six homemade concrete tanks holding garden water. This one is on four metre high piers. Nearby is a 6 metre high tower holding the four PV panels, just off the edge of the tea house where the four 220 amp-hour 12 volt batteries are kept. Also here is a small low roof over a 15 centimetre circular saw bench, run on the 12 volt system and capable of ripping 19 millimetre softwood. A small wood turning lathe also runs off the motor.

One of six homemade concrete tanks for garden water

The path passes the honey processing equipment. We will see the hive later but frames and boxes are kept here, along with the homemade centrifuge for getting the honey out. It only takes about four hours 'work' a year to produce more honey than we can use. Bee keeping is an interesting hobby. You would only need a few enthusiasts to keep your neighbourhood in honey. The bees' wax is very useful, for waterproofing, sealing food containers, and for candles, moulds, sculpture and other hobby work.

We go past another small shed made from poured mud, built for craft-work. Nearby is the caretaker's cottage, which was made without power tools, in six months spare time, in 1989... for about $8000. It is possible to make much cheaper, beautiful, small dwellings, from straw bales or earth. Building your own house, with help from experienced local people, should be one of your most satisfying life adventures. The average Australian new house is now the biggest in the world. Big is ugly and resource wasteful. *The Simpler Way* is to ask, what would be sufficient?

The caretaker's cottage built in 1989

Now to the second chicken area... Moving the chickens and ducks allows the parasites at the old site to die out. They then clean up the new garden ground and fertilise the fruit trees in the pen. The chicken house is an example of wattle and daub earth building and the feed shed is an example of mud brick building. One display board here lists basic permaculture principles, and another shows how we could dig up many of the roads in our neighbourhoods and replace them with gardens, sheds, orchards and fishponds. These are some of the many *commons* we should develop in our settlements, to provide free fruit, nuts, fuel, craft materials, grazing, honey, fish, community sheds, workshops and craft rooms. The *commons* would be maintained by voluntary working bees.

Display boards here show the alarming magnitude of the energy and greenhouse problems. One shows the *peak oil* expectation that world supply will fall far below demand in the next few decades. Another shows that if all the nine billion people expected to live on earth after 2050 were to have the per capita energy consumption that Australians are heading for by then (maybe 400 gigajoules), total world energy production would have to be seven times as great as it is now. But as another display board shows we will probably have to entirely eliminate use of fossil fuels by 2050. Most people think this can be done by replacing fossil fuels with renewables such as the sun and the wind, but there is a strong argument that this cannot be done because we could not afford the amount of generating plant that would be required. This is not an argument against moving to renewables, only an argument that we can't live affluently on them.

The next display we come to indicates the way global resources are distributed. At first the white blocks (resources) are level across the almost seven billion people represented on the base line. But then the blocks are rearranged to show how most resources are used by the few people living in rich countries, while most people get very few of them. More than one billion have dangerously dirty drinking water, are hungry all the time, and have no sewage systems... mainly because they do not get a fair share of the world's resources. Thus the gross injustice of the global economy is evident; it allocates vast resource wealth to the rich countries while it so seriously deprives billions in the Third World that tens of thousands there die avoidably every year.

Many resources are now scarce and getting scarcer, including petroleum, water, fish, food in general, phosphorus, forests, and several minerals. When we realize that world population will probably be nine billion by 2050 it is obvious that there is no chance that all people could ever rise to the per capita rate of use we have in Australia now. It will not be possible for the poor majority of the world's people to get a fair share unless and until we in countries like Australia move down to much lower rates of consumption, that is, until we live on something like our fair share.

The magnitude of the required shift down is show by the 'footprint measure' symbols set up here. About eight ha of productive land is needed to produce the food, water, settlement area and energy each Australian needs. But by 2050 the amount available per capita in the world will be only 0.8 hectares. We are already 10 times over the amount that will be possible for all to have.

Most people do not seem to realise the significance of these basic and well-known resource and footprint facts and figures. There can be no doubt that we in rich countries are far beyond sustainable levels of consumption. It is not plausible that technical advance and conservation effort could reduce our consumption of resources sufficiently. Sustainability and global justice cannot be achieved unless we move to ways of life and to systems that enable us to live well on a small fraction of our present levels.

But back to our walk... We now go over a small bridge. Its approaches were built from broken up footpaths, as a leisure activity. All the public structures and systems around our new neighbourhoods, the windmills, sheds, orchards, community gardens, halls and workshops will be built and maintained by that most powerful institution, the *community working bee*. Imagine what you could have in your area if every Saturday afternoon you got together to build things that would make it a more interesting and productive place to live. In some towns the working bees will be able to look after old people, keep the parks in order, maintain and harvest orchards, build leisure facilities, and actually do some of the educating and policing. Americans watch TV an average of four hours a day and spend more in front of a computer screen. Think how rich their areas could be if they spent that time cooperating on community projects.

The bridge

The path now runs across low ground through a forest of tall Casuarinas. The guide points out that all of this area will probably be under seawater by 2100 because of sea level rise caused by the greenhouse problem.

Signs along the path represent the scale of the solar system, with the sun a 2.5 centimetre diameter sphere and the earth a pinhead three metres away. We walk for about 80 metres until we get to Pluto, and on this scale it would be four kilometres to the nearest star. Muck up this planet and there's nowhere else to go.

Near the river we pass a two-metre diameter water wheel that is slowly driven round by high tide water held in small lakes and channels behind a low dam. When the tide is low a valve automatically releases and a jet of water drives a pump 100 metres away, via a wire belt. When we move off fossil fuels we will have to harvest all the sources of energy available around our settlements. However it is worth remembering that when we live simply we will not need anywhere near as much energy as we use now.

The water wheel

So far the main point made has been that present levels of production and consumption are grossly unsustainable. But our society is obsessed with raising living standards and the GDP – that is, increasing production and consumption as fast as possible and without any limit! Displays at this point show the significance of this commitment. If the Australian economy grows at 3% per annum its normal rate, until 2050 then the amount of producing and consuming going on will be three to four times as great as it is now... but we are already producing and consuming far too much.

One sign here makes the point that if all the nine billion people expected on earth by 2050 were to rise to the per capita income that Australians would have, given 3% per annum growth, then the total amount of producing and consuming going on in the world every year would be about 15 times as great as it is now. This is totally impossible and to continue in that direction would be to exhaust resources and to bring on ecological catastrophe.

The point again is that clearly the need is for dramatic reduction in levels of resource use and consumption. So obviously the problems cannot possibly be solved in a growth economy. Economic growth can only make the already alarming problems worse. There can be no solution to this problem in this system; we can only solve it by changing to a very different system, that is, to an economy that does not need any economic growth. Quite a few economists and scientists are saying this now, and there are movements for *De-growth* and *Steady State* economics but the mainstream takes no notice.

The path now runs along the riverbank past a series of signs indicating another scale, this one representing the last one billion years of evolutionary time. We walk 150 metres until we come to the sign representing the emergence of the first single cell organisms. Over the next 100 metres we pass the emergence of fish, amphibians, reptiles, birds, dinosaurs, mammals, apes and humans. The distance from Neanderthals to Homo sapiens is a centimetre.

Meanwhile we have come to the large wetland. About five hectares, maybe half of it, is visible from here. On the dam is one of our two windmills, pumping garden water, and an experimental 'chain of buckets' pump that was driven by the water wheel we passed 100 metres away.

Wetland, windmill and chain of buckets pump

Another 60 metres through the wetland forest and we come to the Peter Pan path. This area is intended to show how our working bees could landscape our communities to contain rich leisure resources for all. This one has waterways for canoeing, ornamental bridges, gardens, pagodas, a castle, a seven metre crocodile, a flying fox and soon to be made, a cave, and a pirate ship.

Seven metre crocodile

Most neighbourhoods in consumer society are boring leisure-deserts, so we have to drive away for entertainment or watch TV. In our new highly self-sufficient neighbourhoods we would be surrounded by little farms, firms, craft centres, artists, and landscapes similar to those seen on this Peter Pan path. We would have leisure committees organizing concerts, games, talks, field days, picnics, visits and adventures, and researching what other things people thought would make our areas even more interesting. Five minutes on a bike would get you to an inexhaustible number of similar sites people in surrounding neighbourhoods had developed.

In our new neighbourhoods there would be far less desire to travel or consume commercial entertainment. Many leisure activities are also productive, such as arts and crafts.

The path now winds under the trees over four more bridges up to the main house.

Near the teahouse is a display illustrating the huge difference between conventional Third World development and 'appropriate' development. A model island has labels pinned on showing that conventional development gears its productive capacity to the interests of rich world corporations and supermarket shoppers, with very little 'trickle down' benefit to most of the Third World's people. For instance the best land is put into export crops, reducing local food production and yielding only a few jobs... whereas that land should be being used by local people to feed themselves. In the conventional approach the development that takes place is that which will maximize the profits of some investor... it is not the development that is most likely to meet needs. If no corporation thinks it can make good profits there, then there is no development there, even though there might be abundant soils, rainfall and labour.

Bridge to the teahouse

The result is a grossly unjust world economy. The rich countries get most of the resources and most Third World productive capacity is geared to our demand. Those are inevitable outcomes when market forces and profit are allowed to determine development. The point again is that a just situation cannot be achieved within this economic system. The Third World could only get a fair share of the world's resources in a very different economy, one that determined distribution and development according to needs, not profit.

We now are at the halfway point in the tour. Time for morning tea – but morning tea is going to be auctioned. People are given 'money' and told the things they can buy. We ask who would buy the tea and scones, costing a lot, and who would ask for a biscuit, and who only has enough money to afford a glass of water. People look at the amounts of money they have been given, and find that only a few could afford the tea and scones. But that's what we would decide to produce and sell, because we can make most profit on that option. So unfortunately most people would have to get by on a glass of water. Is that a satisfactory way of proceeding?

Teahouse

Well it is precisely the way the market economy does things. The 'money' we gave out was in proportion to the distribution of world income; most people do not have enough to bid for valuable resources, including food so they are ignored while the market provides luxuries for the rich few because that's the most profitable option.

Again the point is that you cannot have global justice in the world while the global economy is driven by market forces. The market allocates resource wealth to the rich, and it develops what benefits the rich. In a good society we would make sure that resources and development go to what is needed, not what maximizes the profits of corporations and stocks rich world supermarkets.

After morning tea we go down past the four metre wide garden pot, holding bushfire safety water, and the main house water tank (all the house water comes from rain on the roof) to the 4.5 metre tall water wheel. Water wheels should be along the gullies in every neighbourhood, doing some work for us when the creeks are running, such as generating electricity or mixing clay.

A pipe from the septic tank shows by a small flame at its tip that useful methane gas is being produced. A well-designed neighbourhood would harvest this energy from all house and animal pen wastes before these are pumped to the gardens and orchards. There is also a mini Pelton wheel and a coil pump here, illustrating different simple alternative technologies.

Large water pot for bushfire safety water

A small, scruffy coil of plastic pipe is rotated, dipping its open end into a water tray, and water is pumped out of the other end a metre higher. This is the simplest but most energy-efficient pump on the property. We discuss the physics, and the principle of always looking for the resource, energy and technically simplest way of doing things. Usually the most satisfying way to do something is with hand tools and craft ways, not high-tech machinery. *The Simpler Way* is not opposed to high tech, and is happy to use computers and solar panels where these make sense. But we do not see sophisticated technology as being important. Certainly it is not necessary to solve our problems. We knew how to grow perfect food and build beautiful houses hundreds of years ago. What we need to solve our problems is not better technology but better ideas and values, which eliminate the need to produce more and more all the time.

At this point the path passes a statue representing Gaia, the Earth-mother goddess who sends the rain and keeps the soil fertile. We are treating Gaia badly. Nearby is a board dealing with the extremely environmentally destructive nature of our society. It makes the point that the environment cannot be saved within or by consumer-capitalist society. The environment is being destroyed because the amount of producing and consuming going on is already far beyond sustainable levels (remember those footprint numbers) and yet this society insists on growth, on constantly and limitlessly increasing these amounts! The environment cannot be saved unless we move to ways that involve far less production and consumption.

"But couldn't better technology solve the problems?" This is what most people assume. Our argument is that the problems are far too big for that. The level of unsustainability and overshoot cannot be remedied by technical wizardry that allows us to all go on merrily trying to get richer and consume more, for ever. Again remember the Australian footprint is already 10 times too big.

Under this shelter there is a small 12 volt car fan motor, geared down by the big wheel to slowly drive a pump. We will soon have it working a washing machine and a saw to slowly cut firewood.

This tank holds water for safety in case of bushfire. Soon we will grow edible fish in it. A neighbourhood can have its own fishing industry, in tanks and small ponds. Beside the tank is our main windmill, 17 metres to the hub, and homemade.

Not far ahead is the beehive. A large macadamia and a bunya nut tree are near the mill. To the west are large paddocks for the animals. We usually have a goat and a sheep as well as the pony. Their important job is to keep the growth down in those areas because that is the fire danger direction.

Billy on bushfire prevention duty

A model, almost two metres by two metres, shows how a small town or village could be highly self-sufficient. The population assumed is 1000 and the main settlement in the middle is 700 metres across. All fruit and vegetables needed could be produced within that town area but just outside the town are the required grain, dairy and forest areas. We estimate that people living simply and self-sufficiently in a town like this might have a 'footprint' and energy consumption rate that is only around 5-10% of the Australian average. In other words *The Simpler Way* would enable huge reductions in use of non-renewable resources and in dollar, energy and environmental costs.

The model also makes the point that the main solutions to the global problem are not to be found at the level of individual lifestyles. They can only be achieved if there is radical change in systems, structures and settlements. Centrally important is change to a new economy, and to new geographies of settlements in which there can be small, highly self-sufficient local economies, run by the people who live there to meet needs and not for profits or wealth accumulation. We think there would still be a place for mostly private small firms, and for markets but they would have to be under careful social control via participatory forms of government not via centralized, authoritarian state bureaucracies.

Now we come to the industrial area. Many of the items we will need manufactured in our new neighbourhoods could be produced in very small firms and cooperatives, using local resources, and allowing many people to enjoy hobby and craft production. Pottery is a good example. In a stable, zero-growth economy not much new crockery would be needed each year and it could all be produced in tiny potteries like ours, from local clay, by people who love making pottery. A kiln outside burns wood from our trees. The clay used, and from which the pottery was made, comes from within a kilometre.

Nearby is a blacksmith's forge and a tiny furnace for melting aluminium and lead to make castings. Air is blown through the fires with a fan from a car. There is a small shed for bush carpentry, making roofing shingles from split wood, furniture, gates, tool handles, etc. Another small shelter is for ornamental cement work including mosaic making, using broken crockery or pebbles. There are three 'lathes' on which circular objects are made from cement, including all the large ornamental garden pots around the house.

Large ornamental garden pots

Some people think that the main fault in humans is a tendency to aggression and domination. We think that although this is a serious problem in Western culture (but it is not a problem in some cultures, such as the Arapesh in New Guinea, or the Amish or Quakers in our own society), there is a bigger problem, which is the desire for affluence, possessions, wealth, consumption. Unless we learn to live happily with what is sufficient and not try to get richer all the time, there will inevitably be conflict between people and between nations. Most people in the Peace Movement don't seem to realize that war cannot be eliminated while all nations strive to get hold of as many resources as they can to be as rich as they can, on a planet where there are nowhere near enough resources for all to be as rich as Australians are now.

A few metres further up the slope we come to the recycling area. Every neighbourhood should have a place where things no longer needed can be put for others to use, or to dismantle for materials.

On top of the hill are the main water tanks, made cheaply from cement thinly plastered over old chicken wire. Their roofs stop leaves getting in and collect rainwater for the house. All of the eight tank and shed roofs in this area feed to a house water tank lower down the hill. (We use four different kinds of water: rain water for the house; salty river water for waterwheels; swamp water for the garden; and washing up water carried to the garden.) In a well-designed settlement all 'black' water, i.e. sewage, would also be run to compost heaps, orchards and fields so that all nutrients are recycled to food production.

On the way down the hill back to the main house we cross a levelled area to which rain water is fed by bunds and swales (low ridges and channels.) It can then soak in to keep the soil moist. Loquat and apple trees have been planted off the edge of the circle. We pass another house, this one less than a metre high and available only for rental to elves.

Elf house

We are now back to near the main house, and we come to the workshop. It shows some of the things that would be available in the community work-shop that we should have on every neighbourhood block, including tools and benches, recycling racks, arts and crafts spaces, library, ping pong table, canoes, an art gallery, a museum, a pot belly stove and coffee pot, easy chairs for just sitting and chatting. The community workshop is where our community committees will meet.

Inside the workshop

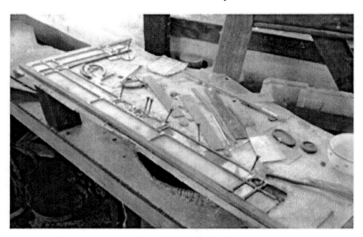

Lead light workbench

Our new neighbourhoods, suburbs and towns will have to be largely self-governing. In the coming era of scarce resources and highly localised and self-sufficient economies it will not be possible for central state governments to run everything. Good decisions for your town will only be possible if they are made by the citizens of the town. The citizens know what the people want and what the town's conditions and problems are. Unless there is good morale and conscientiousness and a sense that we are in control of our own situation, people will not attend working bees, meetings or concerts. In other words the town will not work well unless there is much direct participatory (not representative) self-government. Some things will still be done by much-reduced state and federal governments but most day to day 'governing' will be carried out by ordinary citizens.

Central to *The Simpler Way* vision is the idea of communities in control of and running their own highly self-sufficient local economies, through these participatory or direct democratic procedures, with relatively few functions remaining to be carried out by distant state and federal governments.

When we have control over our economic situation we will be able to get together to solve problems such as unemployment. We will have our own town bank and business incubator so if there are people without work we can simply set up another cooperative in which they can produce useful things for the town. We can identify problems and solve them immediately, making sure no one is poor or lonely and that everyone has a livelihood, a worthwhile and respected contribution to make. These options are not possible in the present economy that leaves many unemployed, poor, stressed and without purpose.

Finally, we have two models that show how we could transform our neighbourhood to make it highly self-sufficient. One shows the normal present form of most neighbourhoods, dominated by roads and cars and by houses that consume a lot and produce little, containing little or no community productive capacity. Most people leave the neighbourhood every day and travel a long way to work in the national economy to earn money to purchase things from the national economy. Many people there are unemployed or over-worked, bored, stressed and depressed.

The second model has the same basic pattern of houses, but most of the streets have been transformed into gardens and community uses, including fish ponds, orchards and animal pens, the park has been stacked with ponds and useful trees. The petrol station has become a neighbourhood workshop. The disused factory has become a small farm. The whole area is crammed with useful trees. The supermarket has become a small factory, meaning people can get to work on foot or by bicycle, and its roof is now a garden.

Model of neighbourhood with streets transformed into gardens

The new neighbourhood would also have cooperative gardens and firms in which all could contribute to producing things the local people need. These along with home gardening would eliminate dependence on the treacherous global economy for food and other necessities. This control over our own situation would enable us to eliminate unemployment, boredom and loneliness. There would be a strong sense of supportive community, with a lot of familiarity, giving away of surpluses, mutual assistance, friendship and sense of looking after each other, because people would derive much satisfaction from cooperating in running their community well.

In these new economies most people would not need to earn much money, because their needs would be few and many of these would be met by free goods from the gardens and commons (which they helped to maintain via the working bees). You might need to work for money only two days a week, so you could spend the rest in art and craft activities, studying, helping on working bees, or just sitting in the sun. In the present consumer society we work about three times too hard!

From our experience as homesteaders at Pigface Point, and our awareness of the global Eco-village and Transition Towns movements, we have no doubt that *The Simpler Way* would enable a far higher quality of life than most people have in our present society.

Consumer-capitalist society is rapidly heading into a time of great troubles, probably triggered by the coming of 'peak oil' supply. The global economy is likely to increasingly fail to provide for people. Your prospects will depend greatly on whether the people where you live can come together to develop the local systems that can produce what you need from local resources.

The most important contribution that each of us can make to the required huge transition in society is to start working here and now to develop local economic self-sufficiency. But just establishing more permaculture gardens, farmer's markets, community gardens, composting, commons etc will achieve little of lasting significance unless these ventures are informed by the understanding that these must be part of massive system and cultural change. Just establishing another community garden does nothing to get rid of the growth economy for instance. We can only do that if people eventually come to realize that sustainability requires a steady-state economy. The reason why activists should join in things like community gardening is not primarily to create another garden, it is to be able to work beside people in order to raise awareness of the need for those big system changes.

---

*Thinking it through*

The premise that underpins this chapter – that we need 'massive system and cultural change' to reach a level of sustainability that is fair for everyone, no matter what society we are born into – is a challenging one. Do you agree with this premise? Where do you stand and why?

How do *you* think we can achieve sustainability that is fair for everyone?

---

*Action: what can I do?*

Discuss the ideas in this chapter with family and friends. Visit the website below to find out more. Decide on *your* first step along the path to sustainable living.

---

## Further reading

Speth, G. (2001). *A Bridge At The End Of The World*. New Haven, Connecticut: Yale University Press.

Trainer, T. (2010). *The Transition to a Sustainable and Just World*. Sydney: Envirobook.

## Resources

A detailed account of The Simpler Way alternative society is given at
http://ssis.arts.unsw.edu.au/tsw/

# Chapter 28
## Doing Nothing, for Sustainability

*Joe Francis*
*Freelance cartoonist, Sydney, Australia*
***Tomorrow, Man***
*Superhero, The Future*

How can *doing nothing* be an actual contribution towards *doing something* to
address unsustainable aspects of our culture? And how can we suggest that
you do nothing when the whole point of this book is to provide you with
things that you can *do* that will make a difference. Your guide through this
quite unlikely perspective on a problem of calamitous importance to humankind (and a great deal of terrestrial and aquatic life too) is naturally
enough a quite unlikely superhero, and that superhero is Tomorrow, Man!

## Tomorrow, Man – Mentor and Guide

It's true of course that this book suggests many pro-active things we can do to promote sustainable living but another purpose of this book is to provide myriad lenses through which to view the world and our place in it. Some writers have applied an economics lens, some an environmental one. Others have looked at our predicament through the world of business or through socio-cultural perspectives including indigenous ones that present us with different ways of seeing and knowing an inter-connected world.

Art is also a way of knowing the world. It is a diverse field and if we focus on the visual arts it includes sculpture, painting, video, performance, street art, cartoon and comic strip. Its language of symbols and metaphor is used to describe our surroundings as well as our philosophical ponderings on life and our understanding of universal truths. A 2011 conference sponsored by the American *National Science Foundation* on this very theme[1] had as its key principle to 'explore and discuss the role of aesthetic inquiry' in public discourse and learning. Susan Hiller, an American born artist and writer, mused on the importance of aesthetic inquiry in society when attempting to answer the questions: 'What is it that artists do? What is our job? What is our function?' She offered these answers:

> "I think what art does is reveal hidden undisclosed, unarticulated codes within a culture ... I think the job of an artist is to make manifest a shared but unarticulated belief or to find a new form for something which is known but not fully understood."[2]

The artist Cecil Collins thought that art could bring about 'a universal awakening of conscience towards life'. His major interest was for a kind of spiritual liberty facilitated by the 'wisdom of art'. This liberty was only possible, he thought, if we create a condition of 'spiritual fertility' through the 'leisure of the soul'. Collins imagined a new world, but:

---

1. *Art as a Way of Knowing*, American National Science Foundation, San Francisco March 3 & 4, 2011, http://www.exploratorium.edu/knowing/logistics.html

2. Hiller, Susan (1996) *Thinking about art: conversations with Susan Hiller*. Edited by Barbara Einzig. Manchester University Press: Manchester.

"Before a new world can be made, first the conditions of spiritual fertility must be created in society. And one of the most important of these conditions of spiritual fertility is 'leisure of the soul', without which there can be no flowering of life, without which no civilization can be built."[3]

In the modern world it is becoming increasingly difficult to form a careful opinion because that requires time – an often scarce commodity. In this context art has an increasingly important role to play because art embodies time. It is the time required for contemplation and the time of creation for the artist. It is also the time of contemplation and the time of appreciation necessary for the artwork to reveal itself to the viewer. This chapter is about finding that leisure of the soul, learning how to slow down, think more, do less, consume less and take time to live a simpler, richer life.

## Take Your Time

This 'leisure of the soul' is something that has been recognized by great thinkers over the centuries. Albert Einstein spoke of the importance of allowing time to be contemplative when he said: "It's not that I'm so smart, it's just that I stay with problems longer."

Tomorrow, Man belongs to this old tradition of artistic and scientific liberty, his message is to allow more contemplative time and act less wherever possible so that we become wiser in our responses to life's challenges. Tomorrow, Man's battle is against a society that is hell bent on moving faster, consuming more and putting catastrophic pressure on the systems we rely on to provide the things that we are so intent on consuming. Therefore if we could slow down we might alleviate some of the pressure on these systems and this may also give us a chance to better understand and more intelligently respond to the problems, challenges and opportunities of the incredible matrix that is life on earth.

---

3. Transcribed by the author from a Cecil Collins' diary entry exhibited at the Tate, London, 2008. This is a partial quote, the full quote can be found at the end of this chapter.

In one way the problem of sustainability is very simple: we must live, as a people, in such a way that allows nature to constantly replenish and restore itself to the condition that is both healthy for us and for the other organisms that replenish and restore nature. The question is how are we going to do this? And, how shall we live in the time between now and when we figure out the answer to this first question? It is out of these questions that Tomorrow, Man was born.

## Primordial Soup

If understanding takes time, how then do we allow time to ponder life's questions – questions that arise in our own personal lives as well as those pertaining to life on Earth?

## Manic Oppression!!

With such a busy life finding time to think about these issues is obviously a job for tomorrow, man!

## The Timely Brilliance of Tomorrow, Man

The social usefulness of Tomorrow, Man is that he provides an important counter balance to the messages we are constantly being bombarded with: 'achieve more'; 'be the most you can be'; 'do it now'; buy this product and receive this one for less'; 'do this'; 'do that'; 'do more'. He provides a contrary perspective on a culture created by advertisers who generate needless competition and insecurity in order to sell us products to resolve this insecurity. Of course, the lack of these products is not the reason why we were feeling these pressures in the first place[4].

## An Out of Character Rant

In contrast to the barrage of information from advertising and marketing it seems that there is very little to counter their messages that ask us to consume more, travel more, earn more. There is very little room for a voice saying: "Why not have a simple life that you enjoy and in your free time you might contemplate life and what it means, because that's how you attain wisdom".

---

4. The reasons why have been expertly explored by Iain Black in his chapter on the psychology of marketing.

The message of Tomorrow, Man alone would, of course, be quite unhelpful. Things do need to be done if we are to continue surviving individually and collectively. Although Tomorrow, Man is undeniably passive, he is nonetheless a life force, existing as a boost of yin to an overstated yang[5]. Global imbalance of yang has already had, and will continue to have, serious ramifications for a sustainable future for humanity as well as for many other species of life. This is because the more typical yang characteristics such as masculinity, high energy, heat and constant movement leave a much larger environmental footprint than would a lifestyle based on typically yin characteristics such as femininity, low energy, receptivity and rest.

## A Very Yin Comic Character

Tomorrow, Man suggests that it would be helpful if we could value simplicity as much as complexity, un-ambition as much as ambition, quietness as much as extravagance, inaction as much as dynamism, contemplation as much as action, passiveness as much as obedience. These messages are very much swimming against our cultural tide, but for these very reasons Tomorrow, Man is a Superhero for our times, demanding our attention: *Tomorrow, Man! Champion of not doing things.*

But marketing is not the only system to influence how we live our lives. We live within a varied collection of cultural and political systems, some of which are more benign than others. However we can't abrogate responsibility for how we live within these systems whatever they are; we have some control over what we do and *do not do* with our lives.

---

5.Yin is the black side with the white dot on it and yang is the white side with the black dot on it. The relationship between yin and yang is often likened to the sun's path across a mountain and valley. Yin is the 'shady place' or 'north slope'. It is the dark area where the sun is blocked by the mountain. Yang is the brightly lit 'sunny place' or 'south slope'. As the sun moves across the sky yin and yang gradually change places revealing what was obscured and obscuring what was previously revealed. "The underlying polarity of Yang and Yin ... begins with light vs. dark and extends not only into high vs. low, creative vs. receptive, firm vs. yielding, moving vs. resting, and masculine vs. feminine, but also into many other areas of human concern, including the sun and the moon, the weather, the parts of the body, and even the distinction between gods (all Yang) and ghosts (all Yin)" (Osgood, C.E. & Richards, M.M. (1973). From Yang and Yin to *and* or *but. Language*, 49, 2, p. 380).

## Quiet Anarchy

Great leaders such as Mohandas Karamchand Gandhi have inspired millions with the steadfast paths they have taken towards the kind of world they want to see. In Gandhi's view "the ideally non-violent state will be an ordered anarchy. That State is the best governed which is governed the least". Tomorrow, Man's ideology rests within a Gandhian worldview, understanding the incredible power of grass roots movements and all things passive – including passive resistance.

He has taken it as his personal challenge to slow down humanity believing that if we live a less pressured, slower-paced life we will consume less. And because our consumption of goods and services is a big part of the sustainability problem, slowing down and consuming less can be a big part of the solution. Viewing life through this lens helps to reveal the often 'unarticulated codes' of consumerism and mindless, frenetic 'progress' within our culture. Taking Tomorrow, Man's advice to slow down will help us find that 'leisure of the soul', without which, Collins believed, "there can be no flowering of life" and "no civilization can be built".

Tomorrow, Man argues that slowing down will give us more time to understand the problems of sustainability and thoughtfully formulate our solutions. When we are able to think calmly, rather than reactively through a barrage of unnecessary and unsolicited information, we can make space to contemplate this incredible world. And through contemplating life on earth we will become a wiser people.

Tomorrow, Man's challenge is to slow down humanity.

## Leading the Leisurelution

### *Leisure of the Soul*

"...for liberty is the control of life by faith, hope and charity. Freedom is the sense of the privacy and holiness of all human identity. Liberty is wisdom of art, and it is then that human society will desire to drink of its poetry and eat of its wisdom. But until that moment, society will continue the degradation of mankind, unless by a miracle of creative effort we can bring about a universal awakening of conscience towards life. The old world having passed away, no other world will be possible to us; we shall have no world at all, unless we change fundamentally our attitude towards life. Before a new world can be made, first the conditions of spiritual fertility must be created in so-

346

ciety. And one of the most important of these conditions of spiritual fertility is 'leisure of the soul', without which there can be no flowering of life, without which no civilization can be built."

(Cecil Collins, complete quotation transcribed by the author from a Cecil Collins' diary entry exhibited at the Tate, London, 2008)

# Part VII

## Out of the Classroom and into a Sustainable World

*the long swim*
pen and ink, watercolour
80cm by 65cm

# Chapter 29
## What should Everyone know about Humanity's Environmental Predicament?[1]

*Paul R Ehrlich*
*Anne H Ehrlich*
Stanford University, California

### The issue

Human society today is challenged in a way never before seen in history. For the first time, humanity is fundamentally altering ecosystems on a global scale that threatens the stability and continuation of our social order. Disruption of the climate has been entrained to such a level that leading climatologists fear that societies will be increasingly unable to deal with its escalating effects. Biodiversity, the working parts of human life-support systems, is being destroyed ad lib. Toxic chemicals are increasingly spread from pole to pole. Population growth itself, growing numbers of undernourished people, and high-speed transport systems are greatly increasing the chances

---

1.Based in part on an article, which includes references to most of the statements here: Ehrlich P R 2011. A personal view: Environmental education - its content and delivery. *Environmental Studies and Sciences* volume 1 number 1, pp. 6-13.

of vast epidemics. And as pressures rise on needed resources from water and petroleum to phosphorous and rare earth metals, the risk of international conflict climbs.

The struggle to develop appropriate modes of behavior that will not erode vital ecological processes and to combat the other diverse global environmental threats to humanity is the great challenge of the $21^{st}$ century. Without major changes in our collective behavior, the present "business as usual" course of human affairs will lead inevitably to a collapse of civilization.

Education is central to meeting this challenge; indeed, it can be argued that no challenge faced by humanity is more critical than generating an environmentally literate public. An appropriate environmental education could equip people with the knowledge and values to understand and address the human predicament. Thus understanding the environmental situation needs to be a vital component of all educational processes in all nations from kindergarten to doctoral studies and continuing to update adults through public education especially via the mainstream and social media. In our view, however, environmental education today is given too little attention in most school systems of the United States and other nations, and is often poorly timed and structured when it is delivered, despite the best efforts of many dedicated teachers and curriculum designers. The situation is only marginally better in colleges and universities, where students may have access to excellent courses but no requirement to take them. Perhaps the best evidence for the inadequacy of environmental education in most places is that, as ecologists Daniel Blumstein and Charlie Saylan put it, "out of the classroom, people have failed to make the link between their individual actions and the environmental condition."

A basic problem is that educational systems for the young are designed to fill students with various packages of "tailored" knowledge, and then send them "out in the world" to use that knowledge, principally to make a living. Systematic thought has rarely been given to the ever-changing needs of citizens who face what we have called "the culture gap" – the enormous and widening gulf between the non-genetic information possessed by each individual and that possessed by the entire society. No adult could possibly know or would need the full complement of information and ideas in one's own culture, let alone those of the hundreds of other cultures in the modern world. But some appreciation of what is known about vital environmental and social issues and a coherent sense of their relevance to one's life is essential to being a responsible citizen. Today, such issues are increasingly important in human affairs and are often bones of contention politically or legally. But with little background understanding of those issues, people often neglect important problems or make poor decisions.

Thus it is insufficient simply to become more aware of the environmental consequences of what we do. Even the most green-minded and enlightened corporate managers, for instance, can't deal properly with environmental issues in the absence of appropriate collective action (public policy). Without policies that level the playing field, well-intentioned corporate decision makers would find their companies losing market share, their stockholders upset, and they might themselves become jobless.

What we outline here is what is required for individuals to gain an adequate environmental education. It reads like a very tall order, but remember, it would be stretched over perhaps 16 years of formal education and should be continually reinforced and updated through the media. On the optimistic side, we have found that a 20-lecture Stanford undergraduate course with no prerequisites but supplemented by a text designed for the course can at least provide the majority of students some familiarity with most important topics and a sense of the big picture – how the "topics" relate to one another and to themselves. Of course, much more could be transmitted if environmental education were integrated into the schooling and lives of everyone before college.

We won't detail the numerous political, financial, logistic, and other barriers that make creating an environmentally literate public so difficult at present. Those of us who are now actually trying to close key parts of the culture gap as educators in schools or colleges, or by communicating with the general public and policy makers, are only too familiar with them.

## *What should everyone know if given an adequate environmental education?*

A basic grasp of some key topics is essential for a critical assessment of current environmental issues. While most of the topics are taught in schools, they are usually not connected to each other or presented within a coherent environmental framework. Some of those key topics are obvious and information on them is broadly available, so their mention can be brief here.

### *Agriculture and the Agricultural Revolution*

Obtaining food is humanity's most basic activity, and for the past 5-10,000 years agriculture has been the main source of food. Nonetheless, aside from the small and shrinking proportion of people directly involved in food production today, many if not most educated people in developed countries have no grasp of what is involved in producing and distributing food, still less what the problems in increasing future production might be. The average university graduate, if asked "where does your food come from?" is likely to answer "the supermarket."

Furthermore, most people are unaware that the gradual transition from gathering and hunting to farming and herding – the "agricultural revolution" – was the most significant transition in at least the last ~50,000 years of the history of our species. As historian Clive Ponting has emphasized, much of human history since the agricultural revolution has been about the acquisition, distribution, and uses of the food surpluses made possible by farming. Education about agriculture (and aquaculture and fisheries) is not often considered "environmental," but since these activities are among the most ecologically destructive ones, care must be taken to see they are woven into curricula from the earliest schooling.

*Energy and the Laws of Thermodynamics*

Energy, the ability to do work or make changes in the physical world, is central to our lives and to most environmental issues, and the basic ways it behaves are critical for us all to know. Everyone should be acquainted with the significance of the first and second laws of thermodynamics (energy can be neither created nor destroyed, but it tends to change into forms that cannot do useful work. The chemical energy in gasoline is converted into the energy of motion of a car, as well as into heat energy from the exhaust, braking, rubbing of tires against the road, etc. The total energy remains the same (first law), but doing useful work with the heat is much more difficult (second law). Armed with such knowledge, people can better grasp issues such as the structure of food chains and the impossibility of recycling energy. Here the ties to agriculture are obvious – especially to the differences in energy flows between plant and animal agriculture, which determine the higher energetic costs of animal products.

*The Key Role of Photosynthesis*

The sun and photosynthesis are the basic sources of energy that runs almost all organisms (and thus farms and fisheries). Photosynthesis in the distant past was the source of the energy in fossil fuels.

*Basic Earth Science*

The fundamentals of mountain-building (orogeny), soil formation (pedogenesis), soil erosion, plate tectonics, ocean circulation, etc should be taught to everyone. This understanding of our planetary home must include how the climate system works, tying back again to both the sun's energy and to plate tectonics.

*Basics of Evolutionary Biology*

An understanding of evolution provides background for learning about topics from pesticide resistance to the capacity for empathy and many other human attributes. The differences between genetic and cultural evolution and the oft-neglected importance of the latter need to be explained and examples pointed out throughout education. Special attention should be called to factors of the prenatal environment that can affect development and later life, an issue scientists are learning is of increasing importance. It turns out that fetuses are terribly sensitive to the environment of the mother, and effects on the unborn can later be passed on to their own children.

*Human Population Growth and Structure*

Basic demography is essential to underscore the importance of one of the three major drivers of environmental deterioration. Issues related to age composition and migration should not be neglected, especially the social changes that accompany the inevitable aging of populations as birth rates fall and growth stops.

*Biodiversity, Natural Capital, and Ecosystem Services*

What these key concepts represent, how they relate to one another, and why they are so important is essential environmental information. People should understand what they are and how they work and be aware of the importance of preserving key ecosystem functions such as pollination, pest control, carbon sequestration, soil regeneration, flood control, and water purification.

*The I=PAT equation in its basic and elaborated forms*

This is a key framework for understanding how population, consumption, and technology interact to cause environmental deterioration. It should be emphasized that *P*opulation size, per-capita consumption ("*A*ffluence"), and the *T*echnological, social, cultural, economic, and political systems involved in servicing the consumption, *multiply together* in generating environmental *I*mpacts such as climate disruption, habitat destruction, wiping out of fish stocks and coral reefs, poisoning of people and natural systems, and so on.

*Negative Externalities*

Negative externalities (such as pollution), side effects of economic activities not counted in the cost of production, tilt the economic system against the environment by encouraging producers and consumers to do the wrong thing environmentally. Citizens should have a basic understanding of how markets yield undesirable environmental outcomes in the presence of externalities and a recognition of ways that public policy can remedy these problems by "leveling the economic playing field."

***Other points that are less obvious, that should be taught, and are often neglected***

*General*

How science Is actually done, as opposed to conventional high-school "scientific method" recipes, and an understanding of probability and uncertainty in general, need to be deeply instilled (e.g. science never proves anything; an introduction to frequentist and Bayesian thinking[2]; the use of models to predict likely outcomes).

*Population*

The nonlinearities associated with population growth, especially the disproportionate impact of additional people on an already stressed natural life support system, need to be explained. Issues surrounding the human carrying capacity of Earth, despite their crucial importance, are generally absent from both education and the media. The impossibility of perpetual population growth and that population control has the classic characteristics of a government function (ensuring that individual decisions don't endanger public welfare) are, sadly, rarely mentioned.

*Consumption*

Some analysts who don't wish to offend various constituencies try to focus on the per capita consumption factor in the I=PAT equation, even though trying to separate its central contribution from that of population size is as impossible as separating the contributions of length and width to the area of a rectangle (of course, if the area is changing size, one can find it informative to analyze what's changing, the length or width or both). Although population size is a central determinant of aggregate consumption, it is the consumption itself that does the vast majority of environmental damage.

The neglect by education systems of the crucial problem of overconsumption by the rich is reflected in the mind of average person (and certainly the average economist) who views consumption as an unalloyed good. While there is a growing literature on consumption (and economic growth among the already wealthy) as a central problem, it needs to be integrated into education with emphasis on the lack of analysis pointing to solutions. Students need to understand that the mix of things we consume is greatly influenced by prices. If individuals had to pay the mostly unseen social and environmental costs paid by society for various forms of energy, the patterns of energy consumption – as well as the total level of such consumption – would be much more in keeping with the social good. Finding ways to reduce unnecessary consumption could be a major topic for paper writing and research projects, starting in grade school.

---

2. Frequentists tend to view probability as the long-run expected frequency of occurrence; how often you'll get heads in a long run of coin tosses. They think there's a "real" answer out there, which is approximated by coin-tossing experiments. Bayesians think probability is related to what one believes, in the face of some ignorance, how likely a certain outcome is (they would consider carefully whether or not the coin was "honest" and would believe that only the data gathered by tossing experiments are real – not a hypothetical value being estimated by them. Bayesian inference depends on having a prior hypothesis about the probability (a pair of dice are "honest" – that is, the chance of getting any face on a given toss is 1/6 for each die) which then can be modified (posterior probability) if a run of tosses shows that 6 comes up on both dice about every other time (dice are "loaded").

The most environmentally damaging form of human consumption is eating. The scale of the agricultural enterprise, its dependence on fossil fuels, and its environmental impacts are unknown to most "educated" people in developed nations. While there is some media coverage of the decline of oceanic fisheries, the ecological damage done by fish farming is rarely mentioned, nor are the benefits of marine reserves (and the threats they face because of climate change).

*Technologies*

The roles of technology in enhancing efficiency but creating environmental disruption and the need to deal with it, and technology's relationship to the economic system, need to be explained. So should the issues related to the environmental Kuznets curve and Jevon's paradox,[3] and the failure of earlier proposed technological "cures" such as "nuclear agro-industrial complexes" that would use nuclear power to desalinate sea water and grow crops in desert areas. Especially critical is making people aware of the extent of the infrastructure that supports civilization, the time, effort, and resources required to produce it, the need to redesign parts of it (especially those parts that deal with energy and water) to be resilient to global change, and the long lead time required to make needed major modifications.

It is important to emphasize that what all societies need is not "energy" but a full range of energy-based services, from cooking, lighting, and transportation to "clean" manufacturing. All this is needed at reasonable prices that incorporate the costs of side effects. How many people can be so supplied sustainably depends on many factors, the most general being "standard of living," and it must be clear that "clean" implies very little emission of $CO_2$ and other greenhouse gases, as well as conventional pollutants. Today many government subsidies and regulations are barriers to achieving the overall goal of a sustainable energy system. Education should make it clear that the fundamental problem is finding the primary energy (that embodied in natural resources, including solar energy) and capital to give everyone affordable energy services – while pricing energy at its true costs.

*Climate*

In discussions of climate disruption, much attention is paid to the danger of sea level rise, because it threatens the lives and well-being of tens of millions of people in low-lying areas. The rise is real, but likely to be mainly gradual, allowing ample time to change coastal settlement patterns and infrastructure. Nonetheless, in science classes, more attention should be given to the fascinating (and still inadequately understood) topic of the dynamics of glaciers and ice sheets, including the possibility of "tipping points" that could lead to imminent danger from very rapid inundation of coastal areas.

More broadly, however, not enough attention is devoted to the influence of changing patterns of precipitation and heating on yields of staple crops, which could potentially endanger *billions* of people. The searing of Russia's

---

3. If you don't know them, easily explained on Google or Wikipedia.

wheat crop in the summer of 2010 is exemplary of events that are likely to occur increasingly often. The same changes also very likely will increase catastrophic flooding, especially threatening to vast numbers of people in overpopulated river valleys and flood plains, as happened in Pakistan, China, and Australia in 2010.

Similarly, the press reports regularly on the "bleaching" caused by heating of spectacular coral reefs, where damage is easily visible to scuba enthusiasts. But the media do not give adequate coverage to acidification of the oceans or the synergisms among the varied assaults on oceanic ecosystems. For example, it is quite possible that a combination of warming and acidification will do four times as much damage to a reef ecosystem as the sum of the damages each would do alone. And almost no attention is given to the importance of time lags and feedbacks in environmental systems. All this, and the absurdity of most "geoengineering" fixes for climate warming, should be part of the knowledge of every adult.

Once the complexities of Earth's climate system and the causes and prospective consequences of its disruption are understood, introducing the complexities of climate politics can begin. Unfortunately, many people erroneously think that previous environmental problems such as conventional air and water pollution have all been "solved." They are therefore convinced that climate disruption is essentially the only serious global environmental problem now, when, in fact, others such as toxic pollution, long recognized but poorly regulated, actually may be equally or more dangerous, especially given the potential for worsening impacts through interactions with other problems.

*Loss of Ecosystem Services*

Extinctions, interacting with climate disruption, thus may create more severe consequences than the disruption alone. Because the key role of the *population diversity* of plants and animals in supplying ecosystem services is mostly unappreciated, the gravity of the population extinction crisis is largely neglected. At the moment, it is more serious and more indicative of the biodiversity crisis than are species extinctions per se. It is organisms, after all, that in concert supply ecosystem services such as soil replenishment, pest control, pollination, flood control, cultural services, and so on in any given place

Students should be introduced to the issue of how ecosystem services can (in some cases) be shored up by human intervention: the complex topic of "intervention ecology." It should be emphasized that the old view of what is sometimes called "restoration ecology" is falling out of favor because of the impossibility of determining exactly what a previous state of an ecosystem was, or of returning an ecosystem to an earlier state, even if it could be determined. Everyone should understand that ecosystems have always been in a state of flux and always will be, although major features may persist for thousands of years. One of the chief ways in which human beings cause environmental degradation (loss of properties desired by human beings) is by greatly increasing the rate of change.

*Toxics*

We know almost nothing about the effects of most of the 100,000 or so potentially toxic synthetic compounds that now permeate the environment from pole to pole. Worse yet, essentially nothing is known about the possible synergisms among toxins, cases where the toxicity of a combination is worse than the sum of the toxicities of the ingredients. This includes not just two-way synergisms among these compounds, but also the possible three-way, four-way, etc synergisms. The importance of toxics that mimic our hormones and often have non-linear dose-response curves is generally ignored. While most people are at least somewhat aware of the threats of poisoning from toxic compounds, most assume that "the dose makes the poison." Yet extremely tiny doses of hormone mimics can disrupt development in young organisms, whereas larger doses may have little or no effect.

Other toxic threats that should be covered in the course of an environmentally sound education include the accumulation of persistent organic pollutants (POPs, such as DDT) and heavy metals (such as lead, mercury, or cadmium) in food chains or soils. Closely related to the toxic problem as classically viewed is the accumulation in the biosphere of almost immortal remains of plastic feedstocks and materials. Much of the plastic debris degrades very slowly if at all and can seriously harm or kill organisms that become entangled in it or ingest it. There is also some sign that other toxins, such as PCBs, can accumulate on the surface of plastic particles.

It is especially important that people understand that the threat of toxification might be as serious, or even more serious, than that of climate disruption. And some research has indicated that a warming climate could mobilize many toxic chemicals that have been released into the environment – an unexpected synergism. For climate disruption, though, we can at least contemplate the science-fiction "cures" of geoengineering. We don't have any similar speculative "solutions" for everyone starting to suffer from fatal cancers, reproductive failures, or other symptoms of poisoning.

*Ozone Depletion*

There has been much confusion about an issue related to the problem of the release of toxic chemicals. That has been the release of chlorofluorocarbons and other chemicals that trigger the destruction of Earth's stratospheric ozone shield. Everyone should know that, although at low altitudes ozone can be a pollutant damaging to plant life, at high altitude it forms a critical barrier against incoming lethal ultraviolet rays from the sun. Release of freons into the atmosphere in the mid to late 20th century started to destroy that shield, threatening humanity and all life on land. The story of the campaign to stop the flow of ozone-destroying gases into the atmosphere, its results (at least partial success so far), and why it was an easier political task than dealing with climate disruption should become familiar to all. It is really important that people learn the differences between ozone depletion and climate disruption, where confusion sometimes reigns because some ozone-destroying chemicals are also greenhouse gases.

*Infectious Disease*

As we indicated at the start, rapid globalization is accelerating the movement of people and bringing previously separated societies together. This and the increasing speed of transportation is facilitating the rapid spread of disease organisms. Deterioration of the epidemiological environment is another problem that might prove more severe than climate disruption. As the human population grows, the probability increases that novel infectious diseases will successfully invade it from animal reservoirs and cause vast epidemics. Heightening that probability is growth in the number of malnourished and thus relatively susceptible individuals. Misuse of antibiotics, leading to serious problems of resistance (a concept that should be introduced early in secondary school in connection with teaching evolution), further darkens the outlook. So does the poleward and altitudinal spread of tropical diseases on a warming planet – another malign interaction.

*Nuclear War*

In the early $21^{st}$ century, the chance of a global nuclear war with catastrophic environmental effects seems very low, although the United States and Russia, while no longer adversaries, still face each other with thousands of "strategic" warheads. On the other hand, the chances of regional nuclear wars (as between India and Pakistan) is probably increasing. Ironically, though, such a conflict, using a hundred or so Hiroshima-sized (~15 kiloton) weapons, we now know could be capable of generating climatic and other effects that could bring down civilization. Thus keeping students updated on the ecological effects of nuclear war should be an ongoing aspect of environmental education; today it is sadly neglected throughout education in general.

*Human Evolution*

Societies evolve culturally as well as biologically. Changing values and institutions must be part of the agenda for reaching sustainability. Issues of race and gender that damage that agenda should be taught in a context of human evolution, focusing on the biological unity of *Homo sapiens*, rather than the great diversity of behaviors generated by cultural evolution. All human beings share possession of a theory of mind (the ability to understand that other individuals have knowledge, viewpoints, beliefs, and intentions) and a capacity for empathy, without which even small societies could never function, let alone a global civilization. Human behavior is key to solving our global environmental problems, and people should understand what is known of its fundamentals. Above all, they should not be fooled by the notion, unhappily too prevalent among scientists, that given the proper information on the state of the environment, people will act in a rational manner. There is massive evidence that this is incorrect and that many "irrational" factors need to be grasped to understand our behavior.

*Economics*

In the context of behavior, some basic background in economics and social processes is essential for everyone. Topics such as externalities, common property (cooperative governance or the tragedy of the commons), and the differences between markets, corporations, and capitalism need to be understood. Environmental or ecological economics also needs to be explained. Sound economic analysis indicates that, contrary to many claims, government intervention can improve the functioning of markets and create social net benefits. People should learn that unfettered markets are far from ideal and often generate anti-environmental and anti-social behavior. Adam Smith's views in *The Theory of Moral Sentiments* should be explained to counter the too common misuse of quotes from *The Wealth of Nations* and can be used to drive home this point.

People also need to grasp the importance of varieties of capital beyond financial and produced capital. The roles of human and social capital, and especially, natural capital and the ecosystem services that are the "interest" flowing from it, are important to understand. That natural capital is rarely depreciated in accounts of the wealth of nations. And what GNP is and is not also should be communicated. In this context, students should be introduced to new measures of progress to replace GNP, both those that have been proposed and those that are needed.

The need for appropriate information – for "getting prices right" – in order for markets to function properly needs to be repeatedly emphasized. If environmentally damaging goods or services could be appropriately priced, with damaging externalities internalized, then consumers would have all the information they need; they could do the right thing just by comparing prices. When externalities are ignored, what turns out to be privately less costly proves socially more costly. For example, a carbon tax on fossil fuels would cause downstream goods and services to be more appropriately priced (at least in terms of the carbon damage associated with their production or use). People should always be aware, however, that even in theory it is impossible to determine exactly the size of negative externalities (e.g. damage to one's great-great grandchildren from driving a car today) and thus to internalize them. In this context it is useful to teach something about the overall scale of the human enterprise, the pattern of its historical development, and the ethical issues now entailed for those who wish it to expand further.

Everyone should realize that people often do not do what most of us would consider "the right thing" just because they know it's right, even when they have appropriate information. A stunning example of this was the refusal of European Jews to believe the Nazis aimed to exterminate them, and thus flee, until it was too late, despite massive and building evidence that that was the German goal. The current failure to address climate disruption shares many features with this tragic example. But sometimes people will do what they consider is right, even if it goes against their economic interests, as doing what was "right" as an important element in the abolition of slavery in the United States illustrates. The same can be said of the acceptance of environmental regulation in the United States, although in both cases opposition was strong, delaying the needed action for decades, and persisted afterward for a long period.

*Governance and Institutions*

The importance of effective governments capable of making environmentally sound policies and enforcing them with sensible regulation should be stressed. Environmental issues in governance should become part and parcel of a continuing effort to inform students of how collective decision-making works, whether by social movements, informal communities, governments, or world bodies. Student experience in voting in elections and making collective decisions can be (and long has been) gained in classrooms as early as middle school or even sooner. Environmental problems can be integrated into these processes though exercises such as deciding about recycling procedures or whether to have a school garden. In later grades, it should be recognized that the nation state (a rather recent development) is often an impediment to achieving sustainability, and that reform is needed at various levels of government. Similarly, influential institutions from chambers of commerce to churches and universities need to be modified to meet the realities of global change.

*Ethics*

Much more attention to ethics is needed both in schools and in adult media, with discussion of such topics as intergenerational equity, environmental justice, empathy, etc. Ethical issues are rarely discussed in our society, and when they are, it is often in the context of an introductory college course or rules passed down in religious texts. Many of the most difficult ethical dilemmas today are closely tied to environmental issues, from animal rights and the exploitation of endangered species to human reproduction rights and migration.

### How should environmental science be made an important focus of everyone's education?

*Starting Early*

In the face of today's knowledge explosion, combined with the "endarkenment" of current anti-education, anti-science political trends, especially in the United States, closing key parts of the culture gap is extremely challenging. As pervasive in our lives as environmental issues are now, they still too often are taught as a separate "package." This results in a compartmentalization of the topic, putting parts of it in "silos," as it's popular to say today, and people accordingly don't relate them to their daily activities unless the connections are pointed out to them. But making the connections as part of general education is not difficult, and, we emphasize, it can start early.

Successful environmental education could start in nursery and grammar school and continue to be integrated into education from then on. As an example, the "see Spot run" approach to early readers, where it still exists, could be transformed into "see the corn grow in the sun" with many equivalent changes made, so that youngsters learn early the basic facts of life on Earth. Primary school students often learn to carry out recycling of paper, cans, bottles, and plastics both at home and at school. This activity presents an opportunity for them to learn that there are limits to the materials our society uses and that they can be re-used or reprocessed for new goods. Similarly, composting and gardening can supply lessons about the ingredients of life and how nature recycles essential nutrients.

Furthermore, starting early and continuing throughout life, society would benefit from more direct exposure of an increasingly urbanized human population to natural systems – to active field trips at all levels, since video and simulations give only a limited glimpse of natural and agricultural environments, let alone their decay.

Students in middle school and even before can start learning how their personal choices can have an influence on the environment. Have a cat for a pet and let it run loose for the night? You are contributing to the decimation of song bird populations. Want to have a cell phone? Cell phones are convenient, but cell phone towers frequently slaughter migrating birds. More remotely, building a road across the Serengeti Plain in Africa for extracting and shipping rare earth minerals now needed by phone technology threatens to end the last great mammal migration on Earth. Love hamburgers? You are contributing to one of the greatest threats to biodiversity and the human food supply, since raising cattle often leads to tropical deforestation, climate disruption, overtaxing of water supplies, and diversion of grain that could benefit hungry people. Want to have three or more children? You'll likely be a contributor to those kids, or their kids, leading a miserable life.

*Tie Environmental Issues into Standard Parts of Curricula*

Environmental concepts and connections can easily be incorporated into conventional curricula. Thus students in middle school mathematics classes should be introduced to exponential growth so they will not only be able to understand interest rate problems but also learn that a long history of exponential growth does not promise a long future of exponential growth. In this context, the norm of believing that perpetual population and economic growth are possible can be challenged, as well as the idea that such unlimited economic growth can be based on energy from fossil fuels. Discussing interest rates opens the door to following up with an explanation of discount rates, with the latter feeding eventually into the ethical issues of intergenerational equity. Needless to say, one would hope that all students would be introduced to basic calculus, especially growth functions, before the end of high school.

Information on the epidemiological environment could be folded into material on how to deal better with medications and the medical system, which themselves badly need to be integrated into school curricula. Sex education is one place where this could be done, and it should be included with related but usually omitted topics such as evolution of the family, ecoethics, reproductive behavior, and so on. Collective human behavior, after all, is fundamentally what is threatening civilization; it would pay for everyone to understand as much as possible its roots, more or less benign variations, and how it plays out in governance.

The importance of regulation of population size as a government function should be introduced early in civics classes, perhaps using the analogy that, just as the government needs to restrict one's freedom to drive on either side of the road or steal from one's neighbors, it has the duty to see to it that the size of the population is not causing social or ecological harm.

At all educational levels, history studies should always include "green history" – that is, such things as the ecological dimensions of past collapses of civilizations and the narrow balance between population growth and food production for most of history.

*Revise Teacher Education*

One of the most challenging tasks we face in the environmental education enterprise is revising the education of teachers. This could probably best be accomplished by dissolving schools and departments of education, integrating what is known about learning (much from the work of psychologists) into general education, as well as requiring more and better education for teachers generally, and (of course) radically improving the status of those who educate the young. Improving the quality and scope of refresher courses for teachers, especially on ways to integrate environmental science into traditional subjects, also could be helpful.

*Reform College/University Curricula*

While the basics of environmental science should be taught in elementary and high schools, a serious challenge for all of us is to deepen understanding at the college level. In particular, this will require modifying the antique disciplinary structure that so hamstrings higher education, especially in the humanities and social sciences. Continuing education, even for tenured professors, is essential for dealing with accelerating environmental issues and to help correct the severe cultural lag that afflicts colleges and universities.

For instance, a dominant theme of international relations in the twenty-first century will clearly be environmental issues, broadly defined to include avoidance of resource wars (potentially nuclear). Nonetheless, in the antique structure of universities, schools of international relations tend to be the domain of political scientists unaware of many environmental issues. This is just one instance of the "siloing" of higher education, tracing in no small part to Aristotle, that all scholars must struggle to reform. A major challenge for environmental educators is to fuse research and education in international relations with environmental studies.

Other failures have to do with taboos and omission of certain topics in curricula. A prime example is the power relations that run the world, whose social, resource, and environmental impacts are rarely considered. Another is the negative aspects of organized religion. They are often neglected despite their frequently dreadful influence on societies, as exemplified by their role in the slaughter of millions. But that's only part of it; consider the waste of vast amounts of human time and talent examining the minutiae of the behavior and wishes of mythical beings.

In our view, the *relative* success of the natural sciences in keeping disciplinary boundaries more flexible is not due to the scientists' having an unusual openness to change, but to their being forced to face change as increased understanding of the world has demanded it. When we first joined Stanford's faculty in 1959, neither biochemistry nor climatology was part of environmental biology; in most universities there were separate departments of zoology, botany, and even entomology, and no one would have imagined economics being an important part of an ecologist's training. Now our "biology" department has many biochemists, climate is a central topic in conservation biology, there are relatively few departments of zoology, botany, or entomology left in first-rate institutions in the United States, and graduate students in ecology are encouraged to learn some economics. Similar restructuring of the social sciences, a need long recognized by some social scientists, is in part a challenge for environmental educators, especially since it now makes little sense to separate natural and social sciences. Fortunately, a small cadre of social scientists have been bringing their expertise into the battle to achieve environmental sustainability.

At the end of formal education, every PhD or postdoctoral fellow, regardless of discipline, should know what the second law of thermodynamics says and how human beings depend upon ecosystem services, just as they should be at least vaguely familiar with MacBeth, Van Gogh, and Plato's cave.

*Beyond Schooling*

As you can see from the perspective of what we think people need to know, current curricula are deeply flawed. Much of the reform needs to be done through school systems, although in many countries the tendency to standardize curricula is a tendency to lock in disaster. The situation in universities is no better, even though curricula there are *relatively* free of outside interference. The sad facts are that, even in the greatest of research universities, students often graduate or even get a doctorate and remain profoundly ignorant of how the world works. At Stanford it is possible to complete an education and know essentially nothing about science (which along with technology is at least half of our culture) – to say nothing of environmental science.

But schooling is not enough. Beyond schooling, public education of adults is necessary for the survival of civilization, and it must be continuing. We need to change the entire concept of education from the present "fill young people up with information for getting and holding a job" view to an essential life-long process of upgrading. This is required by the speed of cultural evolution, especially in the areas of science (including social sciences) and technology. The world is changing so rapidly that other sources of information are required if one is to have at least a basic grasp of what is going on. But in a world of rapidly multiplying sources of information, knowing how to evaluate them and assemble a useful world view is crucial.

Given this situation, students, starting in middle school, need to be made aware that there are powerful propaganda organizations at work and that no single channel, or even set of channels, of information on the environment can be fully trusted (including our own books and articles). Ideally, good citizens will acquire the basic scientific background and then carefully sample books, articles, the media, and the Internet to form their own conclusions. It can be especially helpful to organize groups of friends in which individuals specialize in keeping track of what is happening in different areas, and share their knowledge with others. Social media tools can assist in this endeavor. And promoting the reading of more general environmental literature in the broadest sense can aid greatly in encouraging environmental literacy.

*Taking Environmental Education Global*

Scientific information is necessary but not sufficient to move to a sustainable society. Scholars now know more than enough to say how society could be turning in that direction, but it is not doing so. That's why a new initiative called (following the lead of the Millennium Ecosystem Assessment) the Millennium Assessment of Human Behavior (MAHB) has been established. The objective is to begin a discussion and an assessment of human goals and the barriers to achieving them, including ethical considerations and how and why people are behaving as they do. The goal of the MAHB is to involve not only natural and social scientists, but also scholars from the humanities, decision makers, and members of the general public. Whether or not the MAHB is successful, all citizens should be made critically aware of the behavioral and ethical dimensions of human behavior and how they relate to the culture gap between collective and individual knowledge. Above all, the real possibility that continuing on the business-as-usual course, a growth-oriented, fossil-fueled, weakly-regulated capitalist system, could lead to the first collapse ever of a global civilization. Introducing everyone to that key point, and the cultural behavior that makes it difficult to alter that course, is a central challenge for environmental educators.

### Conclusion

Obviously, fulfilling our view of an appropriate environmental education would not be simple, and likely would simply prove impossible in all its details. But we present it here not as something we think is good, ideal, or doable. We maintain that most of its elements will be *required* if humanity is to achieve a sustainable society in a battered ecosphere. Our small-group animal is struggling to learn how to live in gigantic groups. Unless at least a substantial minority of human beings is familiar with the essentials of how environmental and socio-political systems work and interact, and how their functions can be retained, we do not think we have a hope of succeeding. Retooling education is an utterly necessary but not sufficient requirement for giving us a chance.

## Further reading

Blumstein, D.T. & Saylan, C. (2011). *The Failure of Environmental Education (And How We Can Fix It)*. Berkeley, CA: University of California Press.

Ehrlich, P.R. (2000). *Human Natures: Genes, Cultures, and the Human Prospect*. Washington, DC: Island Press.

Ehrlich, P.R. (2009). Ecoethics: Now central to all ethics. *Journal of Bioethical Inquiry 6*, 417 – 436.

Ehrlich, P.R. & Ehrlich, A.H. (2005). *One with Nineveh: Politics, Consumption, and the Human Future*, (with new afterword). Washington, DC: Island Press.

Ehrlich, P.R. & Ehrlich, A.H. (2009). *The Dominant Animal: Human Evolution and the Environment* (Second Edition). Washington, DC: Island Press.

Ehrlich, P.R. & Ornstein, R.E. (2010). *Humanity on a Tightrope: Thoughts on Empathy, Family, and Big Changes for a Viable Future*. New York, NY: Rowman & Littlefield.

Oreskes, N., & Conway, E.M. (2010). *Merchants of doubt: How a handful of scientists obscured the truth on issues from tobacco smoke to global warming*. New York, NY: Bloomsbury Press.

Ponting, C. (2007). *A New Green History of the World*. New York, NY: Penguin Books.

Weisman, A. (2007). *The World Without Us*. New York, NY: Picador.

## Acknowledgements

We thank Bob Brulle (Sociology, Drexel), Dan Blumstein (Ecology and Evolutionary Biology, UCLA), Corey Bradshaw (Environmental Institute, Adelaide), Tad Fukami (Biology, Stanford), Larry Goulder (Economics, Stanford), Donald Kennedy (Woods Institute, Stanford), Hal Mooney (Biology, Stanford), Dennis Pirages, (Political Science, University of Nevada, Las Vegas),Gene Rosa (Sociology, Washington State, and Woods Institute, Stanford), and Kirk Smith (Global Environmental Health, Berkeley), for extremely helpful comments. This work was supported by the Mertz-Gilmore and Winslow Foundations and Peter and Helen Bing.

# Chapter 30
## Education for Sustainability in Schools

### More Challenges for Teachers

*Syd Smith*
*Consultant in Education for Sustainability and former CEO*
*Environmental Education, NSW Department of Education and Training*

### *The issue*

*There can be few more pressing and critical goals for the future of humankind than to ensure steady improvement in the quality of life for this and future generations, in a way that respects our common heritage – the planet we live on. Education for sustainable development is a life-wide and lifelong endeavour which challenges individuals, institutions and societies to view tomorrow as a day that belongs to all of us, or it will not belong to anyone.*

(United Nations Decade of Education for Sustainable Development 2005-2014)

If we were asked to nominate the most important thing we wanted for the future and present what would we say? If we were asked to make this value a priority for our education system how might we go about implementing it in our schools? This is a big picture question and many people are likely provide more ephemeral answers with such desires as their consumer needs being met along with their requirements for good health, a stable life-style and positive relations with those they know. If we then asked whether we wanted the human race to continue into the future, if wealth could be shared more equitably, if our resources were going to be available and se-cure for future generations or our natural environment would be conserved very few would disagree with these aspirations as being vitally important. What then could be more important in our education system than identify-ing our values, our needs, our wants, our vision for the future and the impact that our activities have on the Earth and its ecosystems? This in fact is what education for sustainability is all about but whether our education systems recognise this and give it the high priority it deserves is somewhat ques-tionable and will vary unfortunately from country to country, state to state, school to school. This chapter examines this question and alleges that edu-cation for sustainability is such a new concept that schools are only just be-ginning to become aware of its significance. In addition those who are genu-inely trying to implement sustainability programs in their schools are often finding the task not only challenging but highly frustrating in a society that has yet to truly embrace it. Ironically most education systems in the world would claim they are preparing our students for the future yet the notion of sustainability or, more specifically, ecological sustainability is still struggling to get some official mandatory status within the total curriculum or even to get some support at all. Certainly the documents issued to schools give offi-cial support to sustainability but the implementation is patchy in Australia, the USA and a number of countries and planners find it difficult to ascertain its success overall.

Assessing the reliability and security of food production, for instance is one of society's major considerations for the future along with its associated farming practices relating directly to ecological sustainability. If this is a ma-jor issue both now and for the future surely our students need to be made aware of it and should be offered the skills and competences to deal with it. One reason for the disjunction between what we know is important and what are the actual priorities for schools is that most education systems still operate on an industrial age model with very distinct inputs, processes and end points, This is a system which is seen by some, but never admitted by systems, as treating students and learning processes as products functioning independently in society.

### Context

It has taken almost a century for the concept of sustainability to become a recognised force to influence government policy and economic planning in Australia and other parts of the world. This is in spite of some politicians still regarding sustainability as unimportant. It has taken even longer for education systems to accept sustainability and to find ways to link it to cur-rent curriculum frameworks. One reason for this is sustainability was deve-loped outside of the academic world and adopted by universities and other tertiary institutions later. Sustainability as an area of concern arose in the area of global politics, not in the lecture theaters of universities, schools or colleges. The last few decades have seen the depletion of oil stocks, a concern for climate change, the loss of biodiversity, a rapid growth in development, increasing global poverty, an increase in social corporate responsibility and a growing debate about pollution issues and carbon emissions.

It is interesting that a century ago a much simpler analysis of sustainability was taught in Australian schools, even if that term in its current context had yet to be coined. In 1909 in Victoria and 1910 in NSW a movement to protect local fauna began at a grass roots level in schools. In the NSW town of Wellington for example, a teacher, Walter Finigan and his principal, Edward Webster began the organisation known as the *Gould League of Bird Lovers*. This arose largely in response to a decline in bird populations due to the collection of eggs, mostly by children for home collections. The new organisation was quickly accepted and adopted by the then NSW Department of Public Instruction and with its departmental head as president it soon became a dominant movement in all primary schools. The protection of birds and later their habitat also became the concern of the *NSW Junior Tree Wardens*. In 1967 the first sign of integration occurred when the two groups amalgamated to become the *Gould League of NSW*.

By 1989 the term, *environmental education* had officially entered the curriculum with most states and territories issuing a curriculum statement of some kind. Within ten years the majority of states and territories had strengthened this to a curriculum policy thanks to the work and coaxing of the then Australian Department of Environment and Heritage (later known as the Department of Environment, Water, Heritage and Arts – DEWHA). The first official national educational document mentioning the word "sustainable" was published by DEWHA in 2005 with the then brave release of the title: *Educating for a Sustainable Future: A National Environmental Education Statement for Australian Schools*. Note however the term, 'environmental education' was not discarded at that time. Changing the term and focus overnight would have been difficult for schools to accommodate but it still paved the way for all state and territory education ministers to accept its principles and allow for it to be used by curriculum designers in each of their systems.

The 2010 document published by DEWHA epitomises the final acceptance of sustainability, at least at policy level. What is interesting in all these developments is they were initiated by DEWHA and not the Commonwealth Department of Education, Employment and Workplace Relations (DEEWR). While DEEWR had no problem in approving the DEWHA documents, (and certainly they were consulted about it), the question remains why this was not at least a joint publication and to what extent was DEEWR really interested in Education for Sustainability? In fact this reflects the trend in most western democracies where the environment portfolio normally funds the bulk of environmental education initiatives or education for sustainability programs and the education portfolio is happy to go along with it, but not necessarily giving it the same attention and commitment.

This brief account of how we have got to where we are helps account for the challenges and issues teachers and education administrators now face when dealing with education for sustainability. This of course assumes that all educators believe it is an issue worthy of special attention. The problems are not insurmountable and some directions for resolving them have begun but there is still a long way to go before we can confidently say that education for sustainability has been accepted by all schools, let alone an Australian society still having doubts about a carbon tax and other environmental issues.

### *The Curriculum and Teaching Education for Sustainability*

Most Australian states and territories have a curriculum framework in which the total curriculum is organised into specific learning areas. The model adopted for the Australian curriculum continues to embrace this framework ensuring that most, if not all learning areas, will be preserved, This is particularly so in the secondary school where each learning area or syllabus will still be taught separately and often according to a recommended time allocation Critics of this framework often call it a *silo curriculum* approach because specific information, knowledge and skills are confined to one discipline or learning area. Teachers and schools have been accustomed to this arrangement for a very long time and have organised their staffing and administrative systems to support it. To change it would be a massive operation now.

Education for sustainability however offers a different paradigm. It is committed to the **integration of knowledge** rather than one area of knowledge residing in a single discipline or learning area. It focuses on a big picture or **holistic approach** to learning, an emphasis on real world issues and above all **taking action** to support the environment or deal concurrently with social or economic issues. In the original *NSW Environmental Education Statement* of 1989 the term, 'taking action' was rejected in its first draft stage because senior educators at that time thought it was too political and might make students radical political advocates. They were concerned that students would try to pull political strings and protest in the streets but this was not the intention at all. When the subsequent NSW *Environmental Education Policy for Schools* was published in 2001 it was made quite clear that schools needed to develop a *school environmental management plan (SEMP)* where both students and the community could collaborate to develop environmental education plans still supporting the centrally developed curriculum models. In addition the SEMP plans had to consider the management of their resources more sustainably and adopt a more ecological approach to redesigning their school grounds. This did not mean, of course, that they would not discuss political issues but, if they did, it would be in the context of looking at all the data and information in a balanced way and trying to resolve a problem or issue where one existed. Since then the idea of taking action has expanded and involves many schools forming partnerships with their councils and local communities. Often these are in the form of projects which tackle problems in their natural environment or activities that may cause the depletion of a resource or a challenge to resolve an equity issue.

Unfortunately this seems to have occurred in only a small percentage of schools with drive from a comparatively few committed teachers and principals. Some of those involved in implementing their plans had to face parent opposition, some who believed that too much time was wasted outside the classroom and not enough attention given to the so called three 'Rs'. Perhaps some parents were concerned that schools of today are not exactly like they were when they went to school.

In one case a school education director was called to a primary school in northern NSW in response to parents complaining about this very issue. After examining the school's programs and teaching methods in great detail the director noted ironically that the students' performance in literacy and numeracy were superior in comparison with other schools in his district. This was in spite of the school's strong emphasis on sustainability programs.

Again this demonstrates the ability of the so called three Rs to permeate the whole curriculum. They do not exist in isolation and neither does education for sustainability. Education for sustainability still struggles to find its place as a core curriculum study in many schools nevertheless even when the principal and staff endeavour to make it the centre of a school's core business. One of the reasons, according to some principals and educators for this is because of the focus on the *National Assessment Program Literacy and Numeracy (NAPLAN)*. This Australia wide national assessment and testing initiative by the Federal Government puts an emphasis on literacy and numeracy results and unfortunately school funding is determined to some extent by student performance according to these results. While literacy and numeracy are without doubt highly important, in some schools, the time allocated to training students for answering these tests is often at the expense of other curriculum priorities. Consequently schools are forced to compete with each other on a statewide basis, in order to aim for higher performance outcomes in numeracy and literacy. This in itself is the result a national concern for improved student and school performance. While this is commendable in one sense it has the danger of influencing schools to change the way they balance the implementation of their total curriculum. One result leading from this is to downgrade the social curriculum, a worrying trend which requires us to look at the testing program more broadly.

National assessment programs overseas are given high prominence in countries like the USA, Britain and Singapore yet Finland which is regarded highly by educators has not given it the same status; yet is ironically considering it now. *The Environment and School Initiative (ENSI)* project operating in Europe and with Australia as one of its members was given high priority by European countries in the 1990s and early 2000s but they are now showing signs of reducing their funding and placing restrictions on their representatives to attend meetings. The value of the organisation was to share initiatives, engage in joint programs at school and tertiary levels and support valuable research projects. There are signs that committed educators are giving up more of their time to support environmental education and sustainability projects as volunteers rather than as paid professionals. With the emergence of the world financial crisis the first projects to be downgraded were those relating to Environmental Education and sustainability. Similarly in New Zealand the conservative government reduced its funding for environmental education although its Enviro Schools Program was allowed to continue. The issue seems to be that governments still see that the traditional model of providing seed funding is sufficient rather than appreciating that sustainability programs require long term support. In spite of this China, India and many South East Asian nations still appreciate the value of sustainability education and still look to the west for ideas and assistance, a somewhat ironic situation given the apparent decline in support for it in some of those western nations. Perhaps governments are still unable to appreciate the links between their growing national debts and the explosion in rampant consumerism fuelled by excessive borrowing and a disregard for the long term management of their finite resources.

## The Integrated Approach

Another feature of education for sustainability is the integrated approach it employs to examining social/political, environmental and economic components. For many years governments had dwelled on economic issues in isolation emphasising growth, living standards, monthly interest rates, financial matters or unemployment statistics. Obviously these matters are extremely important and affect us all but developing our economy with a short sighted approach and forgetting the availability of resources in the future or how we may be harming our ecology are surely even more important issues to consider. Some economists like Clive Hamilton recognise this and note the relevance of other issues like quality of life and happiness indexes. There are two important messages that sustainability delivers: we can't make a living on a dead planet and it is the environment that determines everything we can do in the long run. We as humans are not separate from it; we are in fact part of it.

## Life Cycles and Sustainability

Education for sustainability also looks at the life cycle of products and offers advice on how waste can be recycled or reduced, how transport can be minimised or how we can reduce our usage of fossil fuels. Fossil fuels traditionally provide the bulk of the energy to produce our goods and services along with the distribution and disposal of their byproducts and the final waste they create. One interesting activity that teachers can employ in this regard is to ask students to select their favourite purchase item and examine how it was transported and processed from its source to its final consumption and what happens after it is of no longer use. Take for example a chocolate bar from its harvesting of the cacao bean to its transport to the factory for refinement, the byproducts produced, to the packaging it required, to its further transport to market outlets and shops, to the final disposal of its packaging etc. At each stage of this process some form of energy is required, pesticides might have been employed on the trees and there could be an exploitation of labour or unfair low wages paid. This process is known as *cradle to grave* analysis and facilitates an understanding of the role of the economic, social and environmental forces in producing, transporting, packaging and disposing of a product. Other consumer items may be less demanding on the environment and offer a *cradle to cradle* model. In this case at the end of the first production and distribution cycle much of the product can be used again or recycled. Bricks that were once used in demolished buildings are one example. A deep knowledge and understanding of environmental impacts and social consequences of a market based, production process cannot be fully comprehended and appreciated in terms of environmental and social costs unless students have an authentic relationship and deep connection with nature and the earth. Little of this can be achieved if they only remain seated within the four walls of a classroom.

### Challenges in Defining Sustainability

The term *sustainability* is the buzzword of our times but unfortunately it is often abused, promoted out of context and regularly employed in green washing marketing strategies. One mining company in Australia once claimed to be sustainable because it restored and rehabilitated its former industrial site following the removal of the minerals from the earth. What the company failed to realise was it was extracting from the environment a resource which was finite, took millions of years to form and could never be replaced once it was mined. In addition it is questionable if mining activities could truly remediate one of its former sites or return an ecosystem to its true original state. This is not meant to be a watertight argument supporting the banning of mining but mining can never be seen as sustainable in its present form because in the long run its primary source of wealth will not be there forever. If the source of a mineral is not there forever then it can't be sustainable.

The question then comes down to what exactly is sustainability? Ironically it is easier to recognise what is not sustainable rather than to be sure that a certain sustainable process or activity is actually taking place. Tackling it from the perspective of beginning with a definition is not necessarily the most helpful approach although there is a generally accepted definition from the late 1980s where it is used more in the sense of human sustainability and this has resulted in the most widely quoted example. This was the one presented by the Brundtland Commission of the United

Nations in 1987: that *"sustainable development is development that meets the needs of the present without compromising the ability of future generations to meet their own needs.* As one child said, *"Sustainability is enough for all forever"*

What is challenging for teachers and students alike is that a universally accepted definition of sustainability is elusive because it is expected to achieve many things. On one hand it needs to be factual and scientific, offering a clear statement of a specific "destination". The simple definition *"sustainability is improving the quality of human life while living within the carrying capacity of supporting eco-systems"* is somewhat vague but does have particular significance for farming, yet it does convey the idea of sustainability having quantifiable limits. But sustainability is also a call to action, a task in progress or "journey" and therefore a political process, so some definitions seem to agree with a number of common goals and values. The term is extremely wide in its coverage and is comprised of many variables which can be studied separately but still needs to be seen as an integrated system. Each approach is important and there are strong arguments that the total system should be included as a mandatory subject in every student's education. The last time NSW had an integrated learning course was the HSC course, *General Studies* but this was unfortunately discontinued after the release of the McGaw *Review Report of the HSC* in 2001.

The following topics are neither exclusive nor limited yet all the following can come under the heading of education for sustainability: energy, water, waste, population and carrying capacity, biodiversity, human consumption, consumerism, technology, resources, environmental management, landuse, food production, environmental degradation, economic growth, peace, security, social justice, social ecology and deep ecology.

In terms of food production and farming, education for sustainability examines such issues as encouraging more local food production accompanied by efficient distribution infrastructures and making nutritious food accessible and affordable to all. Furthermore, its operational methods should be humane and just, protecting farmers and other workers, consumers, and communities. Concerns about the environmental impacts of agribusiness and the stark contrast between the obesity problems of the Western world and the poverty and food insecurity of the developing world have generated a strong movement towards healthy, sustainable eating as a major component of overall ethical consumerism.

### Integrating Sustainability Concepts and Principles into the Current Curriculum

There are a number of changes currently taking place in the Australian curriculum. Even before Federation in 1901 each Australian state and territory was responsible for the design and assessment of its curriculum. While there are many similarities across the country curriculum mapping exercises have revealed notable differences which can make it difficult for students whose families transfer from one state/territory to another. Subsequently the Australian Government, in its announcement to embark on an "Education Revolution" in 2008, took responsibility for consulting with the states and territories to develop first a **national curriculum** and later renaming it to the **Australian Curriculum**. The Australian Curriculum and Assessment Reporting Authority (ACARA) was given the task of developing this highly complex curriculum model. ACARA has decided to maintain the learning areas curriculum framework and is in the process of continuing separate learning areas or disciplines which hopefully will reflect the principles, content and priorities of existing education systems across Australia. When it comes down to broad integrated studies like Aboriginal Education and Education for Sustainability ACARA defined these first as *dimensions and then cross curriculum priorities.* In the past they were known as perspectives, integrated studies or cross curriculum areas, although there are semantic differences among each of these terms. The processes adopted are exemplified by ACARA's draft *Geography Shape Paper* where a statement was made on how Geography contributes to education for sustainability.

*Geographers study the environmental, economic and social environment of places. The subject integrates the national and social sciences around studies of human environmental relations, in particular places. It thus brings a holistic perspective to this analysis. For example when exploring the sustainability of the biophysical and built environments geography allows students to learn about the environmental processes involved in phenomena such as climate change and land degradation. (2010)*

Each learning area will be required to make similar statements in support for education for sustainability, some having less relevance and contribution than geography, perhaps but all will have something to contribute. Since ACARA, (like most state and territory curriculum frameworks in the past), has taken a learning areas centric approach it may be difficult for teachers to get a full picture of what sustainability is all about, particularly for secondary teachers who are usually specialised in teaching only the learning area they were trained for. Some history teachers, for example may find the sustainability dimension difficult to implement given that most history syllabuses of the past had not necessarily considered the importance of the environment on changes over time. The issue then comes down to how we can ensure that all students experience the full scope of this new paradigm within the learning areas framework.

While it may take some organisation and a change in attitude or a different school management model, principals and teachers can achieve this successfully once secondary schools establish a cross faculty committee to investigate their total curriculum and to take responsibility for each area of the sustainability process. Similarly in the primary school specific curriculum responsibilities can be allocated to teachers and each staff member can investigate where sustainability would support each learning area. In each case the total picture for sustainability education can be constructed this way along with who will be responsible for each section of the curriculum plan and how the sections fit together and interrelate with each other. In this way an integrated holistic approach can be developed while still maintaining the spirit and goals of each learning area and ensuring that each task does not appear as another layer of knowledge and skills for teachers to deal with. Either way it is essential that all teachers and their principals are supported at every level when they attempt to implement education for sustainability programs in their schools and classrooms. Along with a committed principal this is the only way for it to have any modicum of success or truly become mainstream education. At the same time the plan and structure of the program needs to be **long term**, become part of the school's permanent **culture** and **routines** and have established precautions to ensure it does not degenerate into a one year wonder with one or two teachers left to deal with the program on their own. Even the United Nations has given sustainability a good decade to become even partly effective (*UN Decade of Education for Sustainability 2005-2014*)

## Australian Sustainable Schools Initiative

*The Australian Sustainable Schools Initiative (AuSSI)*.was developed by DEWHA in consultation with the states to facilitate this type of model and is seen to support constructivist learning in schools. Although the program was first trialed in NSW and Victoria it was DEWHA who took it to the states nationally. AuSSI integrates existing education for sustainability initiatives into a holistic program with measurable environmental, economic, social and curriculum outcomes. The initiative implements efficiencies in the school's management of resources (e.g. energy, waste, water, products and materials) and the management of school grounds (e.g. biodiversity, landscape design, soil, noise and human vehicular traffic abatement) It then integrates this approach into state and national curricula and the daily running of the school. Following the principles of sustainability the school is meant to involve its local community and make it a genuine partner. What is notable in this program is that action is the key component and real world issues are investigated. Collecting real world mathematical data and statistics for example is a much preferable option to examining statistics in theoretical isolation. The goal is for students not to be exposed to a surfeit of problems or depressing visions of the world but to give them opportunities and make them aware of, their power to improve environmental and social conditions and resolve problems in a methodical and positive way. School systems have long recognised the importance of a planning cycle that involves reflection and evaluation of all the elements of their activities. Good governance occurs when decision making is distributed across the whole school community and involves students in a meaningful and constructive way. Good governance also requires an intelligent, progressive principal who is committed to the ideas and principles of sustainability.

## Pedagogy and Education for Sustainability

It is not only the knowledge and content of learning areas that align so well with education for sustainability. Education for sustainability is a major supporter of most accepted modern pedagogies in education and quality teaching principles in Australian schools. In addition to developing high levels of intellectual quality, it promotes a quality learning environment and makes explicit the significance of its content. In all aspects it provides a vehicle for **higher order thinking,** develops positive relationships between teachers and students (and among students themselves) as they work together as cooperative teams of joint learners and teachers. Above all education for sustainability demonstrates **connectedness, knowledge integration** and a strong **engagement** in learning, factors which are sometimes harder to cover adequately by a specialised learning areas approach where a certain amount of content has to be treated within a specific time schedule.

Looking more specifically at pedagogies, education for sustainability promotes many accepted quality teaching strategies including the *inquiry based approach to learning.* Often known as *open learning* or *discovery learning*, inquiry based learning fits the sustainability paradigm perfectly. Inquiry based learning occurs when there is no prescribed target or result which students have to achieve. In many conventional traditional science experiments for example, students may be told what the outcome of an experiment should be, or is expected to be, and the student is simply expected to 'confirm' this. In enquiry based learning on the other hand, the students are either left to discover for themselves what the result of an experiment or survey is, or the teacher guides them to the desired learning goal but without making explicit what it should be. Inquiry based learning is an important but difficult skill for teachers to acquire but they do it regularly and with panache knowing it is a much more effective method for students to internalise their learning. Inquiry based learning has many benefits. It means students do not simply perform experiments or analyses in a routine like fashion, but actually think about the results they collect and what they mean.

It is by using inquiry based learning and other modern teaching and learning strategies that teachers can best implement sustainability programs in schools. To some extent it frees teachers temporarily from the set but important objectives or outcomes of the learning areas curriculum framework including the assessment requirements of NAPLAN or any other public examinations set by education systems and schools. Without demeaning the mandated and clearly defined curriculum in the state systems or the national curriculum itself, teachers can still expand student learning by using the inquiry based model, ensuring constructivist learning occurs and to still enrich the approved disciplines and learning areas by integrating a sustainability theme and action process throughout them. However until sustainability content is enshrined in the Australian curriculum and not presented as a suggestion or even an option, then the struggle to find its place in schools will continue. Equally important until sustainability is included as mandatory content in national assessments it will continue to be viewed as a low priority study and process and, with the added difficulty of a crowded curriculum, schools are more likely to ignore it. If a curriculum area or process is seen as a hierarchy then those seen as having low priority will be given some attention only if and when time allows.

### *Critical Thinking and Education for Sustainability*

We all know students learn more efficiently when they are engaged, when they can debate an issue or are encouraged to look at things more critically. One way to do this is to look at a local or national issue and critically assess whether it is sustainable or not. It is prudent therefore to expose students to a relevant case study which gives them a deeper understanding of how sustainability does or doesn't work in the real world. One example recently debated in the NSW Parliament was a new Tourism Bill in which different groups took opposing views on whether to give more prominence to tourism in national parks. The case study raised the issue of how well people understood the concept of conservation and whether nature has a right to exist for itself or is it just something for humans to use? If people believe in the former (a right for nature to exist for itself) then they are said to be *eco-centric*, if the latter and nature is seen as something there for us simply to use then they are *anthropocentric* or focused on themselves.

There are other ways to look at nature as well; we can be resourcist (nature is just a resource to us) or utilitarian (it is all about how we can use nature). These latter two perspectives are known as *modernism* or modernity but most conservationists take the opposite view; they want to protect these places because they think the land has a right to exist only for itself. The utilitarians talk about how an ecosystem services our human society- how it can regulate water flow, which bioresources we can use, how the area can recycle nutrients etc. Hawker and Lovins introduced us to a similar idea in 1999 when they presented the notion of *natural capital* in which they saw the world's economy as being within the larger economy of natural resources and the ecosystem services that sustain us. This implies that we should attribute value to gifts such as human intelligence and cultures to hydrocarbons, minerals, trees, water, soil and air. Some of these things were formerly perceived as free and did not have to be counted in the costs of production but we now know that although we can't always put a price on them they certainly have value and need to be considered when we make important decisions about sustainable production. The authors argued that only through recognising this essential relationship with the Earth's valuable resources can businesses, and the people they support, continue to exist. Dr Haydn Washington from the Nature Conservation Council of NSW reminds us that the State of the World Report (2010) showed that consumerism is spreading quickly to most cultures all around the world. Obviously Dr Washington is very concerned about this development. Going hand in hand with this trend is nature being seen as becoming just a commodity, not something wondrous or sacred, appreciated for its intrinsic worth or worth keeping for future generations. Originally, thanks to pioneers like John Muir and Aldo Leopold in the USA national parks were to be first and foremost for nature conservation. There were opponents to this of course but at the time nature conservation won out.

However, by 2010 the new Tourism Bill in NSW was seen by the Nature Conservation Council of NSW as supporting the *commodification* of nature, not improving nature conservation itself but simply making money for government. So embedded is the consumerist mindset, the Council says, in our modern day market economy it now seems that everything has to be traded. The word "trade" is now creeping into a number of political issues. We talk about carbon trading for example; carbon dioxide, a gas that was once beyond our control in the atmosphere is now something that has economic, environmental and social implications and the level at which it occurs can now be regulated to some extent by the way humans manage their energy and transport systems. In relation to the new bill on national parks the Nature Conservation Council of NSW concluded that the problem is one of failing to understand the ecological limits to this consumerist ideology and an unfortunate omission to consider any ethical or spiritual values to national parks.

Such a case study opens the door to discussing a number of political issues for students but more importantly it goes to the core of what exactly education for sustainability is all about. It makes us question our real commitment to sustainability and whether in the long run, money and economics should override environmental and ethical values. The NSW Government in introducing this bill claimed they did support conservation and were initiating better management practices to protect national parks. The study of this bill facilitates a deep knowledge exercise in which there is an opportunity for senior students to define the meaning of specific terms and whether it is really possible for tourist industries to protect parks. One way to help students appreciate these complex issues is to organise a simulation game in which they take on different roles to lobby the "government". Some may represent the Shooters Party, others the Nature Conservation Council, the government, environmentalists, the Green Party, a group representing the tourist industry while others could represent the National Parks Association and so on. At the end of a simulated lobbying session a debrief should be organised in which the teacher asks students to examine the ethics and values of each group, whether they were resourcists, utilitarians, anthropocentrics or eco-centrics and to look at the long term different outcomes if, over time, each of the groups was to win their lobbying exercise with the "government". There is usually no right or wrong answer to the final decisions the class makes but in the spirit of inquiry based learning students will be able to question, scrutinise and criticise a real life situation which might affect them to some extent in the future. Another activity could be for each group to prepare an action plan demonstrating how they would amend the Bill. This would support the recent DEWHA publication which outlines the components of a sustainability action process. The process includes the generation of ideas, preparing a communication, implementing a proposal and evaluating and reflecting on actions. *(Ref: Sustainability Curriculum Framework: A guide for curriculum developers and policy makers 2010).*

## Case study

While all these activities appear to be feasible and easy to manage in schools it is important to be realistic about the hidden but often unintended barriers that may exist within an education bureaucracy and the difficulties that are caused by the ignorance or poor understanding of what sustainability means to some of those in control of the decision making process in schools. Most educators believe a balanced and open approach when teaching students about the real world. Of course what is regarded as the 'real world' may mean something different to each of us but to illustrate the point it is interesting to see what occurred in a northern Sydney school in 2006. An enthusiastic and well qualified teacher decided to set her students an assignment relating to nuclear energy. She asked them to analyse the arguments both for and against Australia embarking on a nuclear energy program. Resources both for and against were provided to students and in no way did the teacher attempt to influence their decision or comment on the arguments presented in the broad range of resources and literature that was made available. The students' final decision was to reject nuclear energy and to write to the prime minister outlining the reasons for their decision. The result of what began as an innocent classroom activity led to the local Member of Parliament coming to the school, criticising the students' decision, questioning the teacher's objectivity and making a formal complaint. The local press then released the story further encouraging a number of readers to write to the editor claiming such questions were political and should not be raised in schools. In the end after a departmental investigation the teacher was declared unbiased and not guilty of influencing the political thinking of the young minds in her charge.

## Discussion

This and other incidents demonstrate a number of issues where schools have to be highly sensitive and aware. If teachers have to face political opposition when they are correctly implementing a departmental learning policy one has to ask is it worth their while. While it is acceptable to raise controversial issues like nuclear energy, particularly when the Federal Government was initiating an enquiry into the matter at the same time, it is interesting that many members of the community still have a poor understanding of what is happening in schools and the legal right of teachers to undertake investigative and inquiry based activities as in the case study above. Looking at such long term initiatives which will affect us in the future is something our young population should surely be prepared for but in spite of this there are still those in the community who feel schools are there to teach literacy and numeracy and all the rest is of secondary importance. Like so many other developments in education it not only takes a long time for a new idea or policy to be fully implemented at the school level but even longer for the general community to understand and accept it. Society has changed and is continuing to change. With these changes come changes in curriculum and how schools are administered.

## Summary

This chapter began by asking what is our most treasured wish, what is most important to us and how should schools reflect the priorities and values we hold concerning the future of the planet. While we may disagree on how we should prepare for and influence the future there is no doubt ecological and climate changes are upon us. Education is a highly important factor in helping us to manage and understand these changes but unless we educate our population on the complexities of sustainability, to take action for it, work cooperatively on agreed directions for a sustainable future and give sustainability a permanent, high priority and committed place in the total curriculum, we will be selling our students short and ignoring one of the essential elements of their education. If we don't we will be running the risk of an unprepared population to deal with multiple complex issues. Schools and education systems will have a better chance of achieving this if we revive our commitment to learning communities where schools can provide teaching and learning services to their communities and for communities to make a similar input to schools.

There is a plethora of support material for teachers about sustainability and there are impressive programs running in schools across the country and all around the world but there is little evidence on how much it has been adopted universally. It is difficult to verify the number of AuSSI schools in Australia, for instance and there hasn't been an evaluation of how sustainability programs are implemented in schools since environmental education was surveyed for the first time in NSW in 1996.

In 2001 when the *Environmental Education Policy for Schools* was released in NSW every teacher in the state was issued with a copy yet in many schools principals set it aside concerned that teachers had too much on their plates already. Similarly the Department put little pressure on teachers to implement it, again concerned that teachers could not cope with what they thought was too much additional work. This was in spite of the message that to implement environmental education at that time it should not be seen as a burden but simply a teaching activity you did while you were already teaching one of the learning areas at the same time.

To assist teachers we need a commitment from all levels of government to ensure education for sustainability is a permanent and mandatory curriculum component, that a training program is designed for all teachers, principals and senior departmental administrators and it be included in assessment processes at both national, state and school levels. It is essential that every teacher, principal and senior education manager understand the importance of education for sustainability and demonstrate a commitment to it. There is evidence that a number of senior education employees, some in important decision making positions, have little understanding of this new paradigm and are inhibiting developments undertaken by curriculum developers and enthusiastic schools keen to implement the program.

There are several cultural changes needed to help teachers implement education for sustainability without experiencing frustration and interference. First education for sustainability as a priority area for one year is useless. It infers that after a year it is no longer important and can be put aside. Secondly, all training programs should be done with all staff involved and a commitment gained from everyone to work as a team to implement school-community based programs. Alternatively a group of schools can meet to experience a training program. And thirdly, the program needs to be ongoing, continuous and part of the school's culture and values system. All these initiatives are tall orders but when one considers the alternatives and the dangers presented if an ignorant population makes poor, unsustainable decisions the impact on our future and security leave us with no alternative at all.

Finally we need to look at the barriers inhibiting the implementation of education for sustainability in schools. In what way is the sustainability paradigm at odds with the current curriculum framework? Should we continue with the process of education for sustainability currently fitting in with the national curriculum framework or should we design a general management model in which the curriculum and the administrative structure of schools guide policy and influence curriculum in schools? The writer supports the latter but accepts that a major educational reform would need to happen and this is most unlikely to occur at least in the short term. Yet a sustainable future is extremely important for our planet and perhaps this may be the only effective option possible.

## Further reading

Australian Government: Department of Environment, Water, Heritage and the Arts (2010). *Sustainability Curriculum Framework: A guide for curriculum developers and policy makers.* Canberra: Commonwealth of Australia.

Australian Government: Department of the Environment and Heritage (2006). *Educating for a Sustainable Future: A National Environmental Education Statement for Australian Schools.* Carlton South, Victoria Curriculum Corporation.

NSW Department of Education and Training; Curriculum Support Directorate (2001). *Environmental Education Policy for Schools.* Sydney NSW.

## *Resources*

An excellent website on sustainable schools:

> http://www.sustainableschools.com.au/sustainableschools/default.asp?

A useful website on AuSSI:

> http://www.environment.gov.au/education/aussi/index.html

An example of sustainable schools in NSW:

> http://www.sustainableschools.nsw.edu.au/

# Chapter 31

## Implementation

### From the Village to a Global Order[1]

*Manfred Max-Neef*
*Economics Institute, Universidad Austral de Chile*

When introducing in public the alternative paradigm for a more humane economy, people often ask how it would work in practice or how such principles could be articulated into policy. In other words, the concern is about implementation, but in fact such policies are already being implemented in hundreds of places. The point is that policy is generally perceived as a macro top-down process that makes the news, and not as a bottom-up grassroots phenomenon that remains hidden in the consciousness of those directly involved in the actions, and very rarely appears in the media.

What is described in this chapter is essentially a process that involves many projects. Converging around common principles, orientations and values, these projects together build an alternative paradigm of

---

1.This is a reprint of chapter 13 from: Max-Neef, M. & Smith P.B. (2011). *Economics Unmasked: From Power and Greed to Compassion and the Common Good,* Green Books: Totnes, Devon, UK. The chapter is copyright Philip B. Smith and Manfred Max-Neef.

development that goes upwards, from the village to a global order[2]. Despite the fact that the number of cases is enormous, they are generally perceived as being of no more than anecdotal interest. Paul Hawken describes the situation clearly.

> *Movements... have followers. This movement, however, doesn't fit the standard model. It is dispersed, inchoate, and fiercely independent. It has no manifesto or doctrine, no overriding authority to check with. It is taking shape in schoolrooms, farms, jungles, villages, companies, deserts, fisheries, slums – and yes, even fancy New York hotels. One of its distinctive features is that it is tentatively emerging as a global humanitarian movement arising from the bottom up. Historically, social movements have arisen primarily in response to injustice, inequities and corruption. Those woes still remain legion, joined by a new condition that has no precedent: the planet has a life-threatening disease, marked by massive ecological degradation and rapid climate change. As I counted the vast number of organizations it crossed my mind that perhaps I was witnessing the growth of something organic, if not biologic.*
>
> *Many outside the movement critique it as powerless, but the assessment does not stop its growth. When describing it to politicians, academics, and business people, I found that many believe they are already familiar with this movement, how it works, what it consists of, and its approximate size... For them and others the movement is small, known and circumscribed, a new type of charity, with a sprinkling of ragtag activists who occasionally give it a bad name. People inside the movement can also underestimate it, basing their judgment on only the organizations they are linked to, even though their networks can only encompass a fraction of the whole. But after spending years researching this phenomenon, including creating with my colleagues a global database of its constituent organizations, I have come to these conclusions: this is the largest social movement in all of human history. No one knows its scope, and how it functions is more mysterious than what meets the eye.*
>
> *What does meet the eye is compelling: coherent, organic, self-organized congregations involving tens of millions of people dedicated to change. When asked at colleges if I am pessimistic or optimistic about the future, my answer is always the same: if you look at the science that describes what is happening on Earth today and aren't pessimistic, you don't have the correct data. If you meet the people in this unnamed movement and aren't optimistic, you haven't got a heart. What I see are ordinary and some not-so-ordinary individuals willing to confront despair, power and incalculable odds in an attempt to restore some semblance of grace, justice, and beauty to this world[3].*

### *From Power and Greed to Equity and Respect*

What we have is two parallel worlds. One concerned with politics, competition, greed and power, which seems to have everything under its control; and another concerned with equity, well-being, respect for life and solidarity, which doesn't control anything, but grows and expands as an unstoppable underground movement of civil society. The former, despite its overwhelming power and presence is, because of its rigidity, dogmatism and

---

2. 'From the Village to a Global Order' was a programme launched by the Dag Hammarskjöld Foundation of Sweden in the early 1980s, under the sponsorship of which the Theories of Human Scale Development and of Fundamental Human Needs came into existence.

3. Paul Hawken (2007). *Blessed Unrest: how the largest movement in the World came into being and why no one saw it coming.* Viking Press, New York.

growth fetishism[4], vulnerable and unsustainable, as shown by its ever-deeper crises; while the latter, because of its dispersion, its diversity, its fierce independence and its chaotic structure, cannot be beheaded nor can it collapse.

The existence of these parallel worlds reveals that we are moving, or at least intending to move, from a world of power and individualism to one of solidarity and community. Responses are emerging everywhere to environmental disasters and all forms of human suffering. The need for a radical change of the dominant economic model underlies all the components of the movement.

Despite the vigour with which this immense underground grows, one often hears comments to the effect that environmentalism, and more generally a new economics, have failed as a movement and are dead. In fact, the opposite is true. Sooner or later everyone will be an environmentalist as a consequence of necessity and experience. The belief that problems can be solved individually, from the top down is, at this stage, clearly out of the question. "The world is a system, and it will soon be a very different world, driven by millions of communities who believe that democracy and restoration are grassroots movements that connect us to values that we hold in common"[5].

The initiatives for change that emerge from civil society are similar to the immune system of a living being. You don't see it, you don't feel it, but it is there working in order to protect the body to which it belongs. The body feels the disease, which is the enemy, but does not feel the underground army that attacks the disease. We are aware of deep crises and profound problems affecting our lives and, as a consequence, often feel depressed and defeated. But we should also be aware of the fact that if our immune system did not exist, things would be much worse. It is impossible to estimate how many infections and wounds that could harm our social body are avoided every minute and everywhere due to the actions of those invisible millions of the underground network of civil society.

In his Natural Capital Institute in California, Paul Hawken and his colleagues have created an immense database of civil society organizations in 243 countries, territories and regions, which amount to close to 300,000. This is, of course, only a fraction of all the groups that exist worldwide. The classification scheme that emerged from the mapping of the landscape covers literally thousands of disciplines and concerns. The main headings (under each one of which are many subcategories) are: Agriculture and Farming, Air, Biodiversity, Business and Economics, Children and Youth, Coastal Ecosystems, Community Development, Cultural Heritage, Democracy, Ecology, Education, Energy, Fisheries, Forestry, Climate Change, Globalization, Governance, Greening of Industry, Health, Human Rights, Indigenous People, Inland Water Ecosystems, Media, Mining, Plants, Pol-

---

4. See Clive Hamilton (2003), Growth Fetish, Allen and Unwin, Sydney, Australia.

5. Paul Hawken, op. cit.

lution, Population, Poverty Eradication, Property Rights, Seniors, Sustainability, Sustainable Cities, Sustainable Development, Technology, Terrestrial Ecosystems, Water, Wildlife, Women and Work[6].

Such an enormous network of civil society initiatives is a colossal immune system that, once the global top-down power system reaches its final crisis, will be capable of giving rise to a new bottom-up democracy, based on solidarity and cooperation, that will expand from the village to a global order and offer the answers for the construction of a more humane world.

The following are some concrete examples of the concerns and actions of civil groups that relate to our proposed new economy – examples that are coherent with the five principles for 21st century economics outlined in Chapter 10 [of *Economics Unmasked*]. We start with a short history of Human Scale Development, and continue with experiences in Colombia and Sweden – two very different contexts yet with similar aims.

### *Human Scale Development*

During the early 1980s the Dag Hammarskjöld Foundation of Sweden launched a programme under the name of 'From the Village to a Global Order'. Part of that programme was the research team of the Development Alternatives Centre (CEPAUR) that I (Manfred) headed and whose purpose was to propose an alternative economics. In 1986, after three years of work and discussions in several international seminars that convened academics and experts with similar interests, CEPAUR generated a document outlining the principles of Human Scale Development and its Theory of Fundamental Human Needs. The final text was published by the Foundation, firstly in Spanish and two years later in English. Through the Foundation's network the text was distributed in most Latin American countries. It generated an almost immediate interest and enthusiasm, not only among dissident academics and alternative groups but also, to our great surprise, among many peasant and Indian communities in South America. We were absolutely astonished when we realized that the original Spanish version became in those days the most photocopied document on the continent. We used to arrive in Andean communities to be approached by local leaders with a photocopy of a photocopy of a photocopy, almost unreadable, ready to discuss whether their interpretation was correct and whether their projects satisfied the philosophy of Human Scale Development. It was moving to witness how such marginal communities adopted the principles and designed local development projects that conventional experts would have been unable to conceive. Many of those projects have survived and flourished. One of them, the Peasant Development Association, is described later in this chapter.

---

6.Paul Hawken, op. cit., Appendix.

The first lesson we learned from those experiences was that the language of Human Scale Development and its Needs Theory can be easily understood by simple people who lack any formal education beyond a few years of primary school. The second lesson was that no true development can succeed without the understanding, participation and creativity of the people themselves. The third lesson was that what mobilizes common people does not necessarily mobilize academics. In fact, what took the peasants almost no time to understand took about 15 years to generate interest at academic levels. Now Human Scale Development is finally in the academic system, and its Human Needs Theory is recognized as one of the most important contributions in the field[7].

Human needs, quality of life and well-being are what people understand – not the abstractions of macroeconomic indicators that have nothing to do with real life. Development is about people, not about objects. The fact that once again civil society is willing to rediscover and respect human feelings and the value of all manifestations of life means that a better world is possible, even if it is not mentioned in the news delivered by the power-controlled media.

## *The Peasant Development Association*

La Cocha is a lake located in Colombia's Southern Department of Nariño, close to the border with Ecuador. It is surrounded by a large number of small farmer and peasant holdings. Traditionally the main economic activity was the exploitation of the forests in order to use the timber for the production of charcoal. During the late 1980s, when a group of farmers had become aware of the principles of Human Scale Development and realized that deforestation was beginning to have devastating effects, an initiative was undertaken to organize the community around alternative forms of income generation. This led to the constitution in 1991 of an association named Minga Asoyarcocha[8], which declared all its holdings as Private Natural Reserves of Civil Society – a concept unknown at the time in Colombia. As a result, 4,000 hectares became protected land, including wetlands, temperate rainforest and biodiversity, generating what were then identified as biological corridors.

From the very beginning the Minga organized educational programmes promoting social, economic, political and cultural principles based on the respect for all forms of life, the sustainable use of biodiversity, and human-scale development for all members of the community. All holdings were divided according to zones that facilitated the best alternatives for soil use, prioritizing food security and greater levels of self-reliance. The reserves be-

---

7. Google shows about 300,000 pages for Human Scale Development.

8. Minga is an ancestral form of Indian cooperative organization, the purpose of which is to achieve conditions that benefit members of the community, or the community as a whole, through communal work.

came spaces for interdisciplinary work and research about biodiversity, ecology, agroecology and sustainability in the use of natural resources. Politically the Minga is based on a direct democracy, with full participation of all members of the community. This has allowed the strengthening of their power as a civil society to such a degree that they have been able to stop the construction of two megaprojects that would have dramatically altered the whole region.

Family income of the members of the Minga has increased to 2.77 times above the regional average, and 1.8 times above the national average. In terms of self-reliance, traditionally they produced around 40 per cent of the food consumed, and now they produce 83 per cent. The use of chemicals has been totally eliminated, so all agricultural production is organic. All families of the community leave 66 per cent of their holdings for conservation, compared with not more than 20 per cent conserved by non-members. The initiatives of reforestation and regeneration that the Minga has undertaken have facilitated again the movement of migratory birds, which can be observed as a result of the increase in the number and variety of species. This has generated an enormous interest among members of the community, so that now it is common to find adults and children who record the taxonomy, the feeding habits and the migratory routes of the majority of birds that appear in the region.

The Minga Asoyarcocha has had both regional and national impacts. In the department of Nariño, three additional Mingas have been created, following the same principles, and by joining together have given rise to the Peasant Development Association (ADC)[9]. The success of this structure is due to the fact that all productive projects, as well as other initiatives, are designed in coherence with the ecological, geographical and cultural characteristics of the different areas. This is promoted through the voluntary work of different active groups, such as the Network of Natural Reserves, the Soil Recoverers, the Community Communicators, Women in Action, the Agroecological Producers and the Sociocultural Group. At the national level the ADC became the co-founder of the Colombian Network of Natural Reserves of Civil Society, which promotes similar initiatives in other regions of the country.

The concept of sustainability of the ADC is mainly based on intergenerational concerns. This has resulted in what is probably its most beautiful initiative: the Programme of the Inheritors of the Planet, the purpose of which is to create spaces for children and youth in order to give them the opportunity to develop their artistic, cultural, crafts, environmental and playing abilities and capacities, allowing them to take ethically based decisions and become true creators of their own lives. At the time of writing the programme includes 512 children and teenagers linked to five different groups, called the Friends of Nature, the Toucans, the Orchid, Gualmaventura and Green Life.

---

9. ADC, in Spanish 'Asociación de Desarrollo Campesino'.

The ADC must assure the continuity of the organization and its philosophy of community, solidarity and cooperation. A relief generation of 18 young members is already studying at university those disciplines that will allow them to contribute as advisors in order to bring about better leadership, administration and technical efficiency of the Mingas and the ADC. Before going into formal higher education, children and teenagers go through a centre that gives them guidance on how to become capable of generating an attractive and familial social and political context that ensures the tenure of the peasants in their territory and allows for the development of a production model that is environmentally sane, economically viable, socially just and culturally acceptable.

A fundamental principle promoted by the community is what they call the "dialogue of knowledge", as a recognition of the importance of traditional cultural, spiritual and organizational values of the peasants that have been discredited by modern techniques and attitudes. Through this they make a continuing effort to recover and honour ancestral wisdoms.

The ADC has become an outstanding example of successful bottom-up sustainable development, promoting self-reliance, a spirit of community and harmony with nature. In 2007 its project 'Cultivating the diversity of the Colombian Southeast, an alternative of conservation and well-being according to the principles of human scale development' was awarded the national environmental prize, the Blue Planet Prize.

In its effort to promote dialogue and share experiences, since the 1990s the ADC has organized three international seminars: in 1996 with 200 participants from 14 countries, in 1998 with 280 participants from 11 countries, and in 2010 with 250 participants from mainly Latin American countries. The seminars consist of sharing dreams about the future. In fact the participants identify themselves as 'dream designers', and all the presentations and papers must consist of designed dreams. In the sessions and round tables it is interesting to see peasants discussing as equals with politicians, academics and experts; often the interventions of the peasants are the most creative and substantial. The seminars go on for five days, and include, not only discussions but also excursions, exhibitions of crafts, folklore, music, poetry and other cultural expressions.

What is especially fascinating is that while the seminar takes place on one side of the lake, on the opposite side another seminar, with the same topics and questions, is run by the Inheritors of the Planet. At the end of the first day a delegation of four members of the main seminar crosses the lake in order to inform the children about the results of their meeting. At the end of the second day a delegation of the children crosses the lake in order to inform the adults about their discussions and conclusions. The same happens on the following two days. The culmination occurs with a joint final meeting on the fifth day, which becomes an unforgettably enriching experience for the participants.

Emulation of the ADC example is taking place in many rural areas of Latin America. Having worked for the FAO (Food and Agriculture Organization) and ILO (International Labour Organization) as a development expert in the field, I (Manfred) never found a development project organized by official institutions as successful as those that originated as bottom-up self-reliant community initiatives. The case of ADC is in my experience the most conspicuous example, but there are many more all over the world. Why don't they make the news? According to my experience, the answer is that for the development bureaucracy a conventional failure is more acceptable than an unconventional success.

## Eco-municipalities

In the mid-1980s a little town of 6,000 inhabitants in northern Sweden called Övertornea received the national prize of Municipality of the Year. Its history confirms the strengths of the bottom-up process in the sense that a local initiative, no matter how small, can have great and significant impacts – very often even greater and more significant than the top-down approaches practised by large-scale politics. The main speaker in the award ceremony compared the town to a bumblebee. He reminded his listeners of Igor Sikorsky, a famous aeronautical engineer of the early twentieth century, who hung in his office lobby a sign that read: "The bumblebee, according to the calculations of our engineers, cannot fly at all, but the bumblebee doesn't know this and flies."

Övertornea was hit very hard by the 1980 economic recession, which raised unemployment to 20 per cent, losing as a consequence 25 per cent of its population compared with 30 years earlier. Many experts predicted that the region was doomed to die. No solution seemed to exist, and people were affected by apathy and a lack of mutual trust. It was then that the municipal government decided to explore other possibilities for the future.

Together with members of the community, the municipal government made a commitment to create a process of development that was in harmony with nature. It had to be a win-win-win relationship between humans, society and nature. Residents began to realize that investing with an ecological orientation would bring about economically positive effects. To characterize the transformation they were initiating, Övertornea began to call itself an 'eco-municipality'. As related by Torbjörn Lahti:

> Övertornea was discussing and practising ideas such as mobilizing people, taking a bottom-up approach to community planning, collaborative community development, cooperating across department and industrial sector boundaries, investing in local culture, and taking into account the local informal economy. Such ideas were foreign to conventional Swedish town planning and community development practices at that time. What the regional and national establishments could see, without understanding why, was that these strange ideas evidently produced remarkable results.
>
> Key to these successes was widespread community participation. The citizens of Övertornea took on the community development work to become the town they wanted. In the six years following this decision, 200 new companies in Övertornea developed and prospered. These new enterprises included organic farms, beekeeping, fish farms, cheap husbandry and eco-tourism enterprises. Over 600 residents took part in special study circles discussing regional development issues and future possibilities. Out of these study circles emerged village development associations that took charge of the ideas

*sprouting and gradually taking form. The ecological perspective blossomed in a municipal government investment in biofuelled district heating, support for ecological farming such as farmer education and municipal purchasing of organic foods, establishing a 'health home' and building an ecovillage to attract new families*[10].

As proof that there is nothing so small that it cannot produce large and unexpected effects (like the moving wings of a butterfly in China producing a hurricane in the Caribbean), the news of Övertornea's transformation spread through the country over the next few years. Inspired in part by its revitalization as a small town, a national movement of 3,300 similar village development groups evolved. Hundreds of thousands of village inhabitants began to take part in developing their communities in the direction that they wanted.

During the early 1990s similar eco-community developments were started in Norway, Denmark and Finland. Collaboration among these Nordic eco-cities and eco-towns brought about a combined Nordic eco-community presentation at the 1992 United Nations Rio Summit on Sustainable Development. Much of the Agenda 21 produced by the Summit in relation to local sustain-able development emerged from the Nordic contribution. Thus the United Nations' world guide to local sustainable development urges communities to begin to work in the same manner in which Övertornea had begun to work ten years earlier. Again, this is an example of where the work of a single cell of the planet's immune system makes the invisible visible. And it is the visible, of course, that makes the news.

The whole process described here has given rise to institutions that are also important elements for the survival, the strengthening and the diffusion of the process. Some give it scientific backing and orientation; others education and assistance.

*The Natural Step Framework*

The foundations come from The Natural Step Framework's four Conditions for Sustainability or 'System Conditions'. The following description of the Natural Step Framework is given on the Alliance for Sustainability website[11].

The scientific consensus principles on which the Natural Step Framework (NSF) is based were used by Swedish physicist Dr John Holmberg and Natural Step (NS) founder and Swedish medical doctor and oncologist Dr Karl-Henrik Robèrt to generate four basic 'system conditions' or conditions of sustainability, which are the focus of the NSF and have been modified as stated below.

10. Sarah James and Torbjörn Lahti (2004). The Natural Step for Communities: How Cities and Towns can Change to Sustainable Practices, New Society Publishers, Gabriola Island, Canada.

11. Alliance for Sustainability: The Natural Step Framework's Four Conditions for Sustainability or 'System Conditions'. See http://homepages.mtn.org/iasa/tnssystemconditions.html.

The Natural Step Framework holds that in a sustainable society, nature won't be subject to:

1. systematically increasing concentrations of substances extracted from the Earth's crust
2. systematically increasing concentration of substances produced by society
3. degradation by physical means.

And in that society:

4. human needs are met worldwide.

To address the first three, strategies include both dematerialization (using fewer resources to accomplish the same task), substitution of alternatives, more efficient use of materials and the 'three Rs': Reduce, Reuse, Recycle, in addition to composting. Here is an easy-to-understand, practical way of addressing the principles:

**1. What we take from the Earth: mining and fossil fuels.** Avoid systematically increasing concentrations of substances extracted from the Earth's crust. Simply stated, we need to use renewable energy and non-toxic, reusable materials to avoid the spread of hazardous mined metals and pollutants. Why? Mining and burning fossil fuels release a wide range of substances that do not go away, but rather continue to build up and spread in the ecosphere. Nature has adapted over millions of years to specific amounts of materials. Cells don't know how to handle significant amounts of lead, mercury, radioactive materials and other hazardous compounds from mining; this often leads to learning disabilities, the weakening of immune systems and birth defects. The burning of fossil fuels generates dangerous levels of pollutants, contributing to smog, acid rain and global climate change.

We can support policies that take action to reduce our overall energy use. We can drive less, use car pools, use public transportation, ride bicycles or walk. We can conserve energy through energy-efficient lighting, proper insulation, passive solar technologies, and reduced heating and cooling. We can support a shift to renewable energy such as solar and wind power instead of nuclear, coal or petroleum. We can also decrease our use of mined metals and minerals through recycling, reuse and preferably reduced consumption. We can avoid chemical fertilizers.

**2. What we make: chemicals, plastics and other substances.** Nature must not be subject to systematically increasing concentrations of substances produced by society. Simply stated, we need to use safe, biodegradable substances that do not cause the spread of toxins in the environment. Why? Since the Second World War our society has produced more than 85,000 chemicals such as DDT and PCBs. Many of these substances, which are unknown to nature, do not go away but rather spread and bio-accumulate in nature and in the fat cells of animals and humans. Cells don't know how to handle significant amounts of these chemicals, often leading to cancer, hormone disruption, improper development, birth defects and long-term genetic change.

We can support green procurement policies and use non-toxic natural cleaning materials and personal care products. We can decrease our use of plastics and reuse the ones we have, such as plastic bags, plates, cups and eating utensils. We can stop using CFCs and other ozone-depleting substances. We can use safe, natural pest control in our schools, parks, homes, lawns and gardens. We can support farmers in becoming sustainable and eliminating hazardous pesticides by using our money to buy certified organic food and clothing. We can support the elimination of factory farming and slurry ponds that cause air and water pollution.

**3. What we do to the Earth: biodiversity and ecosystems.** Nature must not be subject to degradation by physical means. Simply stated, we need to protect our soils, water and air, or we won't be able to eat, drink or breathe. Why? Forests, soils, wetlands, lakes, oceans and other naturally productive ecosystems provide food, fibres, habitat, oxygen, waste handling, temperature moderation and a host of essential goods and services. For millions of years they have been purifying the planet and creating a habitat suitable for human and other life. When we destroy or deplete these systems, we endanger both our livelihoods and the future of human existence.

We can purchase certified, sustainably harvested forest products rather than destroying rainforests. We can reduce or eliminate our consumption of pro-ducts that are not sustainably harvested, such as certain types of fish and seafood. We can shop with reusable bags rather than using more paper and plastic bags. We can decrease our use of water and use composting toilets that return valuable nutrients to the Earth. We can fight urban sprawl and encourage the cleaning up of brownfield and other contaminated sites. We can support smart growth and safeguard endangered species by protecting wildlife habitats.

**4. Meeting fundamental human needs.** Human needs are to be met worldwide. Simply stated, we can use less stuff and save money while meeting the needs of every human on this planet. Why? The US makes up only 4 per cent of the world's population but consumes over 25 per cent of its resources. The lowest 20 per cent of earners receive only 1.4 per cent of the world's income. In order to survive they can see no alternative to cutting down rainforests, selling endangered species and using polluting energy sources.

We need to make business, government and non-profit-making organizations aware that we can achieve the ten-fold increase in efficiency needed to become sustainable, and in some cases, a hundred-fold increase in productivity that will save money, create jobs and reduce waste as part of a new Industrial Revolution. We can encourage discussion about fundamental needs, as proposed by Manfred Max-Neef in his Theory of Human Scale

Development[12]. We can ask if we really need more stuff, and design our workplaces, homes and organizations to give us less of what we don't want (pollution, stress and expense) and more of what we want (healthy, attractive and nurturing environments) and, above all, a sense of community between ourselves and all forms of life.

### The Institute for Eco-Municipality Education and Assistance

The educational component of the process has been established by the Institute for Eco-Municipality Education and Assistance. The information that follows has been taken from a leaflet of the Institute.

The purpose of the Institute is to provide support for emerging eco-municipalities and those communities interested in a systematic, comprehensive approach for changing to sustainable practices. An eco-municipality is defined as a local government – a municipal or county government – that has officially adopted a particular set of sustainability principles and has committed to a bottom-up, participatory approach for implementing them. As mentioned earlier, the first eco-municipalities developed in northern Sweden in the early 1980s. Their work became the model for Agenda 21 in the 1992 Rio Summit on Sustainable Development.

The process has expanded dramatically during the last two decades. At this stage (2010) there are over 70 eco-municipalities in Sweden – almost one-third of all municipalities in the country, with Stockholm being the most important one. The movement has spread widely. In the United States several cities, towns and county governments have officially declared themselves to be eco-municipalities, adopting the same sustainability principles of their Swedish counterparts and working to systematically change their local government and larger community to sustainable practices. Similar initiatives are taking place in Kenya, Ghana, Japan, Canada and Mexico, and will soon be happening in Chile.

The role of the Institute in this expanding process is to provide education and training in how to become an eco-municipality, to develop leadership skills and municipal staff training in sustainability principles and how to change to sustainable practices – and more.

The services include workshops and presentations on:

- The eco-municipality systems approach to sustainable community change.
- The Natural Step Framework, a science-based system approach to sustainable development.
- A 'bottom-up' participatory approach to sustainable community and municipal change.

---

12. Manfred Max-Neef (1991), *Human Scale Development*, The Apex Press, New York and London.

Municipal training includes:

- A science-based understanding of sustainability and its practical everyday application.
- How to translate sustainability principles into concrete, systematic change in municipal practices.
- How to integrate and institutionalize change toward sustainable practices in departmental and agency operations, policy and regulations.
- 'Train the trainer' sessions.

Community education, planning and strategy development includes:

- Bringing about broad-based community participation.
- Involving businesses and institutions.
- Sustainability education using clear principles to design action.

Eco-municipality process leadership, including:

- Advice and assistance to local governments and community organizations interested in a systematic approach to sustainable community change.
- How to design and carry out multi-year systemic change process.
- 'Process leadership' and guidance during a multi-year change process.
- Educational and training events.

Training is also given to NGOs on request.

### *Final Reflections*

It is a cause for optimism to realize that there is nothing so small and so weak that it cannot provoke an enormous and massive positive change; and that there is nothing so big and strong that it cannot dramatically collapse. Just think of the beautiful positive explosion provoked by the little community of Övertornea, located in one of the remotest places of the Earth, and compare it with the ugly and catastrophic implosion of a giant such as Lehman Brothers, located in New York. Of course, in the case of the latter the media all over the world were reporting about the massive damage to the economy and the resulting global financial disaster. Nothing has ever been reported about the healing processes that have been emerging and expanding from the bottom up, in the case of the former.

Probably the best that can happen to those of us who believe in community, in respect for all forms of life and in a more humane economy, is to remain as invisible as possible as long as the fight goes on. Invisibility, while fighting, may be after all our greatest strength. If we reach victory at the end of the day, visibility may be welcomed again.

As I am writing this chapter, in June 2010, I have just received the news that the proposal to once again legalize the killing of whales went down in flames in an international meeting in Morocco. This was mainly due to the fact that in a few weeks 1.2 million signatures from citizens all over the world

399

were collected, amounting to the biggest whale-saving petition in history. The impact of this campaign was demonstrated by the Australian Environment Minister Peter Garret when he received the petition: "Thank you very much Avaaz[13]. It is a great pleasure to be here and accept this petition... I believe the people of the world's voices need to be heard. I certainly hear them today."

Here again we have our wonderful planetary immune system doing its job.

We end with a final note of advice to those who always want to know how to implement good ideas: make an effort and try to discover what is beyond what you see. There is always much more happening if you awaken all your senses. We may still discover that a better world is possible.

---

13. Avaaz is the name of the NGO that promoted the collection of signatures. It is concerned with many other initiatives of social justice.

# Chapter 32
## A Collarless Workforce

### Teaching and Learning Skills for Sustainability

*Fabian Sack*
*Consultant, Dusseldorp Skills Forum, Honorary Associate,*
*University of Sydney*

### *The Issue*

*"The crisis cannot be solved by the same kind of education that helped create the problems... Schools, colleges and universities are part of the problem."* (Orr, D. (1992). *Ecological Literacy*. Albany: SUNY Press, p. 83.)

Despite growing efforts to integrate sustainability into classroom delivery by teachers across the globe, it is increasingly clear that the educational institutions our societies rely upon to deliver tomorrow's workers need to be reimagined to meet the challenges of the future. The reason for this is at least partially because all around the world political and educational leaders continue to respond to the false lines our communities draw between highly valued academic studies, less well regarded vocational education and often entirely unrecognised socially acquired skills.

Vocational skills are highly sought after by our society, but our education systems struggle to deliver to this demand, focusing instead on preparing school students for academic study. Across the modern world vocational education and training tends to be a poor cousin in the educational hierarchy, a status that has discouraged talented young people for generations. This dysfunctional position – shared across Europe, the UK, Australia, Japan, China, the United States and Canada – values the output of vocational education but not the input or the process of delivery. Perhaps most importantly of all, it is socially acquired skills that will allow young people to take their passion for the future into work places and share it with the existing work force. In the end we face increasing skills shortages at the same time as rising youth unemployment and disengagement.

To drive sustainable change across our economy young people will need to be able to influence others, as well as deliver their technical or academic skills in a work setting. They will need to be part of a wider 'learning community', partnering schools and teachers with community organizations, businesses, unions and Government. It has been recognised for some time that, beyond technical skills, young people entering the workforce require skills like communication, team work, problem solving, initiative and enterprise, planning and organisation, self management, learning and technology. Often we rely on families, peers and friends, as well as schools, to help young people develop these employability skills. Now the need to have young people build sustainability capacity in workplaces around the world, as part of a learning community, adds new skills to the traditional set of employability skills. These new skills are about personal commitment to making the world more sustainable. They are also about leadership and influencing to bring the necessary change about. These are what you might call normative competencies (they establish new norms or ways of behaving socially). An example of the kind of competencies that are required has been developed in Germany as part of their response to the Decade of Education for Sustainable Development. They call these new skills *Gestaltungskompetenz*.

---

### Case study: Gestaltungskompetenz

This German word means variously: shaping, creative, design or structural competencies. A suite of 10 part-competencies making up *Gestaltungskompetenz* have been developed by Transfer 21 to build capacity for sustainability as an element in German secondary schools:

- To create knowledge in a spirit of openness to the world, integrating new perspectives;
- To think and act in a forward-looking manner;
- To acquire knowledge and act in an interdisciplinary manner;
- To be able to plan and act in cooperation with others;
- To be able to participate in decision-making processes;
- To be able to motivate others to become active;
- To be able to reflect upon one's own principles and those of others;
- To be able to plan and act autonomously;
- To be able to show empathy for and solidarity with the disadvantaged; and
- To be able to motivate oneself to become active

---

Finding structured ways of helping young people to develop these normative competencies is a new challenge, but one central to ensuring that young people are equipped with the skills to lead the adoption of emerging solutions to the problems making our world unsustainable. These skills will be practiced right across the economy. Already today:

- Some financial analysts review the carbon risk exposure of investments driving change through the industries they invest in;
- Some hairdressers sort their waste streams and reduce their use of chemicals and energy, thereby educating their clients;
- Some university deans develop campus environment plans that inform students about sustainability through their learning environments;
- Some plumbers install rainwater tanks, thus reminding householders of the need to conserve valuable resources;
- Some travel agents and airlines sell carbon offsets changing the way business people and tourists think about travel; and
- Some builders and architects review forestry certifications, driving changes back through their timber supply chains.

The skills that we as a community ought to value – sustainable skills – are **normative**, they influence the way people act; they are **conceptual**, they rely on analysis and awareness of context; and they are **practical**, they change things in the real world. To learn sustainable skills young people need pathways that link academic studies, vocational education and the social acquisition of skills. These pathways will need to be flexible and they will need to be life long, because people learn differently and sustainability is a journey.

### Context

Much of the debate about skills for sustainability has been conducted in terms of 'green jobs' or 'green collar workers'. For example a headline in Sydney 2010 reads "Green-collar army invades job market" [Sydney Morning Herald, 14/5/2010]. The term 'green collar worker' was first used in hearings before the US Congress in 1976. It comes from the more familiar terms 'white collar worker' and 'blue collar worker', used to describe professional and manual workers respectively. However, this characterisation is politically divisive, it polarises our society along lines of the education people receive and the work they do. The characterisation of 'green collar workers' is also historically backwards looking and limiting, as it suggests that in the future there will be 'not-green' as well as 'green' jobs. So, it is not perhaps very helpful to continue to try and discuss green collar jobs. The workforce that will be building our common future will need to be collarless.

*Historical*

A concerted effort to better understand how sustainability is going to be put into practice through changing the skilled workforce started at the beginning of the 21st century. By 2004 over a hundred international experts on technical and vocational education agreed on the Bonn Declaration, defining the contribution of technical and vocational education and training (TVET) to sustainable development and taking the action necessary for quality skills development that leads to economically viable, environmentally sound and sustainable communities.

In 2008 the United Nation Environment Program (UNEP), the International Labor Organisation (ILO) and other partners published what they saw as the first comprehensive report into the emergence of a sustainable economy and its impact on the world of work in the 21st Century. The report assembles evidence of existing jobs in the key economic sectors of renewable energy, building and construction, transportation, basic industry, agriculture and forestry, providing estimates for future sustainable employment across the world. The report argues that prospective employment may be effected in four ways:

- Some additional jobs will be created, e.g. manufacturing pollution-control devices added to existing equipment.
- Some employment will be substituted, e.g. shifting from fossil fuels to renewable sources of energy, or from truck manufacturing to rail car manufacturing, or from landfill and waste incineration to material recycling.
- Some jobs may be eliminated without direct replacement, e.g. when the production of packaging materials is discouraged or banned.
- Many existing jobs (especially such as plumbers, electricians, metal workers, and construction workers) will be transformed and redefined.

Only the first two of these effects really result in new, 'green' jobs. The emergence of a market for carbon and the substitution of fossil fuel with renewable energy is undoubtedly an area of high employment growth (in 2010 the UN identified more than 2.3 million renewable energy jobs created around the world and 4 million jobs in Europe and the United States devoted to energy resource optimization). However, the transformation of traditional jobs to incorporate the mix of conceptual, practical and social skills required to work in the 21st Century, is by far the largest effect of a transition to a sustainable economy. The transformation of the workforce across the economy to respond and adapt to climate change, resource depletion, pollution, inequality and all the other sustainability drivers, really defies categorisation as 'green collar work'. In the future nearly every one of the 3.18 billion jobs globally (World Bank estimate in 2009) will be at least a bit green.

Around the globe the transition to more sustainable societies, and the transformation of the economies that service our societies, is still at an early stage. Many of the jobs that today's young people will be doing are only just emerging. The jobs of the future will emerge in response to:

- Evolving technologies, social and political arrangements;
- Climate change and other pressures on biodiversity;
- Increasing resource constraints and inequitable distribution of re-sources;
- Rising global populations; and
- Shifting power relations from west to east.

The challenge for educators, employers, parents and others contributing to learning pathways for young people is to continually engage with this changing global reality so that young people are equipped with skills for sustainability. An important way of meeting this challenge is to give young people themselves the competencies to manage and embrace change.

*Political*

The most easily recognised political context for sustainability skills is the very vocal debate about the employment opportunities created by the transition to a low carbon economy. The political counter point to this is the fear of job losses in traditionally carbon intensive industry, or industries that rely in other ways on the carbon economy. One way that jobs may be lost is through what has become know as 'carbon leakage'. This refers to the potential for economic activity to move elsewhere in the world where regulatory or economic constraints on carbon emissions and energy are less costly. Another way jobs may be lost is through changes to the structure of the economy away from the consumption of products with high embodied energy, like steel or concrete, or with high energy demands, like inefficient cars.

Often the debate about the employment impact of sustainable policy change is coloured by ideological distrust of 'greenies'. This underlying political theme is long running and reflects an ongoing trend in politics, the emergence of new 'green' political parties, not aligned to the traditional left or right. 'Green' political parties are regarded as a threat to established politics, which is often simplistically portrayed as pitting the interests of blue-collar workers, educated through vocational education, against university educated white-collar bosses. This is an important reason to move away from loaded terms like 'green skills' and 'green collar workers'.

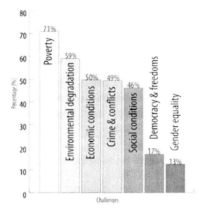

Source: UNEP 2011

Figure 1: Priority issues for youth, global average

Although the world's traditional politics is focused on the global economy and jobs, this does not entirely reflect the priorities and aspirations of the next generation. While significant differences can be observed between countries, a recent UNEP Global Survey on Sustainable Lifestyles found overall agreement amongst young adults from 20 different countries that poverty and environmental degradation are the most important global challenges we face. It is partly this intergenerational commitment to address continuing humanitarian and ecological crises that is driving the rise in new 'green' politics. This changing political landscape highlights the importance to young people of learning about sustainability as they prepare for life after school.

Of course, as figure 1 shows, sustainability is not alone on the emerging political agenda, economic stability and security are also key issues for young people around the world. The 8000 young adults surveyed by UNEP in the Global Survey on Sustainable Lifestyles had an optimistic vision for the future based on simple but fundamental components:

• The capacity to meet one's needs and reach a middle-class standard of living;
• A fulfilling job providing a sense of self-achievement;
• A successful family and social life; and
• A clean environment.

An effective pathway from school to work is essential to allow young people to achieve this vision. Preparation for new occupations, or for growth in demand for some occupations at the expense of others, is particularly important in preparing young men and women entering the labour market. However, young people continue to be overrepresented among the world's unemployed. In 2007, youth comprised only 25 per cent of the working-age population but accounted for more than 40 per cent of those who were jobless, making the youth unemployment rate almost twice that of older workers.

Without employment that translates into income and access to resources, young people lack the capacity to adapt to climate change, let alone tackle the challenges of poverty and environmental degradation. The traditional political issues of job creation and education don't compete with sustainability on the political agenda; they are part of it.

*Geographical*

Education systems vary considerably around the world, not least in the extent to which they formally encompass vocational education and, if they do, the extent to which they combine work based vocational and technical programs into schooling. The share of the upper secondary sector devoted to vocational education in OECD countries (Figure 2) shows that in some countries, for instance Australia and many countries in Central and Northern Europe, vocational education and training plays a very central role in the initial education of young people. In other countries, for instance countries in North America, very few upper secondary students undertake a designated TVET programme.

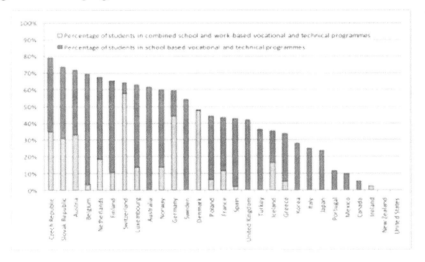

Source: OECD (2008)

Figure 2: Vocational education and training as a share of the upper secondary sector

There are striking parallels between the scale of upper secondary TVET in countries and the aspirations of 15-year-olds towards high-skilled occupations, like plumbing and electrical trades. This suggests that the high regard in which some communities hold academic achievement, and the accompanying low regard given to vocational education, may be reinforced systemically. Pathways that offer young people the conceptual, practical and normative skills they need to navigate our future need to be accessible within the upper secondary educational system, if they are going to be attractive to young people.

Labour market contexts are equally diverse around the world. In some countries, a combination of minimum wages, collective wage bargaining and strong employment protection legislation means that the costs and risks of recruiting a new employee are high, so employers will be reluctant to recruit unskilled workers. Unless the initial secondary, and post secondary education systems can compensate, by ensuring that young people emerge 'job-ready', and in the 21st century this means equipped with skills for sustainability, there may not be a well-structured pathway between school and work, resulting in higher youth unemployment. Schools, technical colleges and universities need to work together and with employers to ensure that young people enter the workforce with the conceptual, practical and normative skills they need, we all need.

The ILO has recently researched skill needs for economies in studies of 21 countries around the world, with a focus on how national policies for sustainable economies are complemented by identification of skills needs and response strategies. Changes in employment, and hence in skills, were found to be the result of four interrelated drivers of change:

- **Physical change in the environment,** which is the basis for policy decisions on environmental regulation.
- **Policies and regulation,** which can affect the development, availability and dissemination of low carbon technology.
- **Markets for greener products and services, and consumer habits,** which affect the way companies do business and encourage them to adopt new technologies.
- **Technology and innovation** that allow them to meet new consumer needs.

The studies of the 21 countries revealed that skill shortages already pose a major barrier to transitions to sustainable economies, a trend that is likely to be exacerbated in the future. Sustainable skill shortages stem from a number of factors, including underestimated growth of certain sectors, for example in energy efficiency in buildings; a general shortage of scientists and engineers – a problem shared by economies at all development levels; the low reputation and attractiveness of some sectors, such as waste management; and the general structure of the national skill base (that is the mix, breadth and depth of different skills available in a national economy). Shortages of teachers and trainers in environmental awareness subjects and in fast-growing sectors (e.g. renewable energy, energy efficiency) are reported in many countries, especially in developing economies. The conclusion from the ILO cross-country comparison is that inclusion of skills development strategies to make national economies more sustainable remains limited to isolated initiatives.

## *Discussion*

The contributors who have written all the chapters in this book come from a wide range of professional backgrounds, ranging from Physics, Energy Science, Chemistry, Zoology, Biology, Ecology, Environmental Science, Epidemiology, Geography, Geo-science, Economics, Political Economy, Marketing, Science and Technology, Environmental Engineering, Cybernetics, Social work, Education, Teaching, English, History and through to Philosophy and Art. This illustrates the incredible range of academic disciplines in which practitioners find sustainability relevant and seek to contribute to making our work and our lives more sustainable. However, many of these professionals are also practicing sustainability by applying what would commonly be considered vocational skills and drawing on the practical knowledge embedded in local cultures. In one case study, Chapter 26, Annukka Alppi describes how pupils and their families have maintained and improved their school using traditional Finnish building and construction techniques, like making their own paint out of ochre. In another case study, Chapter 27, Ted Trainer takes us through some simpler ways of doing the things we need to do, like collecting water. Right at the beginning of this book in Chapter 1, Laklak Burarrwanga, Banbapuy Ganambarr and Merrki Ganambarr explain the Yolŋu way of living where conceptual, practical and normative skills are deeply entwined. They now hunt and fish their bush foods with outboard motors and guns, but the old people still paint the knowledge for the Yolŋu way of learning - by doing and feeling. Sustainability is about more than thinking, it's about doing and, as Harriet Nalukenge in Chapter 9 explains, doing right.

---

*Case study: Sustainable Publishing*

Getting this book to you required the efforts of information technology, forestry, printing and transport workers who also have skills that contribute to sustainability (Thomas Weidmann, Christopher Dey and Manfred Lenzen explore how responsibility can be shared among all these different businesses in Chapter 7). The publisher of this book specialises in publishing that creates communities of knowledge around ideas like sustainability; ideas that require interdisciplinary thinking in ways that are discussed in Chapter 11. In this chapter Ida Kubiszewski and Robert Costanza point out that information is a resource that improves with use. The more the information contained in the chapters of this book is used, the more social good is created and the more new information is formed.

The publisher of this book has gone to some effort to minimise the environmental impact of getting this information to you. Firstly, this book is published simultaneously in print and electronic formats so that those who wish to read on screen can do so without using any paper at all. If these readers require some of the material in hard copy they can print only what they need (for instance a case study to hand out in class). Secondly, the publisher maintains a print on demand (POD) model that offers significant environmental advantages over traditional offset printing.

---

With offset manufacturing books often go unsold and are destroyed, usually after being shipped and handled multiple times. Wasted paper, wasted energy, greenhouse emissions, pulping, and landfill overflows can result. POD technology allows books to be printed to fill an existing demand. POD lessens the possibility of returns, reduces supply chain waste, greenhouse emissions and conserves valuable natural resources.

To further increase the sustainability of this book the paper on which these words are printed comes from timber that is certified as sustainably managed under a number international schemes (the production processes from the forest to printing are also certified). Part of this certification requires that the various companies along the production chain identify the skills and training needs of their staff, and provide or support an appropriate ongoing training programme for employees (including contractors or self-employed) to meet these needs. Other aspects of these certification processes begin to address issues about sustainable agriculture and water management raised in Chapters 15 and 16. In the end it is processes like the ecological footprint discussed by Dan Moran and Mathis Wackernagel in Chapter 3 that will let us know if all these efforts are making a difference.

The authors, editors, publishers, IT workers, foresters, printers and transport workers who have brought you this book have been enabled to do this by their social upbringing, their schooling, their studies and training and their experiences in the workplace. Today's students similarly require upbringing, schooling, studies, training and work experience that address the points made in each of the preceding chapters, if we are to continue our collective journey towards a sustainable future.

It is important to note that only a relatively small cohort of school students will continue to tertiary education that directly relates to the topics discussed in this book (ecological sciences, urban design, etc), but every student will need a pathway that provides them with social, conceptual and practical skills attuned to sustainability. To provide the right pathways to a sustainable future for most secondary students we need to reorient all sources of learning to address economic, environmental, social sustainability and develop the normative competencies that motivate working with others to create a sustainable future. These include developing enhanced competencies in existing skill areas such as:

- Critical thinking, explaining, justifying and negotiating ideas and plans;
- Gender and ethnic equality in the work place; and
- Team work and group skills.

Importantly, all sources of learning need to be reorientated to include new skills:

- Encouraging reflection on the effects of personal values and lifestyle choice;
- Developing an ethic of social responsibility in firms and organisations and in the actions of individual workers;
- Promoting practical citizenship in the wider community;

- Promoting economic literacy, sustainable consumption and managing small enterprises; and
- Understanding a range of environmental concepts, like using resources wisely and minimizing waste and pollution.

All of these are no longer 'nice to have' skills. They are becoming core skills for young people engaging in vocational and academic pathways. It has been clear to many in the TVET community for decades that every young person entering the workforce needs to be equipped with information technology, communications, administrative, business and inter-personal skills as well as technical and manual skills. More recently academic leaders are also recognising the growing expectation of employers, governments and students themselves that university graduates should enjoy a smooth transition to practicing their selected occupations. For this university graduates also require practical and employability skills, as well as normative competencies and traditional research and analytical skills. Making tertiary students 'job ready' requires internships, 'sandwich' courses and other ways of getting practical experiences in workplaces and having this experience recognised.

Computer diagnostics are now standard in many trades – they have been part of automotive mechanics for many years – but now, for instance, smart meters are becoming a standard household electrical fixture. Equally, academic, professional and administrative roles routinely require complex information technology and communications skills. Running the service orientated small to medium businesses that many vocational and tertiary graduates will work in has become increasingly complex and requires business and financial planning skills, customer service and design skills. Technical standards and manuals governing the work of administrators, managers, researchers and technicians (for example guidelines for sustainability reporting, grant applications, environmental management and the standard operating procedures that govern almost all industrial and mechanical processes) are proliferating and changing rapidly. All young people need the skills to track down current versions of these standards on the internet and to interpret them.

Achieving sustainability is a bigger and more complex issue than providing new skills as the demand arises. To help young people build a common future we will need to re-imagine academic and vocational learning communities, dynamically linking them to equally re-imagined industrial and business communities and to a re-imagined civil society. What is needed is a new approach to skill formation that has TVET, secondary and tertiary education, industry, government and community agencies working strategically together to achieve agreed environmental, economic and social goals. The chance of these sorts of reforms being implemented relies ultimately on the willingness of people in education, the community and the private sector to work together in new ways. An example of a partnership bringing industry and TVET together around the world in reimagining skills formation is the WorldSkills movement.

The further we travel into the 21$^{st}$ century the more pressing becomes the need for high order skills that enable young people to reimage the world and for a new way of understanding what education means. Formulating and applying solutions to emerging problems of water and food supply, capturing carbon and recycling materials are matters for high-level skills, deep applied knowledge and the capacity to theorise and solve novel problems. They also require personal commitment and the ability to change existing ways of working so that specialists from different fields, skill types and levels, work together as high-order problem solving teams. The team members won't be green, blue or white collar workers, they'll be collarless.

---

### Case Study: Skills for Sustainability in Australia

In Australia there has been some early success in the shift toward a more comprehensive sustainability agenda across many occupations and industries. Skills for sustainability are increasingly becoming embedded in training, especially on-the-job, but also in more formal training.

To date, Australian Government Skills for Sustainability policy initiatives have emphasised environmental sustainability, relative to the social and economic dimensions of sustainability. As part of the implementation of an inter-Governmental Green Skills Agreement, most Australian vocational training packages now incorporate environmental sustainability considerations. Some have revised qualifications to include sustainable work practices as a core unit; others are developing new qualifications and units of competency, while others are focusing on reviewing the pool of electives in selected training packages. The focus has particularly been on skills required to respond to the wider Government policy agenda in relation to energy efficiency (especially in buildings) and the creation of markets for alternative energy and carbon. Other areas of green skills development have been the skills required for water efficiency and improved waste management.

In addition to Australian Government investment in teaching environmentally sustainable practices at vocational institutes and other places of training, a number of influences are driving Australian businesses to invest in skills for sustainability:

- The rise in new niche markets of consumers who are willing to do and spend more to be environmentally friendly;
- Step increases in energy costs, in water service and in waste disposal costs;
- The continued evolution of environmental protection measures (such as discharge standards and biodiversity offsets); and
- Investment market demands for information about 'carbon risk', for example reporting in the Carbon Disclosure Project.

A recent survey of Australian apprentices and trainees by the Dusseldorp Skills Forum indicates that public policy and business initiatives around skills for sustainability are having an impact. Between 2008 and 2011 Australian young skilled people have seen barriers to sustainability reducing and shifting from cultural factors to technological limitations. They have also seen a significant take up of green skills in workplaces and courses. Apprentices and trainees indicate that their knowledge of sustainability skills has increased substantially, with social sources, such as family and the internet, growing fastest.

This research indicates that there remains a large gap between the aspirations and expectations of young Australians to develop the skills to tackle the challenges of sustainability and available learning opportunities. In particular, respondents said that the skills required to manage the emerging carbon constrained economy, skills such as understanding supply chains, have yet to become common content in their courses and workplace practices. The survey also indicated that apprentices and trainees think some important social and economic skills, such as the skills needed to manage community investment and to operate businesses sustainably, are less common that other skills taught in courses and workplaces. They say that they are mostly exposed to economic and (to a lesser extent) social skills, not environmental skills, in both workplaces and classrooms.

In 2011 the high level of personal interest in sustainability skills among skilled young Australians, and their overall strong recognition of the professional relevance of these skills, still appear to be confounded by a lack of guidance and incentives from employers, the market and educators. This reflects that public policy and business sector responses to sustainability are still in their early development and implementation. There is scope for a broader reimagining of public policy and business culture around skills for sustainability in the future, fostering learning communities that link educational, business and civil society stakeholders.

***Thinking it through: where do I stand?***
Can the mobility traditionally associated with apprentices, the way they learn on the job, be encouraged in your subject area, transforming workplaces into places for sustainability education and training?

Does being an effective practitioner in your subject require normative competencies that change the way other people behave?

Many of the skills required to achieve outcomes described in other chapters and the pathways that students might need to get these skills, are not academic or vocational skills. They will require the inclusion of the community as a source of learning. Think about these neglected skills and how you can encourage and support an environment in which they can flourish.

*Action: what can I do?*

Help your students to identify where jobs in your subject area sit on the framework in Figure 3. Get them to research what skills they will need to get them there, including employability skills and creative competencies. Then get them to map a learning pathway that shows how and when they might learn these skills. Encourage them to be realistic about their expectations of income, influence and advancement – this is a life long learning pathway!

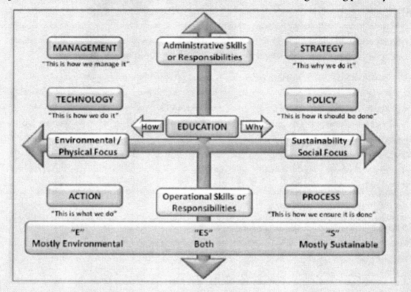

Figure 3: A Sustainability and Environmental Worker Conceptual Framework (From Ehmcke et al (2009). *Who are the Green Collar Workers? A Definition and Taxonomy.* NSW: Connection Research and DECC)

## Further reading

Fien, J., Maclean, R., & Park M-G. (Eds.). (2009). *Work, Learning and Sustainable Development – Opportunities and Challenges.* Netherlands: Springer.

ILO/CEDEFOP (2011). *Skills for Green Jobs: A global view (Executive Summary).* Geneva: International Labour Organization.

Transfer 21 (2007). *Guide - Education for Sustainable Development at Secondary Level: Justifications, Competences, Learning Opportunities.* Berlin: Freie Universitat.

UNESCO /UNEVOC (2004). *The Bonn Declaration on Learning for Work, Citizenship and Sustainabilty.* United Nations Educational, Scientific and Cultural Organisation.

UNEP/ILO/IOE/ITUC (2008). *Green Jobs: Towards Decent Work in a Sustainable, Low-Carbon World.* Nairobi, Kenya: United Nations Environment Programme.

United Nations Department of Economic and Social Affairs (2010). *Youth and Climate Change.* New York: United Nations.

### *Resources*

Green Jobs Programme of the International Labout Organisation (ILO) http://www.ilo.org/empent/units/green-jobs-programme/lang--en/index.htm

German Federal Ministry for Education Portal for Education for Sustainble Development (BNE) http://www.bne-portal.de/coremedia/generator/unesco/en/01__Home/English_20Homepage.html

### *Acknowledgements*

Thanks to Rani De Kalb, New South Wales Department of Education and Communities and Lesley Tobin, Project Partnership Dusseldorp Skills Forum, for their insightful comments on an earlier draft of this chapter.

# Part VIII

## Epilogue

*sally forth*
**watercolour on paper**
**12.5cm by 17cm**

# Epilogue

**The Journey Starts here...**

...or maybe it's simply one continuous journey and we make up beginnings and endings to punctuate the way – places to stop and take stock, reflect on where we've been and where we're heading; bring order out of our serendipitous learning before we plunge back into the messiness of life.

If so then there may be something here that could help you to organise your thoughts about sustainability and provide a schema for use in your teaching.

The book can be worked through in any way that seems appropriate to your needs and interests. You could read from beginning to end or you could take one of the principles (i.e. sections) as a starting point and within that principle take up one of the issues (i.e. chapters) that interests you. This chapter may direct you to another because within the chapter there will be references to interlinked issues. If you're good at mind maps[1] you may be able to link your ideas together that way as you read on. Whatever you do

---

1.A mind-map is a schematic diagram of issues with hierarchies and linkages that can facilitate discussion and show complex structures and connections with an aim to understand opportunities for action. A quick search of the www will provide plenty of advice and examples if you are interested.

you'll probably very soon realise that everything is linked to everything else – change one thing and everything changes. Below are some suggested strategies for organising and consolidating your learning.

### *Four principles for sustainability*

In the Preface we refer to four principles, which may be useful as an organiser for beginning the sustainability discussion with students. Alternatively you could elicit a set of principles from your students and begin the discussion there instead. Either way, principles imply questions, which again are useful organisers. For example:

The principle *Sustainability is everyone's business* (section 2) asks us to grapple with questions such as:

- *How do I measure sustainability and how sustainable is my lifestyle* (chapter 3);
- *What influences us to consume and what can we do about it* (chapter 4);
- *What does it mean to share responsibility fairly among households* (chapter 5);
- *What's the role of business* (chapter 6);
- *How can businesses share responsibility* (chapter 7); and
- *What role should government play?* (chapter 8).

As you can see the chapters within the section address questions implied by the principle. However if your students devise their own principles then they may have a set of different questions for which they need answers. We hope that the book will assist you in supporting your students' research as they pursue the answers to questions that are important in their lives.

Section three *Sharing in a sustainable future* supports our next principle that *we must share equitably the cost and the benefits of living sustainably with nature*

To be able to do this we'll need to know things like:

- *How to work out what is fair and equitable (the ethics of sustainability)* (chapter 9);
- *What constitutes natural capital and how we can invest in it in order to sustain it* (chapter 10);
- *How we create systems in which sustainable and fair decisions can be made about ecosystem services for public good* (chapter 11); and
- *How we should address generational equity* (chapter 12).

Section four is built around our third principle, which states that *people need to be able to live healthy, fulfilling and sustainable lives*

If we think this to be true, then the following questions seemed to us to be important:

- *What's the relationship between our life-style and the environment* (ch13);
- *What are the issues around health* (chapter 14);
- *What are the issues around agriculture and water security* (chapter 15 & 16);

- *What should be done about transport* (chapter 17);
- *How do we need to change our cities* (chapter 18);
- *How can the arts help* (chapter 19); and
- *What is sustainable happiness and how/where do we get it?* (chapter 20).

Finally section five supports the principle that *long-term solutions require a whole system view; they are complex and multi-faceted.* If this is so then we will need to understand:

- *The earth's resilience* (chapter 21); and
- *How a cybernetic/systems framework might help* (chapters 22 & 23).

So many ways to begin the discussion! So many avenues to pursue! All we can do is make a start and one thing will lead on to another.

## *Working through the book*

Many of the chapters end with questions and suggestions. They ask about links to other areas of sustainability, and provide pointers for thinking through the issues. They suggest actions and leave you with further reading and useful resources. Most of the actions can be adapted to a range of age groups. Many can be undertaken by groups of students or by the wider community.

### *Linking the issues*

We suggested in the Preface that a mind map might be a helpful way of linking the different issues in this book. Or you may have your own way of organising the concepts and connections as you go along. Whatever you decide we urge you to have a go at consolidating your learning in some way. This will assist you in helping your students to make links.

### *Taking a stand*

The first principle addressed in this book says that sustainability is everyone's business. It asks you to take a stand, to commit to action. In your role as teacher you will probably also want your students to decide for themselves where they stand. Your job will be to present the arguments and available evidence and provide the resources and processes to help them do this. Many chapters end with the question *Thinking it through: where do I stand?* a question that you might also want to invite students to deliberate on. It is recognition of the belief that learning includes critical reflection, is active and requires the learner to take responsibility for his or her own learning.

### *Action*

Learning is also a social process and involves solving real problems. Some of the invitations to action at the end of the chapters may be suitable for action research projects. Action research is about working with others on something of mutual concern. It is motivated by a desire to improve the world we live in by making changes of some kind. It treats people as autonomous responsible agents who participate in creating the world we share.

The action research process is one of:

- reflecting on what's gone before
- planning future action
- acting
  ○ gathering support and resources
  ○ implementing your plan

- observing (systematically taking note of what's happening)
- reflecting
  ○ thinking about what happened
  ○ evaluating your achievements

- replanning
- continuing the spiral of action and reflection[2].

Often the above steps seem to occur almost simultaneously or else weave in and out of each other within the larger framework of your project. In essence action research means a flexible approach and an iterative creative process of action and reflection. It may be what you always do anyway without even thinking about it however this makes it into a conscious process that you can share with others. It also involves keeping record of the process and outcomes. This could be in the form of a journal or it could be minutes of meetings that provide a way of looking back on where you began and enables everyone to see the learning that has taken place along the way.

A good way to decide on what specific action to take is to discuss and list what concerns people have and then narrow down the concerns by filtering through the lens of what actions are possible in your context. You may want to begin small and then grow as you become more confident. If you are working at a class level this process can give students the initiative in setting the agenda. If working with parents, campus or the wider community this process can help ensure that you are working on something of mutual interest and at the same time is actually do-able. There are many good texts that will help you to conduct action research.

Whatever action you decide to take will inevitably have intended and un-intended consequences. These consequences will probably affect other aspects of the sustainability debate. Your learning can be added to your mind

---

2. This may appear to be a linear sequence of steps, however action research requires what Donald Schön calls 'reflection in action' which means learning and thinking while doing (Schön, D. (1983). *The Reflective Practitioner. How professionals think in action*. London: Temple Smith).

map or other graphical representation, allowing you to plot these connections. And therein lies the central message of this book: everything is connected; we are all connected; we can all make a difference. We just need to start.

CPSIA information can be obtained at www.ICGtesting.com
Printed in the USA
LVOW071822121212

311353LV00004B/233/P

9 781612 290140